Programming from Specifications

Carroll Morgan
Programming Research Group
University of Oxford

Second Edition

Prentice Hall
New York   London   Toronto   Sydney   Tokyo   Singapore

First published 1990
This edition published 1994 by
Prentice Hall International (UK) Limited
Campus 400, Maylands Avenue
Hemel Hempstead
Hertfordshire, HP2 7EZ
A division of
Simon & Schuster International Group

Printed and bound in Great Britain at the
University Press, Cambridge

Library of Congress Cataloging-in-Publication Data

Morgan, Carroll, 1952–
    Programming from specifications / Carroll Morgan. – 2nd ed.
        p.   cm. – (Prentice Hall international series in computer
    science)
    Includes bibliographical references and index.
    ISBN 0-13-123274-6
    1. Electronic digital computers – Programming.   I. Title.
    II. Series.
    QA76.6.M668   1994
    005.13′1–dc20   94-6077
                                                              CIP

British Library Cataloguing in Publication Data

A catalogue record for this book is available from
the British Library

ISBN 0-13-123274-6

---

1   2   3   4   5   98   97   96   95   94

Contents

Preface

In mathematics, one speaks of $x^2 = 1$, an *equation*, as having solutions $x = 1$ and $x = -1$. But $x = 1$ and $x = -1$ are equations too, since they both have the form of two expressions separated by '='. If they are all three equations, then what gives the latter two the additional quality of being solutions?

There are two characteristics of solutions. The first is that they solve something, and in the example above we have the diagram

$$x^2 = 1 \quad \left\{ \begin{array}{ll} \Leftarrow & x = 1 \\ \Leftarrow & x = -1 \end{array} \right. ,$$

showing that we say that '$x = 1$' *solves* '$x^2 = 1$' because of the implication 'if $x = 1$ then $x^2 = 1$'. (Note that the reverse implication does not hold.) The same applies for '$x = -1$'.

The second characteristic of solutions is that the value they determine can be recovered by inspection, without further calculation. It hardly needs saying that '1' is a value for x that makes $x = 1$ true: it can be seen almost without thought.

One can also regard computer programming, or program development as it is known these days, in terms of 'solving' and 'solutions'. Instead of equations, however, we will have programs: some programs will be regarded as solving others (we will say 'refining'); and some programs will be so simple we will regard them as solutions (we will say 'code').

Using a special notation for statements like 'set x so that $x^2 = 1$', we can write specifications in a way that looks like programming. And by equipping them with a carefully defined meaning, we can say that they indeed *are* programs. The above specification, for example, we would write '$x: [x^2 = 1]$' , and the *is refined by* relation '$\sqsubseteq$' between programs would then allow us an analogue of the above 'is solved by' diagram:

$$x: \left[x^2 = 1 \right] \quad \left\{ \begin{array}{ll} \sqsubseteq & x := 1 \\ \sqsubseteq & x := -1 \end{array} \right. .$$

All three components of the above are programs. The first characteristic of solutions is repeated in the implication 'if we require an x such that $x^2 = 1$, then $x := 1$ will deliver one'. The second is repeated in that the value delivered by the programs on the right — they are both *code* — can be discovered by running them on a computer. And that requires no thought at all.

This book teaches elementary programming in the style of the above analogy: that specifications and code are all programs; that there is a refinement order between programs; and that there is a specially restricted sub-language called 'code' that allows programs written in it to be executed with 'no thought at all'. The thinking is necessary elsewhere, to *find* the code that refines a given specification.

The approach rests on the work of Dijkstra, Hoare, and Floyd [Dij76, Hoa69, Flo67]; and the programming language is Dijkstra's *guarded commands*, extended with specification constructs like '$x : [x^2 = 1]$' above. The language itself is presented in the early chapters, and each of its constructs is characterised by the refinement laws that it satisfies. The effect on a computer is described informally, as an aid to the intuition.

Later chapters are split between case studies and more advanced programming techniques. Each case study treats a programming example from beginning to end, using the methods available at that point, and is well known rather than especially intricate. The more advanced programming techniques are *procedures*, *recursion*, *recursive data structures*, *modules* and finally *state transformation* (including *data refinement*).

The other chapters deal with the necessary infrastructure, most notably the predicate calculus and basic types. The former has its own laws, and a large collection of those appears as Appendix A. That avoids relying on any particular method of logical proof from first principles (properly the subject of a different book). Indeed, the introductory Chapter 1 uses the predicate calculus before its proper exposition in Chapter 2: the refinement calculus, not the predicate calculus, is our main subject. Nevertheless Chapter 2 is independent, and may be read first if desired. The basic types are the ordinary sets of numbers from arithmetic, augmented with constructions for powersets, bags, and sequences.

A concluding chapter summarises the main features of our programming style, and discusses its effect on the practices of *documentation*, *modification*, *testing*, and *debugging*.

Beyond the conclusion are several chapters more advanced than the main text. The first two treat fairly complex case studies; the first is iterative (an example of dynamic programming); the second is seriously recursive. The third advanced chapter is a case study in specification itself, thus concentrating on modules, design (of a system), design changes, and both ordinary and data refinement as a tool in careful design.

The final chapter gives the semantics for all the preceding material.

Appendices include a collection of propositional and predicate calculus laws, answers to some exercises, and a summary of the refinement laws introduced in the text. The last is sometimes convenient to have at hand when deriving programs, or studying others' derivations, and for that reason it may be copied and distributed for educational use. Those adopting the book for teaching may obtain from the publisher a separate booklet containing both the summary of refinement laws and answers to all the exercises.

The book is intended to be useful both to those learning to program and to those who — programmers already — would like to make the link between their existing skill and the specifications from which their programs (should) spring. Experience based on nearly 10 years' exposure to second-year computing undergraduates suggests, however, that the best approach is at first to exercise a fairly light touch on the refinement laws. For beginning programmers they should assist, not prescribe: at that stage, the list of refinement laws is for reference, not for certification. And learning to use invariants for iterations is work enough on its own.

Light touch or no, the underlying theme of specification, refinement and code is one that students respond to, and it informs their approach to other courses and to computing generally. More experienced programmers may recognise some of those features in specification and development methods such as *Z* and *VDM* [Jon86, Hay93, Kin90], for parts of which the refinement calculus forms an adjunct or even an alternative.

Differences from the first edition

This second edition represents a rearrangement, modification and augmenting of the first.

The early chapters, on the programming language, have been rearranged so that the programming language features are introduced consecutively, without the intervention of chapters on more technical matters. That technical material has now been delayed, leaving in the original position only just enough to get on with the programming language itself.

The approach to procedures and parameters, including recursive procedures, has been modified considerably, to make it simpler. At the cost of a little generality, the original separate treatment of parameters has been replaced by a more conventional treatment of (recursive) procedures and parameters together.

There is a substantial amount of new material, including: a section on functions and relations (in the 'Z style'); a complete chapter on recursive types (for example, trees), and simple control structures for their use; a section on *functional* refinement, a special and very common case of state transformation whose rules are much simpler than the fully general ones; and two more 'advanced' case studies, adding recursion and data refinement to the techniques illustrated more substantially.

The first extra case study, 'the largest rectangle under a histogram', is well known not to be especially easy whatever technique is used; we develop a proper- (not simply tail-) recursive solution.

The second extra case study, 'a mail system', illustrates at some length the sometimes treacherous interaction of specification, design, re-specification and re-design that leads towards implementation of a system rather than just a program. Data refinement figures prominently.

Acknowledgements

My largest debt remains to my family: Sue, Tristan, Elliot and Ethan.

Many friends and colleagues have contributed to improvements over the first edition, and I am grateful to them all.

The camera-ready copy was made with LaTeX, using mainly BBEdit and OzTeX on an Apple Macintosh.

Carroll Morgan
Easter 1994
Men kan niet weten hoe een koe een haas vangt.

Chapter 1

Programs and refinement

1.1 The traditional view

Traditionally, *programs* are collections of detailed instructions to a computer. They are written in a programming *language*, whose form (syntax) and meaning (semantics) are precisely defined. Programs are easy to execute (computers do that), but hard to understand.

The study of methods for making programs is *programming methodology*. We are concerned with methods that take a *specification* of what the computer is to do, and aim to produce a program which will cause the computer to do it. Specifications might be written in English, or in some more mathematical style. They are hard to execute (computers cannot do that in general), but easy to understand — or they should be.

There would be little need for this book if all programs were understandable, or all specifications executable. But alas neither is true — and matters are likely to stay that way.

Specifications *must* be understood, because each is a contract between a programmer and his client. The client relies on the specification for his *use* of the program; the programmer relies on the specification for his *construction* of the program. A complex specification will spawn subspecifications, each defining a component whose construction the programmer may then delegate to his subordinates. That turns the programmer into a client, and his subordinates become programmers; the subspecifications are contracts between him and them. Ultimately, programs are contracts between the lowest-level programmers and the computer.

1.2 A novel view

Our departure from tradition is a small one: we simply banish the distinction between specifications, subspecifications (super-programs?), and programs. To us,

1

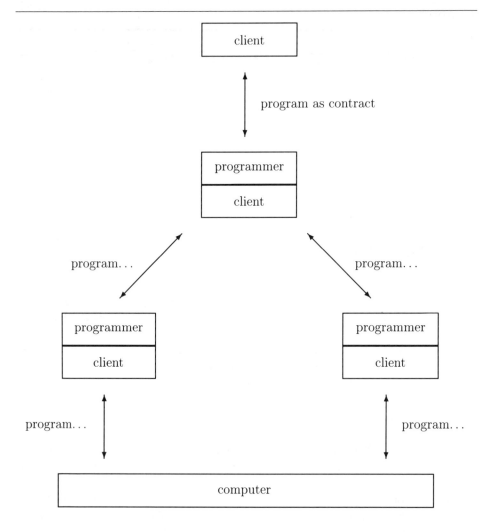

Figure 1.1 A programming hierarchy

they are *all* programs; what we give up is that all programs are directly executable.

What we gain instead is a more uniform approach in which programs play a role at every level. Figure 1.1 illustrates the resulting hierarchy. At the top of the hierarchy we find abstract programs, not necessarily executable. Section 1.4.3 describes some of the constructions they can use.

At the bottom of the hierarchy we find executable programs, which we call *code*. The constructions used there are typical of imperative languages: assignment commands, sequential composition, alternation, iteration, and recursion. Section

cost £10 (paperback)	⊑	cost £10 (paperback), £20 (hardback)
220V outlet	⊑	220/110V outlet
safe working load 1000kg	⊑	safe working load 2000kg
splash-proof	⊑	water-resistant to 50m
needs at least 4Mb	⊑	needs at least 2Mb

Figure 1.2 Informal examples of refinement

1.5.2 describes some code.

In the middle, we find programs in which both abstract and executable constructs appear. They contain too much detail for convenient comprehension, but still too much abstraction to be executed. We meet those later, in our case study chapters.

1.3   Programs as contracts: refinement

A program has two roles: it describes what one person wants, and what another person (or computer) must do. With respect to any particular program, we distinguish the *client* and the *programmer*. Remember that a single person can be both: a systems analyst is a programmer with respect to his firm's clients, but a client with respect to his own programming team.

When a contract is made by negotiation between a client and a programmer, each party has primarily his own interests at heart. The client wants the program to do more: to be more accurate, to apply in more situations, to operate more quickly. The programmer wants more freedom in making the program: more leeway in the selection and presentation of results, more information about the situations in which the program is to run, more access to cheap and standard implementation techniques. Their aims are complementary, and the result is always a compromise.

We take the client's point of view in describing the negotiation: if program *prog*2 is better than program *prog*1, *for the client*, we write *prog*1 ⊑ *prog*2. That relation ⊑, between programs, is called *refinement*: we say that *prog*2 refines *prog*1. In Figure 1.2 are some examples of refinement from more familiar settings. Figure 1.3 illustrates the role of ⊑ in contract negotiation.

Figure 1.3 Refinement in contract negotiation

Figure 1.4 The imperative view of programming

1.4   Abstract programs

1.4.1   Initial and final states

Any program takes a computer from an initial state to a final state. That view, illustrated in Figure 1.4, is called *imperative*, and it is appropriate for most computer languages in general use today. We suppose that the data on which the computer is to operate (the input) are placed in the initial state; the results of the computation (the output) are found subsequently, in the final state.

The *state* of a computer is a collection of named values. The names are called *variables*, and the *values* are taken from ordinary mathematical discourse: natural numbers, integers, real numbers, characters, etc. A state *maps* variables to their values.

For the rest of this chapter, let our variables be just x, y, and z; and let their values be real numbers, from the set $\mathbb{R}$. We shall see later that the set $\mathbb{R}$ is the *type* of x, y, and z. Here are two states that differ in the value of y only:

state0:

x	2
y	17
z	3

state1:

x	2
y	$\sqrt{2}$
z	3

.

An imperative program is used to take *state0* initially to *state1* finally.

1.4.2 Descriptions of states

Pictures of state mappings, however, are not very useful for our development of programs: they say both too much and too little. They say too much because the value of every variable must be given exactly, even the variables in which we might not be interested. They say too little because each gives only *one* state, and to understand a program completely we need to know its behaviour on *all* initial states. That is far too many pictures. . .

We describe states rather than draw them. A formula *describes* a state if it is made true by the mappings in the state. And we say that a state *satisfies* a formula if that formula describes it. Thus each of the formulae $x = 2$, $x + z < y$, and $z \neq 4$ describes *state0*. This formula describes *state0* exactly:

$$x = 2 \land y = 17 \land z = 3 \ .$$

The formula $y^2 = x$, for example, describes *state1*.

As an extreme case, the formula **true** describes *all* states (because it is true in all states). Similarly, the formula **false** describes *no* states (because it is true in no states).

We use the predicate calculus as the language of our formulae. It includes the usual equations (like $x = y$) and relations ($z < 17$), the logical connectives $\land$ (and), $\lor$ (or), $\neg$ (not), and $\Rightarrow$ (implies); and it has the familiar quantifiers $\forall$ (for all) and $\exists$ (there exists).

1.4.3 Specifications

The *specification* is the principal feature of abstract programs. Its *precondition* describes the initial states; its *postcondition* describes the final states; and its *frame* lists the variables whose values may change. If a computer could execute it, this would be the effect:

> *If* the initial state satisfies the precondition *then* change only the variables listed in the frame so that the resulting final state satisfies the postcondition.

It is deliberate that a specification can leave some possibilities unconstrained. If the initial state does not satisfy the precondition, we do not know what will happen; one possibility is that the computer does not deliver any final state at all — that is, it fails to terminate. If there are several possible final states satisfying the postcondition, we do not know which will be chosen (nondeterminism).

Here is a specification which assigns to y the square root of x, provided x lies between 0 and 9:

precondition	$0 \leq x \leq 9$
postcondition	$y^2 = x$
frame	y

$$y\colon \left[0 \leq x \leq 9 \ , \ y^2 = x \right] . \qquad (1.1)$$

x: [**true** , $y^2 = x$]   Make x the square of y.

y: [$x \geq 0$, $y^2 = x$]   Make y a square root of x, provided x is not negative.

e: [$s \neq \{\}$, $e \in s$]   Make e an element of the set s, provided s is non-empty.

x: [$b^2 \geq 4ac$, $ax^2 + bx + c = 0$]   Make x a solution to the quadratic equation, provided the discriminant is non-negative.

Figure 1.5 Example specifications

On the right is the same specification written more compactly: in general, for precondition *pre*, postcondition *post*, and frame w, the compact form is

w: [*pre* , *post*].

Specification (1.1) leaves some possibilities unconstrained: we do not know what would happen if it were applied to an initial state which mapped x to 10, because the precondition would not be true. Even when the precondition is true, there is still some uncertainty: applied to *state0*, it will produce either *state1* (above) or *state2* below — but beforehand we do not know which it will be.

state2:

x	2
y	$-\sqrt{2}$
z	3

Figure 1.5 lists some other examples of specifications. Notice how in those examples (especially the quadratic) the use of formulae allows a specification to capture the intention without necessarily giving the method. It can say 'what' without having to say 'how'.

1.4.4   Refinement of specifications

A specification is improved (for the client) by *strengthening* its postcondition, so that the new postcondition implies the old: *if* a book is available in paperback and hardback, *then* it is available in paperback at least. Requiring the square root to be non-negative is another example: *if* you have a non-negative square root, *then* you at least have a square root. So (1.2) refines (1.1):

$$y: \left[0 \leq x \leq 9 , y^2 = x \wedge y \geq 0\right]. \tag{1.2}$$

Specification (1.2) is better for the customer because he knows more about the final state: he can *depend* on $y \geq 0$, if he wants to, and he could not before.

In general, we have the following law of refinement, of which (1.1) $\sqsubseteq$ (1.2) is an example:

Law 1.1 <u>strengthen postcondition</u> If $post' \Rightarrow post$, then

$$w: [pre\ ,\ post] \quad \sqsubseteq \quad w: [pre\ ,\ post'].$$

$\square$

(For now, read '$\Rightarrow$' as implication; it is defined in Chapter 2.) The requirement $post' \Rightarrow post$ must hold whenever the law is used, and it is called the *proviso*. The symbol $\square$ indicates the end of a law (or similar), and the resumption of normal text.

A different kind of improvement is gained by *weakening* a precondition, so that the old precondition implies the new: *if* at least 4Mb is required, *then* certainly at least 2Mb is required. Requiring our square root program to operate for *any* non-negative x is another example: if x is non-negative and no greater than 9, then x is still non-negative. So (1.3) refines (1.2):

$$y: \left[0 \leq x\ ,\ y^2 = x \wedge y \geq 0\right]. \tag{1.3}$$

Specification (1.3) is better than (1.2) because it works even when $x > 9$.

The general law for preconditions is the following:

Law 1.2 <u>weaken precondition</u> If $pre \Rightarrow pre'$, then

$$w: [pre\ ,\ post] \quad \sqsubseteq \quad w: [pre'\ ,\ post].$$

$\square$

Note that it too has a proviso.

1.5   Executable programs

1.5.1   Code

Specifications are written in a language (predicate calculus) whose meaning is known precisely. They are unambiguous, and very convenient because they are so expressive. Why not build a computer that executes them?

The simple answer to that question is 'it's impossible'. It can be proved that no computer, as the term is presently understood, can be built which could execute all specifications.

The problem is that our formulae are written in too powerful a language: we can say too much with them. We could use a weaker language — but the weaker the language, the more involved become the constructions that we need to say what we must. And the more involved they are, the more likely it is that the client and programmer will misunderstand each other *at the very beginning*, before the design, modularisation, coding, integration, debugging... The enterprise would be doomed before it had started.

Our approach is to have it both ways. The programming language includes specifications, for their expressive power, but has also constructions which are designed to be executable. We call them *code*.

1.5.2   The assignment command

The notation $w := E$ is an *assignment command*, and is our first example of code. It changes the state so that the variable w is mapped to the value E, and all other variables are left unchanged. Assignment commands form the basis of imperative programming languages; they are easy to execute provided the expression E is constructed from constants and operators that the programming language provides (such as 0, 1, 2, $+$, $-$, $\times$ and $\div$). Below we give a law of refinement for assignments.

Law 1.3 <u>assignment</u>   If $pre \Rightarrow post[w \backslash E]$, then

$$w, x: [pre \ , \ post] \quad \sqsubseteq \quad w := E \ .$$

□

The formula $post[w \backslash E]$ is obtained by replacing in $post$ all occurrences of w by E. (Such substitutions are explained more fully in Section A.2.1.) Note that the frame w, x can include variables x not assigned to in the code: the frame says that x *may* change, not that it must.

Law 1.3 allows a programmer to implement a specification $w: [pre \ , \ post]$ by code $w := E$ that is better from the client's point of view — it is better because where $post$ may have allowed several final values for w, now it allows only one, and the customer knows exactly which one it will be. In quite a different sense, it is better for the programmer too: a computer can execute it. Laws like *assignment* 1.3 are the programmer's tools; his expertise is in deciding which to use.

In a programming language with a positive square root operator $\sqrt{\ }$ (and assuming infinite precision arithmetic), Law 1.3 gives us this refinement immediately:

$$y: \left[0 \leq x \leq 9 \ , \ y^2 = x \wedge y \geq 0 \right] \quad \sqsubseteq \quad y := \sqrt{x} \ .$$

That is because we can prove the relevant proviso:

$\qquad 0 \leq x \leq 9$
$\Rightarrow \quad$ "$\sqrt{x}$ well-defined in given range"
$\qquad (\sqrt{x})^2 = x$
$\equiv \quad$ "definition of $\sqrt{\ }$"

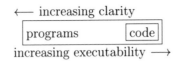

Figure 1.6 Code is the language of *executable* programs

$$(\sqrt{x})^2 = x \land \sqrt{x} \geq 0$$
$$\equiv \quad (y^2 = x \land y \geq 0)[y\backslash\sqrt{x}] .$$

(For now, read '$\equiv$' as equivalence; it is defined in Chapter 2.)

If $\sqrt{}$ is not provided by the programming language, then more complex — but still executable — coding features must be used. And that is the usual case. The overall refinement of specification (eventually) to code is made in steps, each introducing a little more executability, or a little more efficiency. A sequence results, each element refined by the next:

$$spec \sqsubseteq mixed_0 \sqsubseteq \cdots \sqsubseteq mixed_n \sqsubseteq code .$$

We see later that the intermediate steps $mixed_i$ mix specifications and code together. Indeed, in such sequences it is difficult to say when specifying stops and coding begins, and there is nothing to be gained by trying. We call *all* of them programs, whether executable or not, and we reserve the term 'specification' for frame and predicate pairs $w\colon [pre , post]$ only; they can be an entire program (like *spec*), or parts of programs (occurring in $mixed_i$). We use the term 'code' for programs written entirely in our executable language (which we define shortly). Usually, an assignment command is code; a specification is not.

All that is summarised in Figure 1.6. *Program development* moves, via a series of refinement steps, within the outer box (of programs) towards the inner box (of programs that are code as well).

Developing programs, in that sense, is the main topic of this book.

1.6   Mixed programs

Mixed programs occur during development. They contain both abstract and executable constructs, linked by program constructors like *sequential composition*, here defined informally:

> The effect of the program *prog*1; *prog*2 is the effect of *prog*1 followed by the effect of *prog*2.

For example, the mixed program

$$x := 9;$$
$$y: [\textsf{true} ,\ y^2 = x]$$

sets x to 9 and y either to 3 or to -3.

Constructors like sequential composition are introduced by their own laws, which are the subject of later chapters.

1.7   Infeasible programs

Suppose Specification (1.3) is refined still further (by Law 1.2) to

$$y: \left[\textsf{true} ,\ y^2 = x \wedge y \geq 0\right] . \qquad (1.4)$$

Here, the programmer has given up too much. His job in Specification (1.4) is impossible, as we can easily show: since x, y are in $\mathbb{R}$ there are some allowed initial values of x for which *no* final value of y will do. Such a specification is *infeasible*.

Infeasible specifications cannot be refined by *any* code; and so agreeing on a contract containing an infeasible specification means eventual disappointment for the client, and possible financial ruin for the programmer. For that reason it is important to be able to check for feasibility:

Definition 1.4 feasibility The specification w: [*pre* , *post*] is *feasible* iff

$$pre \quad \Rightarrow \quad (\exists\, w : T \cdot post) ,$$

where T is the type[1] of the variables w.
□

The right-hand side is read "there exists a w of type T such that *post*". The symbol $\exists$ is further discussed in Chapter 2, and types are the subject of Chapter 6.

Applying Definition 1.4 to Specification (1.4), the programmer tries to prove

$$\textsf{true} \quad \Rightarrow \quad \left(\exists\, y : \mathbb{R} \cdot y^2 = x \wedge y \geq 0\right)$$

under the assumption that x is of type $\mathbb{R}$. But he cannot: the right-hand side is equivalent to $x \geq 0$, which is not implied by $\textsf{true}$. Hence (1.4) is infeasible. For historical reasons, infeasible programs are sometimes called *miracles*.

Remember that code is designed to be executable: all code, therefore, is feasible. (See Exercise 1.17.)

---

[1]In Chapter 6 the notion of type will be generalised to include so-called 'local invariants', and then a more comprehensive definition (6.5) of feasibility will be appropriate. It does not concern us now, but must be borne in mind if ever referring to the definition above once local invariants have been introduced.

1.8   Some common idioms

We can compact our new notations somewhat by taking advantage of common idioms. Often the precondition of a specification is just true, for example, indicating termination in all circumstances. In that case we just omit it:

Abbreviation 1.5 default precondition

$$w\colon [post] \;\;\widehat{=}\;\; w\colon [\text{true}\,,\; post] \;.$$

□

The symbol '$\widehat{=}$' indicates a definition, and is used in preference to equality when the left-hand side is newly introduced. (Colon ':' is used instead of membership '∈' in the same circumstances.)

When the frame is empty and the postcondition is true, we have a command that either fails to terminate (because its precondition is false), or terminates but changes nothing (because the frame is empty). We call those *assumptions*, and they are related to the practice of 'annotating' a program with formulae that are supposed to hold at various points. With that in mind we have

Abbreviation 1.6 assumption

$$\{pre\} \;\;\widehat{=}\;\; \colon [pre\,,\; \text{true}] \;.$$

□

As a special case (to strengthen further the resemblance to annotating programs), we allow the semicolon that would normally indicate sequential composition to be omitted if it follows an assumption. Thus the program

$$\{0 \le x \le 9\}\; y := \sqrt{x} \tag{1.5}$$

sets y to the non-negative square root of x provided x lies between 0 and 9 inclusive. If x does not fall within that range, then $\{0 \le x \le 9\}$ aborts, effectively aborting the whole of (1.5).

The similarity between (1.5) and (1.2) is not accidental, and suggests some further correspondences. One is

Law 1.7 simple specification   Provided E contains no w,

$$w := E \;\;\;=\;\;\; w\colon [w = E] \;.$$

If w and E are lists, then the formula $w = E$ means the equating of corresponding elements of the lists.
□

Law 1.7 together with a law relating assumptions and preconditions will allow us to show that (1.5) and (1.2) are equal. The law is

Law 1.8 <u>absorb assumption</u> An assumption before a specification can be absorbed directly into its precondition.

$$\{\mathit{pre'}\} \; w{:}\; [\mathit{pre} \; , \; \mathit{post}] \quad = \quad w{:}\; [\mathit{pre'} \wedge \mathit{pre} \; , \; \mathit{post}] \; .$$

□

Law 1.8 highlights the fact that 'aborting now' (at $\{\mathit{pre'}\}$) is the same as 'aborting later' (at $[\mathit{pre'} \wedge \cdots)$ in imperative programs. (See Exercise 1.6.)

With those new laws, the proof of equality runs as follows:

$$\{0 \leq x \leq 9\} \; y := \sqrt{x}$$
$=$ *"simple specification 1.7"*
$$\{0 \leq x \leq 9\} \; y{:}\; [y = \sqrt{x}]$$
$=$ *"absorb assumption 1.8"*
$$y{:}\; [0 \leq x \leq 9 \; , \; y = \sqrt{x}]$$
$=$ "rewrite postcondition"
$$y{:}\; [0 \leq x \leq 9 \; , \; y^2 = x \wedge y \geq 0] \; .$$

With the comment "rewrite postcondition" we are merely relying on the fact that for reals x and y

$$y^2 = x \wedge y \geq 0 \quad \equiv \quad y = \sqrt{x} \; .$$

1.9   Extreme programs

We finish with some specification pathology. From the client's point of view, the worst specification of all is

$$w{:}\; [\mathsf{false} \; , \; \mathsf{true}] \; .$$

It is *never* guaranteed to terminate (precondition **false**); and even when it does, it has complete freedom in its setting of the variables (postcondition **true**). As a contract, it allows any refinement at all: infinite loops, programs setting w to arbitrary values — even programs that change variables other than w. We call it **abort**.

Slightly better is the program that always terminates, but guarantees no particular result:

$$w{:}\; [\mathsf{true} \; , \; \mathsf{true}] \; .$$

It can be refined to any *terminating* program that changes only w; we can imagine that it just chooses w at random. We call it **choose** w.

Better still is the program which always terminates, changing nothing. Its frame is empty:

: [true , true] .

We call it **skip**.

Best of all is the infeasible program that always terminates and establishes the impossible false:

w: [true , false] .

No computer can execute that program; no contract based on it could ever be met. We call it **magic**.

Most of the above are seldom written deliberately in programs (**skip** is the exception). But we need their names if only to reason about them.

1.10 Exercises

Exercises marked with $\heartsuit$ are answered in Appendix B.

Ex. 1.1 $\heartsuit$ 'The programmer's job is to take specifications, via a sequence of refinement steps, to code. Hence the more refined the client's requirements, the fewer refinement steps remain for the programmer to do, and the easier his job.'

The above argument suggests the *opposite* of Figure 1.3. Where is the error?

Ex. 1.2 $\heartsuit$ Recall Specification (1.1) from p.5. Write a new specification that finds a square root y of x if x is non-negative but no more than 9, and sets y to 0 if x is negative.

Ex. 1.3   Revise your answer to Exercise 1.2 so that when x is negative initially the specification does not choose any particular final value for y, but still terminates.

Ex. 1.4 $\heartsuit$ Which of these refinements are valid? (Use *strengthen postcondition* 1.1 and *weaken precondition* 1.2).

1. x: $[x \geq 0] \sqsubseteq ?x$: $[x = 0]$
2. x: $[x \geq 0 , \text{true}] \sqsubseteq ?x$: $[x = 0 , \text{true}]$
3. x: $[x \geq 0 , x = 0] \sqsubseteq ?x$: $[x = 0 , x \geq 0]$
4. x: $[x = 0 , x \geq 0] \sqsubseteq ?x$: $[x \geq 0 , x = 0]$
5. y: $[x > 0 , x > y \geq 0] \sqsubseteq ?y$: $[x > y \geq 0]$
6. y: $[x > y \geq 0] \sqsubseteq ?y$: $[y = 0]$
7. y: $[x > 0 , x > y \geq 0] \sqsubseteq ?y$: $[y = 0]$

Ex. 1.5   What refinement relations hold between Specification (1.1) and those in Exercises 1.2 and 1.3? (You cannot yet prove them.)

Ex. 1.6   Use *absorb assumption* 1.8 to show that

$$\{pre'\} \; w: [pre \, , \; post] \quad = \quad \{pre\} \; w: [pre' \, , \; post] \; .$$

Ex. 1.7 ♡   Give an informal argument to show that *contracting the frame* is a refinement; that is, argue that

$$w, x: [pre \, , \; post] \quad \sqsubseteq \quad w: [pre \, , \; post] \, .$$

(That refinement appears later as *contract frame* 5.4.)

Ex. 1.8 ♡   Prove that your answer to Exercise 1.2 is feasible.

Ex. 1.9   Prove that your answer to Exercise 1.3 is feasible.

Ex. 1.10 ♡   Show that the following is *not* feasible:

$$y: \left[x \geq 0 \, , \; y^2 = x \wedge y > 0 \right] .$$

Explain informally why it is not.

Ex. 1.11 ♡   Describe informally the program

$$: [\mathsf{false} \, , \; \mathsf{false}] \, .$$

Is it **magic**? (Is it feasible?) Is it **skip**? (Can it change w?) Is it **abort**? (Is it ever guaranteed to terminate?)

Ex. 1.12 ♡   What is the effect of adding to a program an assumption that might not be true during execution? Are there circumstances in which that has no effect at all?

Ex. 1.13 ♡   Is it a refinement to strengthen or to weaken assumptions?

Ex. 1.14 ♡   Prove this equality:

Law 1.9 <u>merge assumptions</u>

$$\{pre'\} \; \{pre\} \quad = \quad \{pre' \wedge pre\} \, .$$

□

Ex. 1.15   Show that assumptions can be removed from a program unconditionally, as expressed in this law:

> *Law 1.10* <u>remove assumption</u> Any assumption is refined by **skip**.
>
> $\{pre\} \quad \sqsubseteq \quad \textbf{skip} .$

□

Does that mean that assumptions are code?

Ex. 1.16   Show that neither *strengthen postcondition* 1.1 nor *weaken precondition* 1.2 can refine an infeasible specification to a feasible one.

Ex. 1.17 ♡   'Infeasible specifications cannot be refined by any code' (p.10). From that, show that all code is feasible.

Ex. 1.18 ♡   Show that anything refines **abort**: that is, that

$w\colon [\textsf{false} , \textsf{true}] \quad \sqsubseteq \quad w\colon [pre , post] ,$

for *any* formulae *pre* and *post*.

Ex. 1.19   Show that **magic** refines anything: that is, that

$w\colon [pre , post] \quad \sqsubseteq \quad w\colon [\textsf{true} , \textsf{false}] ,$

for *any* formulae *pre* and *post*.

Chapter 2

The predicate calculus

2.1 Its relevance

The pre- and postconditions of specifications are predicate calculus formulae. And some refinement rules have formulae attached as provisos, meaning that the rule is applicable only if its attached formula is true — which may require a proof. Thus we use the predicate calculus in two ways: for describing, and for reasoning.

Predicate calculus was developed by logicians well before the appearance of computers. With it, they hoped to formalise human reasoning about mathematics at least. The truth or falsity of any conjecture was to be decided as follows:

1. Express the conjecture as a formula $\mathcal{A}$. (That requires a precise notion of the meaning of formulae.)
2. Using a precise system of proof, given beforehand, either prove $\mathcal{A}$ or its negation $\neg\mathcal{A}$.

The system of proof (based on axioms and inference rules) was designed so that there could never be any doubt about whether a text was a proof or not. Finding a proof, however, remained as much a problem as before.

In fact, it became harder to find proofs — and not only because incorrect ones were newly excluded! The rigorous rules each expressed very small reasoning steps, and so proofs required very many of them. But in a theoretical sense that did not matter: every true formula could be proved in that way.

Predicate calculus is of practical concern to computer scientists, however. To use it effectively, we must avoid long proofs. We do that in three ways. First, we choose our laws of program refinement so that they generate few proof obligations. For example, we do not include feasibility checks at every stage, because infeasible programs cannot lead to (incorrect) code — they lead to no code at all. They lose time, but not human life.

Second, we use routinely the more advanced techniques of logical argument (proof by contradiction, etc.) which have themselves been justified formally by others. We will not justify them ourselves.

Finally, in each program to be developed we look for suitable notation of *our* devising, appropriate to the characteristics of the problem. We might assume some properties of the structures involved, calling them 'obvious'; others we might prove.

In summary: We do not use or advocate any particular system of formal logical reasoning with the predicate calculus (axiomatic, natural deduction, tableaux, etc.). Our use of the predicate calculus is based on familiarity (eventually!) with a number of predicate laws, usually equalities between formulae, which are used to reduce a complex formula to a simple one. That is how other calculi in mathematics are employed; we only do the same.

2.2   Terms

Terms (also called expressions) are built from variables, constants, and functions. Thus x on its own is a term (it is a variable); and 1 is a term (it is a constant); and $x + 1$ is a term (it is formed by applying the function $+$ to the two terms x and 1). A state, which maps variables to values (recall Chapter 1), determines the values of terms: one speaks of a term having some value in a state. In a state that maps x to three, the term x has the value three (trivially), and 0 has the value zero (in every state, in fact: that is why it is called a constant), and $x + 1$ has the value four.

Our *variables* will have short lower-case *italic* names, drawn from the Roman alphabet.

Our *constants* will have their usual mathematical names, like 0 and π. (The real number constants e and i will not cause trouble.)

Our *functions* will have their usual mathematical names too, like square root $\sqrt{\ }$, plus $+$, and factorial ! . Some of those take one argument ($\sqrt{\ }$ and !), some take two ($+$), and the position of the arguments can vary: sometimes the function is written before its argument ($\sqrt{\ }$), sometimes between its arguments ($+$), and sometimes after its argument (!). The number of arguments a function takes is called its *arity*.

We often need to introduce new functions, of our own, just for a particular problem. For those, the syntax is more regular: they will have short lower-case sanserif names, in the Roman alphabet. Their arguments follow them, separated by spaces. For uniformity, we use that convention even for the mathematical functions log, sin, etc.

Terms are made from all the above. A *term* is either

1. a variable;
2. a constant; or
3. a function applied to the correct number of other terms, depending on its arity.

Figure 2.1 lists some terms.

$$0$$
$$x$$
$$x + 1$$
$$\log x$$
$$\sin(\pi/2)$$
$$(a + b) \times 3!$$

Figure 2.1 Some terms

$$\text{false}$$
$$1 < (a \div 2)$$
$$(x + 1) = 7$$
$$\text{even } 6$$
$$\pi \in \mathbb{R}$$

Figure 2.2 Some simple formulae

2.3   Simple formulae

Simple formulae[1] are built from terms and predicate symbols. The best-known predicate symbols represent the binary relations from arithmetic: $<$, $=$, $\leq$ etc. Like functions, predicates have an arity; for binary relations, the arity is two. Again like functions, predicates are applied to terms.

Unlike functions, a predicate applied to (the correct number of) terms is not another term: it is a *simple formula*. Simple formulae do not have general values like terms; instead, they take only the values true and false.

For conventional predicates (like binary relations) we use the usual notation. Predicates that we introduce ourselves will be short Roman sanserif names, and their arguments will follow them, separated by spaces (as for our functions).

Finally, there are the two constant predicates true and false. In every state, the first is true and the second is false.

Figure 2.2 lists some simple formulae.

---

[1]They are called *atomic* formulae in the logic literature.

$\mathcal{A}$	$\mathcal{B}$	$\mathcal{A} \wedge \mathcal{B}$
true	true	true
true	false	false
false	true	false
false	false	false

$\mathcal{A}$	$\mathcal{B}$	$\mathcal{A} \vee \mathcal{B}$
true	true	true
true	false	true
false	true	true
false	false	false

$\mathcal{A}$	$\mathcal{B}$	$\mathcal{A} \Rightarrow \mathcal{B}$
true	true	true
true	false	false
false	true	true
false	false	true

$\mathcal{A}$	$\mathcal{B}$	$\mathcal{A} \Leftrightarrow \mathcal{B}$
true	true	true
true	false	false
false	true	false
false	false	true

$\mathcal{A}$	$\neg \mathcal{A}$
true	false
false	true

Figure 2.3 Truth tables for propositional connectives

2.4   Propositional formulae

Propositional formulae are built from simple formulae, using propositional connectives. The connectives are $\wedge$ (and), $\vee$ (or), $\neg$ (not), $\Rightarrow$ (implies), and $\Leftrightarrow$ (if and only if, or iff). (As nouns, they are conjunction, disjunction, negation, implication and equivalence.) Except for $\neg$, all have two arguments, written on either side; the single argument of $\neg$ is written after it.

Like simple formulae, propositional formulae are either true or false, once given a state. If, for example, $\mathcal{A}$ and $\mathcal{B}$ are propositional formulae, then the propositional formula $\mathcal{A} \wedge \mathcal{B}$ is true exactly when both $\mathcal{A}$ *and* $\mathcal{B}$ are true. That is summarised in this table:

$\mathcal{A}$	$\mathcal{B}$	$\mathcal{A} \wedge \mathcal{B}$
true	true	true
true	false	false
false	true	false
false	false	false

A complete set of 'truth tables' for the five connectives is given in Figure 2.3. In a formula $\mathcal{A} \Rightarrow \mathcal{B}$, the subformula $\mathcal{A}$ is the *antecedent*, and $\mathcal{B}$ is the *consequent*.

Following convention, we allow the abbreviation $a < b < c$ (and similar) for the propositional formula $a < b \wedge b < c$.

Figure 2.4 gives some propositional formulae.

$$\text{true}$$
$$x^2 = -1$$
$$(x \leq y) \wedge (y \leq x + 1)$$
$$(x > 0) \Rightarrow (x + y \neq y)$$
$$(0 \leq p < q) \Rightarrow (0 < q)$$
$$(n! = n) \Leftrightarrow (n = 1) \vee (n = 2)$$

Figure 2.4 Some propositional formulae

2.5   Quantifiers

2.5.1   Universal quantification

A *universally quantified* formula is written

$$(\forall x \cdot \mathcal{A}),$$

where x is a variable, called the *bound* variable, and $\mathcal{A}$ is some other formula, called the *body*. It is true exactly when $\mathcal{A}$ is true for all values of x, where it is understood that we know the set from which those values of x are drawn (for example, the real numbers). We also allow a list of bound variables, as in $(\forall x, y \cdot \mathcal{A})$. There, the quantification is true exactly when the body is true for all values of those variables chosen independently. The order in the list does not affect the meaning.

Consider this parody of the distributive law from arithmetic:

$$a + (b \times c) \quad = \quad (a + b) \times (a + c) .$$

Although one would say informally 'that is false', it is in fact true in some states. (Map all three variables to one-third.)

But the quantified formula

$$(\forall a, b, c \cdot a + (b \times c) = (a + b) \times (a + c)) \tag{2.1}$$

is identically false, because it is not the case that the body is true for *all* values of a, b, and c.

Now consider the similar formula

$$(\forall b, c \cdot a + (b \times c) = (a + b) \times (a + c)), \tag{2.2}$$

in which we have quantified only b and c. It depends on a; and it is true when a is zero, and false otherwise.

2.5.2 Free and bound variables

Formula (2.2) depends on a, but not on b or c. Variable a is a *free* variable; variables b and c are not free, because they are bound by the quantifier $\forall$. In fact, variables b and c are just place-holders in that formula, indicating the positions at which all values are to be considered. Changing their names does not affect the formula (provided the new names do not conflict with existing ones). Thus

$$(\forall\, d, e \cdot a + (d \times e) = (a + d) \times (a + e))$$

has the same meaning as (2.2). Formula (2.1) has no free variables, since a, b, c are bound; it does not depend on the value of any variable.

In general, *bound* variables are those bound by a quantifier, as is x in $(\forall\, x \cdot \mathcal{A})$; all free occurrences of x in $\mathcal{A}$ itself become bound occurrences in the larger $(\forall\, x \cdot \mathcal{A})$.

Section A.2.1 further discusses free and bound variables.

2.5.3 Existential quantification

Existential quantification is used to express 'there exists'. An *existentially quantified* formula is written

$$(\exists\, x \cdot \mathcal{A})\,,$$

where x and $\mathcal{A}$ are as before. It is true exactly when there exists a value for x that makes $\mathcal{A}$ true. So the existentially quantified formula

$$(\exists\, a, b, c \cdot a + (b \times c) = (a + b) \times (a + c))$$

is true. Free occurrences of x in $\mathcal{A}$ are bound in $(\exists\, x \cdot \mathcal{A})$ just as they are in $(\forall\, x \cdot \mathcal{A})$.

2.5.4 Typed quantifications

A *typed quantification* indicates explicitly the set from which values for the bound variable are drawn. For example, let $\mathbb{Z}$ denote the set of all integers, and $\mathbb{N}$ the set of all natural numbers (non-negative integers). Then $(\exists\, x : \mathbb{Z} \cdot x < 0)$ is true, but $(\exists\, x : \mathbb{N} \cdot x < 0)$ is false (because 0 is the least natural number). In general, *typed* quantifications are written

$$(\forall\, x : T \cdot \mathcal{A}) \quad \text{and} \quad (\exists\, x : T \cdot \mathcal{A})\,,$$

where T denotes some set of values. The variable x then ranges over that set.

If we know beforehand the set from which values are drawn, we can use the simpler untyped quantifiers; the typing is then understood from context. But when several such sets are involved simultaneously, we use typed quantifiers.

$$\text{true}$$
$$x \neq 3$$
$$y > 0 \Rightarrow y \neq 0$$
$$(\forall\, x : \mathbb{R} \cdot (\exists\, y : \mathbb{C} \cdot y^2 = x))$$
$$a \div b = c \Leftrightarrow (\exists\, r \cdot 0 \leq r < b \wedge a = b \times c + r)$$

Figure 2.5 Some general formulae

2.6   (General) formulae

Now we draw together all the above. A *formula* is any one of the following:

1. A simple formula.
2. $\neg \mathcal{A}$, where $\mathcal{A}$ is a formula.
3. $\mathcal{A} \wedge \mathcal{B}$, $\mathcal{A} \vee \mathcal{B}$, $\mathcal{A} \Rightarrow \mathcal{B}$, or $\mathcal{A} \Leftrightarrow \mathcal{B}$, where $\mathcal{A}$ and $\mathcal{B}$ are formulae.
4. $(\forall\, x : T \cdot \mathcal{A})$ or $(\exists\, x : T \cdot \mathcal{A})$, where x is a list of variables, T denotes a set, and $\mathcal{A}$ is a formula.

That definition allows nested quantifications, such as

$$(\forall\, a : \mathbb{R} \cdot (\exists\, b, c : \mathbb{R} \cdot a + (b \times c) = (a + b) \times (a + c)))$$

(which is true), and the application of propositional operators to quantifications, such as

$$x \neq 0 \Rightarrow (\exists\, y : \mathbb{Z} \cdot 0 \leq y \wedge y < x),$$

true if x is a natural number.

Figure 2.5 gives some general formulae.

2.7   Operator precedence

Strictly speaking, a term like $2 + 3 \times 4$ is ambiguous: is its value fourteen or twenty? Such questions can be resolved by parentheses — $2 + (3 \times 4)$ *vs* $(2 + 3) \times 4$ — but they can be resolved also by general precedence rules. The usual rule from arithmetic is that $\times$ is done before $+$: we say that $\times$ has *higher precedence*.

We adopt all the usual precedence rules from arithmetic, adding to them that functions have highest precedence of all: thus $\sqrt{4} + 5$ is seven, not three. When several functions are used, the rightmost is applied first: thus $\log \sin(\pi/2)$ is zero.[2] We do not require parentheses around function arguments; but note that $\sin \pi/2$ is zero, whereas $\sin(\pi/2)$ is one.

---

[2] Without higher-order functions, the reverse does not make sense anyway.

In propositional formulae, the precedence is (highest) $\neg, \wedge, \vee, \Rightarrow, \Leftrightarrow$ (lowest).

There is no need for precedence rules of quantifiers, because they are always written with enclosing parentheses $(\cdots)$ that give their scope.

2.8   Predicate calculus

2.8.1   Relations between formulae

The two (simple) formulae $x = y \Rightarrow x \neq z$ and $x = z \Rightarrow x \neq y$ are equivalent in this sense: in every state they are both true or both false together. In general, that two formulae $\mathcal{A}$ and $\mathcal{B}$ are *equivalent* is written $\mathcal{A} \equiv \mathcal{B}$, and means

> In every state, $\mathcal{A}$ is true if and only if $\mathcal{B}$ is true .

That is indeed the same as saying 'in every state, $\mathcal{A} \Leftrightarrow \mathcal{B}$ is true'. But there is an important difference between $\equiv$ and $\Leftrightarrow$. The first is a relation between formulae: $\mathcal{A} \equiv \mathcal{B}$ is a statement about $\mathcal{A}$ and $\mathcal{B}$; it is not a formula itself. The second is a propositional connective: $\mathcal{A} \Leftrightarrow \mathcal{B}$ says nothing about formulae; rather it is a formula itself.

Here are two other relations between formulae. The statement $\mathcal{A} \Rrightarrow \mathcal{B}$ means

> In every state, if $\mathcal{A}$ is true then $\mathcal{B}$ is true .

That is the same as 'in every state, $\mathcal{A} \Rightarrow \mathcal{B}$ is true'. And the statement $\mathcal{A} \Lleftarrow \mathcal{B}$ means

> In every state, $\mathcal{A}$ is true if $\mathcal{B}$ is true .

It is the same as 'in every state, $\mathcal{B} \Rightarrow \mathcal{A}$ is true'. The relation $\Rrightarrow$ is known as *entailment*.

Those three relations are used to set out chains of reasoning like this one: for any formulae $\mathcal{A}$, $\mathcal{B}$, and $\mathcal{C}$,

$(\mathcal{A} \Rightarrow \mathcal{C}) \vee (\mathcal{B} \Rightarrow \mathcal{C})$

$\equiv$ "writing implication as disjunction"
$(\neg\mathcal{A} \vee \mathcal{C}) \vee (\neg\mathcal{B} \vee \mathcal{C})$

$\equiv$ "associativity, commutativity of $\vee$"
$(\neg\mathcal{A} \vee \neg\mathcal{B}) \vee (\mathcal{C} \vee \mathcal{C})$

$\equiv$ "de Morgan, idempotence of $\vee$"
$\neg(\mathcal{A} \wedge \mathcal{B}) \vee \mathcal{C}$

$\equiv$ "writing disjunction as implication"
$\mathcal{A} \wedge \mathcal{B} \Rightarrow \mathcal{C}$.

Each formula is related to the one before it by the relation $\equiv$, $\Rightarrow$, or $\Leftarrow$. And each step between formulae carries a decoration, a 'hint', suggesting why it is valid. The quotes "" separate the hints from the proof itself. They are not part of the proof; they are *about* the proof.

The relation $\equiv$ is *transitive*, which means that whenever both $\mathcal{A} \equiv \mathcal{B}$ and $\mathcal{B} \equiv \mathcal{C}$ (which we can write $\mathcal{A} \equiv \mathcal{B} \equiv \mathcal{C}$), then we have $\mathcal{A} \equiv \mathcal{C}$ too. That is why the chain of equivalences above establishes overall that the first formula is equivalent to the last:

$$(\mathcal{A} \Rightarrow \mathcal{C}) \vee (\mathcal{B} \Rightarrow \mathcal{C}) \quad \equiv \quad \mathcal{A} \wedge \mathcal{B} \Rightarrow \mathcal{C} .$$

The other relations $\Rightarrow$ and $\Leftarrow$ are transitive as well, but not if mixed together. Either can be mixed with $\equiv$, however; thus from $\mathcal{A} \equiv \mathcal{B} \Rightarrow \mathcal{C}$ we still have $\mathcal{A} \Rightarrow \mathcal{C}$. Finally, writing just $\Rightarrow \mathcal{A}$ on its own means that $\mathcal{A}$ is true in every state.

2.8.2   Laws for calculation

To reason as above requires some knowledge of the laws to which one can appeal, like "associativity, commutativity of $\vee$". Appendix A contains a collection of them. Each can be used to justify steps in a calculation, and often there are several that will do. One soon acquires favourites.

We do not present all those laws here; indeed, it will be some time before we need many of them. Where helpful, however, we refer to them directly. The reasoning above proved Predicate law A.36; here it is again, by numbers:

$$(\mathcal{A} \Rightarrow \mathcal{C}) \vee (\mathcal{B} \Rightarrow \mathcal{C})$$
$\equiv$ "Predicate law A.22"
$$(\neg\mathcal{A} \vee \mathcal{C}) \vee (\neg\mathcal{B} \vee \mathcal{C})$$
$\equiv$ "Predicate laws A.3, A.5"
$$(\neg\mathcal{A} \vee \neg\mathcal{B}) \vee (\mathcal{C} \vee \mathcal{C})$$
$\equiv$ "Predicate laws A.18, A.1"
$$\neg(\mathcal{A} \wedge \mathcal{B}) \vee \mathcal{C}$$
$\equiv$ "Predicate law A.22"
$$\mathcal{A} \wedge \mathcal{B} \Rightarrow \mathcal{C} .$$

Note the use of equivalence to replace a *part* of a formula, leading to an equivalence for the *whole* formula. That is the usual rule in mathematics: we can substitute equals for equals. But some of our laws are entailments $\Rightarrow$, not equivalences; their substitution within formulae leads either to overall entailment or to its converse $\Leftarrow$. Entailment distributes through quantification, conjunction, disjunction, and the consequent of implication; it is reversed in negations and antecedents of implications. It does not distribute at all through equivalence $\Leftrightarrow$.

Here is an example of distribution. Suppose we have $\mathcal{A} \Rightarrow \mathcal{A}'$, $\mathcal{B} \Leftarrow \mathcal{B}'$, and $\mathcal{C} \equiv \mathcal{C}'$. Then we can proceed as follows:

$(A \Rightarrow B) \Rightarrow C$
$\Rightarrow$ "since $A \Rrightarrow A'$"
$(A' \Rightarrow B) \Rightarrow C$
$\Rightarrow$ "since $B \Lleftarrow B'$"
$(A' \Rightarrow B') \Rightarrow C$
$\equiv$ "since $C \equiv C'$"
$(A' \Rightarrow B') \Rightarrow C'$.

2.9 Exercises

Ex. 2.1   Which of these are terms?

1. true
2. 17
3. $\log^2 x$
4. $\log \log x$
5. $(\log x)^2$
6. $\log x^2$
7. $2x$
8. $x < x + 1$

Ex. 2.2   Write terms for the following:

1. The square root of the factorial of n.
2. The factorial of the square root of n.

Ex. 2.3 ♡   Which of these are propositional formulae?

1. true
2. *true*
3. true
4. $x < y \Rightarrow z$
5. $x < y \Rrightarrow z$
6. $x < y \Rightarrow y < z$
7. $x < y \Rrightarrow y < z$

Ex. 2.4   Assuming that all variables denote natural numbers, which of these propositional formulae are true in all states?

1. $x \geq 0$
2. $x < y \Rightarrow x + 1 \leq y$
3. $x \leq y \vee y \leq x$
4. $x \leq y \wedge y \leq x \Rightarrow x = y$
5. $x < y \wedge y < x \Rightarrow x = y$

6. $x < y \wedge y < x \Rightarrow x \neq y$
7. $x < y \vee y < x \Rightarrow x \neq y$

Ex. 2.5 ♡   Assuming that the one-place predicates **even**, **odd** mean 'is an even number', 'is an odd number' respectively, write general formulae for the following:

1. Every integer is either even or odd.
2. Every odd natural number is one more than some even natural number.
3. There is an even integer that is not one more than any odd natural number.
4. Zero is the least natural number.
5. There is no least integer.
6. Given any positive real number, there is another real number strictly between it and zero.

Ex. 2.6 ♡   Recall that $(\exists\, x \cdot \mathcal{A})$ means 'there is *at least* one x such that $\mathcal{A}$'. Write another formula that means 'there is *at most* one x such that $\mathcal{A}$'.

Ex. 2.7   (Recall Exercise 2.6.) Write a formula that means 'there is *exactly* one x such that $\mathcal{A}$'.

Ex. 2.8 ♡   Use the truth tables of Figure 2.3 to show that these formulae are true in all states:

1. $\mathcal{A} \Rightarrow (\mathcal{B} \Rightarrow \mathcal{A})$
2. $(\mathcal{A} \Rightarrow (\mathcal{B} \Rightarrow \mathcal{C})) \Rightarrow ((\mathcal{A} \Rightarrow \mathcal{B}) \Rightarrow (\mathcal{A} \Rightarrow \mathcal{C}))$
3. $(\neg\mathcal{A} \Rightarrow \neg\mathcal{B}) \Rightarrow (\mathcal{B} \Rightarrow \mathcal{A})$

Ex. 2.9 ♡   Show that $\mathcal{A} \Rightarrow \mathcal{B} \Rightarrow \mathcal{A}$. *Hint*: Recall Exercise 2.8, and the meaning of $\Rightarrow$.

Ex. 2.10 ♡   Prove this, using laws from Appendix A:

$$(\exists\, x \cdot (\mathcal{A} \Rightarrow \mathcal{B}) \wedge (\neg\mathcal{A} \Rightarrow \mathcal{C})) \equiv (\exists\, x \cdot \mathcal{A} \wedge \mathcal{B}) \vee (\exists\, x \cdot \neg\mathcal{A} \wedge \mathcal{C}).$$

Ex. 2.11   Suppose $\mathcal{N}$ contains no free x. Prove this:

$$(\exists\, x \cdot (\mathcal{N} \Rightarrow \mathcal{A}) \wedge (\neg\mathcal{N} \Rightarrow \mathcal{B})) \equiv (\mathcal{N} \Rightarrow (\exists\, x \cdot \mathcal{A})) \wedge (\neg\mathcal{N} \Rightarrow (\exists\, x \cdot \mathcal{B})).$$

Hint: Recall Exercise 2.10.

Ex. 2.12 ♡   Prove this, for any formula $\mathcal{A}$:

$$(\exists\, a \cdot (\forall b \cdot \mathcal{A})) \quad\Rightarrow\quad (\forall b \cdot (\exists\, a \cdot \mathcal{A})).$$

Is the converse true?

Ex. 2.13   Show that $(\exists\, x, y \cdot x \neq y) \equiv (\forall x \cdot (\exists\, y \cdot x \neq y))$. *Hint*: To show $\mathcal{A} \equiv \mathcal{B}$, show $\mathcal{A} \Rightarrow \mathcal{B} \Rightarrow \mathcal{A}$.

Chapter 3

Assignment and sequential composition

3.1 Introduction

In Chapter 1 we saw that *code* is a sub-language in which we write programs that are executable by computer directly. All conventional computer programming languages are examples of code, because all of them were designed to be executed by computers. At least part of our language, however, was designed for program *development*: and so we must be explicit about which part of it is code, and which is not.

Our code will be written in a language that includes assignment, sequential composition, alternation, iteration and recursion. All of those have more or less their conventional meaning, but we do not explain them only in the conventional way.

Each executable construct is introduced in *two* ways: informally, as an operation on some computer; and formally, as a refinement of some specification. The first may aid the intuition, but is not essential for program development. Nor is it sufficient. The second way is essential for program development, however, because only that defines precisely how to reach code from specifications.

In this chapter we meet our first examples of code: assignment, and sequential composition. Others will follow in succeeding chapters.

3.2 Assignment

Informally, an *assignment* changes a single variable, leaving all others unchanged. An expression E is evaluated in the initial state; then in the final state, a variable w is newly mapped to that value, irrespective of its mapping in the initial state. (The initial value of the variable is lost.) Such assignments are written

$$w := E \ ,$$

27

$$x := 1 \qquad \text{Assign 1 to } x.$$

$$x := y \qquad \text{Assign the (initial) value of } y \text{ to } x.$$

$$x := x + 1 \qquad \text{Assign the initial value of } x + 1 \text{ to}$$
$$x \text{ — that is, increment } x.$$

$$x := y \times (x + y) \quad \text{A more complex expression.}$$

Each of the above assignments takes any initial state that satisfies $x = 0 \wedge y = 1$ to a final state satisfying $x = 1 \wedge y = 1$, and changes no variable other than x.

Figure 3.1 Simple assignments

and they are read 'w gets E'. The expression E is built from any constants, variables, and operators available to us; later we will be more explicit about which they are. Figure 3.1 gives some examples of assignments.

A *multiple* assignment changes several variables at once. It is written

$$w_0, \cdots, w_n := E_0, \cdots, E_n .$$

That command assigns E_0 to w_0, $\cdots$, and E_n to w_n simultaneously. (Assigning E_0 to w_0 first, and then later E_n to w_n, does not in general have the same effect.) Figure 3.2 gives examples of multiple assignments. When discussing assignments in general we use the simple form $w := E$, and allow w and E to be lists if appropriate.

We have already met the refinement law for assignment as *assignment* 1.3 in Section 1.5.2 — think of that as a preview of this chapter. The law is based on the observation that in an assignment $w := E$, only w is changed; then *post* describes the final state provided that $post[w \backslash E]$ described the initial state.

Law *assignment* 1.3 shows that each of the assignments of Figure 3.1 refines the specification

$$x \colon [x = 0 \wedge y = 1 \ , \ x = 1 \wedge y = 1] \ ,$$

and similarly each of the multiple assignments of Figure 3.2 refines the specification

$$x, y \colon [x = 0 \wedge y = 1 \ , \ x = 1 \wedge y = 0] \ .$$

In Figure 3.3 there are more examples of refinement to assignment.

$x, y := 1, 0$	Assign 1 to x and 0 to y.
$x, y := y, x$	Swap x and y.
$x, y := x + y, x \times y$	Assign the initial value of $x + y$ to x and the initial value of $x \times y$ to y.

Each of the above assignments takes any initial state that satisfies $x = 0 \land y = 1$ to a final state satisfying $x = 1 \land y = 0$, and changes no variables other than x and y.

Figure 3.2 Multiple assignments

3.3 Open assignment

A slightly mysterious-looking form of (multiple) assignment, but one that we shall find useful later, assigns any value whatever: the command $w, x := E, ?$ assigns E to w but leaves open the value that will be assigned to x. For that reason we call it *open assignment*. (We assume as usual that w and x are disjoint lists of variables.)

Open assignment is used mainly in specifying desired behaviour — although it is code, in fact — because it is a convenient way of writing 'and x may be changed'. Thus the assignment $r, s := \sqrt{s}, ?$ is a command that sets r to the square root of the value found initially in s, and may change s in the process. Similarly, the command $x, y, t := y, x, ?$ swaps the values of x and y using (possibly) a temporary variable t along the way.

The refinement rule for open assignment simply allows the '?' to be replaced by any expression:

Law 3.1 <u>open assignment</u> For any expression F,

$$w, x := E, ? \quad \sqsubseteq \quad w, x := E, F .$$

□

The command **choose** x from Chapter 1 is a special case of open assignment, in which the list w is empty: we could just as well write $x := ?$.

3.4 The skip command

Another unusual command is **skip**, which does nothing: its final state is exactly the same as its initial state. (It was mentioned in Section 1.9.) It can also be regarded

$$x \colon [x = 1] \quad \sqsubseteq \quad x := 1$$

$$x, y \colon [x = X \wedge y = Y \ , \ x = Y \wedge y = X] \quad \sqsubseteq \quad x, y := y, x$$

$$x \colon [y \neq 0 \ , \ x = 1/y] \quad \sqsubseteq \quad x := 1/y$$

$$x \colon [\mathsf{false} \ , \ x = 0] \quad \sqsubseteq \quad x := 17$$

Figure 3.3 Refinement to assignment

as a degenerate assignment, in which the list of changed variables is empty. (It can even be considered to be an assignment of variables to themselves, as in $x := x$.) Its refinement law is as follows:

Law 3.2 <u>skip command</u>   If $pre \Rightarrow post$, then

$$w \colon [pre \ , \ post] \quad \sqsubseteq \quad \mathbf{skip} \ .$$

□

We shall see later that **skip** is a useful command in spite of its doing 'nothing'. (After all, the same holds for '0'.)

3.5   Sequential composition

So far, we have the atomic programs specification, assignment and **skip**. The latter two are code; the first is not. But they are all called *atomic* because they are not formed from still smaller programs: instead, they cannot be broken down any further. Viewing a large program from the bottom up, one first sees atomic programs put together to make *compound* programs. Then those compound programs are themselves put together to form larger compound programs, and so on.

Sequential composition, which we met in Section 1.6, is one way of putting programs together. Informally, the sequential composition of two programs *prog*1 and *prog*2 is a new program which 'first does *prog*1 and then does *prog*2'. It is written *prog*1 ; *prog*2, and operationally one thinks of 'control flowing from left to right'. Figure 3.4 gives examples of sequential compositions.

Sequential composition is an operator which, like addition of numbers for example, is written between its operands. We include it in this chapter on code because it is executable in the sense that if *prog*1 and *prog*2 are executable, then *prog*1; *prog*2 is as well — first *prog*1 is executed, then *prog*2.

In using a *law* for sequential composition, rather than informal reasoning, we are adopting a top-down view instead of bottom-up. A single specification is refined by

$$x := 0; \quad x := 1 \qquad \text{Assign 0 to } x \text{, then assign 1 to } x.$$

$$x := 1; \quad y := x \qquad \text{Assign 1 to } x \text{, then assign that} \\ \text{(new) value of } x \text{ to } y.$$

$$x := y; \quad y := x \qquad \text{Assign the initial value of } y \text{ to } x, \\ \text{then assign that (new) value to } y.$$

$$y := y; \quad x := y \qquad \text{Assign } y \text{ to itself (no change), then} \\ \text{assign that (same) value to } x.$$

Each of these programs takes any initial state that satisfies $x = 0 \wedge y = 1$ to a final state satisfying $x = 1 \wedge y = 1$.

Figure 3.4 Sequential composition

the sequential composition of two others; and they, in turn, are refined by others still. Here is the law:

Law 3.3 <u>sequential composition</u> For any[1] formula *mid*,

$$w\colon [pre \ , \ post] \quad \sqsubseteq \quad w\colon [pre \ , \ mid]; \ w\colon [mid \ , \ post] \ .$$

□

The intuition operating here is that one way of reaching a final state satisfying *post* from an initial state satisfying *pre* is to proceed in two stages, via an intermediate state satisfying *mid*.

The intermediate *mid* can be any formula whatever: if it is strong (tending to false), then the first component in Law 3.3 is hard to refine subsequently, but the second is easy. If *mid* is weak (tending to true), then the reverse is the case. But any choice of *mid* is allowed, even **true** and **false** themselves. Figure 3.5 gives an example of Law 3.3; the resulting program hierarchy is shown in Figure 3.6.

For sequential composition with **skip** specifically, we have the following law:

Law 3.4 <u>skip composition</u> For any program *prog*,

$$prog; \ \textbf{skip} \quad = \quad \textbf{skip}; \ prog \quad = \quad prog \ .$$

□

Note that the three programs are *equal*: each refines both of the others.

---

[1]Neither *mid* nor *post*, however, may contain the so-called 'initial variables' that are the subject of Chapter 8 to come. That does not at all concern us now, but must be remembered if ever referring to this law later, once they have been introduced. Law B.2 on page 275 is the most appropriate replacement for the more general case.

$$x, y \colon [x = 0 \wedge y = 1]$$
$$\sqsubseteq \quad \text{``sequential composition 3.3''}$$
$$x, y \colon [x = 0] \,;$$
$$x, y \colon [x = 0 \,, \ x = 0 \wedge y = 1] \,.$$

We could refine each of those further with *assignment* 1.3, as follows:

$$x, y \colon [x = 0] \quad \sqsubseteq \quad x := 0$$
$$x, y \colon [x = 0 \,, \ x = 0 \wedge y = 1] \quad \sqsubseteq \quad y := 1 \,.$$

Figure 3.5 Example of *sequential composition* 3.3

3.6   Assignment and composition together

As our programming repertoire increases, we will find many other opportunities for laws that combine several constructions. One such is this special case of *assignment* 1.3 and *sequential composition* 3.3, which is useful when one 'knows' that a certain assignment is likely to be appropriate in the final code:

Law 3.5 <u>following assignment</u>   For any term E,

$$w, x \colon [pre \,, \ post]$$
$$\sqsubseteq \quad w, x \colon [pre \,, \ post[x \backslash E]] \,;$$
$$x := E \,.$$

□

What is left after applying Law 3.5 is a specification for the first half of the composition, which must be further developed; the assignment in the second half is code already.

Note that Law 3.5 allows *any* assignment in its second half provided the changed variables lie within the frame of the original specification. The required first half, on the other hand, is calculated by the law. (Ridiculous choices for the assignment in the second half probably lead to infeasible specifications in the first half — but that does not affect the validity of the step.) The laws *sequential composition* 8.4 and *leading assignment* 8.5 (both still to come) allow similar calculations.

3.7   Example: Swapping variables

We illustrate the laws so far by showing, in full, the development of the program which swaps x and y. (Note that the specification below allows the variable t to be changed as well.)

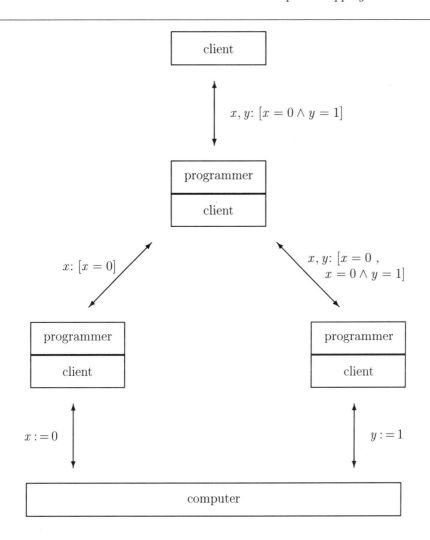

Figure 3.6 A programming hierarchy: recall Figure 1.1.

If the symbol ◁ marks part of a program, then that part alone is next refined, with the rest of the program assumed to be carried forward around it. Decorations in quotes are hints, referring to the law(s) that justify the refinement step:

$$x, y, t\colon [x = X \wedge y = Y \ , \ x = Y \wedge y = X]$$
$\sqsubseteq$ *"following assignment 3.5"*
$$x, y, t\colon [x = X \wedge y = Y \ , \ t = Y \wedge y = X]\,;$$ ◁
$$x\colon = t$$

$\sqsubseteq$ *"following assignment 3.5"*
$x, y, t: [x = X \wedge y = Y \ , \ t = Y \wedge x = X]$;   ◁
$y := x$
$\sqsubseteq$ *"assignment 1.3"*
$t := y$.

Overall, the above development is summarised

$x, y, t: [x = X \wedge y = Y \ , \ x = Y \wedge y = X]$
$\sqsubseteq t := y; \ y := x; \ x := t$.

It is the standard swap via a temporary variable.

3.8   Exercises

Ex. 3.1   Use *assignment* 1.3 to show that each of the assignments of Figure 3.1 refines the specification

$x: [x = 0 \wedge y = 1 \ , \ x = 1 \wedge y = 1]$.

Do the same for Figure 3.2, using the specification

$x, y: [x = 0 \wedge y = 1 \ , \ x = 1 \wedge y = 0]$.

Ex. 3.2   Prove the refinements of Figure 3.3.

Ex. 3.3 ♡   Fill in the details of this refinement, using *sequential composition* 3.3:

$x: \left[x = X \ , \ x = X^4\right] \quad \sqsubseteq \quad x := x^2; \ x := x^2$.

Ex. 3.4   Use *assignment* 1.3 to derive a law specifically for the assignment $w := w$. Comment on its similarity to *skip command* 3.2.

Ex. 3.5   Refine the following specification to a sequential composition of two assignments, neither of which uses the operation 'raise to the fourth power':

$x, y: \left[x = z^2 \wedge y = z^4\right]$.

Ex. 3.6 ♡   Redo the example of Section 3.7 without using *following assignment* 3.5: use *sequential composition* 3.3 directly.

Ex. 3.7 ♡   A *leading* assignment law for multiple assignments is the following:

> *Law 3.6* <u>leading assignment</u>   For disjoint w and x,
>
> $$w, x := E, F[w \backslash E] \quad = \quad w := E; \; x := F \;.$$

□

Note that as a special case we have

$$w, x := E, F \quad = \quad w := E; \; x := F \;,$$

provided F contains no w.

     Use Laws 3.1 and 3.6 to show that

$$x, y, t := y, x, ? \quad \sqsubseteq \quad t := y; \; y := x; \; x := t \;.$$

Ex. 3.8 ♡   Use *sequential composition* 3.3 to prove *following assignment* 3.5.

Chapter 4

Alternation

4.1 Operational description

Alternations (sometimes called '*if* statements') can informally be said to implement a case analysis: based on the initial state, one of several possible commands is selected for execution. They are built from *guarded commands*, each comprising a guard and an associated program called the *command*. A *guard* is a formula which selects those states to which its associated command applies. The guarded command itself is written

$$G \to prog \ ,$$

and it is pronounced 'G then *prog*'; the guard is G and the command is *prog*.

An *alternation* is a collection of guarded commands grouped together. They are separated by the symbol $\|$ (pronounced 'else') and enclosed in the alternation brackets **if** and **fi**. Here is an example:

$$
\begin{aligned}
&\textbf{if } G_0 \to prog_0 \\
&\| \;\; G_1 \to prog_1 \\
&\qquad \vdots \\
&\| \;\; G_n \to prog_n \\
&\textbf{fi} \ .
\end{aligned}
$$

We also write the above as **if** $(\| i \cdot G_i \to prog_i)$ **fi**, with the limits 0 and n understood from context.

The case analysis occurs in this way. In the initial state, none, one, or several of the guards G_i will be true. If exactly one is true, its corresponding command is executed.

If several guards are true, then one of them is selected and its corresponding command is executed. If the alternation has been properly developed, it will not matter which of the several guards is chosen — and one can make no assumptions about which it will be.

If no guard is true, the alternation aborts: in that case it can do *anything*, and one may assume that 'anything' means 'something bad'. (Recall the discussion of **abort** in Section 1.9.) That is not usually the programmer's intention (unless it was the client's too); a proper development will avoid it.

Consider this alternation for calculating the maximum m of two integers a and b:

> **if** $a \geq b \rightarrow m := a$
> $\llbracket$ $\ b \geq a \rightarrow m := b$
> **fi** .

There are two cases — they are $a \geq b$ and $b \geq a$ — and they overlap. Together, they cover all possibilities, thus avoiding **abort**. Whenever $a > b$, the first command is executed; whenever $b > a$, the second is executed. If $a = b$, then *either* can be executed, and of course in this alternation it makes no difference which. (Since the problem is symmetric, it is especially appropriate to have a symmetric solution.)

As a second example, consider

> **if** $2 \mid x \rightarrow x := x \div 2$
> $\llbracket$ $\ 3 \mid x \rightarrow x := x \div 3$
> **fi** .

The formula '$2 \mid x$' means '2 divides x exactly'. If x is initially 2, then finally it will be 1; if initially 3, then the result is the same (but by different means!) If initially x is 6, then finally it could be either 2 or 3, and we cannot predict which. And if initially 7, finally it could be 17... or 289, or nothing at all (because of nontermination).

4.2   Refinement law

Since we deal with the general case, any number of guarded commands, we introduce a notation for the disjunction of all their guards. The name GG abbreviates the formula

$$G_0 \vee G_1 \vee \cdots \vee G_n$$

in the following refinement law:

Law 4.1 <u>alternation</u> If $pre \Rrightarrow GG$, then

> $w \colon [pre\ ,\ post]$
> $\sqsubseteq$ **if** $(\llbracket\ i \cdot G_i \rightarrow w \colon [G_i \wedge pre\ ,\ post])$ **fi** .

$\square$

The precondition of the specification ensures that at least one guard is true; and each command assumes additionally in its precondition the truth of its guard.

Now let us reconsider the maximum-finding program. Using the binary operator $\sqcup$ for *maximum*, we begin

$$m := a \sqcup b$$
$$= \text{``simple specification 1.7''}$$
$$m\colon [m = a \sqcup b]$$
$$\sqsubseteq \text{``alternation 4.1''}$$

$$\textbf{if } a \geq b \rightarrow m\colon [a \geq b , \ m = a \sqcup b] \tag{i}$$
$$[\!]\ b \geq a \rightarrow m\colon [b \geq a , \ m = a \sqcup b] \tag{ii}$$
$$\textbf{fi} \ .$$

Note that each command has in its precondition the corresponding guard.

The numbering (i) and (ii) is to allow those commands to be refined separately below. As with $\lhd$ (a special case), the context is carried forward, and the code can be collected at the end. Continuing, we use *assignment* 1.3 to refine each command:

(i) $\sqsubseteq m := a$
(ii) $\sqsubseteq m := b$.

The resulting program is as shown earlier.

It is deliberate that alternation has no provision for defaults; each case must be explicitly mentioned. If in some case there is 'nothing to do' — because the initial state will serve as the final state — then **skip** is the appropriate command. Consider this development:

$$m := a \sqcup b \sqcup c$$
$$\sqsubseteq \text{``simple specification 1.7; sequential composition 3.3''}$$

$$m := a;$$
$$m\colon [m = a , \ m = a \sqcup b \sqcup c] \qquad\qquad \lhd$$
$$\sqsubseteq \text{``sequential composition 3.3''}$$

$$m\colon [m = a , \ m = a \sqcup b]; \tag{i}$$
$$m\colon [m = a \sqcup b , \ m = a \sqcup b \sqcup c] \tag{ii}$$

(i) $\sqsubseteq$ "alternation 4.1"

$$\textbf{if } m \leq b \rightarrow m\colon [m = a \wedge m \leq b , \ m = a \sqcup b] \tag{iii}$$
$$[\!]\ m \geq b \rightarrow m\colon [m = a \wedge m \geq b , \ m = a \sqcup b] \tag{iv}$$
$$\textbf{fi}$$

(iii) $\sqsubseteq m := b$
(iv) $\sqsubseteq$ **skip**
(ii) $\sqsubseteq$ **if** $m \leq c \rightarrow m := c$ $[\!]$ $m \geq c \rightarrow$ **skip** **fi** .

The resulting code, collected from the derivation above, is

$m := a;$
if $m \leq b \rightarrow m := b$ [] $m \geq b \rightarrow$ **skip fi**;
if $m \leq c \rightarrow m := c$ [] $m \geq c \rightarrow$ **skip fi** .

If we abbreviate **if** $G \rightarrow prog$ [] $\neg G \rightarrow$ **skip fi** by

if G **then** $prog$ **fi** ,

then we can write the above

$m := a;$
if $m \leq b$ **then** $m := b$ **fi**;
if $m \leq c$ **then** $m := c$ **fi** .

4.3   Exercises

Ex. 4.1 ♡   Assuming that x and y are real numbers, refine

$x := \mathsf{abs}\, y$

to an alternation, thence to code.

Ex. 4.2   Assume that x and y are real numbers, and supposing that $\sqrt{}$ takes reals to reals and *always terminates*, refine this to code:

$$y: \left[x \geq 0 \Rightarrow y^2 = x \right].$$

You may use $\sqrt{}$ in expressions.

Ex. 4.3   *Mortgage* Let c, s, b, m be respectively the cost of a house, savings in the bank, borrowing limit, and mortgage granted; they are all integers. Specify using maximum ⊔ and minimum ⊓ a program that determines m in terms of c, s, b. Then refine that program to code in which ⊔ and ⊓ do not appear.

Ex. 4.4 ♡   Prove *alternation* 4.1 from this law:

Law 4.2 alternation

$\{(\bigvee i \cdot G_i)\}\ prog$
$=$ **if** ([] $i \cdot G_i \rightarrow \{G_i\}\ prog$) **fi** .

□

Ex. 4.5   Sometimes one wants to refine one alternation to another, simply re-arranging the guards. The following law can be used for that:

> *Law 4.3* <u>alternation guards</u>   Let GG mean $G_0 \vee \cdots \vee G_n$, and HH similarly. Then provided
>
> 1. $GG \Rightarrow HH$, and
>
> 2. $GG \Rightarrow (H_i \Rightarrow G_i)$ for each i separately,
>
> this refinement is valid:
>
> $$\textbf{if } (\llbracket\, i \cdot G_i \to prog_i) \textbf{ fi} \quad \sqsubseteq \quad \textbf{if } (\llbracket\, i \cdot H_i \to prog_i) \textbf{ fi} \,.$$
>
> $\square$

Use Law 4.3 to show that the second example of Section 4.1 can be refined to

$$\textbf{if } 2 \mid x \textbf{ then } x := x \div 2 \textbf{ else } x := x \div 3 \textbf{ fi} \,.$$

where **if** G **then** $prog1$ **else** $prog2$ **fi** abbreviates

$$\begin{aligned}
&\textbf{if} \quad G \to prog1 \\
&\llbracket \quad \neg G \to prog2 \\
&\textbf{fi} \,.
\end{aligned}$$

Does that mean that we can write our nondeterministic alternations in the programming language C?

Chapter 5

Iteration

5.1 Operational description

Iterations (sometimes called '*while* loops') implement repetition: typically a command is executed repeatedly while a certain condition holds. In their general form iterations are, like alternations, built from guarded commands. We write them as follows:

> **do** $G_0 \rightarrow prog_0$
> $[\!]$ $G_1 \rightarrow prog_1$
> $\vdots$
> $[\!]$ $G_n \rightarrow prog_n$
> **od** .

We can also write **do** $([\!]i \cdot G_i \rightarrow prog_i)$ **od**.

The repetition occurs in this way. In the initial state, none, one, or several guards will be true. If none is true, the command terminates successfully and the state is unchanged. (Note the difference from alternation, which aborts in that case.)

If one or several guards are true, just one is chosen and its corresponding command is executed. Then the process is repeated, beginning with a re-evaluation of all the guards.

It is possible (but usually undesirable) for iterations to repeat forever. From the above, we see that they terminate only when all guards are false; thus as an extreme example (of the opposite)

> **do** true $\rightarrow$ **skip od**

never terminates. By convention, a never-ending iteration is equivalent to **abort**.

Successful iterations finally make all their guards false, and that may occur from some initial states but not others. Consider the following program, which for natural number n establishes $n = 1$ finally whenever n is a power of 2 initially:

$$\textbf{do } 2 \mid n \rightarrow n := n \div 2 \textbf{ od} \ . \tag{5.1}$$

If n is not a power of two initially, then we are not assured of $n = 1$ finally: starting with $n = 12$ for example would lead via $n = 6$ to $n = 3$, where the iteration would terminate successfully because 2 does not divide 3 exactly. And if $n = 0$ initially, there is no finally: variable n is set and reset to 0 forever.

Even from our informal view, we see that an iteration can be *unfolded* without affecting its meaning:

$$
\begin{aligned}
&\textbf{do } G \rightarrow prog \textbf{ od} \\
=\ &\textbf{if } G \textbf{ then} \\
&\quad prog; \\
&\quad \textbf{do } G \rightarrow prog \textbf{ od} \\
&\textbf{fi} \ .
\end{aligned}
$$

Each unfolding makes one more repetition explicit. Thus we can unfold again...

$$
\begin{aligned}
=\ &\textbf{if } G \textbf{ then} \\
&\quad prog; \\
&\quad \textbf{if } G \textbf{ then} \\
&\quad\quad prog; \\
&\quad\quad \textbf{do } G \rightarrow prog \textbf{ od} \\
&\quad \textbf{fi} \\
&\textbf{fi} \ .
\end{aligned}
$$

...any number of times, and that shows that an iteration can be regarded as equivalent to an unbounded nesting of alternations.

5.2   Refinement law: informally

Rather than unfolding as above, we rely instead on a refinement law that abstracts from the number of repetitions: it is all captured in a single formula, the invariant. An *invariant* for an iteration is a formula which, if true initially, is true also after every repetition including the final one. Overall, the iteration *maintains* the invariant, and establishes additionally the negation of the guards — provided it terminates at all. And that is true no matter how many repetitions occur (even 0).

For an example we return to Program (5.1), defining a predicate pt to mean 'is a power of 2':

$$\mathsf{pt}\, n \ \widehat{=}\ \left(\exists\, k : \mathbb{N} \cdot n = 2^k \right).$$

The formula $\mathsf{pt}\, n$ is an invariant for the iteration: if it is true initially, and a repetition occurs (because $2 \mid n$ is true also), then after execution of the iteration body $n := n \div 2$ it is true still. Another way of writing that is

$$n: [2 \mid n \wedge \mathsf{pt}\, n \ , \ \mathsf{pt}\, n] \quad \sqsubseteq \quad n := n \div 2 \ . \tag{5.2}$$

In general, a formula *inv* is an invariant of **do** $G \rightarrow prog$ **od** if for some frame w

$$w: [G \wedge inv \ , \ inv] \quad \sqsubseteq \quad prog \ . \tag{5.3}$$

That is, if the guard G holds, then the iteration body $prog$ preserves the invariant *inv*.

The utility of an invariant is that, assuming termination, its preservation as in (5.3) is sufficient to establish

$$w: [inv \ , \ inv \wedge \neg G] \quad \sqsubseteq \quad \textbf{do}\ G \rightarrow prog\ \textbf{od}\ . \tag{5.4}$$

And in (5.4) we have the essence of our refinement law, which will allow us to replace a specification by an iteration. As an example, we derive (5.1) from the informal specification given earlier:

$$n: [\mathsf{pt}\, n \ , \ n = 1]$$
$\sqsubseteq$ "1 is the only power of 2 not divisible by 2"
$$n: [\mathsf{pt}\, n \ , \ \mathsf{pt}\, n \wedge \neg(2 \mid n)]$$
$\sqsubseteq$ "(5.4), justified by (5.2) in this case"
$$\textbf{do}\ 2 \mid n \rightarrow n := n \div 2\ \textbf{od}\ .$$

Our refinement rule 'if (5.3) then (5.4)' is not yet complete, however: in fact if used in that form it would produce 'refinements' that were invalid. That is because (an extreme case) we could reason

because $\quad w: [\mathsf{false} \wedge \mathsf{true} \ , \ \mathsf{true}] \quad \sqsubseteq \quad \mathbf{skip}$
we 'conclude' $\quad w: [\mathsf{true} \ , \ \mathsf{true} \wedge \mathsf{false}] \quad \sqsubseteq \quad \mathbf{do}\ \mathsf{true} \rightarrow \mathbf{skip}\ \mathbf{od}\ .$

Put more starkly, we would be claiming that

because $\quad \mathbf{abort} \quad \sqsubseteq \quad \mathbf{skip}$
we 'conclude' $\quad \mathbf{magic} \quad \sqsubseteq \quad \mathbf{do}\ \mathsf{true} \rightarrow \mathbf{skip}\ \mathbf{od}\ .$

That is clearly nonsense: the premise is true, but the conclusion is false.

What we are missing is the idea of termination: that the iteration body not only maintains the invariant but cannot be executed indefinitely. For that we need a variant function.

5.3 Termination of iterations: variants

In the example, termination is guaranteed informally by the following observation:

Each repetition of $n := n \div 2$, when $2 \mid n$, strictly decreases the integer n; yet n cannot become negative.

We say therefore that the variant of the iteration is n. In general, some integer-valued[1] variant expression is chosen that is strictly decreased by each repetition, but never below some fixed lower bound (often chosen to be 0).

---

[1]More general variants are possible; they range over well-founded sets.

5.3.1   Specifying decrease of the variant

We have no difficulty writing a command that decreases an integer-valued variable n — the assignment $n := n - 1$ is one of many that would do — but to *specify* that n is strictly decreased is another story. Writing

$$n\colon [n = n - 1] \ ,$$

or more generally $n\colon [n < n]$, would *not* do: both of them are equivalent to **magic**.

We adopt a convention that 0-subscripted variables in a postcondition refer to the *initial* (rather than to the final) values of the variables. With that, the above discussion could be summarised

$$n\colon [n < n_0] \quad \sqsubseteq \quad n := n - 1 \ . \tag{5.5}$$

That is, the assignment $n := n - 1$ (the more refined side) is just one of many ways of strictly decreasing n (expressed by the specification on the left-hand side).

We will meet initial variables in more generality shortly. For now we re-examine just three of our earlier laws, generalising them to take initial variables into account. They become

Law 5.1 strengthen postcondition   If $pre[w \backslash w_0] \wedge post' \Rightarrow post$, then

$$w\colon [pre , post] \quad \sqsubseteq \quad w\colon [pre , post'] \ .$$

□

Law 5.1 strictly generalises our earlier *strengthen postcondition* 1.1 in that the precondition of the left-hand side can now be taken into account.

Law 5.2 assignment   If $(w = w_0) \wedge pre \Rightarrow post[w \backslash E]$, then

$$w, x\colon [pre , post] \quad \sqsubseteq \quad w := E \ .$$

□

Law 5.2 generalises our earlier *assignment* 1.3. Notice that the substitution $[w \backslash E]$ affects only 'final' (*un*subscripted) variables in the postcondition.

Law 5.3 skip command   If $(w = w_0) \wedge pre \Rightarrow post$, then

$$w\colon [pre , post] \quad \sqsubseteq \quad \textbf{skip} \ .$$

□

Law 5.3 generalises *skip command* 3.2, taking advantage of the fact that in a **skip** command the initial and final variables have the same value.

Each of the above reduces to its earlier version if initial variables are not present, and the earlier versions remain valid even when initial variables are present — but they are not as powerful as the newer versions.

Using our new *assignment* 5.2 we can show Refinement (5.5) in just one step:

$$n\colon [n < n_0]$$
$$\sqsubseteq \text{``} n = n_0 \land \mathsf{true} \;\Rightarrow\; (n < n_0)[n\backslash n - 1]\text{''}$$
$$n := n - 1 \;.$$

Simplified, the proviso would be simply $n = n_0 \Rightarrow n - 1 < n_0$.

5.3.2 Initial variables and the frame

We should also mention at this point an interaction between initial variables (values before any change) and the frame (listing which variables may be changed). If a variable x is not in the frame, then x and x_0 may be used interchangeably in the postcondition since the initial and final values of x are equal in that case. Put another way, if we remove x from the frame, then we can replace x_0 by x in the postcondition. That is summarised in the following law:

Law 5.4 <u>contract frame</u>

$$w, x\colon [pre \;,\; post] \quad \sqsubseteq \quad w\colon [pre \;,\; post[x_0 \backslash x]] \;.$$

□

Note that x_0 need not occur in *post* for Law 5.4 to apply — and that means, as a special case, that simply removing a variable from the frame is a refinement too. (Recall Exercise 1.7.)

That concludes our look at initial variables; we return to them in Chapter 8.

5.4 The refinement rule for iteration

With initial variables available for specifying the decrease of the variant, we can now give the full refinement rule. It is

Law 5.5 <u>iteration</u> Let *inv*, the *invariant*, be any formula; let V, the *variant*, be any integer-valued expression. Then if GG is the disjunction of the guards,

$$w\colon [inv \;,\; inv \land \neg GG]$$
$$\sqsubseteq \mathbf{do}\; (\![]i \cdot G_i \to w\colon [inv \land G_i \;,\; inv \land (0 \le V < V_0)]) \;\mathbf{od} \;.$$

Neither *inv* nor G_i may contain initial variables. The expression V_0 is $V[w\backslash w_0]$.
□

In the interests of keeping the amount we must write to a minimum, we introduce an abbreviation that avoids writing *inv* twice in the iteration body. When a formula appears in both the pre- and the postcondition of a specification (as *inv* does in the iteration body above), it can instead be written once in between, as a third formula:

$n\colon [\mathsf{pt}\, n \ , \ n = 1]$

$\sqsubseteq\ n\colon [\mathsf{pt}\, n \ , \ \mathsf{pt}\, n \wedge \neg(2 \mid n)]$

$\sqsubseteq\ \mathbf{do}\ 2 \mid n \rightarrow$

$\qquad n\colon [2 \mid n \ , \ \mathsf{pt}\, n \ , \ 0 \leq n < n_0]$ ◁

$\quad \mathbf{od}$

$\sqsubseteq\ \text{``}2 \mid n \wedge \mathsf{pt}\, n \ \Rrightarrow\ \mathsf{pt}(n \div 2) \wedge 0 \leq n \div 2 < n\text{''}$

$\quad n := n \div 2 \ .$

Figure 5.1 Example iteration development

Abbreviation 5.6 <u>specification invariant</u> Provided *inv* contains no initial variables,

$$w\colon [pre \ , \ inv \ , \ post] \ \hat{=} \ w\colon [pre \wedge inv \ , \ inv \wedge post] \ .$$

□

The iteration body in Law 5.5 can now be written (more briefly as) just

$$w\colon [G_i \ , \ inv \ , \ 0 \leq V < V_0] \ .$$

Figure 5.1 gives a complete development of Program (5.1), including the variant. In the simplified proviso we have used $n = n_0$ on the left-hand side to replace n_0 by n on the right.

5.5   The iteration 'checklist'

In planning one's approach to developing an iteration, it is sometimes useful to consider the following characteristics of iterations that are built in to the iteration law:

1. The invariant holds initially.
2. The invariant and negated guard are sufficient to establish the desired result.
3. The iteration body maintains the invariant provided the guard holds as well.
4. The variant is strictly decreased by execution of the iteration body, provided the invariant and guard hold.
5. The variant cannot be decreased below 0 by the iteration body, provided the invariant and guard hold.

Characteristic 1 is found in the precondition of the specification on the left-hand side: by '$\cdots [inv, \cdots]$' we express that the invariant must hold initially. Similarly,

Characteristic 2 is found in the postcondition: writing '$\cdots, inv \wedge \neg GG] \cdots$' states what is required of the iteration.

In '$\cdots [G_i \wedge inv, inv \wedge \cdots$' of the iteration body is found Characteristic 3; Characteristic 4 is expressed by '$\cdots [G_i \wedge inv, \cdots V < V_0]$', and finally Characteristic 5 is given by '$\cdots [G_i \wedge inv, \cdots 0 \leq V \cdots$'.

When choosing an invariant it is sometimes helpful to run through the checklist[2] informally, before setting out the development in full — one is then (literally) carrying out a feasibility study.

5.6 Exercises

Ex. 5.1   Give a single assignment command that refines

$$n\colon [\text{pt } n \ , \ n = 1] \ .$$

Ex. 5.2 ♡   *Checking for powers of two* Use the invariant $n \neq 0 \wedge (\text{pt } N \Leftrightarrow \text{pt } n)$ to complete the following development, in which N is used to hold the original value of n:

$$n\colon [n \neq 0 \wedge n = N \ , \ n = 1 \Leftrightarrow \text{pt } N]$$
$$\sqsubseteq \ n\colon [n \neq 0 \wedge (\text{pt } N \Leftrightarrow \text{pt } n) \ , \ (\text{pt } N \Leftrightarrow \text{pt } n) \wedge \neg(2 \mid n)]$$
$$\sqsubseteq \ \ldots$$

Hint: You have seen the code before.

Ex. 5.3 ♡   Consider this factorial program, in which we assume f and n are integers. What laws are used for the first refinement step (shown)? (The constant F is used to refer to the desired factorial value.)

$$f, n\colon [F = n! \ , \ f = F]$$
$$\sqsubseteq \ f\colon [F = n! \ , \ f \times n! = F]; \tag{i}$$
$$f, n\colon [f \times n! = F \ , \ f \times n! = F \wedge n = 0] \ . \tag{ii}$$

Complete the refinement to code.

Ex. 5.4 ♡   The law *strengthen postcondition* 5.1 is stronger than *strengthen postcondition* 1.1 because it uses information from the precondition. Assuming $x, y : \mathbb{R}$, use it to show that

$$y\colon [0 \leq x \leq 9 \ , \ y^2 = x]$$
$$\sqsubseteq \ y\colon [0 \leq x \Rightarrow y^2 = x] \ .$$

Explain the fact that the law is called 'strengthen postcondition', yet above the new postcondition is weaker than the old.

---

[2]It is borrowed from [Gri81].

Ex. 5.5 ♡   Assuming $x, y : \mathbb{R}$, prove each of the following:

1. $x\colon [y > x \ , \ x > x_0] \sqsubseteq x := y$
2. $x\colon [x < 0 \ , \ x > x_0] \sqsubseteq x := -x$
3. $x, y\colon [x = y_0 \wedge y = x_0] \sqsubseteq x, y := y, x$
4. $x\colon [x = X + 1 \ , \ x = X + 2] \sqsubseteq x := x + 1$
5. $x\colon [x = X + 1 \ , \ x = X + 2] \sqsubseteq x\colon [x = x_0 + 1]$
6. $\qquad x\colon [x = x_0 + 2]$

$$\sqsubseteq \ x\colon [x = x_0 + 1] \,;$$
$$x\colon [x = x_0 + 1] \ .$$

Ex. 5.6 ♡   Design an *initialised iteration* law of this form:

$$w\colon [pre \ , \ inv \wedge \neg G]$$
$$\sqsubseteq prog1;$$
$$\mathbf{do} \ G \to prog2 \ \mathbf{od} \ .$$

You should supply *prog*1 and *prog*2, as specifications, and you may assume that *inv* and G contain no initial variables.

Ex. 5.7   *Logarithm* Here is a specification of a logarithm-finding program, in which l, n and N are integers:

$$l, n\colon \left[1 \leq n = N \ , \ 2^l \leq N < 2^{l+1}\right] \ .$$

Variable N holds the initial value of n. Develop the specification to code using the invariant

$$n \times 2^l \leq N < (n + 1) \times 2^l \wedge 1 \leq n \ .$$

Ex. 5.8 ♡   *Handing out sweets* Suppose S sweets are to be handed out to C children. If C divides S exactly, then each child should receive S/C (whole!) sweets. But if the division is not exact, then some will receive $\lfloor S/C \rfloor$ and others $\lceil S/C \rceil$, where $\lfloor \ \rfloor$ and $\lceil \ \rceil$ are the *floor* and *ceiling* functions that take a real number to the closest integer no more than and no less than it respectively.

Here is a program for handing out the sweets, using natural number variables s, c and t:

$$s, c := S, C;$$
$$\mathbf{do} \ c \neq 0 \to$$
$$\qquad t\colon [\ \lfloor s/c \rfloor \leq t \leq \lceil s/c \rceil \ ];$$
$$\qquad \text{'hand out } t \text{ sweets to the next child'};$$
$$\qquad s, c := s - t, c - 1$$
$$\mathbf{od} \ .$$

We say the handing out is *fair* if

all the sweets are handed out; and $\qquad$ (5.6)

each child receives between $\lfloor S/C \rfloor$ and $\lceil S/C \rceil$ sweets. $\qquad$ (5.7)

Does the program implement a fair handing out?

Hint: Use *informal* invariant-based reasoning, following the checklist of Section 5.5; consider an invariant resembling[3]

$$\lfloor S/C \rfloor \le \lfloor s/c \rfloor \qquad (5.8)$$
$$\lceil s/c \rceil \le \lceil S/C \rceil \qquad (5.9)$$
$$S = s + \text{'the number of sweets handed out already'}. \qquad (5.10)$$

Useful facts about $\lfloor \ \rfloor$ and $\lceil \ \rceil$ are that for all integers i and reals r

$$i \le \lfloor r \rfloor \ \equiv \ i \le r$$
$$\text{and} \quad \lceil r \rceil \le i \ \equiv \ r \le i \ .$$

---

[3]You may have to alter it slightly...

Chapter 6

Types and declarations

6.1 Types

The only types we have met so far are various numbers, like the reals $\mathbb{R}$, the integers $\mathbb{Z}$ and the natural numbers $\mathbb{N}$. They are examples that we borrow directly from mathematics, more or less taking their existence for granted. Figure 6.1 gives other examples of standard mathematical types; but in general we can use *any* set as a type.

In code, however, the available types are restricted. We make the (idealised) assumption that types $\mathbb{N}$ and $\mathbb{Z}$, at least, are available in code, with the intention that they correspond roughly to types INTEGER or *int* in some everyday programming language. Other types can be constructed from them, as we will see in Chapters 9 and 15. The empty type $\{\}$ is not code, however.

Every type brings with it certain functions and relations which can be applied to its elements. For the types of Figure 6.1 we may use all those from arithmetic, some examples of which are given in Figures 6.2 and 6.3.

Why do we bother with types? They affect program development in several ways. One way is that types provide information about the possible values that variables can take, and the information can be used to make program development easier. For example, the following refinement is not valid in general, but it is valid if m and n are known to be natural numbers, elements of $\mathbb{N}$:

$$n\colon [m \neq 0\ ,\ 0 \leq n < m] \quad \sqsubseteq \quad n\colon [m > 0\ ,\ n < m]\ .$$

The precondition has been weakened because $m \neq 0 \Rrightarrow m > 0$ for any m in $\mathbb{N}$. The postcondition has been strengthened because $n < m \Rrightarrow 0 \leq n < m$ for any n in $\mathbb{N}$. (Actually the two programs are equal, which is a special case of refinement.) Thus having the types declared means that the fact $m, n \in \mathbb{N}$ is available anywhere the usual scope rules allow, and we do not have to carry the information explicitly from place to place.

$\mathbb{N}$ The *natural numbers*, or non-negative integers.

$\mathbb{Z}$ The *integers*, positive, negative, and zero.

$\mathbb{Q}$ The *rational numbers*.

$\mathbb{R}$ The *real numbers*.

$\mathbb{C}$ The *complex numbers*.

Each of the types is a proper subset of the one below it: thus $\mathbb{N} \subset \mathbb{Z} \subset \mathbb{Q} \subset \mathbb{R} \subset \mathbb{C}$. For any type T above except the complex numbers, we write T^+ for the set of *positive* elements of the type, and T^- for the set of *negative* elements of the type. Thus $\mathbb{N}^+ = \mathbb{Z}^+ = \{1, 2, 3, \cdots\}$, and $\mathbb{Z}^- = \{-1, -2, -3, \cdots\}$.

Figure 6.1 Some standard mathematical types

Another way is that types restrict the values that can be assigned to variables, and that makes program development harder: there are fewer assignments to choose from. For example, the code $m := -1$ should not occur in a program where m has type $\mathbb{N}$. That is partly because everyday languages have explicit typing, which therefore we must accommodate.

6.2   Declarations

6.2.1   Variable declarations

To associate a type with a variable we use a *variable declaration*, and for variable x and type T that is written **var** $x : T$. We also have multiple declarations like this:

> **var** $x, y : T$; $z : U$.

It declares x and y to have type T, and z to have type U.

We have earlier met informal declarations, such as at the beginning of Chapter 1: 'let our variables be just x, y, and z; and let their values be real numbers' (p.4). Now we could write that **var** $x, y, z : \mathbb{R}$.

$+$	Addition.
$-$	Subtraction.
$\times$	Multiplication. We allow the conventional $2n$ to abbreviate $2 \times n$.
$/$	Division. Note that dividing two integers does not necessarily yield an integer.
$\lceil\,\rceil$	Ceiling: the least integer no less than.
$\lfloor\,\rfloor$	Floor: the greatest integer no more than.
$\div$	Integer division: $a \div b = \lfloor a/b \rfloor$.
$\ominus$	Natural number subtraction: $a \ominus b = a - b$, provided $a - b \geq 0$.
mod	Modulus: $a = b \times (a \div b) + (a \bmod b)$, provided $b \neq 0$.
abs	Absolute value.
$\sqcup$	Maximum.
$\sqcap$	Minimum.

Figure 6.2 Some standard arithmetic functions

$<$	Less than.
$\leq$	Less than or equal to.
$>$	Greater than.
$\geq$	Greater than or equal to.
$\mid$	Divides exactly: $(a \mid b) \equiv (b \bmod a = 0)$.

Figure 6.3 Some standard arithmetic relations

6.2.2   Invariant declarations

A more advanced form of declaration is the local invariant: instead of writing **var** $x : \mathbb{N}$ we could write

var $x : \mathbb{Z}$; **and** $x \geq 0$.

We could also write just **var** x **and** $x \in \mathbb{N}$, using an untyped declaration of x.

A *local invariant* is any formula written after the keyword **and**, as a declaration. The declaration

and *inv*

allows us subsequently to assume *inv*, as well as any typing information, when applying laws or definitions.

In fact the above examples make it clear that local invariants subsume types: typing a variable just makes invariant that it is an element of its type.

We can write more interesting invariants too. The declaration **and** $2 \mid n$ means that n must always be even. And we can relate different variables to each other; for example, the following declares a rational q, and two integers n and d that always represent it as a fraction:

var $q : \mathbb{Q}$; $n : \mathbb{Z}$; $d : \mathbb{N}$; **and** $q = n/d$.

Finally, invariants can be used to make constants: given a type declaration $g : \mathbb{R}^+$, the additional declaration **and** $g^2 - g - 1 = 0$ makes g the golden ratio $1.618\cdots$. Unlike the conventional constant declaration (for example **const** $g = 1.618$), the distinguishing property of g is declared as well.

Unfortunately, local invariants are not code: they are useful during development, but must at some stage be removed. We return to that later, in Section 6.6.

6.2.3   Logical constants

We have seen in some earlier exercises that it is sometimes useful to have a name, not necessarily a normal program variable, that can be used to refer to values of interest during a development (Exercises 5.2, 5.7 and 5.3). For example, although it is easy enough to write the specification $f, n := n!, ?$ for a program that sets f to the factorial of n (possibly changing n), during the development one might need an invariant along the lines of

$n! \times f \quad = \quad$ 'the factorial of the initial value of n'.

Rewriting the specification as $f, n: [F = n! , f = n_0!]$ is a step in the right direction, since — as long as we do not change F — we can now write the invariant as

$n! \times f \quad = \quad F$.

In fact, a slightly neater specification would be just $f, n: [F = n! , f = F]$ (as in Exercise 5.3).

But, strictly speaking, a precondition $F = n!$ means 'abort if $F \neq n!$', and that certainly is not what we want: we need F to take a value such that the precondition holds. In this case that value would be $n!$.

That 'taking a value such that the precondition holds' is what logical constants are for. Like variables, they are declared — but we indicate their different nature with the keyword **con**: the notation

> **con** F

declares F to be a logical constant, rather than a variable. (Since we declare logical constants explicitly, we can use either upper or lower case for them — but upper case is conventional.)

Unlike **var**, a logical constant declaration **con** is not code, and hence at some later stage of refinement it must be removed. Naturally, that can occur only when all references to those logical constants have been eliminated, since otherwise they would become undeclared. And since logical constants are not code, typing for them is optional.

Our specification above is thus to be interpreted in the context of the declarations **var** $f, n : \mathbb{N}$; **con** F. The development, incidentally, is then

$\qquad f, n \colon [F = n! \,,\, f = F]$
$\sqsubseteq$ "establish invariant"
$\qquad f \colon = 1;$
$\qquad f, n \colon [F = n! \times f \,,\, F = n! \times f \wedge n = 0]$ $\qquad\qquad \triangleleft$
$\sqsubseteq$ "Note we assume $n \geq 0$ because of its declaration."
$\qquad$ **do** $n \neq 0 \rightarrow$
$\qquad\qquad f, n \colon [n > 0 \,,\, F = n! \times f \,,\, n < n_0]$ $\qquad\qquad \triangleleft$
$\qquad$ **od**
$\sqsubseteq$ "How do we know n stays non-negative?"
$\qquad f \colon [n > 0 \wedge F = n! \times f \,,\, F = (n-1)! \times f];$ $\qquad \triangleleft$
$\qquad n \colon = n - 1$
$\sqsubseteq$ "And now the logical constant F disappears, as it must."
$\qquad f \colon = f \times n$.

(What refinement rules were used in the above?)

6.3   Local blocks

6.3.1   Variables and invariants

Declarations of variables, invariants and logical constants are made within local blocks, which indicate precisely the part of the program affected. A *local block* is a program fragment enclosed in the block brackets $|[$ and $]|$; any of the declarations of Section 6.2 may be placed immediately after the opening bracket. They are separated from the following program, the block *body*, by a spot · .

Declarations are limited in effect to the block in which they are declared; such limitations are necessary, for example, whenever a programmer uses extra variables not mentioned in the specification agreed with his client. The specification

$$x, y: [x = X \land y = Y \ , \ x = Y \land y = X] \ ,$$

which swaps the values of x and y, is *not* refined by

$$t := x; \ x := y; \ y := t \ .$$

(Compare Section 3.7, where t was in the frame.)

The specification does not allow t to change, and so its implementation must not either. We must use a local block, and a correct refinement is

$$\|[\ \textbf{var}\ t : T \cdot t := x; \ x := y; \ y := t\ ]\| \ ,$$

where T is the type of x and y. The variable t is significant only within the local block; it is wholly divorced from any variable t declared *outside* the local block. Its initial value is an arbitrary member of its type.

The names of local variables can be systematically altered throughout the block in which they are declared — thus this program also swaps x and y:

$$\|[\ \textbf{var}\ s : T \cdot s := x; \ x := y; \ y := s\ ]\| \ .$$

It is because of that essential arbitrariness in the name of a local variable that it is clear it cannot have anything to do with variables declared outside the block.

In general examples like the above, we may omit types from declarations; in that case, we assume all variables to have the same type.

Here is the law for introducing a local variable, and optionally a local invariant as well:

Law 6.1 <u>introduce local variable</u> If x does not occur in w, *pre* or *post* then

$$w: [pre \ , \ post] \quad \sqsubseteq \quad \|[\ \textbf{var}\ x : T; \textbf{and}\ inv \cdot w, x: [pre \ , \ post]\ ]\| \ .$$

□

It is the proviso of Law 6.1 — that x is 'fresh' — that ensures there is no confusion between the 'new' x and any 'existing' x's. Without it, a reference to an existing x could be captured by the new declaration.

The invariant part of Law 6.1 is optional, of course, and is considered to be **true** if omitted. Remember however that an invariant is not code, and so cannot appear in the final program. (See Section 6.6.)

For laws like *introduce local variable* 6.1, which introduce a block, we can use an abbreviation when setting out refinements: the declaration decorates the refinement step, and the block brackets are omitted. We use the spot · again to separate the decoration from the refined program. Thus we have this alternative layout of the law:

$$w \colon [pre \, , \ post]$$
$$\sqsubseteq \mathbf{var} \ x \colon T; \mathbf{and} \ inv \cdot$$

$$w, x \colon [pre \, , \ post] \, .$$

The advantage of that is a more concise notation, no need for block brackets during the development, and no indentation. (The block brackets are required only if we collect the code and present it linearly: similarly '$2 \times (3 + 4)$' needs parentheses, although expression trees do not contain them.)

6.3.2   Logical constants and blocks

Logical constants are introduced, in general, with this law:

Law 6.2 <u>introduce logical constant</u>   If $pre \Rrightarrow (\exists c \colon T \cdot pre')$, and c does not occur in w, pre or $post$, then

$$w \colon [pre \, , \ post]$$
$$\sqsubseteq \mathbf{con} \ c \colon T \cdot$$
$$w \colon [pre' \, , \ post] \, .$$

If the optional type T is omitted, then the quantification in the proviso should be untyped.
$\square$

Note that we use the abbreviated layout, just as for **var**.

Later we shall see direct applications of Law 6.2; but more often we use this more specialised law, an immediate consequence of it:

Law 6.3 <u>fix initial value</u>   For any term E such that $pre \Rrightarrow E \in T$, and fresh name c,

$$w \colon [pre \, , \ post]$$
$$\sqsubseteq \mathbf{con} \ c \colon T \cdot$$
$$w \colon [pre \wedge c = E \, , \ post] \, .$$

Proof: Law 6.2 requires

$$
\begin{array}{cl}
& pre \\
\Rrightarrow & pre \wedge E \in T \\
\equiv & \text{``}c \text{ fresh''} \\
& (pre \wedge c \in T)[c \backslash E] \\
\equiv & \text{``Predicate law A.56''} \\
& (\exists c \cdot pre \wedge c \in T \wedge c = E) \\
\equiv & (\exists c \colon T \cdot pre \wedge c = E) \, .
\end{array}
$$

$\square$

Law 6.3 is used when it is necessary later in a development to refer to the value that some term E had initially, where the constituent variables of E may be changed by assignments; the logical constant c retains that initial value. Returning to our factorial example above, we could start from $f, n\colon [f = n_0!]$, and use *fix initial value* 6.3 to introduce F, as follows:

$$\sqsubseteq \; f, n\colon [f = n_0!]$$
$$\sqsubseteq \; \textbf{con } F\cdot$$
$$\quad f, n\colon [F = n! \;,\; f = n_0!]$$
$$\sqsubseteq \; \text{``}strengthen\ postcondition\ 5.1\text{''}$$
$$\quad f, n\colon [F = n! \;,\; f = F] \;.$$

In practice, of course, we would not dream of setting out all that detail: it would be sufficient to go from $f, n\colon [f = n_0!]$ (or even $f, n := n!, ?$) to $f, n\colon [F = n! \;,\; f = F]$ in one step directly, quoting '**con** F' as the justification.

Finally, for removing logical constants, we have this law:

Law 6.4 <u>remove logical constant</u> If c occurs nowhere in program *prog*, then

$$|[\ \textbf{con}\ c : T \cdot prog\ ]| \quad \sqsubseteq \quad prog \;.$$

☐

Law 6.4 is the justification for removing declarations **con** c when all occurrences of c have been removed. We will not use it explicitly, however. (We could formulate a similar law for variables, but since they *are* code it would be very seldom that we would want to remove them.)

6.4   Using types and invariants

Within a local block such as

$$|[\ \textbf{var}\ x : T;\ \textbf{and}\ inv \cdot \cdots\ ]|\;,$$

the formula $x \in T \wedge inv$ may be used when proving the provisos of refinement rules. Within several nested blocks, all the enclosing formulae may be used. They are known collectively as the *context*.

Thus in our original example,

$$n\colon [m \neq 0 \;,\; 0 \leq n < m] \quad \sqsubseteq \quad n\colon [m > 0 \;,\; n < m],$$

we may use the context $m, n \in \mathbb{N}$. The provisos for the two refinements, weakening the precondition and strengthening the postcondition, are then

$$m \in \mathbb{N} \wedge m \neq 0 \; \Rightarrow \; m > 0$$
$$n \in \mathbb{N} \wedge n < m \; \Rightarrow \; 0 \le n < m \; .$$

Naturally we need not write in the whole context: only $m \in \mathbb{N}$ was required in the first case, and $n \in \mathbb{N}$ in the second.

A slight difficulty arises if there is danger of variable capture, as in this example:

$$\|[\textbf{var} \; a, b : \mathbb{N}\text{·}$$
$$\quad \|[\textbf{var} \; a : \mathbb{Z}\text{·}$$
$$\quad \quad \cdots$$
$$\quad]|$$
$$]|\text{·}$$

At the point $\cdots$, in the inner block, we cannot refer to the context formula $a \in \mathbb{N}$, because its free variable a would be captured by the inner declaration. One must either rename the inner bound variable, or use only the weaker $b \in \mathbb{N}$ from the outer declaration. In general, we can always use a weaker context than the one we are given, and that allows us to use $a \in \mathbb{Z} \wedge b \in \mathbb{N}$, for example, in the inner block.

6.5 A final note on feasibility

With types and invariants now explicit, and initial variables, we can present a more general definition of feasibility that takes them all into account. It is

Definition 6.5 <u>feasibility</u> The specification $w: [pre \; , \; post]$ is *feasible* in context *inv* iff

$$(w = w_0) \wedge pre \wedge inv \quad \Rightarrow \quad (\exists \, w : T \cdot inv \wedge post) \, ,$$

where T is the type of w.
□

As an example, recall that we have seen that the specification

$$y: \left[y^2 = x \right] \tag{6.1}$$

is infeasible if x, y range over $\mathbb{R}$: the formula $(\exists \, y : \mathbb{R} \cdot y^2 = x)$ is not true for all x in $\mathbb{R}$. But if x, y had type $\mathbb{C}$, the feasibility formula from Definition 6.5 would reduce to $x \in \mathbb{C} \Rightarrow (\exists \, y : \mathbb{C} \cdot y^2 = x)$ instead, quite a different matter.

6.6 Checking types and invariants

Section 6.4 explained the use of context in checking the provisos of refinements, and how that makes proposed refinements more likely to be valid. But there is a price to pay: at some stage we must check that those types are respected and invariants maintained. We call that activity *type checking*, and say that a program successfully checked is *well-typed*. If it fails the check, we call it *ill-typed*.

Experience suggests that type checking is best done at the end of development, rather than during it. Often it is obvious that a program is well-typed; and if types are used in a reasonable way, much of type checking can be done automatically by computer.

We must type-check both types and invariants; we deal first with types. Only assignments can violate types, and so we must be able to tell whether any assignment is well- or ill-typed. In an assignment $w := E$, we always know the type of w because that is given in its declaration. We arrange, as explained below, that we always know a type for E as well. If the type of w is T, and of E is U, then the assignment is well-typed if $U \subseteq T$.

A type for any expression can be deduced provided we know the types of the variables and constants that it contains, and provided the operators have certain properties. For example, we know that the natural numbers are closed under addition, and that 1 is a natural number; therefore we know that in a context containing $a \in \mathbb{N}$ the expression $a + 1$ has type $\mathbb{N}$. Therefore $a := a + 1$ is well-typed. The same applies to $\mathbb{Z}$, $\mathbb{Q}$, $\mathbb{R}$, and $\mathbb{C}$: the constant 1 is an element of them all, and they all are closed under addition.

But type checking is not always so straightforward. Given $m, n : \mathbb{N}$, consider this refinement:

$$ m: [n > 0 \, , \, m = n - 1] \quad \sqsubseteq \quad m := n - 1. $$

Though the refinement is valid, the assignment is ill-typed, because $n \in \mathbb{N} \not\Rightarrow n - 1 \in \mathbb{N}$. Therefore we do not allow subtraction '−' of natural numbers in assignments.

For subtraction of natural numbers we use instead the operator $\ominus$, which agrees with ordinary subtraction '−' as far as possible: $2 \ominus 1 = 2 - 1 = 1$. But $1 - 2$ is not a natural number, while $1 \ominus 2$ *is* a natural number (though we choose not to know which one): therefore they cannot be equal. Still, in the situation above we have this alternative refinement:

$$ m: [n > 0 \, , \, m = n - 1] \quad \sqsubseteq \quad m := n \ominus 1. $$

It too is valid, and this time the resulting assignment is well-typed. The validity rests on the proviso required by *assignment* 1.3, which for the above is

$$ n > 0 \quad \Rightarrow \quad n \ominus 1 = n - 1. $$

That is true given our declaration $m, n : \mathbb{N}$.

Operationally, one would argue that when n is 0 initially, and thus $m := n \ominus 1$ assigns an unknown natural number to m, the refinement still holds: the precondition of the left-hand side is false.

Now we turn to the type-checking of local invariants. Recall that declarations 'and *inv*' are not code, and so must be removed once they have served their purpose (of providing extra context). There are general laws for that; but we do not show them, because our use of invariants will be very modest. Either they refer to variables that are never changed — that do not appear in any frame — or we use operators that maintain them trivially. Under those strong conditions, they can be removed without further checking; we draw attention to that as it arises below (for example, on page 100).

6.7   Undefined expressions

Consider this refinement:

$$x: [x = 1/0] \quad \sqsubseteq \quad x := 1/0.$$

Since the specification terminates (precondition **true**), so must the assignment. Yet that is not the conventional view. Usually, division by 0 is said to be 'undefined', causing assignments like the above to abort.

But recall $1 \ominus 2$ from Section 6.6. It is defined, and is even a natural number; but we do not know which one. Similarly, we say that $1/0$ is a rational number, but we do not know which one. The assignment $x := 1/0$ does terminate, but we simply do not know what value of x results.

Our novel view simplifies program development considerably, but of course complicates programming language implementations. We insist that divisions a/b return a result in all circumstances; they cannot abort when $b = 0$. Thus in programming languages without that property (that is, in most programming languages, regrettably), the command $x := a/b$ cannot be code on its own. Instead, we would have to allow certain specifications as code; in this case, we would allow only

$$x: [B \neq 0 , x = A/B]$$
or the equivalent $\{B \neq 0\}\ x := A/B$ (6.2)

for any variable x and expressions A and B over suitable types. Other partial operators would be handled similarly. Adherence to the strict form could easily be enforced by a compiler, a major part of which is dedicated to syntax checking in any case. (See Exercises 9.15 and following for further discussion of undefinedness.)

6.8   Exercises

Ex. 6.1   Consider this factorial program, in which we assume $f, n : \mathbb{N}$. What laws are used for the first refinement step (shown)?

$$f: [f = n!]$$

$\sqsubseteq$ **var** $i : \mathbb{N}\cdot$

$f, i\colon [i \leq n \wedge f = i!]\,;$ (i)

$f, i\colon [i \leq n \wedge f = i!\,,\; f = i! \wedge i = n]$.   (ii)

Complete the refinement to code.

Ex. 6.2   Repeat Exercise 4.2, but this time assume that $\{x \geq 0\}\; y := \sqrt{x}$ is code, while $y := \sqrt{x}$ (on its own) is not. (Recall Section 6.7.)

Ex. 6.3 $\heartsuit$ Assuming the context $z : \mathbb{Z}$, show the following to be a valid refinement:

$z\colon [z \geq 0]$

$\sqsubseteq$ **var** $n : \mathbb{N}\cdot$

$z := n$.

Ex. 6.4   Show that this refinement is valid:

$w\colon [post]$

$\sqsubseteq$ **and** $post\cdot$

choose w .

Why does that mean that invariants cannot be code? *Hint*: Use the context when checking the proviso of *strengthen postcondition* 1.1.

Ex. 6.5 $\heartsuit$ Some programming languages allow declarations of *constants* as follows:

const $c = 3$.

How can that effect be achieved with the declarations of this chapter? What are the remaining differences?

Ex. 6.6 $\heartsuit$ Suppose we have context $n : \mathbb{N}$. Is the following a valid refinement?

$n\colon \left[n^2 = 1\right] \quad \sqsubseteq \quad n := -1.$

Ex. 6.7 $\heartsuit$ Which of the following specifications are feasible, assuming the declarations $n : \mathbb{N};\; z : \mathbb{Z};\; r : \mathbb{R};\; c : \mathbb{C}$?

1. $n\colon [n = z]$
2. $z\colon [z = n]$
3. $r\colon [z \geq 0\,,\; r^2 = z]$
4. $n\colon [z \geq 0\,,\; n^2 = z]$
5. $r\colon [c^n = 1\,,\; r = c + 1/c]$

Ex. 6.8   Assume that the invariant is $x = 0$. Which of these specifications are feasible?

1. x: $[x = 0]$
2. x: $[x = 1]$
3. x: $[x = 0 , x = 0]$
4. x: $[x = 1 , x = 1]$
5. **choose** x

Ex. 6.9   Suppose we have *type coercion* functions for taking types into their subsets. For example, the function nat takes any natural number to itself, and any other number to *some* natural number. It satisfies these two properties:

1. $n \in \mathbb{N} \Rightarrow n = \mathsf{nat}\, n$
2. $\mathsf{nat}\, c \in \mathbb{N}$, for any c.

The other coercion functions are int, rat, real, and cpx.

Assuming the types $n : \mathbb{N}$; $z : \mathbb{Z}$; $q : \mathbb{Q}$; $r : \mathbb{R}$; $c : \mathbb{C}$, determine whether the following are valid refinements:

1. n: $[n = z]$ $\sqsubseteq$ $n := \mathsf{nat}\, z$
2. n: $[z \geq 0 , n = z]$ $\sqsubseteq$ $n := \mathsf{nat}\, z$
3. n: $[r \geq 0 , n = r]$ $\sqsubseteq$ $n := \mathsf{nat}\, r$
4. z: $[n < 2 , z^2 = n]$ $\sqsubseteq$ $z := \mathsf{int}\, \sqrt{n}$
5. q: $[r \geq 0 , q^2 = r]$ $\sqsubseteq$ $q := \mathsf{rat}\, \sqrt{r}$
6. q: $[r \neq 0 , q = 2/r]$ $\sqsubseteq$ $q := \mathsf{rat}(2/r)$
7. r: $[c^n = 1 , r = c + 1/c]$ $\sqsubseteq$ $r := \mathsf{real}(c + 1/c)$.

Ex. 6.10 ♡   What is wrong with the following 'law' for iterations?

$$w: [I , I \wedge \neg G]$$

$\sqsubseteq$? **con** $e \cdot$

    do $G \rightarrow$

$$w: [G \wedge (e = E) \wedge I , I \wedge (0 \leq E < e)]$$

    od .

Expression E is the variant, captured before each iteration by the logical constant e.

Hint: Unfold the iteration.

Chapter 7

Case study: Square root

In this chapter we follow a small but complete development from beginning to end. The key to success — as is very often the case — will be the finding of an appropriate invariant for an iteration. Application of refinement laws, and the setting out of developments, will become routine with practice; but finding invariants is always a fresh challenge.

7.1 Abstract program: the starting point

We are given a natural number s, and we must set the natural number r to the greatest integer not exceeding $\sqrt{s}$, where $\sqrt{}$ takes the non-negative square root of its argument. Thus starting from $s = 29$, for example, we would expect to finish with $s = 29 \wedge r = 5$.

Here is our abstract program:

> **var** $r, s : \mathbb{N}\cdot$
> $r := \lfloor \sqrt{s} \rfloor$.   (i)

Although an assignment, the command (i) is not code, because in this case study we assume that neither $\sqrt{}$ nor $\lfloor\ \rfloor$ is code. Our aim in the development to follow will be to remove them from the program.

7.2 Remove 'exotic' operators

These first refinement steps remove the square-root and floor functions ('exotic' only because they are not code) from the program by drawing on their mathematical definitions. The steps are routine, and leave us with a specification from which $\sqrt{}$ and $\lfloor\ \rfloor$ have disappeared:

$$= \text{``simple specification 1.7''}$$
$$r\colon [r = \lfloor \sqrt{s} \rfloor]$$
$$= \text{``definition } \lfloor \ \rfloor \text{''}$$
$$r\colon [r \le \sqrt{s} < r + 1]$$
$$= \text{``definition } \sqrt{} \text{''}$$
$$r\colon [r^2 \le s < (r+1)^2] \ . \tag{ii}$$

Comparing (i) and (ii), we can see that the assignment is written for the client: it uses powerful operators, leading to clear and succinct expression. Above all, it is easy to understand. But we have now moved from assignment to specification, and for two reasons: we need the freedom of a formula (rather than just an expression) to exploit the definitions of $\sqrt{}$ and $\lfloor \ \rfloor$; and a specification is easier to develop *from* than an assignment.

7.3   Look for an invariant

The postcondition in *iteration* 5.5 is of the form $inv \wedge \neg GG$, and so we should investigate rewriting our postcondition in (ii) that way. There are two immediate possibilities:

$$r^2 \le s \wedge \neg(s \ge (r+1)^2)$$
$$\text{and} \quad s < (r+1)^2 \wedge \neg(r^2 > s) \ .$$

The first would lead to an iteration

do $s \ge (r+1)^2 \to \cdots$ **od** ,

with invariant $r^2 \le s$. (The assignment $r := 0$ could establish the invariant initially.) The second would lead to

do $r^2 > s \to \cdots$ **od** ,

with invariant $s < (r+1)^2$ (whose initialisation is not so straightforward — but perhaps $r := s$ would do).

Either of those two approaches would succeed (and in the exercises you are invited to try them). But the resulting programs are not as efficient as the one we are about to develop. We rewrite the postcondition as

$$r^2 \le s < q^2 \wedge r + 1 = q \ ,$$

taking advantage of a new variable q that will be introduced for the purpose. (We use 'rewrite' here a bit loosely, since the two postconditions are definitely *not* equivalent. The new one implies the original, as it should — remember *strengthen postcondition* 1.1.) That surprising step is nevertheless a fairly common one in practice: one replaces an expression by a variable, adding a conjunct that makes them equal.

The refinement is the following:

(ii) $\sqsubseteq$ **var** $q : \mathbb{N}\cdot$

$\qquad q, r: [r^2 \leq s < q^2 \wedge r + 1 = q]$.

Now having separate bounds on s gives us more scope: initially, r and q could be far apart. Finally, we should establish $r + 1 = q$, and that will be the source of our increased efficiency: we can move them in big steps.

The next few refinements are routine when introducing an iteration: declare an abbreviation (I for the invariant, just to avoid writing it out again and again), establish the invariant with an assignment (initialisation), and introduce an iteration whose body maintains it.

The abbreviation $I \; \hat{=} \; \cdots$ is written as a decoration of the refinement. Like other decorations there (**var**, **con**), it is available in the development from that point on.

$\qquad \sqsubseteq I \; \hat{=} \; r^2 \leq s < q^2\cdot$

$\qquad\quad q, r: [I \wedge r + 1 = q]$

$\qquad \sqsubseteq q, r: [I]\,;$ $\hspace{5.5cm}$ (iii)

$\qquad\quad q, r: [I \, , \; I \wedge r + 1 = q]$ $\hspace{4.5cm}$ ◁

$\qquad \sqsubseteq$ "invariant I, variant $q - r$"

$\qquad\quad$ **do** $r + 1 \neq q \rightarrow$

$\qquad\qquad\quad q, r: [r + 1 \neq q \, , \; I \, , \; q - r < q_0 - r_0]$ $\hspace{2.5cm}$ ◁

$\qquad\quad$ **od** .

Note that the invariant bounds the variant below — that is, we have $I \Rrightarrow 0 \leq q - r$ — and so we need not write the '$0 \leq \cdots$' explicitly in the postcondition. We leave the refinement of (iii) to Exercise 7.1.

Our next step is motivated by the variant: to decrease it, we must move r and q closer together. If we move one at a time, whichever it is will take a value strictly between r and q. So we introduce a local variable for that new value, and make this step:

$\qquad \sqsubseteq$ **var** $p : \mathbb{N}\cdot$

$\qquad\quad p: [r + 1 < q \, , \; r < p < q]\,;$ $\hspace{4cm}$ (iv)

$\qquad\quad q, r: [r < p < q \, , \; I \, , \; q - r < q_0 - r_0]$. $\hspace{2cm}$ ◁

Strictly speaking, there should be an I in the postcondition of (iv), since in our use of *sequential composition* 3.3 the formula *mid* is clearly $r < p < q \wedge I$. (It is necessarily the same as the precondition of the ◁-marked command, which includes I: recall *specification invariant* 5.6.) But in fact I is established by (iv) whether we write it there or not, since it was in the precondition of the iteration body and does not contain p (the only variable that (iv) can change). Thus informally we can see that (iv) cannot falsify I — but in fact we have appealed (tacitly) to this law:

Law 7.1 <u>remove invariant</u> Provided w does not occur in inv,

$$w\colon [pre \ , \ inv \ , \ post] \quad \sqsubseteq \quad w\colon [pre \ , \ post] \ .$$

□

We now intend to re-establish $r^2 \leq s < q^2$ in the postcondition with an assignment: either $q := p$ or $r := p$. By investigating the proviso of *assignment 5.2*, calculating $(r^2 \leq s < q^2)[q \backslash p]$, we can see that the first requires a precondition $s < p^2$ (or at least as strong as that); similarly, the second requires $s \geq p^2$. That case analysis supplies the guards for our alternation:

$$
\begin{aligned}
&\sqsubseteq \ \textbf{if} \ s < p^2 \rightarrow q\colon [s < p^2 \wedge p < q \ , \ I \ , \ q < q_0] &&\text{(v)}\\
&\phantom{\sqsubseteq \ \textbf{if}} \ \| \ \ s \geq p^2 \rightarrow r\colon [s \geq p^2 \wedge r < p \ , \ I \ , \ r_0 < r] &&\text{(vi)}\\
& \textbf{fi}
\end{aligned}
$$

(v) $\sqsubseteq \ q := p$
(vi) $\sqsubseteq \ r := p$.

Note that the refinement markers (v) and (vi) refer to the bodies of the alternation branches, and do not include the guards.

The simplifications of the variant inequalities are possible because we have used *contract frame 5.4* in each case. In (v) for example, removing r from the frame allows us to rewrite $q - r < q_0 - r_0$ as $q - r < q_0 - r$, thence just $q < q_0$.

Now only (iv) is left, and it has many refinements: the assignment $p := r + 1$ and $p := q - 1$ are two. But a faster decrease in the variant — hence our more efficient program — will result if we choose p midway between q and r:

(iv) $\sqsubseteq \ p := (q + r) \div 2$.

There we have reached code.

7.4   Exercises

Ex. 7.1   Refine (iii) to code.

Ex. 7.2 ♡   Write out the code of the entire square-root program.

Ex. 7.3   Why can we assume $r + 1 < q$ in the precondition of (iv)? Would $r < q$ have been good enough? Why?

Ex. 7.4 ♡   Justify the branches (v) and (vi) of the alternation: where does $p < q$ come from in the precondition of (v)? Why does the postcondition of (vi) contain an *increasing* variant?

Ex. 7.5   Return to (ii) and make instead the refinement

$\sqsubseteq I \;\hat{=}\; r^2 \leq s\text{\textperiodcentered}$
$\quad r\text{: }\left[I \wedge s < (r+1)^2\right] \text{.}$

Refine that to code. Compare the efficiency of the result with the code of Exercise 7.2.

Ex. 7.6   Supply *all* the missing justifications and/or steps in this proof of *remove invariant* 7.1:

$\quad w\text{: }\left[pre \;,\; inv \;,\; post\right]$
$= \; w\text{: }\left[pre \wedge inv \;,\; inv \wedge post\right]$
$\sqsubseteq \; w\text{: }\left[pre \wedge inv \;,\; post\right]$
$\sqsubseteq \; w\text{: }\left[pre \;,\; post\right] \text{.}$

Where does the proof fail when *inv* contains *w*?

Chapter 8

Initial variables

We met initial variables briefly in Chapter 5, where they were necessary to specify the decrease of variants. In this chapter we study them further, presenting generalisations of earlier laws and definitions in order to take initial variables fully into account.

8.1 Simple specifications

We have seen that both initial variables and logical constants can be used to refer in a postcondition to a value based on the initial (rather than the final) state. Just which one is used in any particular situation is a matter of taste: the three commands

$$x := x + 1 \ ,$$
$$x \colon [x = x_0 + 1]$$
$$\text{and} \quad |[\ \mathbf{con} \ X \ \bullet \ x \colon [x = X \ , \ x = X + 1] \ ]|$$

all increment x by 1. They are equal as programs.

That the first two are equal is a consequence of this abbreviation, relating assignments and specifications of a simple kind:

Abbreviation 8.1 <u>simple specification</u> For any relation $\odot$,

$$w \colon \odot E \quad = \quad w \colon [w \odot E_0] \ ,$$

where E_0 is $E[w \backslash w_0]$.
□

As a special case we have that

$$w := E \quad = \quad w \colon [w = E_0] \ ,$$

which explains the equality of $x := x + 1$ and $x: [x = x_0 + 1]$. A further speciali-sation, requiring E to contain no w, returns us to our earlier *simple specification* 1.7.

But there are many other uses of the idiom: the command $x: > x$, for example, increases x strictly. In the context of the declaration $n : \mathbb{N}$, the command $n: < n$ decreases n strictly, but not below 0. Abbreviation 8.1 allows us to write such assignments in abstract programs without losing the opportunity of refining them subsequently.

That latter example above is perhaps slightly surprising, and we should look at precisely how the declaration ensures that n remains non-negative. The simple answer is that in the context $n \in \mathbb{N}$ *nothing* can make n negative, not even the assignment $n := -1$. (Recall the discussion in Section 6.6.) Thus if we refined $n: < n$ to $n := n-1$ in the context $n : \mathbb{N}$ — and it *is* a refinement — the assignment $n := n - 1$ would be miraculous, and would fail the type-checking. Could we refine $n: < n$ to $n := n \ominus 1$, for which type-checking would succeed? We cannot, for after using *simple specification* 8.1 to produce $n: [n < n_0]$, we would by *assignment* 5.2 have to show

$$n \in \mathbb{N} \quad \Rightarrow \quad n \ominus 1 < n \ .$$

That we cannot do, because we do not have in particular that $0 \ominus 1 < 0$.

8.2   Initial variables precisely

The second equality of the previous section is a consequence of this abbreviation, which by using **con** makes our 0-subscript convention precise:

Abbreviation 8.2 <u>initial variable</u> Occurrences of 0-subscripted variables in the post-condition of a specification refer to values held by those variables in the *initial* state. Let x be any variable, probably occurring in the frame w. If X is a fresh name, and T is the type of x, then

$$
\begin{aligned}
&w: [pre \ , \ post] \\
\widehat{=} \ &|[\ \textbf{con} \ X : T \cdot w: [pre \wedge x = X \ , \ post[x_0 \backslash X]] \ ]| \ .
\end{aligned}
$$

$\square$

The frame of a specification has so far been our only reference to initial values: those *not* in the frame are preserved. Now that initial variables allow us to be more explicit, we can give laws for manipulating the frame:

Law 8.3 <u>expand frame</u>

$$w: [pre \ , \ post] \quad = \quad w, x: [pre \ , \ post \wedge x = x_0] \ .$$

$\square$

Note that Law 8.3 is an *equality*: the refinement goes both ways. The conjunct $x = x_0$ in the postcondition prevents x from changing; and so does omitting it from the frame. With Law 8.3 we can prove our earlier *contract frame* 5.4, as follows:

$w, x: [pre \ , \ post]$
$\sqsubseteq$ *"strengthen postcondition 5.1"*
$\quad w, x: [pre \ , \ post \wedge x = x_0]$
$= \ w, x: [pre \ , \ post[x_0 \backslash x] \wedge x = x_0]$
$= $ *"expand frame 8.3 in reverse"*
$\quad w: [pre \ , \ post[x_0 \backslash x]]$.

8.3   Sequential composition revisited

Initial variables bring also a danger: there are some laws in which they must be explicitly banned. Consider the following *incorrect* use of *sequential composition* 3.3:

$x: [x = x_0 + 1]$ $\hspace{4cm}$ (i)
$\sqsubseteq?$ *"sequential composition 3.3"*
$\quad x: [x = 0] \ ;$
$\quad x: [x = 0 \ , \ x = x_0 + 1]$ $\hspace{2.7cm}$ (ii)
$\sqsubseteq \ x := 0; \ x := 1$.

It is incorrect because at (i) the initial variable x_0 refers to the initial value of x, while at (ii) it has come to refer to the *intermediate* value of x, between the two commands.

That is why Law 3.3 carried a warning footnote: it may not be used when initial variables occur in *mid* or *post*.

The correct law for sequential composition, when dealing with initial variables, is the following:

Law 8.4 sequential composition   For fresh constants X,

$w, x: [pre \ , \ post]$
$\sqsubseteq$ **con** $X \cdot$
$\quad x: [pre \ , \ mid] \ ;$
$\quad w, x: [mid[x_0 \backslash X] \ , \ post[x_0 \backslash X]]$.

The formula *mid* must not contain initial variables other than x_0.
$\square$

Law 8.4 is considerably more complicated than *sequential composition* 3.3, and so should be reserved for cases in which its extra power is essential. Other alternatives are *sequential composition* B.2 (probably the most appropriate in general), *leading assignment* 8.5 and *following assignment* 3.5 (good for specific cases).

$$f, n: [n = n_0 + 1 \land f = f_0 \times n]$$
$$\sqsubseteq \; \textbf{con } N \cdot$$
$$n: [n = n_0 + 1] \,;$$
$$f, n: [n = N + 1 \,,\; n = N + 1 \land f = f_0 \times n]$$
$$\sqsubseteq \; n := n + 1;$$
$$f := f \times n \;.$$

Figure 8.1 Sequential composition with initial variables

The constraint of Law 8.4 ensures that $mid[x_0 \backslash X]$ contains no initial variables at all: they would not be meaningful in a precondition. (But see Exercise 8.2.) Figure 8.1 gives an example of using Law 8.4.

Returning to the example that began this section, using Law 8.4 we have

$$x: [x = x_0 + 1]$$
$$\sqsubseteq \; \textbf{con } X \cdot$$
$$x: [x = 0] \,;$$
$$x: [x = 0 \,,\; x = X + 1] \;.$$

No longer can the second command be refined to $x := 1$. In fact, it cannot refine to *any* code, since the logical constant X cannot be eliminated from it. But that is not surprising: we do not expect to increment x by first setting it to 0.

For more examples of *sequential composition* 8.4 see Exercises 5.5 and 8.1.

8.4 Leading assignment

As an example of the use of the fuller form of sequential composition, we give here a law complementary to *following assignment* 3.5; now the assignment comes before, rather than after, the specification:

Law 8.5 <u>leading assignment</u> For any expression E,

$$w, x: [pre[x \backslash E] \,,\; post[x_0 \backslash E_0]]$$
$$\sqsubseteq \; x := E;$$
$$w, x: [pre \,,\; post] \;.$$

The expression E_0 abbreviates $E[w, x \backslash w_0, x_0]$.
□

With *sequential composition* 8.4, we can prove Law 8.5 as follows:

$$w, x: [pre[x\backslash E] \ , \ post[x_0\backslash E_0]]$$
$\sqsubseteq$ "definition of E_0"
$$w, x: [pre[x\backslash E] \ , \ post[x_0\backslash E[w, x\backslash w_0, x_0]]]$$
$\sqsubseteq$ "*sequential composition 8.4*", **con** $X\cdot$
$$x: [pre[x\backslash E] \ , \ pre \wedge x = E[x\backslash x_0]] \ ; \quad\quad\quad\quad\quad\text{(i)}$$
$$w, x: [pre \wedge x = E[x\backslash x_0][x_0\backslash X] \ , $$
$$post[x_0\backslash E[w, x\backslash w_0, x_0]][x_0\backslash X]] \quad\quad\quad\quad\quad\text{(ii)}$$

(i) $\sqsubseteq x := E$

(ii) $\sqsubseteq w, x: [pre \wedge x = E[x\backslash X] \ , \ post[x_0\backslash E[w, x\backslash w_0, X]]]$
$\sqsubseteq$ "*strengthen postcondition 5.1*, using $x_0 = E[x\backslash X][w_0\backslash w]$ from precondition"
$$w, x: [pre \wedge x = E[x\backslash X] \ , \ post]$$
$\sqsubseteq w, x: [pre \ , \ post]$.

Our earlier version *leading assignment 3.6* is a special case of the above, where we start with a simple specification derived from an assignment.

8.5   Exercises

Ex. 8.1   Assuming $x : \mathbb{R}$, prove this:

$$x: \left[x > 0 \ , \ x = 1/\sqrt{x_0} \right]$$
$$\sqsubseteq x: \left[x \geq 0 \ , \ x = \sqrt{x_0} \right] ;$$
$$x: \left[x \neq 0 \ , \ x = 1/x_0 \right] \ .$$

Hint: Use a stronger *mid* than $x = \sqrt{x_0}$.

Ex. 8.2 ♡   Suppose a specification $w: [pre \ , \ post]$ refers to x_0 in the postcondition even though x is not in the frame. Why is that unnecessary? Use *expand frame 8.3* to show that it is equal to $w: [pre \ , \ post[x_0\backslash x]]$.

Ex. 8.3   The abbreviation *initial variable 8.2* gives us this alternative to *expand frame 8.3*:

> *Law 8.6* <u>expand frame</u> For fresh constant X,
>
> $$w: [pre \ , \ post]$$
>
> $\sqsubseteq$ **con** $X\cdot$
>
> $$w, x: [pre \wedge x = X \ , \ post \wedge x = X].$$
>
> □

Use *expand frame 8.6* to show that

skip

$\sqsubseteq$ **con** $N\cdot$

$\quad n := n + 1; \ \ n := n - 1$.

Assume $n : \mathbb{N}$. *Hint*: Recall the formulation of **skip** on p.13.

Ex. 8.4 $\heartsuit$ Prove these equalities:

$$
\begin{array}{lll}
& w \colon [pre \ , \ post] & \text{(i)} \\
= & w \colon [pre \ , \ (\exists\, w \cdot pre) \Rightarrow post] & \text{(ii)} \\
= & w \colon [pre \ , \ (\exists\, w \cdot pre) \wedge post] \ . & \text{(iii)}
\end{array}
$$

Hint: To prove equality, show (i) $\sqsubseteq$ (ii) $\sqsubseteq$ (iii) $\sqsubseteq$ (i).

Ex. 8.5 $\heartsuit$ Write down the law resulting from *sequential composition* 8.4 in the special case that *mid* and *post* contain no x_0. In what way is the result more general than *sequential composition* 3.3?

Ex. 8.6   Assuming $n : \mathbb{N}$, use Definition 6.5 to show that the specification $n \colon [n \neq 0 \ , \ n < n_0]$ is feasible.

Ex. 8.7 $\heartsuit$ Show for any frame w that

$$ w \colon [\textsf{true} \ , \ \textsf{false}] \ \ = \ \ \colon [\textsf{true} \ , \ \textsf{false}] \, , $$

and hence that **magic** need not mention its frame. *Hint*: Use *expand frame* 8.3, and recall the hint of Exercise 8.4.

Ex. 8.8   Repeat Exercise 8.7 for **abort**.

Ex. 8.9   Repeat Exercise 3.8, this time taking initial variables into account.

Chapter 9

Constructed types

In earlier chapters we used basic mathematical types for our variables, all of them numbers of various kinds. In this chapter we are more ambitious, and expand our repertoire considerably by using the types we have already to make other types, and those to make others still. Our tools are powersets, bags, sequences, functions and relations.

9.1 Powersets

9.1.1 Making powersets

Given any type we can form its *powerset*, the type that contains all its subsets: given a type T, the type **set** T has as elements all subsets of T. Thus values of the type **set** $\mathbb{N}$ include $\{\}$, $\{17\}$, $\{2, 6\}$, the set of non-negative even numbers $\{0, 2, 4, \cdots\}$ and of course $\mathbb{N}$ itself.

As a special case, the type **finset** T has as elements all *finite* subsets of T. (Thus $\mathbb{N} \notin$ **finset** $\mathbb{N}$.)

That's all there is to making powersets; but when we introduce a new type, or type construction, we must also decide how to describe individual elements of the type and what operators will be available to use with them.

9.1.2 Using powersets: set enumeration and operators

Finite sets can be written by giving their elements explicitly, by *enumeration* between set brackets $\{\cdots\}$. For example, the set $\{1, 2, 3\}$ contains three elements exactly: 1, 2, and 3. The order of elements does not matter in set enumerations ($\{3, 2, 1\}$ is the same as $\{1, 2, 3\}$); and if by chance a value is written more than once, it makes no difference ($\{1, 2, 2, 3\}$ is still the same).

∪	union	functions
∩	intersection	
−	(set) subtraction	
×	Cartesian product	
∈	membership	relations
⊆	inclusion	
⊂	strict inclusion	
#	cardinality	(a function to ℕ)

Figure 9.1 Basic set operators

Set enumerations cannot describe *infinite* sets, except informally, because we cannot write all the elements down: although we might say that the set of even numbers is

$$\{0, 2, 4, \cdots\} \ ,$$

we cannot really give '⋯' any precise meaning in general.

Our numeric types have operators like + and −, and our set types have their own operators, like ∪ (union) and ∩ (intersection). Those are what we use in terms to combine given sets to form others. Figure 9.1 gives a selection of set operators.

9.1.3   Set comprehension

Set *comprehensions* define sets by some characteristic of their elements, rather than by writing them out, and they apply equally well to both finite and infinite sets. For example, the even numbers are those natural numbers n for each of which there is another natural number m with $n = 2m$:

$$\{n : \mathbb{N} \mid (\exists \, m : \mathbb{N} \cdot n = 2m)\} \ .$$

The general set comprehension has three parts (although the example above had just two). The first is a list of *bound variables* and their types. In the above, that list contains just one variable n and its type $\mathbb{N}$. If there are several variables and types, they are separated by a semicolon, for example $m : \mathbb{N}; \ n : \mathbb{N}^+$. (As in variable declarations, a repeated type may be omitted: thus we can write $m, n : \mathbb{N}$ for $m : \mathbb{N}; \ n : \mathbb{N}$.)

The set is formed by allowing the bound variables to range over their types.

The second part is a formula, called the *range*; in the comprehension above, it is $(\exists \, m : \mathbb{N} \cdot n = 2m)$. The formula usually refers to bound variables of the

$$
\begin{aligned}
\{n : \mathbb{N} \mid n > 0\} &= \{1, 2, 3, \cdots\} = \mathbb{N}^{+} \\
\{n : \mathbb{N} \mid n < 0\} &= \{\} \\
\{m, n : \mathbb{N} \mid m < n\} &= \{(0, 1), (0, 2), \cdots, (1, 2), (1, 3), \cdots\} \\
\{n, m : \mathbb{N} \mid m < n\} &= \{(1, 0), (2, 0), \cdots, (2, 1), (3, 1), \cdots\} \\
\{n : \mathbb{N} \bullet -n\} &= \{0, -1, -2, \cdots\} \\
\{m, n : \mathbb{N} \bullet m + n\} &= \{0, 1, 2, \cdots\} = \mathbb{N} \\
\{m, n : \mathbb{N} \mid m \geq n \bullet m^2 - n^2\} &= \{0, 1, 3, 4, 5, 7, \cdots\} \\
\{m : \mathbb{N}; \ n : \{0, 1, 3\} \bullet 4m + n\} &= \{0, 1, 3, 4, 5, 7, \cdots\}
\end{aligned}
$$

Figure 9.2 Set comprehensions

comprehension (but need not). It can also refer to other variables, in which case the set formed depends on the value of those. In any case, only values that satisfy the formula are considered while the bound variables range over their types; other values are just ignored. Sometimes the formula is just the formula true, in which case it (and the |, pronounced 'such that') can be left out.

The third part of the comprehension is a *term*. For each possible value of the bound variables, it is the value of the term that is put into the set. In the above, the term is left out because it is just the bound variable n itself. In general, a missing term is understood to be the *tuple* formed from the bound variables taken in order. (A 'monotuple', containing just one component, is just the component itself.)

If the term is present, it is preceded by a spot $\bullet$ (pronounced 'make'). Here is another definition of the set of even numbers:

$$\{m : \mathbb{N} \bullet 2m\} \ .$$

Figure 9.2 gives further examples.

9.1.4 Promoted relations

If we have a type T with some relation $\odot$ on its elements, we can use the same symbol $\odot$ for a *promoted* relation between sets $s1, s2 : \mathbf{set}\ T$ as follows:

$$s1 \odot s2 \ \hat{=}\ (\forall\, t1 : s1;\ t2 : s2 \bullet t1 \odot t2) \ .$$

And given a single element $t : T$ we further define

$$
\begin{aligned}
t \odot s2 &\ \hat{=}\ (\forall\, t2 : s2 \bullet t \odot t2) \\
s1 \odot t &\ \hat{=}\ (\forall\, t1 : s1 \bullet t1 \odot t) \ .
\end{aligned}
$$

The convenience of promotion usually outweighs the danger of confusing the two relations denoted by the symbol.

Often the relation $\odot$ is a total order, and the promoted relation allows formulae of this kind:

1. $s1 < s2$: every element of $s1$ is less than every element of $s2$.
2. $n \in s \wedge n \leq s$: the minimum value in s is n.

One must be especially careful, however, with transitivity: a promoted relation is not necessarily transitive, even if it is based on a transitive relation: from $1 < \{\}$ and $\{\} < 0$ (both true) we cannot conclude that $1 < 0$. (See Exercise 9.3.)

9.2 Bags

9.2.1 Bag enumeration and operators

A *bag*, like a set, is a collection of elements. Unlike a set, however, an element can belong to a bag 'more than once'. Given a type T, the type of all bags of its elements is written **bag** T.

For bag b and element e, we write $b.e$ for the number of times e occurs in b, and the formula $e \in b$ is true if and only if $b.e \neq 0$. Traditional set operators carry across to bags:

$$
\begin{aligned}
(b1 \cup b2).e &= b1.e \sqcup b2.e \\
(b1 \cap b2).e &= b1.e \sqcap b2.e \\
(b1 - b2).e &= (b1.e - b2.e) \sqcup 0 \;.
\end{aligned}
$$

As well, there is a new operation of *bag addition*:

$$(b1 + b2).e \; \hat{=} \; b1.e + b2.e \;.$$

Like sets, bags can be explicitly enumerated; the elements are written between bag brackets $\lVert$ and $\rVert$. Unlike set enumerations, bag enumerations are sensitive to how many times an element is written: if it is written twice, then it occurs twice in the bag. But order is still ignored. Figure 9.3 gives examples of bags and bag operations.

9.2.2 Conversion between bags and sets

The function **set** converts a bag to a set by 'forgetting' multiplicity:

$$\mathsf{set} : \mathbf{bag}\ T \to \mathbf{set}\ T \;.$$

For example, $\mathsf{set}\lVert 1, 2, 2, 3 \rVert = \{1, 2, 3\}$. In general, for $s = \mathsf{set}\ b$ we have that $e \in s$ iff $e \in b$.

The function bag_n goes the other way, converting a set into a bag:

$$\lfloor 1,2,2,3 \rfloor .1 \;=\; 1$$
$$\lfloor 1,2,2,3 \rfloor .2 \;=\; 2$$
$$\lfloor 1,2,2,3 \rfloor .3 \;=\; 1$$
$$\lfloor 1,2,2,3 \rfloor .4 \;=\; 0$$
$$\lfloor 1 \rfloor \cup \lfloor 1 \rfloor \;=\; \lfloor 1 \rfloor$$
$$\lfloor 1 \rfloor + \lfloor 1 \rfloor \;=\; \lfloor 1,1 \rfloor$$
$$\lfloor 1 \rfloor - \lfloor 1,1 \rfloor \;=\; \lfloor \; \rfloor$$
$$\lfloor 1,1 \rfloor - \lfloor 1 \rfloor \;=\; \lfloor 1 \rfloor$$

Figure 9.3 Examples of bags and bag operations

$$\mathsf{bag} : \mathbb{N} \rightarrow \mathsf{set}\ T \rightarrow \mathsf{bag}\ T\ .$$

Each element in the set is given multiplicity n in the resulting bag; if n is omitted, it is taken to be 1. For example, $\mathsf{bag}_2\ \{1,2\} = \lfloor 1,1,2,2 \rfloor$. Whenever $b = \mathsf{bag}_n\ s$, we have that $b.e = n$ if $e \in s$, and $b.e = 0$ if $e \notin s$. Finally, the two functions are complementary in the sense that for any set s, $\mathsf{set}\ \mathsf{bag}\ s = s$.

Promoted relations between bags are available as for sets.

9.2.3   Bag comprehension

Bag comprehensions, like set comprehensions, define bags by some characteristic of their elements; the difference is that they are written between bag brackets instead of set brackets. Unlike set comprehensions, the types of the bound variables are bags themselves. (If they are written as sets, then they are first implicitly converted to bags by the function **bag**.)

Multiplicity in bag comprehensions can arise in two ways. First, particular values of bound variables can occur more than once (since they are themselves taken from bags). Second, if the comprehension makes a term, it is possible for the same value to result from evaluations of the term with *different* values for the bound variables: thus $\lfloor n : \lfloor -1,0,1 \rfloor \cdot n^2 \rfloor = \lfloor 1,0,1 \rfloor$.

Figure 9.4 gives examples of bag comprehensions.

9.3   Sequences

9.3.1   Sequence enumerations and operations

A *sequence* is a collection of elements in which the order (and multiplicity) is significant. Given a type T, the type **seq** T has as elements all finite sequences of

$$\begin{aligned}
\lfloor n : \lfloor 1, 2, 2, 3 \rfloor \cdot 2n \rfloor &= \lfloor 2, 4, 4, 6 \rfloor \\
\lfloor m, n : \mathbb{N} \cdot m + n \rfloor &= \lfloor 0, 1, 1, 2, 2, 2, \cdots \rfloor \\
\lfloor m, n : \mathbb{N} \mid m < n \cdot m + n \rfloor &= \lfloor 1, 2, 3, 3, 4, 4, \cdots \rfloor \\
\lfloor m, n : \mathbb{N} \mid m < n \cdot n \rfloor &= \lfloor 1, 2, 2, 3, 3, 3, 4, 4, 4, 4, \cdots \rfloor
\end{aligned}$$

Figure 9.4 Examples of bag comprehensions

elements of T (of any length, including 0). For the type of all sequences of T with fixed length L we write $\mathbf{seq}_L \, T$. As a special case we use $\mathbf{seq}_\infty \, T$ for the type of all strictly infinite sequences of T.

Sequence enumerations are written between the sequence brackets $\langle$ and $\rangle$. For sequence q and natural number n, we write $q[n]$ for the element occupying the nth position of q, with the first position being index 0.

For sequences of integers, we allow a special ellipsis notation: the term $m \rightarrow n$ denotes the sequence starting at m and ending *just before* n. Thus $1 \rightarrow 4$ is the same as $\langle 1, 2, 3 \rangle$.

The principal operations on sequences are cons ':', concatenation '$+\!\!+$', head hd, tail tl, front fr, last lt, and length '#'. They are summarised in Figure 9.5, and Figure 9.6 gives examples of their use.

9.3.2   Conversions between sequences, bags, and sets

The function $\mathbf{seq}_\leq$ converts a bag or set to a sequence whose elements are ascending in the total order $\leq$: if a occurs before b in the sequence, then $a \leq b$. If the order $\leq$ is omitted, it is understood to be the standard order on the element type of the bag or set. For $\mathbf{seq}_\leq$ to be well-defined, the order $\leq$ should be such that every non-empty set has a least element with respect to the order.

If an element occurs n times in the bag, it is repeated n times in the sequence; when $\mathbf{seq}$ is applied to a set, however, each element occurs exactly once in the resulting sequence.

The function **bag** takes sequences to bags (as well as sets to bags), and the multiplicity in the sequence is preserved. Similarly, the function **set** takes a sequence to the set of its elements (in which case the multiplicity is not preserved).

Those functions too are complementary: for any set s and bag b,

$$\begin{aligned}
\mathbf{bag} \, \mathbf{seq}_\leq \, b &= b \\
\mathbf{set} \, \mathbf{seq}_\leq \, s &= s \, .
\end{aligned}$$

We may omit the conversion functions altogether if their use is implicit in the context, and that allows some compact (and possibly confusing) idioms. Some examples are given in Figure 9.7.

$\#q$	The number of elements in q.
$e{:}q$	The sequence whose first element is e, and whose subsequent elements are those of q. We have $(e{:}q)[0] = e$ and for $0 < i \leq \#q$, $(e{:}q)[i] = q[i-1]$.
$q1 \mathbin{+\!\!+} q2$	The sequence that begins with $q1$ and carries on with $q2$. We have $(q1 \mathbin{+\!\!+} q2)[i]$ equals $q1[i]$, if $0 \leq i < \#q1$, and equals $q2[i - \#q1]$ if $0 \leq i - \#q1 < \#q2$.
hd q	The first element of q, provided q is not empty. We have $\mathsf{hd}(\langle e \rangle \mathbin{+\!\!+} q) = e$.
tl q	The second and subsequent elements of q, provided q is not empty. We have $\mathsf{tl}(\langle e \rangle \mathbin{+\!\!+} q) = q$.
fr q	All but the last element of q, provided q is not empty. We have $\mathsf{fr}(q \mathbin{+\!\!+} \langle e \rangle) = q$.
lt q	The last element of q, provided q is not empty. We have $\mathsf{lt}(q \mathbin{+\!\!+} \langle e \rangle) = e$.

Figure 9.5 Operations on sequences: definitions

$$
\begin{aligned}
\#\langle\rangle &= 0 \\
\langle 1,2 \rangle \mathbin{+\!\!+} \langle\rangle &= \langle 1,2 \rangle \\
\langle\rangle \mathbin{+\!\!+} \langle 1,2 \rangle &= \langle 1,2 \rangle \\
1{:}\langle 2,3 \rangle &= \langle 1,2,3 \rangle \\
\langle 1 \rangle \mathbin{+\!\!+} \langle 2,3 \rangle &= \langle 1,2,3 \rangle \\
\mathsf{hd}\langle 1,2,3 \rangle &= 1 \\
\mathsf{tl}\langle 1,2,3 \rangle &= \langle 2,3 \rangle \\
\mathsf{fr}\langle 1,2,3 \rangle &= \langle 1,2 \rangle \\
\mathsf{lt}\langle 1,2,3 \rangle &= 3
\end{aligned}
$$

Figure 9.6 Examples of operations on sequences

Promoted relations are available between sequences as for sets and bags. (That

$$
\begin{aligned}
e \in q &\qquad e \text{ occurs in the sequence } q. \\
q.e &\qquad \text{the number of times } e \text{ occurs in sequence } q. \\
s[n] &\qquad \text{the } n^{th}\text{-from-least element of the set } s. \\
b[n] &\qquad \text{the } n^{th}\text{-from-least element of the bag } b. \\
q = \mathsf{bag}\ q &\qquad \text{the sequence } q \text{ is in order.} \\
\mathsf{bag}\ q = \mathsf{set}\ q &\qquad \text{the sequence is without repetition.} \\
b = \mathsf{set}\ b &\qquad \text{the bag is without repetition.}
\end{aligned}
$$

Note that in the final three cases, it is the right-hand side that is converted implicitly, rather than the left (though either would achieve type compatibility). Where there is a choice, we take the conversion that *adds* information (for example, from bag to sequence).

Figure 9.7 Implicit conversion idioms

$$
\begin{aligned}
\langle n : \mathbb{N} \cdot 2n \rangle &= \langle 0, 2, 4, \cdots \rangle \\
\langle i : 0{\to}10 \mid i^2 > 50 \rangle &= \langle 8, 9 \rangle \\
\langle i, j : \mathbb{N} \mid j < i \rangle &= \langle (1,0), (2,0), (2,1), (3,0), \cdots \rangle \\
\langle n : \mathbb{N} \cdot n^2 \rangle &= \langle 0, 1, 4, \cdots \rangle\ (= sq, \text{say}) \\
\langle n : \mathbb{N} \cdot n^3 \rangle &= \langle 0, 1, 8, \cdots \rangle\ (= cb, \text{say}) \\
\langle i : sq;\ j : cb \mid i = j \cdot i \rangle &= \langle 0, 1, 64, 729, \cdots \rangle
\end{aligned}
$$

Figure 9.8 Sequence comprehensions

follows in fact from the implicit conversion convention: the sequences are converted to sets first.)

9.3.3   Sequence comprehension

Sequence comprehensions define sequences by some characteristic of their elements. The bound variables should be sequences themselves (though implicit conversion may operate, if the element types have standard orders); then the order of the resulting sequence is determined by taking the values of the bound variables, in order, from their types. If there are several bound variables, then the rightmost varies fastest. Figure 9.8 gives examples of sequence comprehensions.

Sequences of sequences allow multi-dimensional structures, and for $q[i][j]$ we allow the abbreviation $q[i,j]$. The 'i^{th} row' of q is just $q[i]$. The 'j^{th} column' of q is $\langle i : 0{\to}\#q \cdot q[i,j] \rangle$.

9.3.4   Sequence idioms

We list below some convenient operations on sequences that can be defined by comprehension.

Filter

A *filter* is a one-place predicate p which can be used to select those elements of a sequence to be retained, in their original order. For sequence q, its filter by p is $\langle e : q \mid \mathsf{p}\, e\rangle$. More succinctly, we can write just $\mathsf{p} \triangleleft q$.

Composition

Given some sequence i of natural numbers, the *composition* of a sequence q with i is made by taking the elements of q indexed by the elements of i. It is written $q[i]$ (distinguished from the ordinary indexing by the fact that i is a sequence), and is equal to $\langle n : i \cdot q[n]\rangle$. Note that $q[i]$ is not necessarily a subsequence of q, because i itself might be out of order:

$$\langle 0, 2, 4, 6, 8\rangle[\langle 2, 1\rangle] \quad = \quad \langle 4, 2\rangle \ .$$

The operation is called composition because of its being related to functional composition when the sequences are considered to be functions from their indices to their elements.

Subsequence

A *subsequence* is a sequence composition taken in the original order. For that, we take a set s of natural numbers, and write $q[s]$. The implicit conversion takes s to a sequence — in ascending order — and the resulting composition then selects the elements in that order. A sequence $q2$ is a subsequence of another $q1$ iff there is a set of natural numbers that produces $q2$ from $q1$ in the above way; in that case we write $q2 \ll q1$, which is defined to be $(\exists s : \mathbf{set}\, \mathbb{N} \cdot q2 = q1[s])$. For example,

$$\langle 0, 2, 4, 6, 8\rangle[\{3, 1\}] \quad = \quad \langle 2, 6\rangle$$
$$\langle 2, 6\rangle \quad \ll \quad \langle 0, 2, 4, 6, 8\rangle \ .$$

We also allow the complementary $q \backslash s$, which is the subsequence formed by excluding the indices in s: it is $\langle i : 0 \rightarrow \#q \mid i \notin s \cdot q[i]\rangle$. For example,

$$\langle 0, 2, 4, 6, 8\rangle \backslash \{3, 1\} \quad = \quad \langle 0, 4, 8\rangle \ .$$

Subsegment

A *subsegment* is a contiguous subsequence (without 'gaps'). For that, we compose with a sequence $m \rightarrow n$ for some natural numbers m and n; the resulting subsegment of q is $q[m \rightarrow n]$. A sequence $q2$ is a subsegment of another $q1$ iff there is a pair of natural numbers that produces $q2$ from $q1$ in the above way; in that case we write $q2 \preceq q1$, which is defined to be $(\exists m, n : \mathbb{N} \cdot q2 = q1[m \rightarrow n])$. For example,

$$\langle 0, 2, 4, 6, 8\rangle[1 \rightarrow 3] \quad = \quad \langle 2, 4\rangle$$
$$\langle 2, 4\rangle \quad \preceq \quad \langle 0, 2, 4, 6, 8\rangle \ .$$

Prefix

A *prefix* is a subsegment that begins the sequence. We compose with a sequence $0 \to n$ for some natural number n; the resulting prefix is $q[0 \to n]$, which we can write $q \uparrow n$ and pronounce 'q take n'. A sequence $q2$ is a prefix of another $q1$ iff there is a natural number that produces $q2$ from $q1$ in the above way; in that case we write $q2 \subseteq q1$, which is defined to be $(\exists n : \mathbb{N} \cdot q2 = q1 \uparrow n)$. For example,

$$\langle 0, 2, 4, 6, 8 \rangle \uparrow 4 = \langle 0, 2, 4, 6 \rangle$$
$$\langle 0, 2, 4, 6 \rangle \subseteq \langle 0, 2, 4, 6, 8 \rangle \ .$$

Suffix

A *suffix* is a subsegment that ends the sequence. For sequence q, we compose with a sequence $n \to \# q$ that removes the first n elements; thus the suffix is $q[n \to \# q]$. We can write that $q \downarrow n$; it is pronounced 'q drop n'. Note that $q \uparrow n \mathbin{+\!\!+} q \downarrow n = q$ for all n such that $0 \leq n \leq \# q$. For example,

$$\langle 0, 2, 4, 6, 8 \rangle \downarrow 4 = \langle 8 \rangle \ .$$

9.4 Distributed operators

The set, bag, and sequence comprehensions have in common the ideas of bound variable, range, and term: each makes a set, bag, or sequence respectively as indicated by the surrounding brackets: $\{\cdots\}$, $[\![\cdots]\!]$, or $\langle\cdots\rangle$. That convention can be generalised, as we see below. But first we consider some properties of binary operators on their own.

A binary operator $\oplus$ is *associative* if for all a,b,c of appropriate type we have

$$(a \oplus b) \oplus c = a \oplus (b \oplus c) \ .$$

Many of the arithmetic operators are associative (Figure 6.2); in particular we have associative $+$, $\times$, $\sqcup$ and $\sqcap$. The set operators $\cup$, $\cap$, the bag operator $+$, and the sequence operator $\mathbin{+\!\!+}$ are associative as well.

To each associative operator corresponds a *distributed* operator that can be applied to a whole sequence. For example, corresponding to $+$, which sums two numbers, we have $\sum$, which sums a sequence of numbers. In general, distributed operators are written

$$(\oplus x : q \mid \mathcal{R} \cdot E) \ ,$$

where $\oplus$ is the associative binary operator, x is the bound variable, $\mathcal{R}$ is the range formula, and E is the term. The elements x of the sequence q are considered, one-by-one, in order; those satisfying $\mathcal{R}$ are retained; the term E is formed for each; and finally $\oplus$ is applied 'between' the resulting values, in order. Since $\oplus$ is associative, it does not matter how the applications of $\oplus$ are grouped.

$(+i : 0 {\rightarrow} n \cdot i^2)$ The sum of the first n squares.

$(\times d : \mathbb{N} \mid (d \mid n))$ The product of the divisors of $n : \mathbb{N}$.

$(\sqcap z : \mathbb{Z} \mid z \geq r)$ The ceiling $\lceil\ \rceil$ of $r : \mathbb{R}$.

$(\sqcup q' : \mathbf{seq}\,\mathbb{Z} \mid q' \preceq q \wedge q' < 0 \cdot \#q')$ The length of the longest sub-segment of $q : \mathbf{seq}\,\mathbb{Z}$ all of whose elements are negative.

Figure 9.9 Examples of distributed operators

The same conventions apply to distributed operators as to comprehensions: the range $\mathcal{R}$ defaults to **true**, and the term E defaults to the bound variable x. Hence we can define the sum of a sequence $q : \mathbf{seq}\,\mathbb{Z}$, say, as

$$\sum q \;\triangleq\; (+x : q \mid \mathsf{true} \cdot x) = (+x : q) \ .$$

Distributed operators are applicable to the empty sequence only if the original operator has an identity, a value e such that for all a we have $e \oplus a = a \oplus e = a$. In that case the result is the identity e, and for example we have therefore that $\sum\langle\rangle = 0$.

An operator $\oplus$ is *commutative* if for all a and b we have

$$a \oplus b \;=\; b \oplus a \ .$$

If an operator is commutative and associative, it can be distributed over bags as well as sequences. A non-commutative operator (like $+\!\!+$) cannot be distributed over a bag, because the result depends on the order in which elements are taken, and a bag has no order.

Finally, an operator $\oplus$ is *idempotent* if for all a

$$a \oplus a \;=\; a \ .$$

Any operator having all three properties can be distributed over sets as well. Thus the maximum of a set s of numbers is simply

$$(\sqcup x : s) \ .$$

If a non-commutative operator is distributed over a bag, or a non-idempotent operator over a set, we implicitly convert the bag to a sequence, or set to a bag, as appropriate. Thus $(+x : s)$ is the sum of the elements in the set s.

Figure 9.9 gives examples of distributed operators.

9.4.1   Quantifiers with ranges

Conjunction ∧ and disjunction ∨ are associative, commutative, and idempotent too, and they are operators over the Boolean type {true, false}. They are also propositional connectives — symbols we use within formulae — and we can exploit their properties there as well: we say that distributing ∧ gives ∀, and distributing ∨ gives ∃.

In fact, the notations of Sections 2.5.1 and 2.5.3 are deliberately close already to that for distributed operators, and the correspondence can be made exact by introducing ranges for quantifiers. (See Predicate laws A.54 and A.55.)

9.5   Functions

9.5.1   Partial functions, domain and range

The square root function $\sqrt{}$, taking real numbers to real numbers, has type

$$\mathbb{R} \nrightarrow \mathbb{R} \ .$$

The left-hand $\mathbb{R}$, the *source*, is the set from which the arguments are drawn; the right-hand $\mathbb{R}$, the *target*, is the set within which the results lie. The direction of the arrow indicates which is which (*from* source *to* target), and the stroke on the arrow indicates that the function is *partial*: there are some elements of its domain for which it is undefined.

There is no reason in principle, given the freedom we already allow ourselves with abstract programs, that we could not declare a variable of that same type and assign $\sqrt{}$ to it:

var $f : \mathbb{R} \nrightarrow \mathbb{R}$·
$f := (\sqrt{})$.

(We have enclosed $\sqrt{}$ in parentheses to make it clear that we mean $\sqrt{}$ *as a function*, not $\sqrt{}$ expecting some further argument.)

In fact we shall do exactly what is suggested above, allowing for any two types S and T the function type $S \nrightarrow T$ which, itself a type, can be used in declarations or to build still further types.

Our mathematical view of functions is that they are sets of pairs, with each pair containing one element from the domain and the corresponding element from the range. Thus these pairs are some of the elements of $\sqrt{}$:

$(0, 0)$
$(1, 1)$
$(1.21, 1.1)$
$(\pi^2, \pi) \cdots$

All of the pairs are elements of the Cartesian product of $\mathbb{R}$ with $\mathbb{R}$, written $\mathbb{R} \times \mathbb{R}$: in general the elements of the set $S \times T$ are pairs (s, t) with one element drawn from S and the other from T. Thus any function in $S \nrightarrow T$ is a subset of $S \times T$.

Associated with functions, as a type, are certain operations. The *domain* of a function is that subset of its source on which it is defined: for $f : S \nrightarrow T$,

$$\operatorname{dom} f \; \widehat{=} \; \{s : S; \, t : T \mid (s, t) \in f \cdot s\} \; .$$

Since f is itself a set, we can write that more succinctly as

$$\{(s, t) : f \cdot s\}$$

if we allow tuples as bound variables (which therefore we do).

The *range* of a function is that subset of the target which it might actually produce (given the right arguments):

$$\operatorname{ran} f \; \widehat{=} \; \{(s, t) : f \cdot t\} \; .$$

Thus $\operatorname{dom}(\sqrt{}) = \operatorname{ran}(\sqrt{}) = $ 'the non-negative reals'.

Note that $\operatorname{ran}(\sqrt{}) = $ 'the non-negative reals' means in particular that every non-negative real number is the square root of something.

9.5.2   Total functions

For any function $f : S \nrightarrow T$, we have $\operatorname{dom} f \subseteq S$ and $\operatorname{ran} f \subseteq T$. When equality holds in either case, we can be more specific: function f above is total when it is defined on all its source. In other words,

f is *total* means that $\operatorname{dom} f = S$.

If f can produce every element of its range, we say that it is onto (or surjective):

f is *onto*, or *surjective*, means that $\operatorname{ran} f = T$.

For total functions we have the special notation of 'uncrossed' arrow, so that declaring $f : S \rightarrow T$ is the same as declaring $f : S \nrightarrow T$ and stating additionally that f is total. Put another way,

var $f : S \rightarrow T$

has the same effect as **var** $f : S \nrightarrow T$; **and** $\operatorname{dom} f = S$.

Totality of a function is relative to its declared source: although partial over $\mathbb{R}$, the square root function is total over the non-negative reals. The same applies to whether the function is onto: thus square root is total and onto if declared from non-negative reals to non-negative reals.

9.5.3 Function application and overriding

Given $f : S \nrightarrow T$ and some $s : \mathsf{dom}\, f$ (which implies that $s \in S$ as well), we apply the function f to its argument s by writing $f\ s$. The result is an element of $\mathsf{ran}\, f$, and of T (since $\mathsf{ran}\, f \subseteq T$). An alternative way of writing the application is $f[s]$.

('Ordinarily', such function application is written $f(s)$. We have chosen instead to reserve parentheses for grouping, and indicate application by simple juxtaposition. The $f[s]$ variant is suggested by analogy with sequences, since they are functions from their indices to their values.)

As an 'abuse' of notation (actually a convenience), we allow $f[ss]$, given $ss : \mathsf{set}\, S$ as a *set* of values, and by it we mean the set of results obtained by applying f to elements of ss separately (and ignoring those that are undefined). Thus

$$f[ss] \;\hat{=}\; \{(s,t) : f \mid s \in ss \cdot t\} \ .$$

We can modify a function at one or more of its source values, so that

$$f[s := t]$$

is the function f *overridden* by $s := t$. Letting g be $f[s := t]$, we have

$$\begin{aligned} g[s] &= t &&\text{(no matter what } f[s] \text{ is)},\\ \text{and}\quad g[s'] &= f[s'] &&\text{for any } s' \neq s. \end{aligned}$$

If $s \neq s'$ and f is not defined at s', then neither is g.

Similarly,

$$\begin{aligned} (f[ss := t])[s] &= t &&\text{if } s \in ss\\ &= f[s] &&\text{if } s \notin ss \ . \end{aligned}$$

More generally still, we can override f by another function g; the resulting function $f \oplus g$ behaves like g if it can (if g is defined at that argument), otherwise like f. Thus

$$\begin{aligned} (f \oplus g)[s] &= g[s] &&\text{if } s \in \mathsf{dom}\, g\\ &= f[s] &&\text{otherwise.} \end{aligned}$$

If neither f nor g is defined at s, then $f \oplus g$ is undefined there also.

In terms of sets,

$$f \oplus g \;=\; \{(s,t) : f \cup g \mid s \in \mathsf{dom}\, g \Rightarrow (s,t) \in g\} \ .$$

That last formulation takes undefinedness automatically into account.

Our earlier notations for overriding can now be seen as special cases of the above, because $f[s := t]$ is just f overridden by the (singleton) function $\{(s,t)\}$, which takes s to t but is undefined everywhere else. In the $f[ss := t]$ case the overriding function is $\{s : ss \cdot (s,t)\}$, defined only on ss.

The overriding notations '$[s := \cdots]$' apply to sequences also, as they are a special case of functions.

9.5.4   Restriction and corestriction

Finally we have operators for restricting functions to smaller domains and ranges. Given $f : S \nrightarrow T$, $ss : \mathbf{set}\, S$ and $tt : \mathbf{set}\, T$, we define

$$
\begin{aligned}
ss \vartriangleleft f &\;\;\widehat{=}\;\; \{(s,t) : f \mid s \in ss\} \\
ss \ntriangleleft f &\;\;\widehat{=}\;\; \{(s,t) : f \mid s \notin ss\} \\
f \vartriangleright tt &\;\;\widehat{=}\;\; \{(s,t) : f \mid t \in tt\} \\
f \ntriangleright tt &\;\;\widehat{=}\;\; \{(s,t) : f \mid t \notin tt\} \;.
\end{aligned}
$$

An immediate use for $\vartriangleleft$ is an even more compact definition of overriding:

$$
f \oplus g \;\;=\;\; ((\mathbf{dom}\; g) \ntriangleleft f) \cup g \;.
$$

9.6   Relations

9.6.1   Generalised functions

Relations are a generalisation of functions: for source S and target T the corresponding relational type is written

$$
S \leftrightarrow T \;,
$$

and, like functions, relations are sets of pairs. In fact,

$$
S \leftrightarrow T \;\;=\;\; \mathbf{set}(S \times T) \;,
$$

which means that *any* subset of $S \times T$ is a relation. In contrast, only some subsets of $S \times T$ are functions; just which subsets they are we shall see shortly.

The generalisation of relations beyond functions is that relations are 'multi-valued': whereas for function f and source value s there is at most one $f[s]$, for relation r there may be many related target values.

Compare for example the function **pred** of type $\mathbb{N} \nrightarrow \mathbb{N}$ (it subtracts 1 from positive natural numbers) with the relation 'less than' $<$, of type $\mathbb{N} \leftrightarrow \mathbb{N}$. The two agree on source element 0 (because **pred** is undefined there, and no natural number is less than 0), and on source element 1 (because $\mathbf{pred}\, 1 = 0$ and the only natural number less than 1 is 0). But beyond 1 we find that $<$ is more generous:

source value s	pred s	less than s
2	1	0,1
3	2	0,1,2
4	3	0,1,2,3

The function returns just one value, whereas the relation relates s to many values: the predecessor of s is *one of* the values less than it.

As sets, we have

$$\mathsf{pred} \;=\; \{(1,0),(2,1),(3,2),\cdots\}$$
$$(<) \;=\; \{(1,0),(2,1),(2,0),(3,2),(3,1),(3,0),\cdots\}\;,$$

and thus we see clearly the difference between a relation and a function: in this case it is just that $\mathsf{pred} \subseteq (<)$.

9.6.2 Functions are relations

Functions and relations are both sets of pairs — but functions have the special property of being single-valued: for relation r in $S \leftrightarrow T$, we say that r is *functional*, or *single-valued*, if for all s in S there is at most one r-related t in T. That is, $r : S \leftrightarrow T$ is *functional* iff

$$(\forall\, s : S;\, t, t' : T \cdot (s,t) \in r \wedge (s,t') \in r \Rightarrow t = t')\;.$$

Thus a function is just a functional relation.

A related property is injectivity (or being one-to-one): a relation $r : S \leftrightarrow T$ is *injective* if

$$(\forall\, s, s' : S;\, t : T \cdot (s,t) \in r \wedge (s',t) \in r \Rightarrow s = s')\;.$$

The same notion applies to functions — because they are relations — and so an injection (or one-to-one) function is one that cannot deliver the same result for different arguments. Thus pred is injective, because $a - 1 = b - 1 \Rightarrow a = b$; but sqr is not, because for example

$$\mathsf{sqr}(-1) \;=\; 1 \;=\; \mathsf{sqr}\,1\;,$$

but $-1 \neq 1$. (Function sqr returns the square of its argument. Don't worry about the font convention for functions — it is only a convention, after all — but we are using sans serif for specific, named functions like sqr, and italic for function variables like f.)

Most of the operators and notations we have defined for functions work for relations as well, and we summarise them here: for $r : S \leftrightarrow T$,

$$
\begin{aligned}
\mathsf{dom}\ r &\;=\; \{(s,t) : r \cdot s\} \\
\mathsf{ran}\ r &\;=\; \{(s,t) : r \cdot t\} \\
r \text{ is total} &\;\text{iff}\;\; \mathsf{dom}\ r = S \\
r \text{ is onto} &\;\text{iff}\;\; \mathsf{ran}\ r = T \\
\text{if } ss : \mathsf{set}\ S, \text{ then } r[ss] &\;=\; \{(s,t) : r \mid s \in ss \cdot t\}\;.
\end{aligned}
$$

For overriding we have

$$r \oplus r' \;=\; ((\mathsf{dom}\ r') \mathbin{\lhd\!\!\!-} r) \cup r'\;,$$

and for the more specific cases then

$$
\begin{aligned}
r[s := t] &= r \oplus \{(s, t)\} \\
r[ss := t] &= r \oplus \{s : ss \cdot (s, t)\} \ .
\end{aligned}
$$

Thus for example $r[s := t]$ replaces *all* associations from s with a *single* new association to t.

Finally, for *applying* a relation one might be inclined to define

$$
r[s] = \{t : T \mid (s, t) \in r\} \ ,
$$

but there is a potential confusion there in that we would not know for example whether **pred** 1 was 0 (taking **pred** as a function) or $\{0\}$ (taking **pred** as a relation).

For writing that s and t are related by r, we have two possibilities: either $(s, t) \in r$, relying on the set-based nature of r, or $s\langle r\rangle t$, a special notation for relations.

The fact that functions are relations causes no problems here, since $1\langle \text{pred}\rangle 0$ means the same as $0 = \text{pred}\, 1$. (Note however the confusion caused by the general convention of writing function types from *left* to right, but supplying their arguments on the *right!*)

9.6.3 Inverses

Given $r : S \leftrightarrow T$, its inverse is written r^{-1} and is of type $T \leftrightarrow S$. The value of r^{-1} is obtained from r simply by reversing the pairs:

$$
r^{-1} = \{(s, t) : r \cdot (t, s)\} \ .
$$

Thus $(<)^{-1} = (>)$, and $\text{pred}^{-1} = \text{succ}$ (where function **succ** adds 1 to its argument).

That pred^{-1} is a function (rather than a relation) is just a bit of good luck: it is because **pred** is injective. In contrast, inverting **sqr** does not give a function, because for example

$$
\{(1, -1), (1, 1)\} \subset \text{sqr}^{-1} \ .
$$

Since **sqr** is not injective, its inverse is not functional: it is a proper relation that for any argument supplies both the positive and the negative square root. Our earlier function $\sqrt{\ }$ is a proper subset of sqr^{-1}.

9.7 Exercises

Ex. 9.1 Evaluate these terms:

1. $\text{bag}\{\}$
2. $\text{set}\lfloor\!\lfloor\ \rfloor\!\rfloor$
3. $\text{bag}_0\, s$

4. $\mathsf{bag}\{1,1\}$
5. $\mathsf{set}\lfloor\!\lfloor 1,1 \rfloor\!\rfloor$
6. $\mathsf{set}\lfloor\!\lfloor m,n:\mathbb{N}\cdot m+n \rfloor\!\rfloor$.

Ex. 9.2 ♡   Write set comprehensions for the following:

1. The perfect squares.
2. The natural numbers whose prime factors are in the set $\{2,3,5\}$.
3. The prime numbers.
4. The complex n^{th} roots of unity.

Ex. 9.3 ♡   Consider this alternative definition of the promoted relation ⊙:

$$s1 \odot s2 \;\hat{=}\; s1 \neq \{\} \wedge s2 \neq \{\} \wedge (\forall\, t1:s1;\; t2:s2 \cdot t1 \odot t2) \;.$$

Now suppose that ⊙ is transitive; is its promotion transitive as well? Why don't we define promotion as above?

Ex. 9.4   Evaluate these terms:

1. $\mathsf{seq}\,\mathbb{N}$.
2. $\mathsf{seq}\,\mathsf{bag}\langle 2,1,3,1 \rangle$.
3. $\mathsf{seq}\,\mathsf{set}\langle 2,1,3,1 \rangle$.
4. $\{n:\mathbb{N}\cdot 2n\}\,[7]$ (The 7th element of the sequence formed from that set.)
5. $\langle m,n:\mathbb{N}\cdot m+n\rangle.99$ (The number of occurrences of 99 in the bag formed from that sequence.)

Ex. 9.5   Show that the operations ∪, ∩, and −, applied to bags without repetitions, yield bags without repetitions. (That is why we can use the same symbols for operations on sets.)

Ex. 9.6 ♡   Consider a set comprehension in which *no* bound variables are given. What is the value of $\{|\; \mathsf{true}\cdot x\}$? Of $\{|\; \mathsf{false}\cdot x\}$? What is the value of $\langle i:0{\to}n\cdot x\rangle$?

Ex. 9.7 ♡   Define the *product* $\prod q$ of a sequence $q:\mathbf{seq}\,\mathbb{Z}$. What is $\prod\langle\rangle$?

Ex. 9.8   If we restrict the distributed maximum $\bigsqcup$ to sets $s:\mathbb{N}$ of *natural* numbers, what would $\bigsqcup\{\}$ be? Why?

Ex. 9.9   Write as a set comprehension the set of all permutations of a given sequence q.

Ex. 9.10 ♡   What is the effect of this operator on sets s:

$$(+x:s\cdot 1)\;?$$

On bags? On sequences?

Ex. 9.11   In type expressions, we let Cartesian product bind more tightly than $\twoheadrightarrow$ or $\rightarrow$, and the latter two both associate to the right.

Give the sizes of these types in terms of the sizes of their components:

1. $S1 \times S2 \rightarrow T$ — that is, $(S1 \times S2) \rightarrow T$
2. $S1 \rightarrow S2 \rightarrow T$ — that is, $S1 \rightarrow (S2 \rightarrow T)$
3. $S1 \times S2 \twoheadrightarrow T$
4. $S1 \twoheadrightarrow S2 \twoheadrightarrow T$
5. $S1 \rightarrow S2 \twoheadrightarrow T$
6. $S1 \twoheadrightarrow S2 \rightarrow T$.

Explain carefully any discrepancy in size between types 3 and 4.

Ex. 9.12   A sequence $s : \mathbf{seq}_N\ T$ can be regarded as a function of type $\mathbb{N} \twoheadrightarrow T$. What subset precisely of $\mathbb{N} \twoheadrightarrow T$ is the set $\mathbf{seq}\ T$?

With s declared as above, what is $\mathbf{dom}\ s$?

Ex. 9.13   Which of these declarations are of total functions over $\mathbb{N}$?

1. $s : \mathbf{seq}_N\ T$
2. $s : \mathbf{seq}\ T$
3. $s : \mathbf{seq}_\infty\ T$

Ex. 9.14   Consider $f : \mathbb{N} \twoheadrightarrow T$ and $s : \mathbf{seq}\ T$. For $n : \mathbb{N}$, when is $f[n] := t$ meaningful but $s[n] := t$ not?

Ex. 9.15   *Linear search* Assuming declarations $as : \mathbf{seq}_N\ A$ and $i : \mathbb{N}$; $a : A$, show that

$$i\colon [a \in as \Rightarrow a = as[i]]$$
$$\sqsubseteq\ i := 0;$$
$$\mathbf{do}\ i < N \wedge a \neq as[i] \rightarrow i := i + 1\ \mathbf{od}\ .$$

Hint: Note that termination is required even if $a \notin as$: use invariant $a \notin as{\uparrow}i$. Do not worry about possible 'undefinedness' of $as[i]$ when $i = N$, since the first conjunct $i < N$ is false in that case anyway. (See Exercises 9.16 and 9.17 however in that connection.)

Ex. 9.16 ♡   *Linear search* Assume our programming language treats $as[i]$ as 'undefined' when i is not in the domain of as, and that programs evaluating $as[i]$ under those circumstances will behave unpredictably (like **abort**).[1] Thus (recalling Section 6.7) an evaluation of $as[i]$ will not be accepted *on its own* as code by our compiler: if as were declared $\mathbf{seq}_N\ A$, for example, then

---

[1]That is the usual situation, but differs from the convention in this text that all expressions terminate: we would say for i outside the domain of as that $as[i]$ returned some value but we do not know which. Our view is convenient for development, but requires more from compilers: either they must generate always-terminating code for expressions (as in Exercise 9.15), or they must carry out compile-time checks as illustrated in this exercise.

$$a := as[i]$$

would not be code, and would be treated as a syntax error (although it is nevertheless meaningful). We would have to write instead

$$\{i < N\} \ a := as[i] \ ,$$

assuming the declaration $i : \mathbb{N}$ (which guarantees $0 \leq i$).

For possibly 'undefined' iteration guards the compiler would insist on 'wellformedness assumptions' (like $\{i < N\}$ above) placed as follows:

$$\{`G \text{ is defined}'\}$$
do $G \rightarrow$
$\quad prog$
$\quad \{`G \text{ is defined}'\}$
od .

Explain briefly why they should be placed like that.

Show that

$$i\colon [a \in as \ , \ a = as[i]]$$
$\sqsubseteq \ i := 0;$
$\quad \{i < N\}$
$\quad$ **do** $a \neq as[i] \rightarrow$
$\quad\quad i := i + 1$
$\quad\quad \{i < N\}$
$\quad$ **od** ,

and explain informally why the possible evaluation of the 'undefined' $as[i]$ is now acceptable. What general rule can you formulate about the connection between iteration invariants and definedness conditions for the iteration guards?

Ex. 9.17 ♡   Can Exercise 9.15 be done under the conditions of Exercise 9.16? Putting it rigorously, we are asking whether this refinement is valid:

$$i\colon [a \in as \Rightarrow a = as[i]]$$
$\sqsubseteq \ i := 0;$
$\quad \{i < N\}$
$\quad$ **do** $i < N \wedge a \neq as[i] \rightarrow$
$\quad\quad i := i + 1$
$\quad\quad \{i < N\}$
$\quad$ **od** .

If it is valid, show it to be so; if it is not, *show* it to be invalid, and give an operational explanation for the failure.

Chapter 10

Case study: Insertion Sort

Insertion Sort is one of the simplest sorting algorithms, and will be our first case study involving sequences (or arrays).

The number of comparisons it makes is proportional on average to the square of the number of elements to be sorted. Later we will do better than that; but for now we study Insertion Sort as our first example of nested iterations.

10.1   What it means to be sorted

We are given sequence as of integers, and we must rearrange its elements so that they are 'sorted'. To be more precise, we define a predicate 'is in non-strict ascending order',

$$\text{up } as \;\widehat{=}\; (\forall\, i, j : 0 \rightarrow \#as \cdot i \leq j \Rightarrow as[i] \leq as[j]) \;,$$

by which we mean 'if the index of one element is no greater than the index of some other element, then the value of that element is no greater than the value of the other'.

With up, we can start with the following abstract program:

> **var** $as : \text{seq}_N \, \mathbb{Z};$ **con** $A;$
> **and** $A = \text{bag } as\cdot$
> $as\colon [\text{up } as]\,.$

The variable as is, of course, the sequence we are to sort.

The logical constant A is the bag of elements in the sequence, and the invariant $A = \text{bag } as$ means therefore that elements may neither be added to nor removed from as. Thus the sequence can be rearranged but not otherwise altered, and so we exclude trivial code such as $as := 0 \rightarrow N$.

10.2 Similar pre- and postconditions

We approach the problem by successively sorting larger prefixes of *as*: at first, no matter what values *as* contains, still its empty prefix is sorted. What we want is to make its 'longest prefix' sorted, since the longest prefix of a sequence is the sequence itself.

The approach above is suggested to us, in fact, by the text of the abstract program, if we try to make its pre- and postconditions similar. By introducing prefixes explicitly,

$$\sqsubseteq \; as\colon [\mathsf{up} \; as{\uparrow}0 \; , \; \mathsf{up} \; as{\uparrow}N] \; ,$$

we can see that somehow we want 'to change the 0 into an N'.

Both 0 and N are constants, yet we want them to vary — therefore we replace them both by a new variable k, and vary *that*: variable k can move from 0 to N, allowing us to write ${\uparrow}k$ in the pre- and postcondition. From there, the development of our first iteration is routine:

$\sqsubseteq$ **var** $k : \mathbb{N}$·
  $\quad k := 0;$ (i)
  $\quad as, k\colon [k = 0 \; , \; \mathsf{up} \; as{\uparrow}k \; , \; k = N]$ $\lhd$
$\sqsubseteq$ $I \; \hat{=} \; k \leq N \wedge \mathsf{up} \; as{\uparrow}k$·
  $\quad as, k\colon [I \; , \; I \wedge k = N]$
$\sqsubseteq$ "invariant I, variant $N - k$"
  $\quad$**do** $k \neq N \rightarrow$
    $\quad\quad as, k\colon [k < N \; , \; I \; , \; k > k_0]$ $\lhd$
  $\quad$**od** .

(See Exercise 10.1 if you are puzzled about (i).)

Note how in the precondition above (writing $k < N$ rather than $k \neq N$) and in the postcondition (omitting $N \geq k$) we have made use of the invariant I.

10.3 Decreasing the variant

In many cases the easiest way is to deal with a variant is to decrease it explicitly, and we do that here with *following assignment* 3.5. After applying *specification invariant* 5.6, we proceed as follows:

$\sqsubseteq$ "*following assignment* 3.5"
  $\quad as, k\colon [k < N \wedge I \; , \; I[k \backslash k + 1] \wedge (k + 1) > k_0];$ $\lhd$
  $\quad k := k + 1$
$\sqsubseteq$ "*contract frame* 5.4"
  $\quad as\colon [k < N \wedge I \; , \; I[k \backslash k + 1]]$ (ii)
(ii) $\sqsubseteq$ $as\colon [k < N \wedge \mathsf{up} \; as{\uparrow}k \; , \; \mathsf{up} \; as{\uparrow}(k + 1)]$.   (iii)

Specification (ii) is an extremely common pattern in iteration bodies: assume truth of the invariant at k, then establish its truth at $k + 1$.

10.4   Iterating up, and down

If the pattern so far is such a common one, then we really should see whether we can generalise it for later use. Suppose $N \geq 0$; then given a specification

$$as, k: [k = 0 , I , k = N] ,$$

we can by choosing invariant $I \wedge 0 \leq k \leq N$ develop the iteration

> **do** $k \neq N \rightarrow$
> $as: [I \wedge 0 \leq k < N , I[k \backslash k + 1]]$;
> $k := k + 1$ ◁
> **od**

by following steps like those in the previous section; the marked statement — where development continues — produces code to ensure that, when the subsequent $k := k+1$ is executed, the invariant will be re-established. Let us call the refinement above *iterate up*.

A second possibility for iterating up is to increase k first, then re-establish the invariant. Then we have instead

> **do** $k \neq N \rightarrow$
> $k := k + 1$;
> $as: [I[k \backslash k - 1] \wedge 0 < k \leq N , I]$
> **od** .

Similar possibilities, for decreasing k (from N to 0 rather than from 0 to N), are examined in Exercise 10.9, where we call them *iterating down*.

With our 'packaged' up-iteration, we could redo our development so far as follows:

> **var** $as : \mathbf{seq}_N \, \mathbb{Z}$; **con** A;
> **and** $A = \mathbf{bag} \, as \cdot$
> $as: [\mathbf{up} \, as]$ ◁
> $\sqsubseteq$ **var** $k : \mathbb{N} \cdot$
> $k := 0$;
> $as, k: [k = 0 , \mathbf{up} \, as{\uparrow}k , k = N]$ ◁
> $\sqsubseteq$ "iterate up"
>   **do** $k \neq N \rightarrow$
> $as: [k < N \wedge \mathbf{up} \, as{\uparrow}k , \mathbf{up} \, as{\uparrow}(k + 1)]$;   (iii)
> $k := k + 1$
>   **od** .

10.5   A tricky invariant

With the iteration body (iii) we are left with what appears to be a fairly straight-forward problem: given a sequence of length $k + 1$ whose first k elements are in order, effect a rearrangement that brings all $k+1$ of its elements into order. (The 'sequence of length $k + 1$' is the prefix $as{\uparrow}(k + 1)$; in casting the problem as we have, we are taking a (small) chance by ignoring the possibility of using elements beyond the prefix (from $as{\downarrow}(k + 1)$). But the chance we are taking is not that we will develop the *wrong* code — rather it is that we will develop no code at all.)

An obvious move for 'making the pre- and postconditions similar' is to write the postcondition as 'the first k elements are sorted, and the last one is too':

$$\textsf{up } as{\uparrow}(k + 1) \quad \equiv \quad \textsf{up } as{\uparrow}k \wedge as{\uparrow}k \leq as[k] .$$

The resulting iteration would begin $\textbf{do } \neg((as{\uparrow}k) \leq as[k]) \rightarrow \cdots$, and the body would have to maintain $\textsf{up } as{\uparrow}k$. Thinking about it operationally, however, there seems no way to move $as[k]$ *gradually* to its correct place in sequence as while maintaining the order of $as{\uparrow}k$ — it would just have to be moved all at once, and then there would be no need for an iteration at all.

A slightly less obvious approach (but we are now forced to try a bit harder) is to generalise slightly: let the invariant be 'all but one of the elements are sorted' (so to speak — we will be more precise in a moment). Then initially the one element that is not is $as[k]$; finally it will be some other — say $as[l]$ — but we will add a conjunct to the postcondition 'element $as[l]$ is sorted as well'.

Now we must make that idea a bit more precise.

Again we try to make the precondition and postcondition similar. Since our concern is mainly with the prefix $as{\uparrow}(k + 1)$, we call that P (for 'prefix'), and the precondition can be written $\textsf{up } P\backslash\{k\}$, meaning '$P$ is sorted except at k'. (We use upper case for P to remind us that it is an expression, not a variable, and so cannot be assigned to.) In the postcondition we want, for some local variable l,

$$\textsf{up } P\backslash\{l\} \wedge P{\uparrow}l \leq P[l] \leq P{\downarrow}(l + 1) .$$

The first conjunct expresses that the prefix P is sorted except at l; the second expresses that it is sorted at l as well.

After all that preparation, we now have the refinement step, in which we add the local variable l. In the postcondition we constrain it to lie within the bounds of P (it is non-negative anyway, because of its type):

$$(\text{iii}) \sqsubseteq \left\{ \begin{array}{rcll} P & \widehat{=} & as{\uparrow}(k + 1) & \text{an expression} \\ J & \widehat{=} & P{\uparrow}l \leq P[l] & \text{a formula} \\ K & \widehat{=} & P[l] \leq P{\downarrow}(l + 1) & \text{a formula} \\ \multicolumn{4}{l}{\textbf{var } l : \mathbb{N}\text{·}} \end{array} \right. .$$

$$as, l\colon [\textsf{up } P\backslash\{k\} ,\ l \leq k \wedge \textsf{up } P\backslash\{l\} \wedge J \wedge K] .$$

precondition	$\neg(P\!\uparrow\! l \leq P[l])$ $l \leq k$ up $P\backslash\{l\}$ $P[l] \leq P\!\downarrow\!(l+1)$
postcondition	$l \ominus 1 \leq k$ up $P\backslash\{l \ominus 1\}$ $P[l \ominus 1] \leq P\!\downarrow\! l$

Figure 10.1 Pre- and postcondition of inner iteration body

Looking at the precondition, we see that l should start at k, and so tend to 0. Looking at the postcondition, we see that there are two possibilities for the guard: either the negation of J (leaving K in the invariant), or the other way around. Since $l = 0 \Rightarrow J$, we will take $\neg J$ as the guard, call the invariant L, and proceed:

$$\sqsubseteq\ L \ \widehat{=}\ l \leq k \wedge \text{up } P\backslash\{l\} \wedge K \cdot$$
$$l := k;$$
$$\mathbf{do}\ \neg J \rightarrow$$
$$\quad as, l\colon [\neg J\ ,\ L\ ,\ l < l_0] \qquad\qquad\qquad \triangleleft$$
$$\mathbf{od}$$
$$\sqsubseteq\ as\colon [\neg J \wedge L\ ,\ L[l\backslash l \ominus 1]]; \qquad\qquad\qquad\qquad\qquad \text{(iv)}$$
$$l := l \ominus 1\ .$$

In (iv), we have met the pattern of (ii) again, this time decreasing. (It is not strictly speaking in the form of our simple 'iterate down', because the guard is not just $l \neq 0$. But they have many features in common.)

To make progress we must now, at last, expand our abbreviations to reveal in more detail what we have to work with: Figure 10.1 sets them out in tabular form. The main difference between the two is that the precondition is concerned with l, and the postcondition with $l \ominus 1$. To bring the two formulae closer together, we widen the sequence exclusions to $\{l \ominus 1, l\}$ in each case, adding back a conjunct to constrain $P[l \ominus 1]$ in the precondition, $P[l]$ in the postcondition. Doing that, and some simplification, results in Figure 10.2. (See Exercise 10.2.)

Comparing the four conjuncts one-by-one between pre- and postcondition, we find:

1. The first in the precondition implies the first in the postcondition.
2. The second conjuncts are complementary with respect to l and $l \ominus 1$, suggesting a swap.
3. The third conjuncts are the same, even if we swap.

precondition	$0 < l \le k$ $P[l \ominus 1] > P[l]$ up $P \backslash \{l \ominus 1, l\}$ $P{\uparrow}(l \ominus 1) \le P[l \ominus 1] \le P{\downarrow}(l+1)$
postcondition	$0 < l \le k+1$ $P[l \ominus 1] \le P[l]$ up $P \backslash \{l \ominus 1, l\}$ $P{\uparrow}(l \ominus 1) \le P[l] \le P{\downarrow}(l+1)$

Figure 10.2 Rewriting of Figure 10.1.

4. The fourth conjunct in the precondition implies the fourth in the postcondition if we swap.

So 'swap' it is: we exchange elements $l \ominus 1$ and l of P, and that is accomplished by exchanging them in as:

(iv) $\sqsubseteq$ *Swap* $(as, l \ominus 1, l)$.

That leaves only the definition of *Swap* itself.

10.6   Assignment to sequences

In many programming languages, *Swap* $(as, l \ominus 1, l)$ would be written

$as[l \ominus 1], as[l] := as[l], as[l \ominus 1]$,

in spite of there being *expressions* on the left of assignment. In general, what is meant by $as[i] := E$ is

$as := as[i := E]$,

where $as[i := E]$ is the sequence got by replacing the ith element of as by E. (Recall Section 9.5.3.) It is defined as follows:

Abbreviation 10.1 <u>sequence assignment</u>   For any sequence as, if $0 \le i, j \le \#as$ then

$as[i := E][j] \;\hat{=}\; \begin{array}{ll} E & \text{when} \quad i = j \\ as[j] & \text{when} \quad i \ne j \end{array}$.

□

Sequence assignment extends to multiple indices as in *Swap*: we have

$Swap\ (as, l \ominus 1, l)$
$=\ as := as[l \ominus 1, l := as[l], as[l \ominus 1]]$.   (v)

10.7   Removing the local invariant

All now is code except the local invariant $A = \mathbf{bag}\ as$. To remove it, we must check that every command in its scope maintains it. Since the only assignment made to as is the one above, the swap, and clearly cannot violate the invariant $A = \mathbf{bag}\ as$, the local invariant can be removed, finally, leaving code.

10.8   Exercises

Ex. 10.1 ♡   Explain the introduction of (i). What laws are used?

Ex. 10.2 ♡   Recall Figure 10.2, rewritten from Figure 10.1. Why are the following true?

1. In the precondition, $P{\uparrow}l \not\preceq P[l]$ can be replaced by $P[l \ominus 1] > P[l]$.
2. In the postcondition, $P[l \ominus 1] \leq P{\downarrow}l$ can be replaced by $P[l \ominus 1] \leq P[l]$.
3. In the precondition, $P[l] \leq P{\downarrow}(l+1)$ is not needed.

Hint: Use the other conjuncts too.

Ex. 10.3   Use *sequence assignment* 10.1 and Figure 10.2 to check that (iv) $\sqsubseteq$ (v).

Ex. 10.4 ♡   Replace the guard $\neg J$ with code. *Hint*: Use the invariant, and recall Exercise 10.2.

Ex. 10.5 ♡   Here is the inner iteration of Insertion Sort:

do $(l \neq 0) \wedge (as[l \ominus 1] > as[l]) \rightarrow$
    $as := as[l \ominus 1, l := as[l], as[l \ominus 1]];$
    $l := l \ominus 1$
od .

Note that the value of $as[l]$ is the same on each iteration. We can 'tune' the algorithm to take advantage of that:

$= \mathbf{var}\ t : \mathbb{Z}{\cdot}$
    $t := as[l];$
    do $(l \neq 0) \wedge (as[l \ominus 1] > t) \rightarrow$
        $as := as[l := as[l \ominus 1]];$
        $l := l \ominus 1$
    od;
    $as := as[l := t]$.

On each iteration we avoid two array index operations and one assignment.

Give the invariant for the tuned iteration. *Hint*: Consider the expression $P[l := t]$.

Why must the local invariant $A = \mathsf{bag}\ as$ have been removed *before* the program is changed as above?

Ex. 10.6 ♡   Modify the predicate **up** so that it expresses *strict* order: moving from lower to higher indices must strictly increase the corresponding elements. (In other words, in the sorted sequence there may not be repeated elements.)

Why doesn't our development go through with the new definition? Find *precisely* the step that is in error.

Ex. 10.7   *Binary search* You have a sorted sequence as of integers, and must find the position i of a given value x in it. If x is not in as, then i should index the least element of as greater than x, if any. Here is the abstract program:

> **var** $as : \mathbf{seq}_N\ \mathbb{Z};\ x : \mathbb{Z};\ i : \mathbb{N};$
> **and** up $as\cdot$
> $i:\ [as{\uparrow}i < x \leq as{\downarrow}i]$.

Refine it to code; it should take time proportional to $\log N$ to execute. *Hint*: Recall Chapter 7.

Ex. 10.8   As for assignment to sequences, for relation r we allow an abbreviation for $r := r[s := t]$ — we just write

> $r[s] := t$.

Similarly $r[ss] := t$ abbreviates $r := r[ss := t]$.

Now suppose that $g[s]$ equals some constant c for all $s : S$ (hence $\mathsf{dom}\ g = S$). How could $f := f \oplus g$ be written in the style of $f[?] := ??$

What is the effect of $f[\{\}] := t$?

Ex. 10.9   *Iterate down* Show that, provided $0 \leq N$,

> $as, k:\ [k = N\ ,\ I\ ,\ k = 0]$
> $\sqsubseteq\ \mathbf{do}\ k \neq 0 \rightarrow$
> $\qquad as:\ [0 < k \leq N \wedge I\ ,\ I[k \backslash k - 1]]\ ;$
> $\qquad k := k - 1$
> $\mathbf{od}$.

Where *precisely* is $0 \leq N$ used?

Ex. 10.10 ♡   Why aren't *iterate up* and *iterate down* made into laws?

Ex. 10.11 ♡   In Exercise 10.9 the statement $k := k - 1$ appears in the body of the down iteration. Shouldn't it be $k := k \ominus 1$?

Chapter 11

Procedures and parameters

For any programming problem other than the very smallest, the size of the development will in itself require careful management if we are not to find that a rigorous approach is more trouble than it is worth.

One of the most basic ways of controlling size and structure in programming is the use of procedures: a procedure is defined in just one place, but used in many. For us, with our broader perspective allowing abstract programs as well as code, we will find procedures convenient for avoiding repeated developments: a specification whose body is a specification may be refined in just one place, but used in many.

There are many advantages of such economy. One is that the structure of the program is more clearly revealed, since sections of identical purpose are clearly labelled as such. Another advantage is that an implementation can save space (perhaps at the expense of some time) by keeping only one copy of the machine code.

But the most significant advantage for us is the one mentioned above. Without procedures, the refinement of a repeated specification must be carried out at its every occurrence; that at the very least involves a lot of copying. With procedures, refinement of the declaration alone gives 'automatic' refinement of all its calls.

The basic principle is that if a text is repeated many times in a program, the program may be improved by *naming* the text and then using the name many times instead. The association of a name with program text is *procedure declaration*. The use of the name to stand for the text is *procedure call*.

If a text is repeated not identically, but with systematic variation — say a renaming of its variables — then there still may be possibilities for reuse of a single declaration. We can use *substitution*, which allows a 'reference copy' of a program text to be adapted to slightly differing uses. When substitution is applied to procedures, we have what are usually called *parametrized procedures*.

In this chapter we look first at procedures, then substitution, and finally the two together: parametrized procedures.

11.1 Procedures without parameters

11.1.1 Declaring procedures

The basic declaration is extremely simple: a procedure is *declared* by associating a *name* with a program fragment, and the fragment is then called the *body* of the procedure. For declarations we use the syntax

procedure $N \ \widehat{=} \ prog$,

where N is the name of the procedure, and *prog* is its body. Like the declaration of ordinary variables (for example **var** declarations), procedure declarations are made within a local block that indicates their scope. There are no restrictions on what may be declared a procedure, or where.

11.1.2 Why one bothers

Suppose we are given three integers p, q, r, and are to sort them into increasing order. We might try

$$p, q, r: \left[\begin{array}{c} p \le q \le r \\ \lfloor p, q, r \rfloor = \lfloor p_0, q_0, r_0 \rfloor \end{array} \right]$$
$$\sqsubseteq \ p, q := p \sqcap q, p \sqcup q;$$
$$q, r := q \sqcap r, q \sqcup r;$$
$$p, q := p \sqcap q, p \sqcup q \ ,$$

which is effectively Insertion Sort specialised to three elements. (Note the $\lfloor p, q, r \rfloor = \lfloor p_0, q_0, r_0 \rfloor$ corresponding to our more general $A = $ **bag** *as* of Chapter 10.)

Because the first and third commands are the same, we introduce a procedure (in the spirit of this chapter) and continue the development:

$\sqsubseteq$ **procedure** *Sort* $\widehat{=} \ p, q := p \sqcap q, p \sqcup q$. (i)

Sort;
$q, r := q \sqcap r, q \sqcup r$;
Sort .

As for **var** declarations, we can write the declaration as a decoration, and add the block brackets, later, when we collect the code.

Having defined the procedure, we can leave until later the development of its body. When finally that moment comes, and assuming for now that $\sqcup$ and $\sqcap$ are not code, we might conclude with

(i) $\sqsubseteq$ **if** $p \ge q$ **then** $p, q := q, p$ **fi** .

$\lVert$ **procedure** *Sort*
    $\mathrel{\widehat{=}}$ **if** $p \geq q$ **then** $p, q := q, p$ **fi**$\cdot$

Sort;
$q, r := q \sqcap r, q \sqcup r$;
Sort
$\rVert$

Figure 11.1 Procedure call

if $p \geq q$ **then** $p, q := q, p$ **fi**;
$q, r := q \sqcap r, q \sqcup r$;
if $p \geq q$ **then** $p, q := q, p$ **fi**

Figure 11.2 Procedure removed from Figure 11.1.

The code resulting from those refinements overall is shown in Figure 11.1, where the middle assignment $q, r := \cdots$ stands tantalisingly untouched. We shall return to it.

All the above can be undone if we replace every occurrence of a procedure name by its text.[1] Applied to Figure 11.1, the result is Figure 11.2, where it is clear how the refinement of a procedure body (in one place) has in effect refined its (two) calls.

11.1.3   Variable capture

When declaring a procedure, or removing it, it is essential that the movement of its text — between point of call and point of declaration — does not move variables into or out of the blocks in which they are declared. The following will not do, for example:

$\lVert$ **var** $p \cdot p := p + 1$ $\rVert$
$\sqsubseteq?$ **procedure** *Inc* $\mathrel{\widehat{=}}$ $p := p + 1\cdot$
    $\lVert$ **var** $p \cdot Inc$ $\rVert$.

---

[1]That technique, known as the *Copy Rule*, comes from the definition of the programming language *ALGOL-60*.

Moving $p := p + 1$ out of the block $\lVert$ **var** $p \cdots$ in which p is declared (out of 'scope') results in code that increments a different p altogether: the reference to p originally is within the local block, but in the 'refined' program, the reference to p is outside the local block. We see later that parametrization can avoid that kind of difficulty.

11.2   Substitution by value

Now we return to the problem of the second command in Figure 11.1, which looks so much like the other two. What we need is a way of altering *Sort* systematically, so that it affects q and r rather than p and q. Such alterations can be made by *substitution*, and we will examine three kinds: by value, by result, and by value-result.

Underlying all three substitutions is the notion of *simple* substitution of one variable for another. Section 11.8 explains why, simple though it is, it cannot be used directly in programming.

Our first kind of substitution, by value, is used in situations where the code we have involves some variable f, say, but we would like to replace the f by an expression A. For example, we may have a command

$$r := \sqrt{f} \tag{11.1}$$

that assigns to r the square root of f — but really we would like the square root of 2 instead. Substituting 2 by *value* for f in (11.1) will get us what we are after, because (as we shall soon see)

$$(r := \sqrt{f})[\mathbf{value}\ f : \mathbb{R}\backslash 2] \quad = \quad r := \sqrt{2}\ .$$

(Our choice of $\mathbb{R}$ for the type of the parameter is fairly arbitrary here: it has 2 as an element, and the operation $\sqrt{}$ is defined for it.)

In general, we speak of replacing the *formal* parameter f (a variable) by the *actual* parameter A — and *provided A itself contains no f*, we can define *prog*[**value** $f : T\backslash A$] to be

$$\lVert\ \ \mathbf{var}\ f : T\cdot$$
$$\qquad f := A;$$
$$\qquad prog$$
$$\rVert\ .$$

The type T of f is used, just as any other type declaration would be, for subsequent refinement steps involving f within the procedure body.

If A does contain f (which is very common), then we must go to just a little more trouble, to avoid capturing the f in A with the **var** f declaration. We use a simple substitution to change the f in *prog* to some new local variable l, say. In that case, we would have

$$
\begin{aligned}
&\|[\quad \mathbf{var} \; l : T \boldsymbol{\cdot} \\
&\quad l := A; \\
&\quad prog[f \backslash l] \\
&\|] \; .
\end{aligned}
$$

The $[f \backslash l]$ is a simple substitution, replacing *all* occurrences of f by the fresh local variable l. ('All' means occurrences on the left of assignments as well as on the right, and 0-subscripted (initial) variables as well.)

If for example *prog* is $s := n^2$, but we need the square of $n + 1$ instead, we might use

$$
(s := n^2)[\mathbf{value} \; n : \mathbb{N} \backslash n + 1]
$$

which, by the above, is

$$
\begin{aligned}
&\|[\quad \mathbf{var} \; l : \mathbb{N} \boldsymbol{\cdot} \\
&\quad l := n + 1; \\
&\quad s := l^2 \\
&\|] \; ,
\end{aligned}
$$

and that, in turn, equals $s := (n + 1)^2$.

Note that both 'obvious' alternatives to using the fresh variable would be wrong; the first,

$$
\begin{aligned}
&\|[\quad \mathbf{var} \; n : \mathbb{N} \boldsymbol{\cdot} \\
&\quad n := n + 1; \\
&\quad s := n^2 \\
&\|] \; ,
\end{aligned}
$$

improperly captures n so that the resulting code finds the square of one more than an uninitialised local variable. The other alternative, just

$$
\begin{aligned}
&n := n + 1; \\
&s := n^2 \; ,
\end{aligned}
$$

indeed finds the square of $n + 1$, but changes n in the process — something that the desired $s := (n + 1)^2$ does not do.

11.3 Procedures with parameters

Our principal use of substitution will be when calling procedures whose bodies are not quite what we want. Suppose we have two procedures, for example, one for finding square roots, and one for finding squares:

$$
\begin{aligned}
&\mathbf{procedure} \quad Sqrt \quad \hat{=} \quad r := \sqrt{f} \\
&\mathbf{procedure} \quad Sqr \quad \hat{=} \quad s := n^2 \; .
\end{aligned}
$$

Then, as we have seen, $Sqrt[\textbf{value}\ f : \mathbb{R}\backslash 2]$ assigns to r the square root of 2, and $Sqr[\textbf{value}\ n : \mathbb{N}\backslash n + 1]$ assigns to s the square of $n + 1$. Since we are likely to use those procedures more than once (why else declare them?), and we do not want to write $[\textbf{value}\ f : \mathbb{R}\backslash \cdots$ or $[\textbf{value}\ s : \mathbb{N}\backslash \cdots$ each time, we use the following syntax instead. The 'substituted for' part of the substitution is written with the procedure body, as in

$$\textbf{procedure}\ Sqrt\ (\textbf{value}\ f : \mathbb{R}) \;\widehat{=}\; r := \sqrt{f}$$
$$\vdots$$
$$Sqrt\ (2)\ ,$$

and

$$\textbf{procedure}\ Sqr\ (\textbf{value}\ n : \mathbb{N}) \;\widehat{=}\; s := n^2$$
$$\vdots$$
$$Sqr\ (n + 1)\ .$$

(It is no coincidence that these now look like conventional procedure calls.)

To find out now what exactly is meant above by $Sqr\ (n + 1)$, for example, we could reason

$$Sqr\ (n + 1)$$
$= \text{``parameter declaration with procedure''}$
$$Sqr[\textbf{value}\ n : \mathbb{N}\backslash n + 1]$$
$= \text{``body of } Sqr\text{''}$
$$(s := n^2)[\textbf{value}\ n : \mathbb{N}\backslash n + 1]$$
$= \text{``definition of value substitution''}$
$$\begin{aligned} &\lvert[\quad \textbf{var}\ l : \mathbb{N}\text{\textbullet} \\ &\qquad l := n + 1; \\ &\qquad s := l^2 \\ &\rvert\rvert \end{aligned}$$
$= s := (n + 1)^2\ .$

That is the reasoning which forms the bedrock of our treatment of procedures and parameters — but in practice we need not always involve ourselves in quite so much tortuous detail.

11.4   Setting out refinements to procedure calls

Our examples so far have shown the effect of a substitution on a given procedure body. In practice, we will need to go in precisely the opposite direction, setting out our refinements in this fashion:

$$s := (n + 1)^2 \tag{i}$$

$$\sqsubseteq \; [\![\; \textbf{var } l : \mathbb{N}\cdot$$
$$l := n + 1;$$
$$s := l^2$$
$$]\!]$$
$$\sqsubseteq \; \text{``assuming declaration } Sqr \, (\textbf{value } n : \mathbb{N}) \; \widehat{=} \; s := n^{2}\text{''}$$
$$Sqr \, (n + 1) \; . \tag{ii}$$

Command (i) is where we start; and given a procedure declaration as shown, we finish with $Sqr \, (n{+}1)$. The intermediate step is precisely the form of a substitution by value of $n + 1$ for n, and it is that whole block that is refined to $Sqr \, (n + 1)$.

To help with setting refinements out that way, we can make the move from (i) to (ii) in a single step, thus avoiding having to deal with the intermediate local block explicitly. We have for example

Law 11.1 value assignment   Given a procedure declaration that refines

$$\textbf{procedure } Proc \, (\textbf{value } f : T) \; \widehat{=} \; w, f := E, ? \; ,$$

we have the following refinement:

$$w := E[f \backslash A] \quad \sqsubseteq \quad Proc \, (A) \; .$$

The actual parameter A may be an expression, and it should have type T. (If it does not, the refinement remains valid but subsequent type checking will fail.) As usual, variables w and f must be disjoint.
□

That the procedure body in Law 11.1 may alter f may seem odd for a value parameter; but such alterations have no effect outside the procedure, since f is not in the frame of the left-hand side of the law.

Independently of procedures, Law 11.1 could have been written

$$(w, f := E, ?)[\textbf{value } f \backslash T] \quad = \quad w := E[f \backslash A] \; ,$$

but as we shall usually be using parameters and procedures together, we give the combined form in the law.

In speaking above about 'a procedure body that refines', we mean one whose *body* is a refinement of $w, f := E, ?$. One such refinement is $w, f := E, ?$ itself; another is $w := E$ (forgoing the opportunity of changing f); yet another is $w, f := E, F$ for any expression F whatever.

Our squaring example above would now be set out (assuming the same procedure declaration)

$$s := (n + 1)^2$$
$$= \; s := (n^2)[n \backslash n + 1]$$
$$\sqsubseteq \; \text{``}value \; assignment \; 11.1\text{''}$$
$$Sqr \, (n + 1) \; .$$

$$\begin{array}{rcl}
\mathbf{skip} & \sqsubseteq & (p := q)[\mathbf{value}\ q \backslash p] \\
p := r & \sqsubseteq & (p := q)[\mathbf{value}\ q \backslash r] \\
p\colon [p = p_0] & \sqsubseteq & p\colon [p = q]\,[\mathbf{value}\ q \backslash p] \\
\mathbf{skip} & \sqsubseteq & (\mathbf{choose}\ p)[\mathbf{value}\ p \backslash p]
\end{array}$$

Figure 11.3 Value substitutions

Note that we have used the fact that $s, n := n^2, ? \ \sqsubseteq\ s := n^2$.

A similar package exists for specifications: it is given by

Law 11.2 <u>value specification</u> Given a procedure declaration that refines

$$\mathbf{procedure}\ Proc\ (\mathbf{value}\ f : T) \ \hat{=}\ w, f\colon [pre\ ,\ post]\ ,$$

with *post* containing no f (but possibly f_0), the following refinement is valid:

$$w\colon [pre[f \backslash A]\ ,\ post[f_0 \backslash A_0]] \ \sqsubseteq\ Proc\ (A)\ ,$$

where A_0 is $A[w \backslash w_0]$.
□

As in *value assignment* 11.1, the procedure body can alter f, and here is an example of where that is useful. Suppose we have a procedure declaration

$$\mathbf{procedure}\ Fact\ (\mathbf{value}\ n : \mathbb{N}) \ \hat{=}\ p, n\colon [0 \le n\ ,\ p = n_0!]\ ,$$

which we might have used to make the following refinement steps:

$$\begin{array}{ll}
& \{0 < q\}\ p := (q \ominus 1)! \\
= & p\colon [0 < q\ ,\ p = (q \ominus 1)!] \\
\sqsubseteq & p\colon [(0 \le n)[n \backslash (q \ominus 1)]\ ,\ (p = n_0!)[n_0 \backslash (q_0 \ominus 1)]] \\
\sqsubseteq & \text{``declaration of } Fact\text{''} \\
& Fact\ (q \ominus 1)\ .
\end{array}$$

Later, we could return to *Fact* itself and, since n is in the frame, develop the procedure body as follows:

$$\begin{array}{ll}
& p, n\colon [0 \le n\ ,\ p = n_0!] \\
\sqsubseteq & p := 1; \\
& \mathbf{do}\ n \ne 0 \to p, n := p \times n, n \ominus 1\ \mathbf{od}\ .
\end{array}$$

In Figure 11.3 are some other examples of value substitutions.

11.4.1   Substitution by result

Useful though it is, our substitution by value cannot by itself take us from Procedure *Sort* to the remaining assignment $q, r := q \sqcap r, q \sqcup r$. The procedure assigns to p and q, but we want an assignment to q and r — and value substitution cannot change that.

Substitution by result is complementary to substitution by value: it takes a value 'out of' a procedure rather than 'into' it. Thus, for example, if we want to adapt our assignment $r := \sqrt{f}$ to assign to s rather than to r, we could use $(r := \sqrt{f})[\mathbf{result}\ r : \mathbb{R}\backslash s]$. That follows from the general form of substitution by result, given by defining $prog[\mathbf{result} f : T\backslash a]$ to be

$$
\begin{aligned}
&\|[\quad \mathbf{var}\ l : T\cdot \\
&\quad\quad prog[f\backslash l]; \\
&\quad\quad a := l \\
&\|] \ .
\end{aligned}
$$

The actual parameter this time must be a simple variable, since it is assigned to. (That is why we write a, rather than A as before.) For $r := \sqrt{f}$, the local block would be

$$
\begin{aligned}
&\|[\quad \mathbf{var}\ l : \mathbb{R}\cdot \\
&\quad\quad l := \sqrt{f}; \\
&\quad\quad s := l \\
&\|] \ ,
\end{aligned}
$$

which equals $s := \sqrt{f}$, just as we hoped.

As with substitution by value, however, we can avoid setting out the intermediate local blocks (if we want to). The law for assignments is

Law 11.3 result assignment   Given a procedure declaration that refines

$$\mathbf{procedure}\ Proc\ (\mathbf{result}\ f : T)\ \mathrel{\widehat{=}}\ w, f := E, F \ ,$$

with f not occurring in E or in F, we have the following refinement:

$$w, a := E, F \quad \sqsubseteq \quad Proc\ (a) \ .$$

Variables a and f need not be different from each other, but w must be disjoint from both.
□

The reason that f cannot appear in the expressions E, F is that they would then depend on the initial value of f; and glancing at the local-block form of substitution by result shows that the procedure body can have no access to those initial values.

For procedures whose bodies are specifications, we have this law:

$$
\begin{aligned}
\textbf{skip} &\sqsubseteq (p := q)[\textbf{result } p\backslash q] \\
r, q := q, r &\sqsubseteq (p, q := q, r)[\textbf{result } p\backslash r] \\
q\colon [q \neq 0] &\sqsubseteq p\colon [p \neq 0]\,[\textbf{result } p\backslash q] \\
q\colon [q = q_0] &\sqsubseteq p\colon [p = q_0]\,[\textbf{result } p\backslash q]
\end{aligned}
$$

Figure 11.4 Result substitutions

Law 11.4 <u>result specification</u> Given a procedure declaration that refines

> **procedure** *Proc* (**result** $f : T$) $\;\hat{=}\; w, f\colon [pre \;,\; post[a\backslash f]]$,

with f not occurring in *pre*, and neither f nor f_0 occurring in *post*, we have the following refinement:

> $w, a\colon [pre \;,\; post] \quad\sqsubseteq\quad Proc\ (a)$.

Again, variables a and f need not be different from each other, but w must be disjoint from both.
□

With Law 11.3, the square root example would be done in just one step:

> $s := \sqrt{f}$
> $\sqsubseteq$ *"result assignment* 11.3*"*
> $Sqrt\ (s)$.

Figure 11.4 gives further examples of result substitutions.

Note that in all substitutions, if the formal parameter f is actually a list then it cannot contain repeated variables. That is because the same restriction applies to the simple substitution $[f\backslash a]$ from which the others are constructed: $[x, x\backslash 0, 1]$, for example, is meaningless. Since in result substitution the assignment $a := f$ appears as well, also the actual parameters must be distinct from each other; but that restriction does not apply to value substitution.

11.5 Multiple substitutions

An obvious possibility with the square root procedure is now to parametrize both its 'input' and its 'output' — then it would be much more useful, and we could for example realise $s := \sqrt{2}$. We do that by putting our two kinds of substitution together: in this case, the effect of $[\textbf{value } f : \mathbb{R}; \;\; \textbf{result } r : \mathbb{R}\backslash 2, s]$ on $r := \sqrt{f}$ would be

$$\begin{aligned}
&|[\ \ \textbf{var } l, m : \mathbb{R}. \\
&\quad l := 2; \\
&\quad m := \sqrt{l}; \\
&\quad s := m \\
&]| \ ,
\end{aligned}$$

where the simple substitution used was $[f, r \backslash l, m]$. That means our general square-root-finding procedure might be declared

$$\textbf{procedure } Sqrt \ (\textbf{value } f : \mathbb{R}; \ \ \textbf{result } r : \mathbb{R}) \ \ \widehat{=} \ \ r := \sqrt{f} \ ,$$

and we would write just $Sqrt \ (2, s)$ to invoke it as above.

Although there are laws (of course!) for dealing directly with multiple substitutions, they tend to be more trouble than they are worth: they simply pile up the various simple substitutions in the separate laws. For multiple substitutions, therefore, we will stick with the local-block form of development.

11.6   Substitution by value-result

We still have our original $q, r := q \sqcap r, q \sqcup r$ to deal with, and at this stage it is tempting to suggest declaring

$$\textbf{procedure } Sort \ (\textbf{value } p, q : T; \textbf{result } p, q : T) \ ,$$

so that $Sort \ (q, r, q, r)$ would mean

$$\begin{aligned}
&|[\ \ \textbf{var } l, m : T. \\
&\quad l, m := p, q; \\
&\quad p, q := p \sqcap q, p \sqcup q; \\
&\quad p, q := l, m \\
&]| \ .
\end{aligned}$$

In doing so, we would be brushing aside the feeling that somehow we should be declaring four local variables, one for each formal parameter, rather than just two.

In fact for situations like the above, we use our third kind of substitution, value-result. The local block above would then result from declaring

$$\textbf{procedure } Sort \ (\textbf{value result } p, q : T) \ ,$$

and using $Sort \ (q, r)$. In general, $prog[\textbf{value result } f : T \backslash a]$ means

$$\begin{aligned}
&|[\ \ \textbf{var } l : T. \\
&\quad l := a; \\
&\quad prog[f \backslash l]; \\
&\quad a := l \\
&]| \ .
\end{aligned}$$

$$p := r \quad \sqsubseteq \quad (p := q)[\textbf{value result } q \backslash r]$$
$$r := q \quad \sqsubseteq \quad (p := q)[\textbf{value result } p \backslash r]$$
$$q := p \quad \sqsubseteq \quad (p := q)[\textbf{value result } p, q \backslash q, p]$$
$$p \colon [r \geq 0 \, , \, p = r_0] \quad \sqsubseteq \quad p \colon [q \geq 0 \, , \, p = q_0] \, [\textbf{value result } q \backslash r]$$
$$r \colon [q \geq 0 \, , \, r = q_0] \quad \sqsubseteq \quad p \colon [q \geq 0 \, , \, p = q_0] \, [\textbf{value result } p \backslash r]$$
$$r \colon [s \geq 0 \, , \, r = s_0] \quad \sqsubseteq \quad p \colon [q \geq 0 \, , \, p = q_0] \, [\textbf{value result } p, q \backslash r, s]$$

Figure 11.5 Value-result substitutions

It is indeed a combination of value and result.

As usual, there are laws for the special cases in which the procedure body is an assignment or a specification and, as earlier, we assume that the variables w are distinct from f and a. Here is a law for assignments:

Law 11.5 value-result assignment Given a procedure declaration that refines

$$\textbf{procedure } \textit{Proc} \, (\textbf{value result } f : T) \; \mathrel{\widehat{=}} \; w, f := E, F \; ,$$

we have the following refinement:

$$w, a := E[f \backslash a], F[f \backslash a] \quad \sqsubseteq \quad \textit{Proc} \, (a) \; .$$

$\square$

And for specification-bodied procedures we have

Law 11.6 value-result specification Given a procedure declaration that refines

$$\textbf{procedure } \textit{Proc} \, (\textbf{value result } f : T) \; \mathrel{\widehat{=}} \; w, f \colon [\textit{pre} \, , \, \textit{post}[a \backslash f]] \; ,$$

with *post* not containing f, we have the following refinement:

$$w, a \colon [\textit{pre}[f \backslash a] \, , \, \textit{post}[f_0 \backslash a_0]] \quad \sqsubseteq \quad \textit{Proc} \, (a) \; .$$

$\square$

Figure 11.5 gives examples of value-result substitutions.

11.7 Syntactic issues

We follow common practice and use parentheses $(\cdots)$ for procedure parametrization, reserving brackets $[\cdots]$ for substitution. Formal parameters (that is, in the declaration, or on the left of the '$\backslash$') will be separated by ';' except that we allow for example $(\cdots \textbf{value } x; \; \textbf{value } y \cdots)$ to be written $(\cdots \textbf{value } x, y \cdots)$, and so

$[$ **procedure** *Sort* (**value result** $x, y : T$)
$\quad \widehat{=}$ **if** $p \geq q$ **then** $p, q := q, p$ **fi**·

$\quad$ *Sort* (p, q);
$\quad$ *Sort* (q, r);
$\quad$ *Sort* (p, q)
$]|$

Figure 11.6 Parametrized procedure calls

on. Actual parameters (at the point of call, or on the right of the '$\backslash$') are as before separated by ','. The correspondence between actual and formal parameter is therefore by position.

The formal parameters, with their types, act as local variables for the procedure body. Those types should be chosen so that an assignment taking actual to formal parameters (for value and value-result), or taking formal to actual parameters (for result and value-result), would be well-typed.

Returning finally to our original example, we have Figure 11.6, in which we have changed the name of the formal parameters. (Such name changes make no difference as long as variable capture does not result.) Note that all three calls must be parametrized.

11.8 Substitution by reference

The most common substitution techniques provided in programming languages are call by value and call by *reference*.

For variables, substitution by reference is identical to simple substitution, and it is dangerous.

Consider the following:

$\quad z := 0$
$\sqsubseteq\ z := 1;\ z := 0$
$\sqsubseteq\ (y := 1;\ x := 0)[\textbf{reference}\ x, y \backslash z, z]$
$\sqsubseteq\ \textbf{procedure}\ \textit{Wrong}\ (\textbf{reference}\ x, y)\ \widehat{=}\ y := 1;\ x := 0$·
$\quad \textit{Wrong}\ (z, z)$.

(We have omitted types.)

Now if we refine the body of *Wrong* as follows, the resulting program is equivalent to $z := 1$ (see Exercise 11.5):

$\quad \textit{Wrong}\quad \sqsubseteq\quad x := 0;\ y := 1$.

Our difficulty is due to *aliasing*: the substitutions in each case have identified two variables that were distinct. This can occur explicitly — as in [**reference** $x, y \backslash z, z$] above — or implicitly as in the substitution $(a := f!)[\textbf{reference } f \backslash a]$.

Aliasing is permitted with any of the substitutions of Section 11.2 however, and that is why we use them: there is no need to check. The problem is that substitution by reference is often more efficient, and certainly is more common.[2] Fortunately, we have the following:

> When aliasing is *absent*, substitution by reference is identical to substitution by value-result.

Thus our techniques are available in most practical cases.

11.9 Exercises

Ex. 11.1 ♡   Simplify the following:

1. $(a := f + 1)[\textbf{value } f \backslash a]$
2. $(f := a + 1)[\textbf{result } f \backslash a]$
3. $(f := a + 1)[\textbf{value result } f \backslash a]$
4. $(f := f + 1)[\textbf{value result } f \backslash a]$

Ex. 11.2 ♡   Supply the missing substitution(s):

1. $n := (n + 1)! \sqsubseteq (f := a!)[\textbf{value } ?; \textbf{result } ? \backslash ?, ?]$
2. $a :> a \sqsubseteq (a :> b)[\textbf{value } ? \backslash ?]$
3. $\quad x: [x \neq 0 , \ x = 1/x_0]$
   $\quad \sqsubseteq \quad q: [p \neq 0 , \ p \times q = 1] [\textbf{value } ?; \textbf{result } ? \backslash ?, ?]$

Ex. 11.3 ♡   Assuming the procedure declaration

> **procedure** *Sqrts* (**value** $a : \mathbb{R}$; **result** $b : \mathbb{R}$) $\ \hat{=}\ b: [0 \le a , \ b^2 = a]$

is in scope, show that the following refinement is valid:

$$x: \left[0 \le x , \ x^2 = x_0\right] \quad \sqsubseteq \quad Sqrts \ (x, x) .$$

Ex. 11.4 ♡   We noted that 'procedureless' programs can be recovered by replacing procedure names with their bodies. Consider the following case:

$$\|[\textbf{ procedure } One \ \hat{=}\ a := 1 \cdot \|[\textbf{ var } a \cdot One \ ]| \ ]|$$
$$=? \ \|[\textbf{ var } a \cdot a := 1 \ ]|$$
$$\sqsubseteq \ \textbf{skip} .$$

---

[2]In *Pascal* and *Modula-2* it is call by *var*, for example, and it is the default in *FORTRAN*. In *C*, however, call by value is used; but the effect of call by reference is regained by using pointers.

Explain why the equality is dubious. Argue instead that the correct result is $a := 1$.
Hint: Rename the local variable.

Ex. 11.5   Verify that the program of Section 11.8 is equivalent to $z := 1$ by removing the procedure *Wrong* from it.

Ex. 11.6 ♡   Show that

$$p, q, r: \left[\begin{array}{c} p \leq q \leq r \\ \llbracket p, q, r \rrbracket = \llbracket p_0, q_0, r_0 \rrbracket \end{array} \right]$$
$$\sqsubseteq\ p, q := p \sqcap q, p \sqcup q;$$
$$q, r := q \sqcap r, q \sqcup r;$$
$$p, q := p \sqcap q, p \sqcup q\ .$$

   Hint: Recall Insertion Sort.

Ex. 11.7 ♡   What is the invariant needed for the refinement in Section 11.4 of *Fact* to the iteration

$$p := 1;$$
$$\textbf{do}\ n \neq 0 \rightarrow p, n := p \times n, n \ominus 1\ \textbf{od}\ ?$$

Chapter 12

Case study: Heap Sort

Our earlier sorting case study, Insertion Sort in Chapter 10, took time proportional to the square of the number of elements sorted. The code developed in this chapter, Heap Sort, does considerably better: if N elements are to be sorted, then the time taken is proportional to $N \log N$.

That alone is worth the extra trouble needed to develop Heap Sort; but it is also worth seeing how radically different code can be reached from the same initial specification.

12.1   Time complexity of code

The outer iteration of Insertion Sort is executed N times: thus its inner iteration, on average, is executed $k/2$ times for each k from 0 to $N - 1$. Overall, therefore, the code performs this many comparisons (one for each inner iteration):

$$\frac{1}{2}(0 + 1 + 2 + \cdots + N - 1) \quad = \quad N(N - 1)/4 .$$

Thus if the sequence is doubled in length, the time taken to sort it is roughly quadrupled.

In general, the number of operations required to execute code is expressed as some function of the size N of the data given to it. For two such functions f and g, we write $f \preceq g$ if there are two numbers $M : \mathbb{N}$ and $c : \mathbb{R}^+$ such that for all $N \geq M$,

$$f N \leq c \times g N .$$

Put informally, that reads 'up to a constant factor $(c\times)$, the function f is less than or equal to g for sufficiently large arguments $(\geq M)$'. We write $f \succeq g$ if $g \preceq f$, and $f \approx g$ if both $f \preceq g$ and $f \succeq g$, and finally $f \prec g$ if $f \preceq g$ but $f \not\approx g$. Thus in this case we have

$$N(N-1)/4 \approx N^2 \ ,$$

and we say that Insertion Sort has N^2, or *quadratic*, time complexity.

Heap Sort has complexity $N \log N$, and is therefore asymptotically more efficient than Insertion Sort, since

$$N \log N \prec N^2 \ .$$

Even better, it can be shown that $N \log N$ is the lowest complexity possible[1] for sorting sequences: in that sense, Heap Sort cannot be improved. Its complexity is *optimal.*

With that background, we now present our abstract program, exactly the same as for Insertion Sort:

> **var** $as : \mathbf{seq}_N \ \mathbb{Z}; \ \mathbf{con} \ A;$
> **and** $A = \mathbf{bag} \ as \cdot$
> $as \colon [\mathbf{up} \ as] \ .$

But our development is completely different.

12.2   Heaps

Heap Sort achieves its better-than-quadratic $N \log N$ complexity by sorting a *balanced tree*, rather than a sequence, of values. That is where the $\log N$ comes from in its complexity $N \log N$: a balanced binary tree of N nodes has depth $\lceil \log N \rceil$. (The N factor comes from the fact that it has N nodes.)

Surprisingly, it is possible to lay a balanced tree out entirely within our given sequence as. The arrangement is easily observed in a sequence numbered from 1: in that case, element $as[i]$ is the *parent* of element $as[j]$ exactly when $i = j \div 2$. And element $as[i]$ is an *ancestor* of element $as[j]$ exactly when $\left(\exists k \cdot i = j \div 2^k \right)$. *Child* and *descendant* are the complementary terms; note that an element is both an ancestor and a descendant of itself.

Our sequences begin at 0, and so we define a relation $\rightsquigarrow$ as follows: for $i, j : \mathbb{N}$,

$$i \rightsquigarrow j \ \mathrel{\hat=} \ \left(\exists k : \mathbb{N} \cdot i + 1 = (j+1) \div 2^k \right) \ .$$

The relation is illustrated in Figure 12.1.

We say that a sequence as is a *heap* whenever the balanced binary tree within it is *ordered* so that ancestors are no smaller than their descendants: for that we write $\mathsf{hp} \ as$, where

$$\mathsf{hp} \ as \ \mathrel{\hat=} \ (\forall \, i, j : 0 {\rightarrow} \# as \cdot i \rightsquigarrow j \Rightarrow as[i] \geq as[j]) \ .$$

That means incidentally that for any non-empty heap as, its first element is its largest: thus $\mathsf{hd} \ as \geq \mathsf{tl} \ as$.

---

[1]Better performance is possible, however, if several computers are used at once.

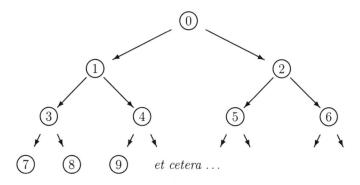

Figure 12.1 Parent–child relation in a heap

12.3 Shrinking a heap

Our strategy is to form the sequence into a heap, and then sort that; thus the first step is

$$\sqsubseteq \quad as\colon [\mathsf{hp}\ as]\ ; \qquad\qquad\qquad\qquad\qquad\qquad\qquad\text{(i)}$$
$$as\colon [\mathsf{hp}\ as\ ,\ \mathsf{up}\ as]\ . \qquad\qquad\qquad\qquad\qquad\text{(ii)}$$

Note that we have diverged immediately from the path taken earlier with Insertion Sort. Motivation for it is the suspicion that sorting a heap is faster than sorting a sequence; naturally we hope that our advantage is not eaten up by the cost of (i), the making of the heap in the first place.

Since (ii) has more detail, we work first on it. The operational idea is to pluck successive greatest elements from the root of the heap, at $as[0]$, reforming the heap each time. (There are N elements, and each reforming of the heap takes no more than $\log N$ comparisons.)

Using the form of (ii) as a guide, we bring its pre- and postcondition together by introducing **up** on the left and **hp** on the right:

(ii) $\sqsubseteq\ as\colon [\mathsf{hp}\ as{\uparrow}N \wedge \mathsf{up}\ as{\downarrow}N\ ,\ \mathsf{hp}\ as{\uparrow}0 \wedge \mathsf{up}\ as{\downarrow}0]\ .$

Rushing into an iteration here may be premature, however. The specification above suggests shrinking the heap towards 0, leaving sorted elements in a suffix behind it. That suffix should contain elements which need not be moved again: they should be in their final positions. We add that to the invariant, just to be sure,[2] and now proceed

---

[2]That sounds a bit imprecise: it means only that if we had not added it, we would have been stuck later on. It does *not* mean that if we had not added it we would have developed incorrect code.

$\sqsubseteq$ fn $i \;\hat{=}\; as{\uparrow}i \leq as{\downarrow}i \wedge$ up $as{\downarrow}i \cdot$

$\quad as\colon [\textsf{hp } as{\uparrow}N \wedge \textsf{fn } N \; , \; \textsf{hp } as{\uparrow}0 \wedge \textsf{fn } 0]$

$\sqsubseteq$ **var** $i : \mathbb{N} \cdot$

$\quad i := N;$

$\quad as, i\colon [i = N \; , \; \textsf{hp } as{\uparrow}i \wedge \textsf{fn } i \; , \; i = 0]$ $\vartriangleleft$

$\sqsubseteq$ "iterate down"

$\quad$ **do** $i \neq 0 \rightarrow$

$\qquad i := i \ominus 1;$

$\qquad as\colon [i < N \wedge \textsf{hp } as{\uparrow}(i+1) \wedge \textsf{fn}(i+1) \; , \; \textsf{hp } as{\uparrow}i \wedge \textsf{fn } i]$ $\vartriangleleft$

$\quad$ **od** .

In the precondition we have $\textsf{fn}(i+1)$, and in the postcondition we have $\textsf{fn } i$: therefore we need to place the maximum $as[0]$ of $as{\uparrow}(i+1)$ at index i. But $as[i]$ must go somewhere — perhaps to index 0. Unfortunately, that does not establish the remaining conjunct $\textsf{hp } as{\uparrow}i$: the new $as[0]$ is more likely to be the minimum than the maximum of $a{\uparrow}i$!

As for Insertion Sort, we need to say 'as is ... except at 0'. Just $\textsf{hp}(\textsf{tl } as)$ will not do, since the ancestor relation in $\textsf{tl } as$ is quite different. Thus we must define a *partial heap* as follows: for $s \subseteq 0{\rightarrow}N$,

$$\textsf{ph } s \;\hat{=}\; (\forall\, i, j : s \cdot i \rightsquigarrow j \Rightarrow as[i] \geq as[j]) \,.$$

Remember that $0{\rightarrow}N$ does not contain N (p.79), and note that $\textsf{ph } 0{\rightarrow}N \equiv \textsf{hp } as$. Now we can proceed by swapping elements i and 0:

$\quad \sqsubseteq$ *Swap* $(as, 0, i);$

$\qquad as\colon [\textsf{ph } 1{\rightarrow}i \; , \; \textsf{fn } i \; , \; \textsf{ph } 0{\rightarrow}i]$.   (iii)

Specification (iii) requires us to 'repair the heapiness' of $as[0{\rightarrow}i]$, without disturbing the elements at i and beyond.

(It is that last step that needed $\textsf{fn } i$ in the invariant rather than the weaker up $as{\downarrow}i$: having only up $as{\downarrow}(i+1)$ is not sufficient for a *Swap* $(as, 0, i)$ to establish up $as{\downarrow}i$ even when $as[0] \geq as{\uparrow}(i+1)$.)

12.4   Establishing the heap

Now we return to (i): in fact specification (iii) above suggests an approach, since it extends a heap towards lower indices. We are further encouraged by the fact that $\textsf{ph}(N \div 2){\rightarrow}N$ is identically true (since there are no ancestors to consider): any sequence is 'half a heap' already. So we proceed

(i) $\sqsubseteq$ **var** $j : \mathbb{N} \cdot$

$\quad j := N \div 2;$

$\quad as, j\colon [j = N \div 2 \; , \; \textsf{ph } j{\rightarrow}N \; , \; j = 0]$ $\vartriangleleft$

⊑ "iterate down"
  do $j \neq 0 \rightarrow$
    $j := j \ominus 1;$
    $as: [j < N \div 2 \wedge \mathsf{ph}(j+1) \rightarrow N \ , \ \mathsf{ph}\,j \rightarrow N]$ ⠀⠀⠀⠀⠀⠀⠀⠀⠀⠀⠀(iv)
  od .

Specification (iv) looks very much like (iii); and since fn N is identically true, we can bring the two closer still, as follows:

(iv) ⊑ $as: [\mathsf{ph}(j+1) \rightarrow N \ , \ \mathsf{fn}\,N \ , \ \mathsf{ph}\,j \rightarrow N]$. ⠀⠀⠀⠀⠀⠀⠀⠀⠀⠀⠀(v)

We are now ripe for a procedure.

12.5⠀⠀**Procedure** *Sift*

The similarity of Specifications (iii) and (v) suggests a procedure defined as follows:

⠀⠀**procedure** *Sift* (**value** $l, h : \mathbb{N}$) ≙
⠀⠀⠀⠀$as: [\mathsf{ph}(l+1) \rightarrow h \ , \ \mathsf{fn}\,h \ , \ \mathsf{ph}\,l \rightarrow h]$,

and that gives the following refinements immediately:

(iii) ⊑ *Sift* $(0, i)$
(v) ⊑ *Sift* (j, N) .

We have used value substitution for both parameters.

Now of course we still must develop *Sift* itself; but at least we need do that only once, and not twice as would have been necessary had we treated (iii) and (v) separately.

The invariant fn h of *Sift* suggests that we confine our attention to the prefix $0 \rightarrow h$ of *as*, just leaving the suffix from h on alone. The pre- and postcondition suggest that we need to say "*as* is a partial heap $l \rightarrow h$ at some k as well", and so we define

⠀⠀$\mathsf{lo}\,k \ ≙ \ (\forall i : l \rightarrow h \cdot i \rightsquigarrow k \Rightarrow as[i] \geq as[k])$
⠀⠀$\mathsf{hi}\,k \ ≙ \ (\forall j : l \rightarrow h \cdot k \rightsquigarrow j \Rightarrow as[k] \geq as[j])$,

so that lo k means that element k is correctly ordered with respect to elements below it, and hi k means the same for elements above it.

Then we continue as we did for Insertion Sort:

⠀⠀*Sift*
⊑ $\left\{ \begin{array}{l} \textbf{var } k : \mathbb{N} \\ J \ ≙ \ \mathsf{ph}(l \rightarrow h - \{k\}) \wedge \mathsf{lo}\,k \wedge \mathsf{fn}\,h\cdot \end{array} \right.$

$$k := l;$$
$$\textbf{do } \neg \textsf{hi } k \rightarrow$$
$$as, k: [\neg \textsf{hi } k \ , \ J \ , \ k_0 < k \leq h]$$
$$\textbf{od } .$$

$\lhd$

Now if $\neg \textsf{hi } k$ holds, we know two things:

1. $as[k]$ has a child in $l \rightarrow h$ (otherwise, $\textsf{hi } k$ would be vacuously true); hence $2k + 1 < h$.
2. $as[k]$ is less than one of its children; certainly it is less than the greater of its children.

Accordingly, we make our final refinement by swapping $as[k]$ with the greater of its children, say $as[m]$. Since that establishes $\textsf{ph}(l \rightarrow h - \{m\})$, we also assign m to k (thus increasing k, but not beyond h).

$$\sqsubseteq \quad \textbf{var } m : \mathbb{N} \cdot$$
$$\textbf{if } 2k + 2 = h \rightarrow m := 2k + 1$$
$$\quad [\!] \quad 2k + 2 < h \wedge as[2k + 1] \geq as[2k + 2] \rightarrow m := 2k + 1$$
$$\quad [\!] \quad 2k + 2 < h \wedge as[2k + 1] \leq as[2k + 2] \rightarrow m := 2k + 2$$
$$\textbf{fi};$$
$$Swap \ (as, k, m);$$
$$k := m \ .$$

That concludes the development of *Sift*, and thus of Heap Sort itself.

12.6   Exercises

Ex. 12.1   Prove that $\textsf{hp } as \Rightarrow \textsf{hd } as \geq \textsf{tl } as$, if as is not empty.

Ex. 12.2 ♡   Use the invariant J to code the guard $\neg \textsf{hi } k$. *Hint*: Recall Exercise 10.4.

Ex. 12.3   Make *Sift* more efficient, as we did for Insertion Sort.

Ex. 12.4 ♡   Show that if

$$\lim_{N \rightarrow \infty} (\textsf{f } N / \textsf{g } N) = 0,$$

then $\textsf{f} \prec \textsf{g}$.

Ex. 12.5   Show that $N \log N \prec N^2$.

Ex. 12.6   Show that $\log_a N \approx \log_b N$ for any logarithmic bases $a, b > 1$.

Ex. 12.7   Prove that *polynomial* complexity is always better than *exponential* complexity by showing that, for all $e \geq 0$ (no matter how large) and all $b > 1$ (no matter how small),

$$N^e \prec b^N .$$

Hint: Use l'Hôpital's Rule.

Ex. 12.8 ♡   The conventional notation for $f \preceq g$ is $f = O(g)$, and for $f \succeq g$ it is $f = \Omega(g)$. Finally, $f \approx g$ is written $f = \Theta(g)$. What makes those notations unusual? *Hint*: Consider the properties of equality.

How could the conventional notations be improved? *Hint*: Suppose $O(f)$ were a *set* of functions; how would $f \preceq g$ be written then?

Ex. 12.9   Give two functions f and g such that neither $f \preceq g$ nor $g \preceq f$.

Ex. 12.10 ♡   In spite of its optimal complexity, Heap Sort is not the fastest sorting code. (Quick Sort, for example, is considerably faster in most cases.) How can anything be faster than optimal?

Ex. 12.11   *Bubble Sort* Using the definitions of this chapter, complete the following development:

$$as: [up\ as]$$
$$\sqsubseteq \textbf{var}\ i : \mathbb{N}$$
$$i := N;$$
$$as, i: [i = N\ ,\ \text{fn}\ i\ ,\ i = 0]\ .$$

Hint: Imagine Heap Sort with no heap: in the inner iteration, you must nevertheless establish $as\uparrow i \leq as[i]$.

Chapter 13

Recursive procedures

Recursive procedures are those that 'call themselves', and the following factorial procedure is perhaps one of the best-known examples:

> **procedure** *Fact* (**value** $n : \mathbb{N}$)
> $\mathrel{\hat{=}}$ **if** $n = 0 \rightarrow f := 1$
> $[\!]$ $n > 0 \rightarrow$
>   *Fact* $(n \ominus 1)$;
> $f := f \times n$
> **fi** .

If we know that *Fact* $(n \ominus 1)$ assigns $(n \ominus 1)!$ to f, then we can deduce that *Fact* (n) assigns $n!$ to f; and to know that *Fact* $(n \ominus 1)$ assigns $(n \ominus 1)!$ to f we must know. . .

In this chapter we see how to develop recursive procedures directly from their specifications (without the '. . .' above). The principal feature, beyond what we know about procedures already, is the use of a variant expression to ensure that the recursion terminates properly. It is essentially the same technique we used in iterations.

13.1 Partial correctness

Here is how we might develop the factorial procedure above, using a straightforward case analysis into an alternation:

> **procedure** *Fact* (**value** $n : \mathbb{N}$) $\mathrel{\hat{=}} f := n!$
> $\sqsubseteq$ "the type $\mathbb{N}$ of n gives cases $n = 0$ and $n > 0$"
> **if** $n = 0 \rightarrow \{n = 0\}\, f := n!$ (i)
> $[\!]$ $n > 0 \rightarrow \{n > 0\}\, f := n!$ (ii)
> **fi**

(i) $\sqsubseteq$ "$0! = 1$"

    $f := 1$

(ii) $\sqsubseteq$ "*following assignment 3.5*"

    $f: [n > 0 \ , \ f \times n = n!]$;

    $f := f \times n$ $\lhd$

    $\sqsubseteq f: [n \ominus 1 \geq 0 \ , \ f = (n_0 \ominus 1)!]$

    $\sqsubseteq$? "*value specification 11.2*"

    $Fact \ (n \ominus 1)$.

Only the last step is dubious, using the specification of *Fact* within its own development — yet clearly we must do something of that kind for recursive procedures. Before seeing exactly what it is, however, we should find out why we cannot accept developments like the above just as they are. Consider therefore this alternative development of *Fact*:

      procedure *Fact* (**value** $n : \mathbb{N}$) $\ \widehat{=}\ f := n!$

  $\sqsubseteq$?! "recursive reference to *Fact*"

    $Fact \ (n)$.

That astonishingly short development gives the code

      procedure *Fact* (**value** $n : \mathbb{N}$) $\ \widehat{=}\ Fact \ (n)$,

and — what is worse — the same strategy would 'work' for any procedure at all.

The reason it does *not* work is that we have taken no account of termination; both versions of *Fact* have the effect of assigning $n!$ to f if they terminate, but only the first version terminates. The second recurses forever, so that any statement about its effect on termination is vacuously true.

Similarly ignoring termination for iterations would have allowed us to argue that

    $f := n!$ $\sqsubseteq$?   **do** true $\rightarrow$ **skip od** .

If that iteration terminated it would indeed assign $n!$ to f — but it never does terminate.

Such 'refinements', ignoring termination, establish what is known as *partial correctness*: that one program refines another 'except for termination'. Unhelpful as it sounds, such partial refinements (as we might call them) are useful ways of having a quick look ahead in a development to see whether it is worth proceeding that way[1] — for if one cannot reach even partial correctness, there is clearly no point in trying the approach at all.

Our normal refinement relation expresses *total* correctness, however, and takes termination into account. For that, we need variants.

---

[1] Partial correctness was the basis, in [Hoa69], of early arguments for rigour in program development. It has the advantage that its rules are simpler; but then one gets less from them.

13.2   Variants for recursion

The extra we pay for total correctness is that we must declare a named variant expression for the development of any recursive procedure. In the factorial example, it would look like this:

> **procedure** *Fact* (**value** $n : \mathbb{N}$) $\;\hat{=}\; f := n!$
> $\sqsubseteq$ **variant** N **is** $n \cdot$
>
> $\cdots$

In general, the effect of a variant declaration **variant** V **is** E, for name V and integer-valued expression E, is to require that any recursive reference to the procedure be formulated as if the procedure included $0 \leq E < V$ in its precondition. (References from *outside* the procedure itself, however, need not include the extra precondition.) In the factorial example, therefore, we would have had to refer to

$$\{0 \leq n < N\}\, f := n!$$
$$\text{or equivalently} \quad f : [0 \leq n < N \,,\, f = n!]$$

at the point of recursive reference to *Fact*, rather than just $f := n!$ on its own. In doing so we are stipulating (as with iterations) that the variant (n) must have decreased strictly ($\cdots < N$), but not below 0 ($0 \leq \cdots$), before the recursive call is made.

In order to be able to include such an assertion, we allow the introduction of $\{V = E\}$ at the point immediately after the declaration of the variant. (Alternatively, it is just included as a conjunct in the precondition, if that first step is a specification.) The effect on the factorial development would be

> $\sqsubseteq$ **variant** N **is** $n \cdot$
> $\{n = N\}$
> **if** $n = 0 \rightarrow \{n = 0\}\, f := n!$ ◁
> $[\!]$ $\;\; n > 0 \rightarrow \{n > 0\}\, f := n!$ (i)
> **fi** ,

and in fact there is no reason it cannot immediately be distributed through the guard of the second branch of the alternation in that same step; we would write (instead of the above) just

> $\sqsubseteq$ **variant** N **is** $n \cdot$
> **if** $n = 0 \rightarrow \{n = 0\}\, f := n!$ ◁
> $[\!]$ $\;\; n > 0 \rightarrow \{N = n > 0\}\, f := n!$ (i)
> **fi** .

(Since the first branch does not lead to a recursive call, we have no need of the variant there.) Then the development would continue as before, but this time carrying the variant along:

(i) $\sqsubseteq$ *"following assignment 3.5"*

$\quad f: [N = n > 0\ ,\ f \times n = n!]\ ;$ $\qquad\qquad\qquad\qquad\qquad\qquad\quad \triangleleft$

$\quad f := f \times n$

$\sqsubseteq f: [N > n \ominus 1 \geq 0\ ,\ f = (n \ominus 1)!]$

$\sqsubseteq$ *"value specification 11.2"*

$\quad f: [N > n \geq 0\ ,\ f = n!]\,[\textbf{value}\ n : \mathbb{N}\backslash n \ominus 1]$

$\sqsubseteq$ "note that $N > n \geq 0$ is correctly placed"

$\quad Fact\ (n \ominus 1)\ .$

The second, bogus, development of *Fact* is no longer possible:

$\qquad \textbf{procedure}\ Fact\ (\textbf{value}\ n : \mathbb{N})\ \,\hat{=}\ f := n!$

$\sqsubseteq \textbf{variant}\ N\ \textbf{is}\ n\cdot$

$\qquad \{n = N\}\ f := n!$

$\sqsubseteq$ "What now?"

The assignment cannot be replaced by *Fact* (n), as we did before, because the precondition is not $N > n \geq 0$ as it must be.

13.3 A complete example

Here, as a second example, we develop a recursive searching procedure. Consider a finite set es of type **finset** E, each of whose elements might satisfy a given property p. (The elements could be integers, for example, and the property 'is even'.) For $e : E$, the formula $\mathsf{p}\,e$ means "p holds for e".

We develop a recursive procedure which, assuming that some element of s satisfies p, assigns to e one such element; the abstract declaration is

$\qquad \textbf{procedure}\ Find\ (\textbf{value}\ es : \textbf{finset}\ E)$
$\quad \hat{=}\ e: [(\exists\,e : es \cdot \mathsf{p}\,e)\ ,\ e \in es \wedge \mathsf{p}\,e]\ .$

Our strategy is simply to choose an element e from es at random. If it satisfies p then we are finished; if it does not, we invoke *Find* recursively on es with the non-p-satisfying e removed. For conciseness, we define $\mathsf{P}\,es$ to be $(\exists\,e : s \cdot \mathsf{p}\,e)$, a convenient abbreviation for 'es contains an element satisfying p'. Here is our first step:

$\qquad \sqsubseteq \textbf{variant}\ V\ \textbf{is}\ \#es\cdot$

$\quad e: [es \neq \{\}\ ,\ e \in es]\ ;$

$\quad e: [V = \#es \wedge e \in es \wedge \mathsf{P}\,es\ ,\ e \in es \wedge \mathsf{p}\,e]\ .$ $\qquad\qquad\qquad \triangleleft$

We have moved both $V = \#es$ and $\mathsf{P}\,es$ through to the precondition of the second command, since neither contains variables in the frame of the first command. The precondition $es \neq \{\}$ of the first command itself follows from the original precondition $\mathsf{P}\,es$.

Now we have chosen an element e, and there are two cases: either e satisfies p or it doesn't. We treat them with an alternation:

$$\sqsubseteq \textbf{ if } \textsf{p}\, e \rightarrow e \colon [e \in es \land \textsf{p}\, e\, ,\, e \in es \land \textsf{p}\, e]$$
$$\textbf{[} \neg \textsf{p}\, e \rightarrow$$
$$e \colon [V = \#es \land e \in es \land \textsf{P}\, es \land \neg \textsf{p}\, e\, ,\, e \in s \land \textsf{p}\, e] \qquad \text{(i)}$$
$$\textbf{fi}$$
$$\sqsubseteq \textbf{ skip} \ .$$

The first branch has been easily disposed of.

Consider now the precondition of the second branch: if there is *some* element of es satisfying p, but it is not e, then that element must lie in $es - \{e\}$ and so $\textsf{P}(es - \{e\})$. We can also strengthen the postcondition, allowing us to make the recursive call:

$$\text{(i)} \sqsubseteq e \colon [V > \#(es - \{e\}) \land \textsf{P}(es - \{e\})\, ,\, e \in es - \{e_0\} \land \textsf{p}\, e]$$
$$\sqsubseteq \textit{Find } (s - \{e\}) \ .$$

We have not bothered with $0 \le \#es$, since set sizes are non-negative by definition.

13.4   Epilogue: recursion blocks

What we have seen above is all we need for developing recursive procedures, but there is a special case that deserves a closer look. Sometimes the recursive procedure is declared 'just to be able to recurse', rather than to make the procedure widely available. As matters stand, we have to do that in order to have a name with which to indicate the point of recursion.

We will allow ourselves to write parameterless recursions that are *not* procedures as follows:

$$\textbf{re } R \cdot \textit{prog } \textbf{er} \ ,$$

for some name R and program fragment *prog*. The effect is precisely as if R had been declared locally, as a procedure, called once, and then forgotten about:

$$\textbf{[[} \textbf{procedure } R \mathrel{\hat{=}} \textit{prog}\cdot$$
$$R$$
$$\textbf{]] } \cdot$$

If we were to develop a recursion block directly, rather than first developing a 'temporary' procedure as above, we would set it out as in this example:

$$f, n := n!, ?$$
$$\sqsubseteq f := 1;$$
$$f, n := f \times n!, ? \qquad \triangleleft$$

⊑ **re** F **variant** N **is** $n\cdot$
  if $n = 0 \rightarrow$ **skip**
  [] $n > 0 \rightarrow \{N = n > 0\}\, f, n := f \times n!, ?$ ◁
  fi
⊑ $f, n := f \times n, n \ominus 1;$
  $\{N > n \geq 0\}\, f, n := f \times n!, ?$ ◁
⊑ F .

Collecting the code, and collapsing the development, we can see that we have shown

$$f, n := n!, ?$$
⊑ $f := 1;$
  re $F\cdot$
    if $n = 0 \rightarrow$ **skip**
    [] $n > 0 \rightarrow f, n := f \times n, n \ominus 1;\ F$
    fi
  er ,

and it is interesting to note that, since we began developing the recursion block only *after* the first refinement step, the final code is not in its entirety a recursion: only the second half is.

In fact what we have seen above is an example of a more general phenomenon known as *tail recursion*, and summed up in this equality:

    do $G \rightarrow prog$ **od**
= **re** $D\cdot$
    if G **then** $prog;\ \ D$ **fi**
  er

Using the equality (and remembering that n is a natural number, so that we can rewrite the guards $n = 0$ and $n \neq 0$) converts the above factorial program to the more familiar

  $f := 1;$
  do $n \neq 0 \rightarrow f, n := f \times n, n \ominus 1$ **od** .

Tail recursion is more general than 'ordinary' iteration, however, as illustrated by this second equality:

  loop
    $prog1;$
    if G **then** **exit** **fi**;
    $prog2$
  end

$$= \mathbf{re}\ L\cdot$$
$$\quad prog1;$$
$$\quad \mathbf{if}\ \neg G\ \mathbf{then}\ prog2;\ L\ \mathbf{fi}$$
$$\mathbf{er}\ .$$

The **loop** $\cdots$ **exit** $\cdots$ **end** construction iterates its body 'until an **exit** is executed'. The above not only makes that precise, but shows how to develop programs of that form.

13.5   Exercises

Ex. 13.1 ♡   Would *Find* terminate if *es* were infinite? Where in its development do we use the fact that *es* is finite?

Ex. 13.2 ♡   For $f, n : \mathbb{N}$, show that

$$f\colon [f = n!] \quad \sqsubseteq \quad Fact'(n, 1)\ ,$$

where

$$\mathbf{procedure}\ Fact'\ (\mathbf{value}\ m, k : \mathbb{N})$$
$$\widehat{=}\ \mathbf{if}\ m = 0 \rightarrow f := k$$
$$[\!]\ \ m > 0 \rightarrow Fact'\ (m \ominus 1, m \times k)$$
$$\mathbf{fi}\ .$$

Hint: Consider $f := m! \times k$.

Ex. 13.3   *Linear search* Assuming declarations as : $\mathbf{seq}_N\ A$ and i : $\mathbb{N}$; a : A, show that

$$i\colon [a \in as \Rightarrow a = as[i]]$$
$$\sqsubseteq\ i := 0;$$
$$\mathbf{loop}$$
$$\quad \mathbf{if}\ i \geq N\ \mathbf{then}\ \mathbf{exit}\ \mathbf{fi};$$
$$\quad \{i < N\}\ \mathbf{if}\ a = as[i]\ \mathbf{then}\ \mathbf{exit}\ \mathbf{fi};$$
$$\quad i := i + 1$$
$$\mathbf{end}$$

by refining the left-hand side to the tail-recursive code

$i := 0;$
re L ·
    if $i \geq N \rightarrow$ **skip**
    [] $\quad i < N \rightarrow$
        $\{i < N\}$
        if $a = as[i] \rightarrow$ **skip**
        [] $\quad a \neq as[i] \rightarrow i := i + 1; L$
        fi
    fi
er .

Hint: Do not bother about the 'obvious' rewriting of the recursion block to introduce the **loop** and **exit**s as given above; concentrate on reaching the recursion-block itself. Its specification should be $i: [a \in as\!\downarrow\!i_0 \Rightarrow a = as[i]]$.

What is the point of the assumption $\{i < N\}$? Need it be there? *Hint*: See Exercise 9.17 concerning undefined expressions.

Ex. 13.4   Develop an iteration (rather than a recursion) from the specification

$$e, es: [\mathsf{P}\ es\ ,\ e \in es_0 \wedge \mathsf{p}e]\ ,$$

similar to *Find* in Section 13.3 except that *es* may now be changed. *Hint*: Introduce a logical constant S to capture the initial value of the set *es*, and use the invariant $e \in es \wedge es \subseteq S \wedge \mathsf{P}\ es$.

Ex. 13.5   Show that

$$w: [inv\ ,\ inv \wedge \neg G]$$
$\sqsubseteq$ **re** D·
    if G **then** $w: [G\ ,\ inv\ ,\ 0 \leq E < E_0];\ D$ **fi**
    er

by carrying on after this first step:

$$w: [inv\ ,\ inv \wedge \neg G]$$
$\sqsubseteq$ **re** D **variant** V **is** E·
$w: [V = E\ ,\ inv\ ,\ \neg G]$.

Chapter 14

Case study: The Gray code

.

In this chapter we use our new techniques for recursion in a slightly out-of-the-way case study, and in passing examine the issues of input and output.

14.1 The Gray code

The *Gray code* represents natural numbers as sequences of digits 0 or 1, but not in the usual way. If we let the function $\mathsf{gc} : \mathbb{N} \rightarrow \mathbf{seq}\{0, 1\}$ take a natural number to its Gray code, then we find it has these properties:

1. As for the usual binary code,

$$\begin{aligned} \mathsf{gc}\,0 &= \langle 0 \rangle \\ \mathsf{gc}\,1 &= \langle 1 \rangle, \end{aligned}$$

and for $n \geq 2$,

$$\mathsf{gc}\,n = \mathsf{gc}(n \div 2) \mathbin{+\!\!+} \langle d \rangle, \text{ for } d \text{ either 0 or 1.}$$

Alternatively, we could say $\mathsf{fr}\,\mathsf{gc}\,n = \mathsf{gc}(n \div 2)$.

2. But $\mathsf{gc}\,n$ and $\mathsf{gc}(n + 1)$ differ in exactly one position, for all n.

Property 1 applies to both Gray and binary codes, with the difference being only the choice of d. Property 2, on the other hand, applies to the Gray code alone. Figure 14.1 lists the first few Gray codes, comparing them with the corresponding binary codes.

The Gray code is used in applications where it is important that only one bit changes at a time in counting up or down. We shall develop a program to output Gray codes; but first, we examine input and output in general.

132

n	gc n	binary
0	0	0
1	1	1
2	1 1	1 0
3	1 0	1 1
4	1 1 0	1 0 0
5	1 1 1	1 0 1
6	1 0 1	1 1 0
7	1 0 0	1 1 1
8	1 1 0 0	1 0 0 0
9	1 1 0 1	1 0 0 1

Figure 14.1 The first Gray codes

14.2 Input and output

For programs using input and output we introduce two special-purpose variables named, by convention, α and ω. Their types will depend on the problem at hand, but usually α is a sequence of input values, and ω is a sequence of output values.

Input is performed by removing the first element of α, and that may be abbreviated as follows for any variable x:

$$\textbf{input } x \;\hat{=}\; \{\alpha \neq \langle\rangle\} \; x, \alpha := \mathsf{hd}\,\alpha, \mathsf{tl}\,\alpha \;.$$

Testing for end of file on input is just testing for emptiness of α:

$$\textbf{eof} \;\hat{=}\; \alpha = \langle\rangle \;.$$

Output is performed by appending an expression E to ω:

$$\textbf{output } E \;\hat{=}\; \omega := \omega + \langle E \rangle \;.$$

And output may be initialised by setting it to empty:

$$\textbf{rewrite} \;\hat{=}\; \omega := \langle\rangle \;.$$

Finally note that, since **input** x changes α (by removing an element), programs performing input should include α in the frame.

Our abstract program for this case study — a procedure — outputs the Gray code corresponding to a given integer n:

$$\textbf{procedure } \textit{Gray} \; (\textbf{value } n : \mathbb{N}) \;\hat{=}\; \omega := \omega + \mathsf{gc}\, n \;.$$

We are assuming in this case that ω is a sequence of binary digits (thus $\omega : \textbf{seq}\{0, 1\}$).

14.3   Isolate the base cases

Since the first two Gray codes are given explicitly, we treat them on their own, using an alternation. Our variant (for the recursion) is n itself:

$\sqsubseteq$ **variant** N is n.
 if $n < 2 \rightarrow$ **output** n
 $[\![\quad n \geq 2 \rightarrow \{2 \leq n = N\} \; \omega := \omega \mathbin{+\!\!+} \mathsf{gc}\, n$ $\lhd$
 fi .

To make further progress, however, we must return to Properties 1 and 2. From Property 2, the number of 1's in $\mathsf{gc}\, n$ must alternate between even and odd. Let the *parity* of a sequence *as*, written $\mathsf{pr}\, as$, be 0 if the number of 1's in *as* is even, 1 if it is odd. Thus $\mathsf{pr}\, \mathsf{gc}\, n$ alternates as n increases. Since from Property 1 we know $\mathsf{gc}\, 0 = 0$, we have by a simple induction that

$$\mathsf{pr}\, \mathsf{gc}\, n \quad = \quad n \bmod 2 . \tag{14.1}$$

The above suggests that to calculate $\mathsf{gc}\, n$, we could first calculate $\mathsf{gc}(n \div 2)$ and then use its parity to calculate the final bit d. That leads to

$\sqsubseteq \; \omega : [2 \leq n = N \; , \; \omega = \omega_0 \mathbin{+\!\!+} \mathsf{gc}\, n]$
$\sqsubseteq$ *"sequential composition 8.4"*; **con** $\Omega : \mathbf{seq}\{0, 1\}$.
 $\omega : [2 \leq n = N \; , \; \omega = \omega_0 \mathbin{+\!\!+} \mathsf{gc}(n \div 2)];$ (i)
 $\omega : [\omega = \Omega \mathbin{+\!\!+} \mathsf{gc}(n \div 2) \; , \; \omega = \Omega \mathbin{+\!\!+} \mathsf{gc}\, n]$ (ii)
(i) $\sqsubseteq \{0 \leq n \div 2 < N\} \; \omega := \omega \mathbin{+\!\!+} \mathsf{gc}(n \div 2)$
 $\sqsubseteq$ *Gray* $(n \div 2)$.

To refine (ii) we need a small calculation. For $a, b : \mathbb{N}$ let $a \oplus b$ be the sum $(a + b) \bmod 2$; then we have

 $\mathsf{gc}(n \div 2) \mathbin{+\!\!+} \langle d \rangle = \mathsf{gc}\, n$
$\Rightarrow$ $\mathsf{pr}(\mathsf{gc}(n \div 2) \mathbin{+\!\!+} \langle d \rangle) = \mathsf{pr}\, \mathsf{gc}\, n$
$\equiv$ *"from (14.1)"*
 $(n \div 2) \bmod 2 \oplus d = n \bmod 2$
$\Rightarrow$ $d = n \div 2 \oplus n$.

Hence, with that equality, we have finally

(ii) $\sqsubseteq$ **output** $(n \div 2) \oplus n$.

That concludes the development, which is summarised in Figure 14.2.

```
procedure Gray (value n : ℕ)
≙ if n < 2 → output n
  ∥ n ≥ 2 →
      Gray (n ÷ 2);
      output (n ÷ 2) ⊕ n
  fi .
```

Figure 14.2 Recursive Gray-code code

14.4   Exercises

Ex. 14.1 ♡   Continue Figure 14.1 up to $n = 15$.

Ex. 14.2 ♡   The base case in recursions is often 0, but for the Gray code it is 0 and 1 together. Why?

Ex. 14.3   Develop recursive code for the following, where br n is the (ordinary) binary representation of n:

> **var** n : ℕ; ω : **seq**$\{0, 1\}$·
> $\omega := \omega + $ br n .

Of course, br itself is not code!

Ex. 14.4   Let gcb : **seq**$\{0, 1\} \to$ **seq**$\{0, 1\}$ take the binary representation of n to the sequence gc n. For example,

> gcb$\langle 1, 0 \rangle$ $=$ $\langle 1, 1 \rangle$.

Develop *iterative* code for

> **var** n, g : **seq**$\{0, 1\}$·
> $\{n \neq \langle \rangle\}$ $g, n := $ gcb $n, ?$.

Ex. 14.5   Refine the following to iterative code:

> **var** n : ℕ; α : **seq**$\{0, 1\}$·
> α, n : $[\neg \textbf{eof}$, gc $n = \alpha_0]$.

Ex. 14.6 ♡   For sequence q, define its reverse rv q as follows:

> rv$\langle \rangle$ $\widehat{=}$ $\langle \rangle$
> rv$(\langle e \rangle + q)$ $\widehat{=}$ rv $q + \langle e \rangle$.

Refine this program to recursive code, using a recursion block:

> **var** α, ω : **seq** E·
> $\alpha, \omega := ?, $ rv α .

Hint: Rewrite output first.

Chapter 15

Recursive types

We have already seen a number of basic ways of making types for use in variable declarations. As well as the 'standard' types like the natural numbers $\mathbb{N}$ and the reals $\mathbb{R}$, we encountered the type-constructing functions **set**, **bag** and **seq** that make new types from existing ones, and we considered functional and relational types.

In this chapter we go further, showing how to invent such structuring tools for ourselves.

15.1 Disjoint union

The principal new ingredients of our type constructions will be disjoint union and recursion. Normal set union forms a new set from two given sets by including in the new set exactly those elements that are in either of the two given sets: thus for sets A, B and elements x, we have the equivalence $x \in A \cup B \equiv x \in A \lor x \in B$. One property that normal set union does *not* have in general, however, is equality between $\#(A \cup B)$ and $\#A + \#B$: that property holds only when A and B are disjoint. (Recall that the size of the (finite) type S is written $\#S$.)

Disjoint union resembles ordinary union in that it aggregates the elements of its two operands; but it makes them disjoint by giving each operand a distinct 'tag'. Thus, while the elements of the (ordinary) union $\{0, 1\} \cup \{1, 2\}$ are 0, 1 and 2, the elements of the disjoint union

left $\{0, 1\}$ | right $\{1, 2\}$

are left 0, left 1, right 1 and right 2. The names left and right are the *tags*, made up by the programmer (or mathematician) specifically to keep the two sides disjoint: elements left 1 and right 1 are not equal.

In fact left and right are *injection functions*, because they inject the component types ($\{0, 1\}$ and $\{1, 2\}$) into the disjoint union type (and because they are injective). If we let the disjoint union above be X then we have the following function types for the injections:

left : $\quad \{0,1\} \to X$
right : $\quad \{1,2\} \to X$.

Notice that X has four elements (not just three); and more generally, for any (finite) sets A and B we have

$$\#(\text{left } A \mid \text{right } B) \quad = \quad \#A + \#B \ .$$

If we write several types following a tag, rather than just one, then the injection functions take values of those types successively.[1] Thus for example

nats $\mathbb{N} \mathbb{N}$ | reals $\mathbb{R} \mathbb{R}$ $\hspace{6cm}$ (15.1)

is a type including the elements nats 2 3 and reals 1.5 π. (Writing nats $(\mathbb{N} \times \mathbb{N})$ | reals $(\mathbb{R} \times \mathbb{R})$ would have had a similar effect, but there the elements would have been nats$(2,3)$ and reals$(1.5, \pi)$ instead.)

It is also possible to have a tag just on its own, in which case just a single element, of that name, is contributed to the type. (Think of the injection function in that case as a constant, which is after all just a function of no arguments.)

Here are some examples of disjoint unions:

1. The type of days of the week is

    sunday | monday | tuesday | wednesday | thursday | friday | saturday .

    Typical elements are sunday and monday.
2. A value that is either an integer or is 'undefined' could be typed

    ok $\mathbb{Z}$ | undefined .

    Typical values are ok 3 and undefined.
3. A collection of currencies could be typed

    pounds $\mathbb{Z}$ | guilders $\mathbb{Z}$ | ecu $\mathbb{Z}$ | lira $\mathbb{Z}$.

    Typical values would be pounds 3 and lira(-1000000).
4. A database entry might either be empty or associate a key of type K with a datum of type D; its type would be

    empty | full K D .

    Typical values are empty and full k d, with k of type K and d of type D.

Note that the injections are written in the function font, just as other functions and predicates are.

---

[1]That is, the injection functions are *Curried*.

15.2   Testing for tags

Consider the type empty | full K D in the final example above. Given an element x of it, we may wish to know which alternative it inhabits ('what its tag is'). Although the formulae

$$x = \text{empty}$$
$$\text{and} \quad x = \text{full } k \ d \ ,$$

make sense for $k : K$ and $d : D$, they are not exactly what we want. The first formula indeed determines whether x is in the first alternative. But the second is too specific, depending on a particular k and d: instead we need the existential quantification $(\exists k : K; d : D \cdot x = \text{full } k \ d)$, asking whether $x = \text{full } k \ d$ for *some* k and d.

We therefore introduce the abbreviation

x is full,

for $(\exists k : K; d : D \cdot x = \text{full } k \ d)$, using a new two-place predicate is for the purpose: it tests for membership of an alternative.

15.3   Pattern-matching in alternations

Testing as in the previous section is not yet enough to make our disjoint unions useful: the truth of m is guilders tells us what kind of money we have, but not how much. Consider for example the type definition

first | second A | third B C ,

and suppose E is some expression of that type; then the program

```
if E is
    first      → prog1
 ▯  second a → prog2
 ▯  third b c → prog3
fi
```

executes *prog*1, *prog*2, or *prog*3 depending on the the tag of E. In addition, the variables a, b, and c are local in their respective branches of the alternation, and are initialised appropriately. Thus in general we access the components of elements of such types with a *tagged alternation*, as above.

Note that (sanserif) is (of the previous section) is a binary predicate, while (bold) **is** simply distinguishes the tagged alternation from the ordinary one. Although the effect of the tagged alternation can be partially achieved using the predicate is instead, the expression E in that case must be repeated, and in *prog*2′, for example, the variable a is not available as it is in *prog*2:

if E is first $\rightarrow prog1'$
[] E is second $\rightarrow prog2'$
[] E is third $\rightarrow prog3'$
fi

is less useful. That shows the advantage of the pattern matching.

If the expression E does not match any of the supplied patterns in a tagged alternation, then the alternation aborts (just as ordinary alternation aborts when no guard is true).

Although the use of tagged alternation should not need much formal justification in practice, it does — like the other constructs of our language — have an associated refinement law.

Law 15.1 <u>tagged alternation</u> Let first, middle and last be tags from a typical type declaration

> first $A \cdots H$ | middle $I \cdots P$ | last $Q \cdots Z$.

Provided none of $a \cdots h, q \cdots z$ appear free in E or *prog*, this refinement is valid:

> $\{E$ is first $\vee E$ is last$\}$ *prog*
> $\sqsubseteq$ **if** E **is**
>   first $a \cdots h \rightarrow \{E = $ first $a \cdots h\}$ *prog*
>   [] last $q \cdots z \rightarrow \{E = $ last $q \cdots z\}$ *prog*
>   **fi** .

□

We have of necessity given just an example of the types to which law *tagged alternation* 15.1 applies, but the principle should be clear: the assumption $\{E$ is first $\vee E$ is last$\}$ makes explicit the possible tags of E — which need not be all that the type allows. (We have left out middle, for example.) The guards of the alternation then correspond exactly to the disjuncts of the assumption.

Here are some alternations based on the example types mentioned earlier:

1.   **if** dd **is**
        wednesday $\rightarrow prog1$
        [] tuesday $\rightarrow prog2$
        fi
    executes $prog1$ if dd is wednesday holds, and $prog2$ if dd is tuesday holds; it aborts otherwise.

2.   **if** nn **is**
        undefined $\rightarrow$ **skip**
        [] ok n $\rightarrow nn := \mathsf{ok}(n+1)$
        fi
    'increments' nn if it is not undefined; if undefined it is left so.

3.   **if** mm **is**
        guilders $m \;\rightarrow\; mm := \mathsf{ecu}(.45 \times m)$
        [] pounds $m \;\rightarrow\; mm := \mathsf{ecu}(1.3 \times m)$
        [] lira $m \quad\;\;\rightarrow\; mm := \mathsf{ecu}(m/1885)$
        [] ecu $m \quad\;\rightarrow$ **skip**
        fi

converts m into European Currency Units. (The ecu branch does nothing;
but what would happen if it were not there?)

4. Suppose we represent a database db as a sequence of length N of entries,
   each either empty or containing a key/datum pair:

$$db : \mathsf{seq}_N(\mathsf{empty}\,|\,\mathsf{full}\;K\;D) \;.$$

Then for given $k : K$ the following program searches the database for the
associated datum d in D:

        $i := 0;$
        re $S\cdot$
            if $db[i]$ **is**
                empty $\rightarrow i := i + 1;\; S$
            [] full $k'\;d' \rightarrow$
                    if $k = k' \rightarrow d := d'$
                    [] $\;k \neq k' \rightarrow i := i + 1;\; S$
                    fi
            fi
        er .

Note how in the pattern-matching guards the local variables are k' and d',
allowing a distinction to be made between the values found in the sequence
and the original k and d. The program behaves unpredictably if the key does
not occur in the database.

    As an example of the use of *tagged alternation* 15.1, we will now look at the
development steps that led to the last of the four program fragments above. First
we define for convenience a predicate expressing the presence (or absence) of k in
db:

$$k \;\mathsf{in}\; db \;\widehat{=}\; (\exists\, d \cdot \mathsf{full}\; k\; d \in db) \;.$$

Then, starting with a specification that allows abortion (hence, unpredictable behaviour) if k does not occur, we proceed:

        $d\colon [\,k \;\mathsf{in}\; db\,,\; \mathsf{full}\; k\; d \in db\,]$
        $\sqsubseteq$ **var** $i : \mathbb{N}\cdot$
            $i := 0;$
            $d, i\colon [\,k \;\mathsf{in}\; db{\downarrow}i\,,\; \mathsf{full}\; k\; d \in db\,]$ ◁

$\sqsubseteq$ **re** S **variant** I **is** $i\cdot$

$\quad$ $d, i \colon [I = i \land k$ in $db{\downarrow}i$, full k $d \in db]$ $\quad\quad\quad\quad\quad\quad\quad\quad\quad$ ◁

$\sqsubseteq$ "k in $db{\downarrow}i \Rightarrow i < N \Rightarrow db[i]$ is empty $\lor$ $db[i]$ is full"

$\quad$ **if** $db[i]$ **is**

$$\text{empty} \to d, i \colon \begin{bmatrix} db[i] = \text{empty} \\ I = i < N \\ k \text{ in } db{\downarrow}i \end{bmatrix}, \text{ full } k \ d \in db \qquad \text{(i)}$$

$$[\!]\ \text{ full } k'\ d' \to d, i \colon \begin{bmatrix} db[i] = \text{full } k'\ d' \\ I = i < N \\ k \text{ in } db{\downarrow}i \end{bmatrix}, \text{ full } k \ d \in db \qquad \text{(ii)}$$

$\quad$ **fi**

(i) $\sqsubseteq$ $i := i + 1;$

$\quad\quad$ $d, i \colon [I < i \leq N \land k$ in $db{\downarrow}i$, full k $d \in db]$ $\quad\quad\quad\quad\quad$ ◁

$\quad$ $\sqsubseteq$ S

(ii) $\sqsubseteq$ **if** $k = k' \to d, i \colon \begin{bmatrix} i < N \\ db[i] = \text{full } k\ d' \end{bmatrix}$, full k $d \in db$ $\qquad$ (iii)

$$[\!]\ \ k \neq k' \to d, i \colon \begin{bmatrix} k \neq k' \\ db[i] = \text{full } k'\ d' \\ I = i < N \\ k \text{ in } db{\downarrow}i \end{bmatrix}, \text{ full } k \ d \in db \qquad \text{(iv)}$$

$\quad$ **fi**

(iii) $\sqsubseteq$ $d := d'$

(iv) $\sqsubseteq$ "as for (i)"

$\quad\quad$ $i := i + 1;$

$\quad\quad$ S .

The variant I is increasing, in this example: it starts at i and is bounded above by N. (Following the earlier presentation strictly, our variant would have been $N - i$, bounded below by 0.)

15.4   Type declarations

With the introduction of our new type-forming mechanisms it becomes more important that we allow types to be named and reused. The syntax is, by analogy with procedures,

$\quad\quad$ **type** *Name* $\ \hat{=}\ $ *type−expression* ,

thus allowing declarations like

$$\textbf{type } \textit{Money} \;\hat{=}\; \text{pounds } \mathbb{Z} \mid \text{guilders } \mathbb{Z} \mid \text{ecu } \mathbb{Z} \mid \text{lira } \mathbb{Z}$$

$$\textit{Days} \;\hat{=}\; \text{sunday} \mid \text{monday} \mid \text{tuesday}$$
$$\mid \text{wednesday} \mid \text{thursday} \mid \text{friday} \mid \text{saturday}$$

$$\textit{Entry} \;\hat{=}\; \text{empty} \mid \text{full } K \; D$$

$$\textit{DataBase} \;\hat{=}\; \textbf{seq}_N \; \textit{Entry} \;.$$

Unless the types refer to each other recursively (a case we treat shortly), the meanings of programs with such declarations can be recovered simply by replacing type names by the expressions they stand for. Thus the declaration

$$\textbf{var } \textit{db} : \textit{DataBase}$$

means

$$\textbf{var } \textit{db} : \textbf{seq}_N \; \textit{Entry}$$

which in turn means

$$\textbf{var } \textit{db} : \textbf{seq}_N(\text{empty} \mid \text{full } K \; D) \;.$$

We allow type parameters as well, writing for example

$$\textit{Maybe } T \;\hat{=}\; \text{ok } T \mid \text{undefined} \;,$$

and, again in the absence of recursion, the meaning is recovered by substitution:

$$\textbf{var } \textit{marks} : \textbf{seq}_N \; \textit{Maybe } \mathbb{N}$$
$$\text{means} \quad \textbf{var } \textit{marks} : \textbf{seq}_N(\text{ok } \mathbb{N} \mid \text{undefined}) \;.$$

15.5   Recursive types

We are now well-enough equipped to discuss type declarations that refer to themselves. Consider, as our first example, the recursive declaration

$$\textbf{type } \textit{Tree} \;\hat{=}\; \text{empty} \mid \text{node } \mathbb{N} \; \textit{Tree } \textit{Tree} \;. \tag{15.2}$$

Typical elements of the type are

```
empty
node 3 empty empty
node 7 (node 3 empty empty) empty .
```

One might depict them as in Figure 15.1, where their tree-like nature is evident.

In fact we define the elements of a recursive (or any other) type to be exactly those whose membership in the type can be demonstrated by (perhaps repeated, but only finitely often) reference to the type definition. In the case above, for example, we know that empty is a *Tree* from the left alternative of the declaration, and it does not matter what the right alternative says. Once we do know that empty

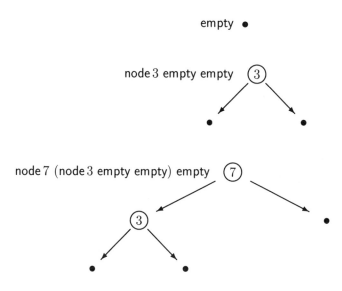

empty ●

node 3 empty empty

node 7 (node 3 empty empty) empty

Figure 15.1 Elements of type *Tree*

is a *Tree*, we can use the right alternative to deduce that node 3 empty empty is as well (and the same holds of course for other natural numbers, not only 3). Once we know *that*, we consider node 7 (node 3 empty empty) empty, and so on.

The above is just about the simplest view one could take to recursively defined types, and it does restrict us to finite structures, excluding for example the 'infinite' tree of Figure 15.2: node 0 empty (node 1 empty (node 2 (···))).   There is nothing inherently wrong with such infinite structures, although we do not treat them here; but there can be problems however with declarations such as

type *TooBig* ≙ one | several (**set** *TooBig*) .

Since no set (or type) can be big enough to contain representations of all subsets of itself, it is not at all certain that the type *TooBig* exists, in spite of the fact that we can enumerate elements as before:

one
several{}
several{one}
several{several{}}
several{one, several{}} .

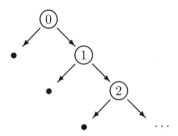

Figure 15.2 An 'infinite' tree

We avoid such problems by restricting our use of type functions within recursive definitions, avoiding **set** and **bag** in particular. (The function **seq** we allow, however.)

15.6   Structural order

Along with a definition such as (15.2) of *Tree* comes an ordering relation which we will write as $\lessdot$: it is the 'is-a-component-of' order, relating two elements whenever one occurs structurally within the other. For example,

$$
\begin{array}{ll}
& \mathsf{empty} \\
\lessdot & \mathsf{node}\,3\;\mathsf{empty}\;\mathsf{empty} \\
\lessdot & \mathsf{node}\,7\;(\mathsf{node}\,3\;\mathsf{empty}\;\mathsf{empty})\;\mathsf{empty}\ .
\end{array}
$$

The order $\lessdot$ has these properties in common with the (strict) order $<$ over the integers, for example:

- It is *irreflexive*: for all x we have $\neg(x \lessdot x)$;
- It is *antisymmetric*: for all x and y we have $x \lessdot y \wedge y \lessdot x \Rightarrow \mathsf{false}$;
- It is *transitive*: for all x, y and z we have $x \lessdot y \wedge y \lessdot z \Rightarrow x \lessdot z$.

The order $<$ has one property that $\lessdot$ does not share, however: it is a *total* order, which means that for all distinct x and y we have that either $x < y$ or $y < x$. Because the same is not true for $\lessdot$, we call it a (strict) *partial* order, and strict partial orders are characterised exactly by the three properties above.

To see that $\lessdot$ is partial, consider

$$\mathsf{node}\,0\;\mathsf{empty}\;\mathsf{empty}\quad\text{and}\quad\mathsf{node}\,1\;\mathsf{empty}\;\mathsf{empty}\ .$$

Neither occurs as a component of the other, and so they are unrelated by $\lessdot$.

When developing programs over recursive data structures — as we shall do shortly — often the variant function is not an integer expression. Instead it is some element of the recursive type itself, and rather than use $<$, as we would over integers, we use the structural order $\lessdot$ over the recursive type. For that to be sound, we use one additional property of $\lessdot$ as a structural order, that it is *well-founded*: for no starting point x is there an infinite descending chain

$$\cdots \lessdot x''' \lessdot x'' \lessdot x' \lessdot x \;.$$

Note that our total order $<$ is well-founded over the natural numbers, since no natural number is negative. Thus our usual technique, writing $0 \leq v < v_0$ for integer-valued v, is a special case of the more general approach we are examining at the moment: the $0 \leq v$ restricts attention to the natural numbers (rather than the integers as a whole including negatives), and $<$ is well-founded over the natural numbers.

15.7   Pattern matching in iterations

By analogy with tagged alternations, we can define tagged iterations: where a tagged alternation would abort in the case of no match, a tagged iteration simply terminates ('successfully'). Consider for example the type

$$NatList \;\hat{=}\; \mathsf{empty} \mid \mathsf{cons}\; \mathbb{N}\; NatList \;, \tag{15.3}$$

whose typical elements include

> empty
> cons 0 empty
> cons 1 (cons 0 empty) .

Given the declarations $n : \mathbb{N}$; $nl : NatList$, the following iteration assigns to n the sum of the elements originally in nl:

> $n := 0$;
> **do** nl **is** cons $n'\; nl' \rightarrow$
> $\qquad n, nl := n + n', nl'$
> **od** .

(Note that nl is modified in the process.) The iteration guard covers only one of the two possible tags for nl, and so termination occurs when nl has the tag of the other alternative: that is, termination occurs when nl **is** empty.

The law for the introduction of tagged iterations is

Law 15.2 <u>tagged iteration</u> Let first, middle and last be tags from a type declaration

$$Type \;\hat{=}\; \mathsf{first}\; A \cdots H \mid \mathsf{middle}\; I \cdots P \mid \mathsf{last}\; Q \cdots Y \;.$$

Provided none of $a \cdots h, q \cdots y$ appears free in z, inv, E, or V, this refinement is valid:

$$z\colon [inv \ , \ inv \wedge \neg(E \text{ is first} \vee E \text{ is last})]$$
$$\sqsubseteq \ \textbf{do} \ E \ \textbf{is}$$
$$\text{first } a \cdots h \rightarrow z\colon [E = \text{first } a \cdots h \ , \ inv \ , \ V \otimes V_0]$$
$$[\!] \quad \text{last } q \cdots y \rightarrow z\colon [E = \text{last } q \cdots y \ , \ inv \ , \ V \otimes V_0]$$
$$\textbf{od} \ .$$

The formula inv is the invariant, the expression V is the variant, and the relation $\otimes$ must be well-founded.
□

Note that, as in tagged alternation, the guards of the iteration correspond exactly to the disjunction (negated) in the postcondition, and that they need not exhaust the type. (Indeed, if they did then the iteration would never terminate!)

As an example, we define the function sumI : $NatList \rightarrow \mathbb{N}$, for summing a list, as

$$
\begin{aligned}
\text{sumI empty} \quad &\mathrel{\hat{=}} \quad 0 \\
\text{sumI(cons } n \ nl) \quad &\mathrel{\hat{=}} \quad n + \text{sumI } nl \ ,
\end{aligned}
\tag{15.4}
$$

and develop the program above as follows:

$$n, nl := \text{sumI } nl, ?$$
$$\sqsubseteq \ \textbf{con } N : \mathbb{N}\text{·}$$
$$n, nl\colon [N = \text{sumI } nl \ , \ n = N]$$
$$\sqsubseteq \ I \ \mathrel{\hat{=}} \ N = n + \text{sumI } nl\text{·}$$
$$n := 0;$$
$$n, nl\colon [I \ , \ I \wedge nl \text{ is empty}] \qquad\qquad\qquad\qquad \triangleleft$$
$$\sqsubseteq \ n, nl\colon [I \ , \ I \wedge \neg(nl \text{ is cons})]$$
$$\sqsubseteq \ \text{“tagged iteration 15.2”}$$
$$\textbf{do } nl \text{ is cons } n' \ nl' \rightarrow$$
$$n, nl\colon [nl = \text{cons } n' \ nl' \ , \ I \ , \ nl \otimes nl_0] \qquad\qquad \triangleleft$$
$$\textbf{od}$$
$$\sqsubseteq \ n, nl\colon \left[\begin{array}{c} nl' \otimes nl \\ N = n + n' + \text{sumI } nl' \end{array} \ , \ N = n + \text{sumI } nl \wedge nl \otimes nl_0 \right]$$
$$\sqsubseteq \ n, nl := n + n', nl' \ .$$

Since the type $NatList$ is structurally identical to $\textbf{seq} \ \mathbb{N}$, we could almost have 'defined' the latter

$$\textbf{seq} \ \mathbb{N} \ \mathrel{\hat{=}} \ \langle\rangle \mid \mathbb{N}\colon(\textbf{seq} \ \mathbb{N}) \ .$$

Continuing that analogy, if nl were declared of type $\textbf{seq} \ \mathbb{N}$ we could have written for the above program

$$n := 0;$$
$$\textbf{do } nl \text{ is } n'\colon\!nl' \rightarrow n, nl := n + n', nl' \ \textbf{od} \ ,$$

which is a very compact imperative notation for summing a sequence.

15.8 Example: Summing a tree

We return now to our definition (15.2) of trees of $\mathbb{N}$, and we develop code to sum the node values. As one would expect, the recursive code is straightforward (type *Tree* is recursive, after all); iterative code will require some ingenuity, however. In this section we investigate both approaches.

15.8.1 Recursive tree-summing

First, we define sumt ('sum for trees' as opposed to lists)

$$
\begin{aligned}
\text{sumt empty} \quad &= \quad 0 \\
\text{sumt(node } n \ nt1 \ nt2) \quad &= \quad n + \text{sumt } nt1 + \text{sumt } nt2 \ ,
\end{aligned}
\tag{15.5}
$$

and then begin the development using a procedure:

> **procedure** $SumT$ (**value** $nt : Tree$; **result** $n : \mathbb{N}$)
> $\;\widehat{=}\; n := \text{sumt } nt$
> $\sqsubseteq$ **variant** NT **is** $nt\cdot$
> $n{:}\ [nt = NT \ , \ n = \text{sumt } nt]$
> $\sqsubseteq$ **if** nt **is**
>   empty $\to n := 0$
> $[\!]$ node $n'\ nt1\ nt2 \to$
> $n{:}\ [NT = nt = \text{node } n'\ nt1\ nt2 \ , \ n = \text{sumt } nt]$ $\triangleleft$
>   **fi**
> $\sqsubseteq n{:}\ \left[\begin{matrix} nt1 \oslash NT \\ nt2 \oslash NT \end{matrix} \ , \ n = n' + \text{sumt } nt1 + \text{sumt } nt2 \right]$
> $\sqsubseteq$ **var** $n1, n2 : \mathbb{N}$
> $n1{:}\ [nt1 \oslash NT \ , \ n1 = \text{sumt } nt1]\,;$ (i)
> $n2{:}\ [nt2 \oslash NT \ , \ n2 = \text{sumt } nt2]\,;$ (ii)
> $n := n' + n1 + n2$
> (i) $\sqsubseteq SumT\ (nt1, n1)$
> (ii) $\sqsubseteq SumT\ (nt2, n2)$.

The result is shown in Figure 15.3.

15.8.2 Iterative tree-summing

Matters are not so straightforward for the iterative development. Comparing the two types of sum (15.4) and (15.5), the first for lists and the second for trees, we find one recursive occurrence in the first case but two in the second. (That is, sumt 'calls itself' *twice* on the right-hand side.) Such multiple occurrences are not so easily dealt with by iteration.

---

procedure *SumT* (**value** *nt* : *Tree*; **result** *n* : $\mathbb{N}$) $\;\widehat{=}$
$|[$ **var** *n1, n2* : $\mathbb{N}$.
   if *nt* **is**
      empty $\rightarrow$ *n* := 0
   $[\![$ node *n'* *nt1* *nt2* $\rightarrow$
         SumT (*nt1, n1*);
         SumT (*nt2, n2*);
         n := *n'* + *n1* + *n2*
   fi
$]|$

Figure 15.3 Recursive tree-summing

Thus we look at replacing (15.5) by something more like (15.4). On the right-hand side of (15.5) we find

sumt *nt1* + sumt *nt2* ,

and note that it can be rewritten

suml$\langle$sumt *nt1*, sumt *nt2*$\rangle$.

We are generalising, in other words, and if we carry on for more than two we would define[2]

$$
\begin{array}{lll}
\text{sumlt}\langle\rangle & \widehat{=} & 0 \\
\text{sumlt}(nt{:}ntl) & \widehat{=} & \text{sumt } nt + \text{sumlt } ntl \ .
\end{array}
\tag{15.6}
$$

We now have only one recursive occurrence of sumlt, and we can obtain our original sumt as a special case of it.

Our iterative development is thus

> $n := \text{sumt } nt$
> $\sqsubseteq$ **var** *ntl* : **seq** *Tree*.
> $ntl := \langle nt\rangle;$
> $n, ntl := \text{sumlt } ntl, ?$ $\triangleleft$
> $\sqsubseteq$ **con** $N : \mathbb{N}$.
> $n, ntl{:}\ [N = \text{sumlt } ntl\ ,\ n = N]$
> $\sqsubseteq I \;\widehat{=}\; N = n + \text{sumlt } ntl \cdot$
> $n := 0;$
> $n, ntl{:}\ [I\ ,\ I \wedge ntl = \langle\rangle]$ $\triangleleft$

---

[2]Functional programmers will recognise this as just suml $\circ$ map sumt.

```
|[  var ntl : seq Tree·
    ntl := ⟨nt⟩;
    do ntl is
        empty:ntl′ → ntl := ntl′
    []  (node n′nt1 nt2):ntl′ → n, ntl := n + n′, nt1:nt2:ntl′
    od
]|
```

Figure 15.4 Iterative tree-summing

⊑ "invariant I; variant V (later)"
   do ntl **is**
      empty:$ntl′$ → n, ntl: $[ntl = $empty:$ntl′$, I , $0 \leq V < V_0]$ (i)
   [] (node $n′$ $nt1$ $nt2$):$ntl′$ →
        n, ntl: $[ntl = ($node $n′$ $nt1$ $nt2$):$ntl′$, I , $0 \leq V < V_0]$ (ii)
   od

(i) ⊑ $ntl := ntl′$
(ii) ⊑ $n, ntl := n + n′, nt1$:$nt2$:$ntl′$.   (iii)

Those last two steps, perhaps rather large at first sight, are easily justified (still leaving aside the variant). For the second, we could have proceeded more slowly

(ii) ⊑ n, ntl: $[N = n + $sumlt$(($node $n′$ $nt1$ $nt2$):$ntl′)$,
        $N = n + $sumlt $ntl \wedge 0 \leq V < V_0]$
  ⊑ n, ntl: $[N = n + n′ + $sumt $nt1 + $sumt $nt2 + $sumlt $ntl′$,
        $N = n + $sumlt $ntl \wedge 0 \leq V < V_0]$
  ⊑ n, ntl: $[N = n + n′ + $sumlt$(nt1$:$nt2$:$ntl′)$,
        $N = n + $sumlt $ntl \wedge 0 \leq V < V_0]$
  ⊑ "ignoring the variant part"
    (iii) above.

The collected code for the iterative version is shown in Figure 15.4. The sequence *ntl* that occurs there is typical of imperative implementations of problems that are inherently recursive: examination of the code shows that *ntl* is accessed as a stack.

But that does leave the variant V. The 'obvious' choice of *ntl* itself (using the structural order for lists) does not work, since the second branch of the iteration actually *increases* the size of *ntl*, albeit with structurally smaller elements. What is decreased is in fact the *overall* size of *ntl*, taking its components into account:

$$\text{sizelt}\langle\rangle \quad \hat{=} \quad 0$$
$$\text{sizelt}(nt{:}ntl) \quad \hat{=} \quad \text{sizet } nt + \text{sizelt } ntl$$

$$\text{sizet empty} \quad \hat{=} \quad 1$$
$$\text{sizet}(\text{node } n \; nt1 \; nt2) \quad \hat{=} \quad 1 + \text{sizet } nt1 + \text{sizet } nt2 \;.$$

Thus our variant V is sizelt ntl: with these more elaborate structures, variants are not as easily found as before!

15.9   Exercises

Ex. 15.1   What is the size of the type

first | second A | third B C,

in terms of $\#A$, $\#B$, and $\#C$?

Ex. 15.2 ♡   Give types for each of the following:

1. A one-place buffer which either is empty or contains a natural number;
2. The finite binary trees with real numbers at the tips (a recursive type);
3. The colours of the spectrum.

Ex. 15.3 ♡   Example alternation 2 of Section 15.3 leaves n untouched if it is undefined. Write an alternation that instead *aborts* if n is 'undefined'.

Ex. 15.4 ♡   Recall the code of example alternation 4 in Section 15.3. How would you *specify* such a search so that termination is guaranteed even if key k does not occur in the database db? (In that case d may be given a value arbitrarily.)

Ex. 15.5   How would you implement the specification of Exercise 15.4?

Ex. 15.6 ♡   Use a type similar to that of example alternation 2 in Section 15.3 to modify your answer to Exercise 15.4 so that ok d is returned when full k d ∈ db, and undefined is returned otherwise.

Ex. 15.7   How would you implement the specification Exercise 15.6?

Ex. 15.8   Write your answers to Exercises 15.5 and 15.7 as **loop · exit · end** constructions.

Ex. 15.9 ♡   Recall the type of Section 15.5

type *TooBig* $\hat{=}$ one | several (**set** *TooBig*) ,

and consider the following subset of it:

$$paradox \ \hat{=} \ \{t : TooBig \mid (\exists \, ts : \mathbf{set} \ TooBig \cdot t = \mathsf{several} \ ts \wedge t \notin ts)\} \ .$$

Because *paradox* is a subset of *TooBig* we have that several *paradox* is an *element* of *TooBig*, and we can then reason

>   several *paradox* $\in$ *paradox*

$\equiv$ "definition of *paradox* as set comprehension"
> $(\exists \, ts : \mathbf{set} \ TooBig \cdot \mathsf{several} \ paradox = \mathsf{several} \ ts \wedge \mathsf{several} \ paradox \notin ts)$

$\equiv$ "several is injective"
> $(\exists \, ts : \mathbf{set} \ TooBig \cdot paradox = ts \wedge \mathsf{several} \ paradox \notin ts)$

$\equiv$ "Predicate law ???"
>   ???

What can we deduce at ??? What can we then conclude about *TooBig* itself?
   (The above construction is an example of *Russell's paradox.*)

Ex. 15.10   Recall Exercise 15.9, concerning the type *TooBig*. Consider now the declaration

>   **type** *QuiteBig* $\hat{=}$ one | several (**finset** *QuiteBig*) ,

which differs from *TooBig* only in its using **finset** in place of **set**. Replay from here the argument of Exercise 15.9; do we reach the same conclusion?

Ex. 15.11   In Section 15.6 we introduced the notion of (strict) partial order, together with its three defining properties (page 144). Show that, given *transitivity*, properties *irreflexivity* and *antisymmetry* are equivalent: each implies the other.

Ex. 15.12   A *non-strict* partial order is obtained from a strict one by allowing equality; thus we could define

$$x \oslash y \ \hat{=} \ x \oslash y \vee x = y \ . \tag{15.7}$$

Show that $\oslash$, defined as above, satisfies these three properties:

- It is *reflexive*: for all x we have $x \oslash x$;
- It is *antisymmetric*: for all x and y we have $x \oslash y \wedge y \oslash x \Rightarrow x = y$;
- It is *transitive*: for all x, y and z we have $x \oslash y \wedge y \oslash z \Rightarrow x \oslash z$.

Then show that *any* non-strict partial order $\oslash$ satisfying those three properties may be written as (15.7) for some strict partial order $\oslash$ satisfying the three properties of Section 15.6.

Ex. 15.13   In Exercise 15.12 there were three properties given to characterise a non-strict partial order. In Exercise 15.11 you were asked to show that the first two of the corresponding properties for a *strict* partial order were equivalent. Does that equivalence hold for the non-strict case as well? If not, propose a slight modification to the three (non-strict) properties so that equivalence of *reflexivity* and *antisymmetry* follows from *transitivity*.

Ex. 15.14 ♡   Is strict subset inclusion $\subset$ a strict partial order? Is it well founded?

Ex. 15.15   In Section 15.7 it was pointed out that *NatList* as defined at (15.3) is structurally equivalent to **seq** $\mathbb{N}$, and as a result we used from then on their notations interchangeably.

Can you define a type *Nat* that is structurally equivalent to $\mathbb{N}$ itself, and would justify the notation used in the following factorial calculator?

$$f := 1;$$
$$\textbf{do } n \textbf{ is } n' + 1 \rightarrow f, n := f \times n, n' \textbf{ od} .$$

Ex. 15.16 ♡   Usually in Law *tagged iteration* 15.2 the variant is the expression E itself, and the relation $\oslash$ is 'is a component of'. Use the law to show that the following tagged iteration is a refinement of $r, s := \mathsf{rv}\ s, ?$, where rv is the list-reverse function:

$$r := \langle\rangle;$$
$$\textbf{do } s \textbf{ is } h{:}t \rightarrow r, s := h{:}r, t \textbf{ od} .$$

Hint: You will need a logical constant in the invariant.

Ex. 15.17   Consider the binary tree type

$$BT\ X \ \hat{=}\ \mathsf{tip}\ X \mid \mathsf{node}\ (BT\ X)\ (BT\ X) .$$

The *frontier* of such a tree is the sequence of tip-values in left-to-right order. The following recursive procedure puts out the frontier of a given binary tree *bt* in *BT X*:

```
procedure Frontier (value bt : BT X)
≙ if bt is
       tip a → output a
  ▯ node bt1 bt2 →
       Frontier (bt1);
       Frontier (bt2)
  fi .
```

Develop *iterative* code (neither recursive nor parametrized) with the same effect, using a local variable $s : \textbf{seq}\ BT\ X$ as a stack. *Hint*: To express the invariant, use a recursive mathematical function $\mathsf{frontier}$ that you define yourself. You will need a logical constant.

Harder: What is the variant of your iteration?

Ex. 15.18 ♡   Recall Exercise 15.17. Develop *iterative* code, using two stacks, that determines whether the frontiers of two binary trees are equal:

var $bt1, bt2 : BT\ X$;
  $eq : Boolean$;

$eq := (\mathsf{frontier}\ bt1 = \mathsf{frontier}\ bt2)$

Your solution should be as space-efficient as possible: do not just 'output' into two sequences and then compare them.

Ex. 15.19 ♡   Verify the strict decrease of the variant $\mathsf{sizelt}\ ntl$ in Section 15.8.2.

Chapter 16

Modules and encapsulation

We have seen already how procedures act as a structuring tool for large programs, and that they simplify the development process. Going further, groups of procedures can themselves be organised, usually into units corresponding to data abstractions. We call those *modules*, and they are the subject of this chapter and the next.

16.1 Module declarations

Suppose in a large program there were a need for uniquely allocated natural number tags. The program would declare a set u of used tag values:

> declaration: **var** $u : \mathbf{set}\,\mathbb{N}$.

It would contain commands for acquiring and returning tags (assume that t is in $\mathbb{N}$):

> acquire new tag: $t, u \colon [u \neq \mathbb{N} \,,\; t \notin u_0 \wedge u = u_0 \cup \{t\}]$
> return tag: $u := u - \{t\}$.

And it would contain an initialisation of u, placed before any other use of it:

> initialisation: $u := \{\}$.

Finally — an important point — the variable u would not be used in any other way.

If the commands occur often, they could be made procedures. But there would still be a lack of organisation in the program: the three aspects of u (declaration, use, initialisation) would be widely separated, though they are all to do with a single abstraction. With a module they can be brought together.

Modules contain all three features: local variable declarations, procedure declarations, and initialisations. They *encapsulate* their data and all aspects of their

154

module *Tag*
    var $u : \mathbf{set}\ \mathbb{N}$;

    procedure *Acquire* (**result** $t : \mathbb{N}$)
    $\mathrel{\widehat{=}} t, u \colon [u \neq \mathbb{N}\ ,\ t \notin u_0 \wedge u = u_0 \cup \{t\}]$;

    procedure *Return* (**value** $t : \mathbb{N}$)
    $\mathrel{\widehat{=}} u := u - \{t\}$;

    initially $u = \{\}$
end

Figure 16.1 Module declaration

use. Figure 16.1 gives an example; note that a module is a declaration, not a command.

A local block containing a module declaration is equivalent in meaning to one in which the components are distributed back to their normal positions. Its variable declarations are placed with the other variable declarations of the block; its procedure declarations are placed with the other procedure declarations; and its initialisation (made a command) is placed at the beginning of the block body. Figures 16.2 and 16.3 illustrate that distribution. Normally in program development, however, we would move in precisely the reverse direction, from Figure 16.3 to 16.2.

16.2   Exported and local procedures

In Figure 16.2 it is not possible for *prog* to refer to the variable b, because *prog* is outside the module but b is inside the module. The procedures $P1$ and $P2$ can be used in *prog*, however; that is precisely what they are for. They are *exported* from the module. In general, we indicate explicitly the procedures to be exported: an *export list* gives their names. It is written

    export $P1, P2$,

and is placed inside the module. If it is missing, then by default all procedures are exported.

Procedures not exported are *local*, and are available for use only within the module. As for local variables, they can be given fresh names if the module is removed. Figure 16.4 gives an example of the use of a local procedure; it is equivalent to Figure 16.1.

```
‖[   var a;

     module M
        var b;
        procedure P1 ⋯ ;
        procedure P2 ⋯ ;
        initially init
     end;

     var c;

     procedure P ⋯⋯

     prog
]‖
```

Figure 16.2 Local block with module

```
‖[   var a;
     var b;
     var c;

     procedure P ⋯ ;
     procedure P1 ⋯ ;
     procedure P2 ⋯⋯

     b: [init] ;
     prog
]‖
```

Figure 16.3 Equivalent local block without module

Variables may be exported also, in which case they may be accessed but not changed ('read' but not 'written') by commands outside of the module. They may be changed by commands within the module.

module *Tag*
    export *Acquire*, *Return*;

    var u : **set** $\mathbb{N}$;

    procedure *Acquire* (**result** t : $\mathbb{N}$)
    $\mathrel{\widehat{=}}$ *Choose* (t); $u := u \cup \{t\}$;

    procedure *Return* (**value** t : $\mathbb{N}$)
    $\mathrel{\widehat{=}}$ $u := u - \{t\}$;

    procedure *Choose* (**result** t : $\mathbb{N}$)
    $\mathrel{\widehat{=}}$ $t : [\, u \neq \mathbb{N}\, ,\ t \notin u \,]$;

    initially $u = \{\}$
end

Figure 16.4 Module with local procedure

16.3 Refinement of modules

We saw in Chapter 11 that refining a procedure body refines the program containing it, and we regard that as refining the procedure itself.

Similarly, we can refine a module, as a whole, by refining its exported procedures. The local procedures can be changed in any way we please (as long as that results in refinement of the exported procedures). The initialisation is refined by strengthening it:

Law 16.1 <u>refine initialisation</u> If $init' \Rightarrow init$, then

    initially $init$ $\sqsubseteq$ **initially** $init'$.

$\square$

Figure 16.5 contains a refinement of the module in Figure 16.4. By refining *Choose*, we refine the exported *Acquire*, which uses it. The refined module acquires the *least* unused tag.

16.4 Imported procedures and variables

Modules developed for one program can often be reused in another, because their encapsulation makes them largely independent of the surrounding program.

---

module *Tag*

⋮

procedure *Choose* (**result** $t : \mathbb{N}$)
$\;\hat{=}\; t := (\sqcap e : \mathbb{N} \mid e \in \mathbb{N} - u)$

⋮

end

Figure 16.5 Refinement of Figure 16.4

For reuse, however, we must be explicit about the dependencies there are. References made by the module to its environment are *imported* using an *import list*. Both variables and procedures may be imported.

An imported variable is redeclared within the module, and that declaration must be implied[1] by the original declaration of the variable.

An imported procedure is redeclared within the module, and its original declaration must refine its redeclaration. The effect of an imported procedure on a module is given by the text associated with its (re)declaration *in the module*, not for example by the text of the actual (external) procedure — a necessary precaution if we are to allow modules to be refined in isolation, without direct reference to the context in which they will be placed.[2]

Both sorts of redeclarations — of variables and procedures — are to make reasoning about the module independent of the surrounding program, and the import list distinguishes redeclarations from declarations.

Imported procedures cannot refer directly to local variables of the module (because of variable capture); for that, they must use parameters. Figure 16.6 continues the example by importing *Choose*. The redeclaration of *Choose*, within the module, records the assumptions made about it. Refining the module means assuming *less*:

Law 16.2 <u>refine module</u> Let E be the list of exported procedures from module M, I its imported procedures, and *init* its initialisation. A module M' refines M if the following three conditions are satisfied:

1. Its exported variables are unchanged.

---

[1] Consider types as local invariants for that purpose, so that for example the declaration $a : \mathbb{N}$ 'implies' the declaration $a : \mathbb{Z}$.

[2] Naturally an implementor is likely to resolve calls to the imported procedure by using the actual external procedure. Given our rule about imported procedures being refined by the procedures they redeclare, the effect of that is a refinement of the whole program — but one on which the developer *cannot depend*. No more can he depend on the fact that a particular compiler might implement all assumptions as **skip**, or all nondeterministic choices as a deterministic choice of the first enabled alternative.

---

module *Tag*
  export *Acquire*, *Return*;
  import *Choose*;

  var u : set $\mathbb{N}$;

  procedure *Acquire* (result $t : \mathbb{N}$)
  $\hat{=}$ *Choose* $(\mathbb{N} - u, t)$;
    $u := u \cup \{t\}$

  procedure *Return* (value $t : \mathbb{N}$)
  $\hat{=}$ $u := u - \{t\}$;

  procedure *Choose* (value s : set $\mathbb{N}$; result $e : \mathbb{N}$)
  $\hat{=}$ $e : [s \neq \{\}$, $e \in s]$;

  initially $u = \{\}$
end

Figure 16.6 Module with imported procedure

---

2. Its exported procedures E' refine E.

3. Its initialisation *init'* refines *init*.

In addition, the following changes may be made provided the three conditions above are not invalidated as a result:

1. Its imported variables' declarations are weakened.

2. Its imported procedures I' are refined by I.

3. An imported procedure I is replaced by a *local* (neither imported nor exported) procedure I' that refines I.

□

(In fact the third change cannot invalidate any of the earlier conditions, but is mentioned for completeness: in that way a module can be decoupled from parts of its context.)

Note that Law 16.2 says 'if', and not 'only if': we see in the next chapter that there are other much more general ways of achieving $M \sqsubseteq M'$.

module $M1$	module $M2$
export $P1$;	**export** $P2$;
import $P2$;	**import** $P1$;
procedure $P1 \mathrel{\hat{=}}$ **magic**;	**procedure** $P2 \mathrel{\hat{=}}$ **magic**;
procedure $P2 \mathrel{\hat{=}}$ **magic**	**procedure** $P1 \mathrel{\hat{=}}$ **magic**
end	**end**

Figure 16.7 Circular export/import

16.5   Definition and implementation modules

In fact we do not need a technical meaning for 'definition' and 'implementation' when applied to modules. They refer only to a discipline of module reuse.

When a module is first formulated, it is likely to be during the development of some program, and will be abstract. Using an import list, it can be extracted from the program, and left for later refinement. That is a definition module.

Later, we can refine the definition module. The refined version can be inserted back into the program, replacing the original. That is an implementation module.

If in the development of some other program the same (definition) module is reached, it can immediately be replaced by its refinement, the implementation module. If the implementation module is code, as often will be the case, then that replacement can be done by linking in machine code just before execution. Thus the discipline we refer to is simply this:

> If for modules D and I we have $D \sqsubseteq I$, then we can call D a *definition* module and I (one of) its *implementation* module(s).

Definition/implementation pairs can be saved for future program developments. The definition module is published, but the implementation module is supplied. Since a module can have many refinements, a definition module can have many corresponding implementation modules.

16.6   Circular export/import

Consider Figure 16.7, and its refinement by *refine module* 16.2 to Figure 16.8. Figure 16.7 is infeasible (it contains **magic**), but Figure 16.8 is code — remember that the imported procedures (for example, $P2$ into $M1$) are there only for reasoning (about $M1$). Imported procedures need not be code.

Recall however from Chapter 1 that infeasible programs can never be refined to code.

module $M1$	module $M2$
export $P1$;	**export** $P2$;
import $P2$;	**import** $P1$;
procedure $P1 \mathrel{\hat=} P2$;	**procedure** $P2 \mathrel{\hat=} P1$;
procedure $P2 \mathrel{\hat=}$ **magic**	**procedure** $P1 \mathrel{\hat=}$ **magic**
end	**end**

Figure 16.8 Apparent refinement of Figure 16.7

The contradiction is due to the circular export/import between $M1$ and $M2$; and a simple way of avoiding that is to forgo such circularities between modules. If more care is taken, that can be relaxed to banning only circularities between procedures in separate modules. The most general solution involves variants, as for recursion; but it is seldom needed in practice.

16.7 Initialisation in code

We allow only certain initialisations in code. One is

> **initially** true,

which allows any initial values of the variables consistent with their types. An initialisation true can be omitted.

The other initialisation allowed in code is

> **initially** $w = E$,

where the variables w are all local, and the code expressions E are consistent with their types. The initialisation true is a special case of that, where w is empty.

16.8 Exercises

Ex. 16.1   The law *refine initialisation* 16.1 allows any initialisation to be refined to false. Why isn't that a good idea?

Ex. 16.2 ♡   Is it possible to refine *Tag* so that it acquires only *even* numbers? Is the result feasible?

Ex. 16.3   Modify *Tag* so that it can abort if 'too many' numbers are acquired but not returned. Is that a refinement? Does the original version refine your modified version?

Ex. 16.4 ♡   Write a module for acquiring pseudo-random numbers. Does it refine *Tag*?

Ex. 16.5 ♡   Recall Figure 16.7. In Module $M1$, can the imported procedure $P2$ be refined to **abort**? Can that be done in Figure 16.8?

Ex. 16.6 ♡   Suppose a module contained the declarations

> **var** $n : \mathbb{N}$;
> **import** *In*;
> **export** *Out*, n;
>
> **procedure** *In* (**result** $m : \mathbb{N}$) $\mathrel{\widehat{=}}$ $m{:}\, [m = 0 \vee m = 1]$;
> **procedure** *Out* $\mathrel{\widehat{=}}$ *In* (n) ,

and that the actual procedure supplied for *In*, by the context, was

> **procedure** *In* (**result** $m : \mathbb{N}$) $\mathrel{\widehat{=}}$ $m := 0$.

What value would a call of *Out* assign to n under those circumstances?

Suppose now a programmer refined *Out* to the assignment $n := 1$. Does that refine the module, according to Law 16.2? Is the new behaviour — of the module and its actual procedure — a refinement of the original behaviour?

Can you explain?

Chapter 17

State transformation and data refinement

In the last chapter, where we met modules for the first time, the notion of module refinement was introduced: it was argued that refinement of a module's individual procedures refined the module overall.

We now consider a much more radical possibility, in which we can carry out quite startling changes within the module while still being sure of its overall refinement. The technique is known as state transformation, or data refinement.

17.1   What we cannot yet show

Consider the module Tag' of Figure 17.1. It is a refinement of module Tag of Figure 16.1, although we cannot yet show it to be — for suppose the contrary, that $Tag \not\sqsubseteq Tag'$: then a client expecting Tag would have to be disappointed by Tag'. That means in turn that there is some program whose behaviour would be detectably different if Tag were replaced by Tag' — otherwise, the client would have no grounds for complaint! But there is no such program: using Tag', any series of $Acquire$ and $Return$ will produce successively higher values of t, starting from some randomly chosen value. And using Tag, exactly the same could have happened. (One might argue that it is unlikely: but still it is *possible*.) Thus $Tag \not\sqsubseteq Tag'$ is *not* true.

On the other hand, we can see easily that $Tag' \not\sqsubseteq Tag$ is indeed the case. For Tag can $Acquire$ 1 then 0, and that is something Tag' could never do. Thus $Tag \sqsubseteq Tag'$ but $Tag' \not\sqsubseteq Tag$, and so $Tag \sqsubset Tag'$: a strict refinement. The former could be a definition module, and the latter one of its implementation modules.

Although we have argued that $Tag \sqsubseteq Tag'$, indeed we cannot show that rigorously with our techniques so far: the individual procedures Tag' do not refine their counterparts in Tag; moreover, the states of the two modules are completely different. Such differences, however, are of great importance in program development. Module Tag contains a *set* of natural numbers, and few programming languages

163

---

module *Tag'*
  var $n : \mathbb{N}$;

  procedure *Acquire* (**result** $t : \mathbb{N}$)
  $\cong t, n := n, n + 1$;

  procedure *Return* (**value** $t : \mathbb{N}$)
  $\cong$ **skip**
end

Figure 17.1 A refinement of Figure 16.1

---

accept that as code. But *Tag'* contains only a single natural number, and that is far more realistic.

We see shortly that it is precisely because the state of a module cannot be accessed directly — its local variables — that we are free to change that state; we can replace more abstract variables (like sets) by more concrete variables (like simple numbers), provided the difference cannot be detected by use of the exported procedures.

Such a change of state is sometimes known as *change of representation*; if the change tends from abstract to concrete (towards code, in other words), it is known as *data refinement*.

17.2   State transformation

State transformation, carried out on the interior of a module, results in refinement of its external behaviour. We consider two specific transformations: one adds variables to a module; the other removes variables from a module.

To add variables, a *coupling invariant* is chosen, relating the existing variables to the new ones; it can be any formula over the local and exported variables of the module. (It may not refer to imported variables.) Declarations of the new variables are added; the initialisation is strengthened by conjoining the coupling invariant; every guard may assume the coupling invariant; and every command is extended by modifications to the new variables that *maintain* the coupling invariant. The resulting module then refines the original.

To remove variables, they must be first made auxiliary by refining the procedures of the module individually. A set of variables is *auxiliary* if its elements occur only in assignments or specifications whose changing variables are in the same set, so that other variables cannot depend on them. Then the declarations and all occurrences of those variables are removed. Again, the resulting module refines the original.

Often the two steps are carried out in succession — augmentation to add variables, then diminution to remove them — though in special cases we can bundle them together in one step.

Before we look at augmentation however, the first of the two, we must take a brief detour.

17.3 Coercions

We have already met assumptions, formulae {*pre*} between braces that act as **abort** unless the formula holds as that point in the program. Complementary to assumptions are *coercions*, which *make* a formula true at that point in the program. Here is the abbreviation:

Abbreviation 17.1 <u>coercion</u> Provided *post* contains no initial variables,

$$[post] \ \widehat{=} \ : [\mathsf{true} \ , \ post] \ .$$

□

A coercion to *post* behaves like **skip** if *post* is true, and **magic** otherwise. As do assumptions, coercions have an empty frame, and **true** as one of their constituent formulae. For both, the explicit appearance of the sequential composition operator is optional.

Here are two simple laws for coercions:

Law 17.2 <u>absorb coercion</u> A coercion following a specification can be absorbed into its postcondition.

$$w\colon [pre \ , \ post]\,; \ [post'] \quad = \quad w\colon [pre \ , \ post \wedge post'] \ .$$

□

(Compare *absorb assumption* 1.8.)

Law 17.3 <u>introduce coercion</u> **skip** is refined by any coercion.

$$\mathbf{skip} \quad \sqsubseteq \quad [post] \ .$$

□

(Compare *remove assumption* 1.10.)

We should also mention the following law for absorbing an assumption *following* (rather than preceding) a specification. It is

Law 17.4 <u>establish assumption</u>   An assumption after a specification can be removed after suitable strengthening of the precondition.

$$w\colon [pre\ ,\ post]\ ; \ \{pre'\}$$
$$=\ w\colon [pre \wedge (\forall\, w \cdot post \Rightarrow pre')\,[w_0 \backslash w]\ ,\ post]\ .$$

□

Law 17.4 exploits the fact that we do not distinguish a program that can abort later (because *post* can be true but *pre'* false) from one that aborts sooner (because in its precondition $(\forall\, w \cdot post \Rightarrow pre')\,[w_0 \backslash w]$ is false).

Assumptions and coercions are together known as *annotations*. Coercions in particular have many surprising — and useful — properties that are explored in the exercises for this chapter. One specific use is in augmentation, to which we now turn.

17.4   Adding variables: augmentation

Each of the following laws deals with an aspect of adding new variables. We assume throughout that the new variables are *c*, and that the coupling invariant is *CI*. Note that they are not *refinement* laws, and so do not contain the symbol ⊑. Rather they are transformations, for which we use the word '*becomes*'.

In our examples below, we suppose the module already contains a variable p, and that the new variables are q and r. The coupling invariant is $p = q + r$, and all three variables have type $\mathbb{N}$.

17.4.1   Declarations

Declarations of the new variables are added to the module. For the example, we would add **var** $q, r : \mathbb{N}$.

17.4.2   Initialisation

The coupling invariant is conjoined to the initialisation.

Law 17.5 <u>augment initialisation</u>   The initialisation I *becomes* $I \wedge CI$.
□

If the initialisation were $p = 1$, it would become $p = 1 \wedge p = q + r$.

17.4.3   Specifications

The coupling invariant is conjoined to both the pre- and postcondition of specifications, and the frame is extended to allow the new variables to change.

Law 17.6 <u>augment specification</u>   The specification $w\colon [pre \ , \ post]$ *becomes*

$$w, c\colon [pre \ , \ CI \ , \ post] \ .$$

□

For example, the command $p\colon [p > 0 \ , \ p < p_0]$ *becomes*

$$p, q, r\colon [p > 0 \ , \ p = q + r \ , \ p < p_0] \ .$$

17.4.4   Assignments

Assignments are extended so that they can change the new concrete variable, but they too must preserve the coupling invariant:

Law 17.7 <u>augment assignment</u>   The assignment $w := E$ can be replaced by the fragment

$$\{CI\} \ w, c := E, ? \ [CI] \ .$$

□

Note the similarity between Laws 17.6 and 17.7: in each, the frame is widened to include c, and the coupling invariant appears before (in the precondition, or assumption) and after (in the postcondition, or coercion). As a special case of *augment assignment* 17.7, however, we have

Law 17.8 <u>augment assignment</u>   The assignment $w := E$ can be replaced by the assignment $w, c := E, F$ provided that

$$CI \quad \Rightarrow \quad CI[w, c \backslash E, F] \ .$$

□

Law 17.8 is easily obtained by refining the right-hand side of Law 17.7. (See Exercise 17.32.)

As an example of augmenting assignments, the command $p := p + 1$ can be replaced by

$$\{p = q + r\} \ p, q, r := p + 1, ?, ? \ [p = q + r] \ ,$$

which in turn can be refined to

$$p, q := p + 1, q + 1 \ ,$$

for example. The effect of the coercion is to force the two open assignments $?, ?$ to resolve to values that make the formula hold (the formula is $p = q + r$, in this case). There may be many such values, and so there are of course other possibilities for the augmentation. If the notion of coercion seems too surprising, remember that the alternative, *augment assignment* 17.8, reaches $p, q := p + 1, q + 1$ in a single step.

17.4.5   Guards

Each guard can be replaced by another whose equivalence to the first follows from the coupling invariant.

Law 17.9 <u>augment guard</u>   The guard G may be replaced by G' provided that

$$CI \quad \Rightarrow \quad (G \Leftrightarrow G') \,.$$

☐

Note that $CI \wedge G$ is always a suitable G' above, as is $CI \Rightarrow G$. The guards $p > 0$ and $p < 0$ could become $p > 0 \wedge p = q + r$ and $p < 0 \wedge p = q + r$.

17.5   Removing auxiliary variables: diminution

Each of the following laws deals with an aspect of removing variables. In each one we assume that the auxiliary variables are a and that their type is A, and we continue with the example of the previous section. There is no coupling invariant for diminutions.

17.5.1   Declarations

The declarations of auxiliary variables are simply deleted. In our example, the declaration **var** $p : \mathbb{N}$ is removed.

17.5.2   Initialisation

Existential quantification removes auxiliary variables from the initialisation.

Law 17.10 <u>diminish initialisation</u>   The initialisation I *becomes*

$$(\exists\, a : A \cdot I) \,.$$

☐

The example initialisation, augmented in Section 17.4.2, *becomes* $q + r = 1$ when p is removed.

17.5.3   Specifications

The following laws remove variables from a specification. In many practical cases, however, these laws are not needed: often the variables can be removed by ordinary refinement. (See our more substantial example, in Section 17.6.2.)

The first law is used when the variable a, to be removed, is in the frame:

Law 17.11 <u>diminish specification</u> The specification $w, a: [pre\ ,\ post]$ *becomes*

$$w: [(\exists\, a : A \cdot pre)\ ,\ (\forall\, a_0 : A \cdot pre_0 \Rightarrow (\exists\, a : A \cdot post))]\ ,$$

where pre_0 is $pre[w, a\backslash w_0, a_0]$. The frame beforehand *must* include a.
□

Law 17.11 may appear surprisingly complex (a good reason perhaps to use ordinary refinement where possible to eliminate the abstract variables, and to reserve *diminish specification* 17.11 as a last resort). In fact it performs three operations: first, since a is auxiliary, we can have no interest in its final value — we care only that there *is* one. That explains the quantification $\exists\, a$ in the postcondition.

Second, we strengthen the postcondition so that it no longer depends on the initial value of a; it must apply for *all* such values. That explains the quantification $\forall\, a_0$ in the postcondition. The antecedent pre_0 is optional (and *strengthen postcondition* 5.1 allows it in any case); it makes the postcondition weaker, and less likely to be infeasible.

Finally, we cannot refer in the precondition to the actual value of a, although we can be sure it has *some* value. That explains the quantification $\exists\, a$ in the precondition, which weakens it.

The example from Section 17.4.3 yields, after several applications of Predicate law A.56,

$$q, r: [q + r > 0\ ,\ q_0 + r_0 > 0 \Rightarrow q + r < q_0 + r_0]\ .$$

And by strengthening the postcondition that refines to

$$q, r: [q + r > 0\ ,\ q + r < q_0 + r_0]\ .$$

If a specification does not contain a in the frame, we can still use Law 17.11 provided we use *expand frame* 8.3 first. Or we can use this law, derived from those:

Law 17.12 <u>diminish specification</u> The specification $w: [pre\ ,\ post]$ *becomes*

$$w: [(\exists\, a : A \cdot pre)\ ,\ (\forall\, a : A \cdot pre_0 \Rightarrow post)]\ ,$$

where pre_0 is $pre[w\backslash w_0]$. The frame beforehand must not include a, and *post* must not contain a_0.

Proof:

$\qquad w: [pre\ ,\ post]$
$\quad \sqsubseteq$ *"expand frame 8.3"*
$\qquad w, a: [pre\ ,\ post \wedge a = a_0]$
$\quad becomes$ *"diminish specification 17.11"*
$\qquad w, a: [(\exists\, a : A \cdot pre)\ ,$
$$\left(\forall\, a_0 : A \cdot \begin{array}{l} pre[w, a\backslash w_0, a_0] \\ \Rightarrow (\exists\, a : A \cdot post \wedge a = a_0) \end{array}\right)]$$

$\sqsubseteq$ "Predicate law A.56"

$$w, a\colon [(\exists\, a : A \cdot pre)\ , \\ \left(\forall\, a_0 : A \cdot \begin{array}{l} pre[w, a\backslash w_0, a_0] \\ \Rightarrow\ a_0 \in A \wedge post[a\backslash a_0] \end{array}\right)]$$

$\sqsubseteq$ "remove $a_0 \in A$, rename bound variable"

$$w, a\colon [(\exists\, a : A \cdot pre)\ ,\ (\forall\, a : A \cdot pre[w\backslash w_0] \Rightarrow post)]\ .$$

$\square$

For example, $n\colon [p > 0\ ,\ 0 \leq n < p]$ is taken by *augment specification* 17.6 to

$$n, q, r\colon [p > 0\ ,\ p = q + r\ ,\ 0 \leq n < p]\ ,$$

and then by *diminish specification* 17.12, *strengthen postcondition* 5.1, and *contract frame* 5.4 to

$$n\colon [q + r > 0\ ,\ 0 \leq n < q + r]\ .$$

17.5.4 Assignments

The auxiliary part of the assignment is removed.

Law 17.13 diminish assignment If E contains no variables a, then the assignment $w, a := E, F$ can be replaced by the assignment $w := E$.
$\square$

The example yields $q := q + 1$.

17.5.5 Guards

Guards must be rewritten so that they contain no auxiliary variables. Our earlier law *alternation guards* 4.3 can be used for that, since it is applicable to the refinement of alternations generally. In the example, we get $q+r > 0$ and $q+r < 0$.

17.6 An example of data refinement

As our first serious[1] example, consider the module of Figure 17.2 for calculating the mean of a sample of real numbers. We write $\sum b$ and $\#b$ for the sum and size respectively of bag b.

The module is operated by: first *clearing*; then *entering* the sample values, one at a time; then finally taking the *mean* of all those values.

---

[1]It is serious: the refinement we calculate here is exactly the one used in pocket calculators.

module *Calculator*
  var b : **bag** $\mathbb{R}$;

  procedure *Clear* $\;\widehat{=}\; b := \lfloor\!\rfloor$;

  procedure *Enter* (**value** $r : \mathbb{R}$)
    $\widehat{=}\; b := b + \lfloor r \rfloor$;

  procedure *Mean* (**result** $m : \mathbb{R}$)
    $\widehat{=}\; \{b \neq \lfloor\!\rfloor\}\; m := \sum b / \#b$
end

Figure 17.2 The mean module

We transform the module, replacing the abstract bag b by a more concrete representation s, n, a pair of numbers. Throughout, we refer to b as the abstract variable, and to s, n as the concrete variables. First s and n are added, then b is removed.

17.6.1   Adding concrete variables

We shall represent the bag by its sum s and size n:

abstract variable:	b : **bag** $\mathbb{R}$
concrete variables:	$s : \mathbb{R}$; $n : \mathbb{N}$
coupling invariant:	$s = \sum b \wedge n = \#b$.

The first step is to add the declarations of new variables s, n and apply the augmentation techniques of Section 17.4 to the initialisation and the three procedures.

- For the initialisation, we have from *augment initialisation* 17.5

$$s = \sum b \wedge n = \#b \ .$$

- For *Clear*, we have from *augment assignment* 17.8

$$b, s, n := \lfloor\!\rfloor, 0, 0 \ .$$

- For *Enter*, we have from *augment assignment* 17.8

$$b, s, n := b + \lfloor r \rfloor, s + r, n + 1 \ .$$

- For *Mean* we have from *augment specification* 17.6 (after rewriting)

$$m, s, n \colon [b \neq \lfloor\!\rfloor \;,\; s = \textstyle\sum b \wedge n = \#b \;,\; m = \textstyle\sum b / \#b] \;,$$

and we can carry on, making these refinements immediately:

$$\sqsubseteq \; m, s, n \colon [n \neq 0 \;,\; s = \textstyle\sum b \wedge n = \#b \;,\; m = s/n]$$

$$\sqsubseteq \; m \colon [n \neq 0 \;,\; s = \textstyle\sum b \wedge n = \#b \;,\; m = s/n]$$

$$\sqsubseteq \; \text{``}remove\ invariant\ 7.1\text{''}$$

$$\qquad m \colon [n \neq 0 \;,\; m = s/n] \;.$$

The result is shown in Figure 17.3.

Remember that augmentation (or diminution) is not in itself a refinement: the assignment $\{b \neq \lfloor\!\rfloor\} \; m := \sum b / \#b$ is *not* refined by $\{n \neq 0\} \; m := s/n$. The relation between them is augmentation (or diminution), relative to the abstract and concrete variables and the coupling invariant. That is why we write *becomes* rather than $\sqsubseteq$.[2]

17.6.2   Removing abstract variables

The abstract variable is b, and its removal from Figure 17.3 is straightforward for the assignment commands, because it is auxiliary (*diminish assignment* 17.13). Its removal from *Mean* is unnecessary — it has been removed already! That leaves only the initialisation. We use *diminish initialisation* 17.10, giving

$$n = 0 \Rightarrow s = 0 \;.$$

Now the abstract b has been removed altogether; the result is given in Figure 17.4. But the appearance of an explicit initialisation may be surprising, and it is in circumstances like this that being careful pays off. Suppose at some later stage an alternative abstract definition of *Clear* were given, such as this one:

procedure *Clear*
$\widehat{=}$ **if** $b \neq \lfloor\!\rfloor \rightarrow b := \lfloor\!\rfloor$
$\quad[\!]\quad b = \lfloor\!\rfloor \rightarrow$ **skip**
$\quad$ **fi** .

It is equal to the original, in Figure 17.2, but it could be more efficient if the operation $b := \lfloor\!\rfloor$ were very expensive, to be avoided if at all possible. With our augmentation and diminution it *becomes*

---

[2]Compare change of variable in an integral: faced with $\int_a^b dx/\sqrt{1-x^2}$ we might consider the substitution $x = \sin\theta$ (which is the analogue of the coupling invariant). But it would be wrong to claim that $dx/\sqrt{1-x^2}$ and $(\cos\theta\,d\theta)/\cos\theta$ were *equal*, even though the two definite integrals as a whole are equal.

module *Calculator*
   var b : **bag** $\mathbb{R}$;
      s : $\mathbb{R}$; n : $\mathbb{N}$;

   procedure *Clear* $\mathrel{\widehat{=}}$ $b, s, n := \lfloor\!\lfloor\,\rfloor\!\rfloor, 0, 0$;

   procedure *Enter* (**value** r : $\mathbb{R}$)
   $\mathrel{\widehat{=}}$ $b, s, n := b + \lfloor\!\lfloor r \rfloor\!\rfloor, s + r, n + 1$;

   procedure *Mean* (**result** m : $\mathbb{R}$)
   $\mathrel{\widehat{=}}$ $m\colon [n \neq 0\ ,\ m = s/n]$;

   initially $s = \sum b \wedge n = \# b$
end

Figure 17.3 After addition of concrete variables

---

procedure *Clear*
$\mathrel{\widehat{=}}$ **if** $n \neq 0 \to s, n := 0, 0$
   [] $n = 0 \to$ **skip**
   fi ,

and a subtle bug has crept in — suppose n and s were initially 0 and 1, for example (as they might be with no *explicit* initialisation)!

So our explicit concrete initialisation is necessary, after all, even though there was no abstract initialisation (other than **true**); and it is our good fortune that a rigorous approach brings that naturally to our attention. Note however that by *refine initialisation* 16.1 we could replace it by the simpler $s = 0$.

17.7   Abstraction functions

The laws of Section 17.4 dealt with a very general case of data refinement, in which the coupling invariant linking the abstract and concrete states could be anything whatever. In particular, several abstract variables could be collapsed onto a single concrete representation, as shown in the example of Section 17.6:

   both $b = \lfloor\!\lfloor 1, 2, 3 \rfloor\!\rfloor$
   and $b = \lfloor\!\lfloor 2, 2, 2 \rfloor\!\rfloor$ are represented by $s = 6 \wedge n = 3$.

That is actually a fairly rare occurrence in everyday program development however: it is much more common for the coupling invariant to be functional from

---

module *Calculator*
  var $s : \mathbb{R}; \ n : \mathbb{N};$

  procedure *Clear* $\ \widehat{=}\ s, n := 0, 0;$

  procedure *Enter* (**value** $r : \mathbb{R}$)
  $\widehat{=}\ s, n := s + r, n + 1;$

  procedure *Mean* (**result** $m : \mathbb{R}$)
  $\widehat{=}\ m: [n \neq 0 \ , \ m = s/n];$

  initially $n = 0 \Rightarrow s = 0$
end

Figure 17.4 The mean module, after transformation

---

concrete to abstract. (The above is not, but our earlier example $p = q + r$ is.) An example is the representation of sets by sequences, in which many distinct sequences may represent a given set: the elements may appear in different orders, may be duplicated, or even both. But to each sequence there corresponds at most one set; that is the functional nature of the abstraction, and what distinguishes it from the calculator example at the beginning of Section 17.6.

The general form for such coupling invariants, called *functional abstractions* is

$$a = \mathsf{af}\ c \wedge \mathsf{dti}\ c\ , \tag{17.1}$$

where af is a function, called the *abstraction function* and dti is a predicate, in which a does not appear, called the *data-type invariant*. In the case of sets and sequences, for example, the abstraction function is set, the function that makes a set from a sequence. Various data-type invariants may be included as well, for example that the sequences are kept in order (in which case we would write $a = \mathsf{set}\ c \wedge \mathsf{up}\ c$), or that the sequences contain no duplicated elements.

The reason for our interest in the special cases of data refinement is that when the augmentation and diminution laws are specialised to coupling invariants of the form (17.1) they become very much simpler, and the augmentation and diminution may be done together in one step.

17.7.1   Data-refining initialisations

Suppose that here (and in the following subsections) the coupling invariant is in the form (17.1), whence we may speak of abstraction function af and a data-type invariant dti. Given abstract initialisation I we would with *augment initialisation* 17.5 calculate $I \wedge a = \mathsf{af}\ c \wedge \mathsf{dti}\ c$; then *diminish initialisation* 17.10 would produce

$$(\exists\, a \cdot I \wedge a = \mathsf{af}\ c \wedge \mathsf{dti}\ c)\ .$$

But we can simplify that as follows:

$\equiv$ "Predicate law A.80"
     $(\exists\, a \cdot I \wedge a = \mathsf{af}\ c) \wedge \mathsf{dti}\ c$
$\equiv$ "Predicate law A.56"
     $I[a\backslash\, \mathsf{af}\ c] \wedge \mathsf{dti}\ c\ .$

Thus one merely replaces all occurrences of abstract variables a by their concrete counterparts $\mathsf{af}\ c$, conjoining the data-type invariant $\mathsf{dti}\ c$ to the result. That gives

Law 17.14 <u>data-refine initialisation</u>   Under abstraction function af and data-type invariant dti, the initialisation I *becomes*

     $I[a\backslash\, \mathsf{af}\ c] \wedge \mathsf{dti}\ c\ .$

$\square$

In our original example (Section 17.4.2) that would take us in just one step from abstract initialisation $p = 1$ to concrete initialisation $q + r = 1$. (The data-type invariant is just true.)

As an example, let us represent a set $as : \mathbf{set}\ A$ by a sequence $aq : \mathbf{seq}\ A$ kept in strictly ascending order (thus excluding duplicates, and making the assumption that A is an ordered type). By analogy with up, we define

$$\mathsf{sup}\ aq \ \widehat{=}\ (\forall\, i, j : 0 \rightarrow \# aq \cdot i < j \Rightarrow aq[i] < aq[j])\ ,$$

and so take as our coupling invariant

$$as = \mathsf{set}\ aq \wedge \mathsf{sup}\ aq\ . \tag{17.2}$$

If we now suppose that our abstract initialisation was $as = \{\}$, we calculate the formula $\mathsf{set}\ aq = \{\} \wedge \mathsf{sup}\ aq$ for the concrete initialisation, and continue

$\equiv$ $aq = \langle\rangle \wedge \mathsf{sup}\ aq$
$\equiv$ $aq = \langle\rangle\ .$

Thus to implement an abstract initialisation to the empty set, we provide a concrete initialisation to the empty sequence, whose strictly ascending order is trivial.

17.7.2   Data-refining specifications

Here as above we are going to carry out augmentation and diminution in succession; since *diminish specification* 17.11 will require an abstract a in the frame, we shall start with one there in readiness. Thus we begin with $w, a: [pre , post]$ and apply *augment specification* 17.6 to get

$$w, a, c: [pre , a = \mathsf{af}\ c \wedge \mathsf{dti}\ c , post] .$$

Law *diminish specification* 17.12 then produces the (rather complicated-looking)

$$w, c: [(\exists\, a \cdot pre \wedge a = \mathsf{af}\ c \wedge \mathsf{dti}\ c) ,$$
$$\left(\forall\, a_0 \cdot \begin{array}{l} pre_0 \wedge a_0 = \mathsf{af}\ c_0 \wedge \mathsf{dti}\ c_0 \\ \Rightarrow\ (\exists\, a \cdot post \wedge a = \mathsf{af}\ c \wedge \mathsf{dti}\ c) \end{array} \right)] .$$

As before, however, the one-point laws A.56 apply, and we can simplify as follows:

$\sqsubseteq$ "Predicate laws A.78, A.80, A.56"

$$w, c: \left[pre[a \backslash \mathsf{af}\ c] \wedge \mathsf{dti}\ c , \begin{array}{l} pre_0[a_0 \backslash \mathsf{af}\ c_0] \wedge \mathsf{dti}\ c_0 \\ \Rightarrow\ post[a_0, a \backslash \mathsf{af}\ c_0, \mathsf{af}\ c] \wedge \mathsf{dti}\ c \end{array} \right] .$$

$\sqsubseteq$ "*strengthen postcondition 5.1*"

$$w, c: [pre[a \backslash \mathsf{af}\ c] , \mathsf{dti}\ c , post[a_0, a \backslash \mathsf{af}\ c_0, \mathsf{af}\ c]] .$$

The pattern is again substitution (abstraction function) and conjunction (data-type invariant). The law is thus

Law 17.15 <u>data-refine specification</u>   Under abstraction function af and data-type invariant dti, the specification $w, a: [pre , post]$ *becomes*

$$w, c: [pre[a \backslash \mathsf{af}\ c] , \mathsf{dti}\ c , post[a_0, a \backslash \mathsf{af}\ c_0, \mathsf{af}\ c]] ..$$

$\square$

Earlier that would have taken us from

$$p: [p > 0 , p < p_0]$$

directly to $q, r: [q + r > 0 , q + r < q_0 + r_0]$ in just a single step.

Continuing with our more recent example above, we consider now the specification

$$as: [a \in as , a \notin as \wedge \{a\} \cup as = as_0]$$

that removes a given element a from our abstract set as (and which may abort if the element is not there). With the coupling invariant (17.2) we proceed

becomes "*data-refine specification 17.15*"

$$aq: [a \in \mathsf{set}\ aq , \mathsf{sup}\ aq , a \notin \mathsf{set}\ aq \wedge \{a\} \cup \mathsf{set}\ aq = \mathsf{set}\ aq_0] ,$$

and are confronted immediately with one of the 'facts of life' in such derivations: after a calculated data refinement there still may be considerable work to do at the concrete level. In this case, we carry on as follows:

$\sqsubseteq$ **var** $n : \mathbb{N}\cdot$

$\quad n\colon [a \in aq \ , \ aq[n] = a]\,;$ (i)

$\quad aq, n\colon [aq[n] = a \wedge \mathsf{sup}\ aq \ ,$

$\qquad \mathsf{sup}\ aq \wedge a \notin \mathsf{set}\ aq \wedge \{a\} \cup \mathsf{set}\ aq = \mathsf{set}\ aq_0]$ (ii)

(i) $\sqsubseteq$ "invariant $a \in aq{\downarrow}n$"

$\quad n := 0;$

$\quad$ **do** $aq[n] \neq a \rightarrow n := n + 1$ **od**

(ii) $\sqsubseteq n, aq := ?, aq{\uparrow}n \mathbin{+\!\!+} aq{\downarrow}(n+1)$

$\quad \sqsubseteq$ **con** $AQ : \mathbf{seq}\ A\cdot$

$\qquad n, aq\colon [AQ = aq{\uparrow}n \mathbin{+\!\!+} aq{\downarrow}(n+1) \ , \ aq = AQ]$

$\quad \sqsubseteq I \ \hat{=} \ AQ = aq{\uparrow}n \mathbin{+\!\!+} aq{\downarrow}(n+1)\cdot$

$\qquad n, aq\colon [I \ , \ I \wedge n \geq \#aq - 1]\,;$ $\qquad\qquad\quad \triangleleft$

$\qquad aq := \mathsf{fr}\ aq$

$\quad \sqsubseteq$ "invariant I"

$\qquad$ **do** $n < \#aq - 1 \rightarrow$

$\qquad\qquad aq[n], n := aq[n+1], n + 1$

$\qquad$ **od** .

17.7.3 Data-refinement of assignments

In this case by *augment assignment* 17.8 we can replace $w, a := E, F$ by the assignment $w, a, c := E, F, G$ provided

$$a = \mathsf{af}\ c \wedge \mathsf{dti}\ c \Rightarrow F = \mathsf{af}\ G \wedge \mathsf{dti}\ G \ . \tag{17.3}$$

(Note that w, a here are together playing the role of w in *augment assignment* 17.8.)

If we assume additionally that E, G contain no a, then *diminish assignment* 17.13 takes us immediately from $w, a, c := E, F, G$ to $w, c := E, G$. The law is thus, after simplification of the proviso,

Law 17.16 <u>data-refine assignment</u> Under abstraction function af and data-type invariant dti, the assignment $w, a := E, F$ can be replaced by the assignment $w, c := E, G$ provided that E and G contain no a, and that

$$\mathsf{dti}\ c \Rightarrow F[a \backslash \mathsf{af}\ c] = \mathsf{af}\ G$$
$$\text{and} \quad \mathsf{dti}\ c \Rightarrow \mathsf{dti}\ G \ .$$

$\square$

That our earlier $p := p + 1$ *becomes* $q := q + 1$ follows immediately.

For our later example we take the abstract $a := \{2, 0\}$ (with A as $\mathbb{N}$), and we propose $aq := \langle 0, 2 \rangle$ for the concrete assignment. The proviso is (the two taken together)

$$\text{sup } aq \quad \Rightarrow \quad \{2, 0\} = \text{set}\langle 0, 2 \rangle \wedge \text{sup}\langle 0, 2 \rangle \ ,$$

and is easily verified (even without its antecedent). But note how the proviso would not hold had we chosen $aq := \langle 2, 0 \rangle$, where the sequence is not in order.

17.7.4   Data-refinement of guards

Law *augment guard* 17.9 allows us to replace G by $G[a \backslash \text{af } c] \wedge \text{dti } c$, where as in *augment guard* 17.9 there is some flexibility: the conjunct dti c is optional. Subsequent adjustments may be made by *alternation guards* 4.3 as before. We have

Law 17.17 data-refine guard   Under abstraction function af and data-type invariant dti, the guard G may be replaced by $G[a \backslash \text{af } c] \wedge \text{dti } c$, or if desired simply by $G[a \backslash \text{af } c]$ on its own.
□

Consider for example the alternation

>   **if** $a \in as \rightarrow prog1$
>   [] $\quad a \notin as \rightarrow prog2$
>   **fi** .

By *data-refine guard* 17.17 (and other laws) that *becomes*

>   **if** $a \in \text{set } aq \rightarrow prog1'$
>   [] $\quad a \notin \text{set } aq \rightarrow prog2'$
>   **fi** ,

where $prog1'$ and $prog2'$ data-refine $prog1$ and $prog2$ respectively. We could continue

> $\sqsubseteq$ **var** $n : \mathbb{N}\cdot$
> $\quad n\colon [\text{sup } aq \ , \ a \in \text{set } aq \Leftrightarrow a = aq[n]] \ ;$ ◁
> $\quad$ **if** $a = aq[n] \rightarrow prog1'$
> $\quad$ [] $\quad a \neq aq[n] \rightarrow prog2'$
> $\quad$ **fi**
> $\sqsubseteq$ $n\colon [\text{sup } aq \ , \ aq{\uparrow}n < a \leq aq{\downarrow}n]$
> $\sqsubseteq$??? .

17.8 Exercises

Ex. 17.1 Give other possible new assignment commands for the example $p := p + 1$ in Section 17.4.4.

Ex. 17.2 Use *diminish specification* 17.12 to remove the variable a from the following:

$$x: [x = a \ , \ x = a + 1] \ .$$

Ex. 17.3 (See Exercise 17.2.) Remove a from that specification *without* using *diminish specification* 17.12.

Ex. 17.4 ♡ Use *diminish specification* 17.11 to remove a from

$$a, x: [x = a_0] \ .$$

Now remove it from $a, x: [x = a]$. Comment on the difference: is a auxiliary in both?

Ex. 17.5 ♡ *Log-time multiplication* The following program terminates in time proportional to $\log N$:

$$l, m, n := 0, 1, N;$$
$$\mathbf{do} \ n \neq 0 \rightarrow$$
$$\qquad \mathbf{if} \ \text{even} \ n \rightarrow m, n := 2 \times m, n \div 2$$
$$\qquad [\!] \quad \text{odd} \ n \ \rightarrow l, n := l + m, n - 1$$
$$\qquad \mathbf{fi}$$
$$\mathbf{od} \ .$$

Propose an iteration invariant that could be used to show that the program refines

$$l, m, n: [l = N] \ ,$$

given the declarations $l, m, n, N : \mathbb{N}$.

Augment the program by variables l' and m', coupled as follows:

$$l' \ = \ M \times l$$
$$m' \ = \ M \times m \ .$$

What is the resulting program, and what value is then found in l' on its termination?

Now go on to diminish the program by removing all variables not needed for the calculation of l'; then rename variables to remove primes. What is the resulting program?

Ex. 17.6 *Log-time exponentiation* Augment the program of Exercise 17.5 by variables l' and m', coupled as follows:

$$l' = M^l$$
$$m' = M^m .$$

What is the resulting program, and what value is then found in l' on its termination?

Diminish the program by removing all variables not needed for the calculation of l'; then rename variables to remove primes. What is the resulting program?

Ex. 17.7   Log-time transitive closure Let A be given, and define

$$\mathsf{tc}\, n \; \hat{=} \; (+i : \mathbb{N} \mid i < n \cdot A^i) .$$

(The function tc could be said to be forming the transitive closure of A, if A were an incidence matrix for a graph; but that point of view is not necessary for this exercise.)

Augment the program of Exercise 17.5 by variables l' and m', coupled as follows:

$$l' = \mathsf{tc}\, l$$
$$m' = \mathsf{tc}\, m .$$

What is the resulting program, and what value is then found in l' on its termination?

You will need an identity that gives $\mathsf{tc}(a + b)$ in terms of $\mathsf{tc}\, a$, $\mathsf{tc}\, b$ and A^b; what is it? How does that identity help you to decide what the 'definition' of $\mathsf{tc}\, 0$ should be?

Your augmented program should not contain any occurrences of tc, but may contain expressions A^m.

Further augment the program — add another variable, suitably coupled — so that the exponentiation can be removed. Note that the coupling invariant may be assumed when simplifying expressions.

Now diminish the program so that, after suitable renaming, a program remains that calculates $\mathsf{tc}\, N$ in logarithmic time.

Ex. 17.8 ♡   Exercise 17.6 showed that A^N can be calculated in time logarithmic in N, and so the equality

$$\mathsf{tc}\, N \;\; = \;\; (A^N - 1)/(A - 1)$$

appears to extend that logarithmic efficiency to the calculation of $\mathsf{tc}\, N$ itself, where tc is as defined in Exercise 17.7.

Under what circumstances might the program of Exercise 17.7 still be a better way to proceed? (The case $A = 1$ is on its own not a sufficient answer!)

Ex. 17.9 ♡   Suppose *pre* and *post* and w contain no a or a_0. What effect does *diminish specification* 17.12 have on the following?

$$w: [pre \; , \;\; post]$$

Ex. 17.10 ♡   Use *assumption* 1.6 to formulate laws for adding and removing variables from assumptions.

Ex. 17.11 ♡   Use *coercion* 17.1 to formulate laws for adding and removing variables from coercions.

Ex. 17.12   Apply *diminish specification* 17.12 directly to

$$m, s, n: \left[b \neq \lfloor \rfloor \,, \; s = \sum b \wedge n = \#b \,, \; m = \sum b / \#b \right] ,$$

without first doing the refinements on p.172. Then simplify the result. Which is easier: this exercise, or p.172?

Ex. 17.13 ♡   Suppose the mean procedure were instead

> **procedure** *Mean* (**result** $m : \mathbb{R}$)
> $\mathrel{\widehat{=}}$ **if** $b \neq \lfloor \rfloor \rightarrow m := \sum b / \#b$
> $\quad \mathbin{[\!]} \quad b = \lfloor \rfloor \rightarrow$ **error**
> **fi** ,

where **error** is some definite error indication unaffected by data refinement. Use *augment guard* 17.9 and *alternation guards* 4.3 to calculate the concrete procedure.

Ex. 17.14 ♡   In Exercise 16.2, Module *Tag* of Figure 16.1 was refined so that *Acquire* acquired only even numbers. The result was infeasible, because the precondition $u \neq \mathbb{N}$ was not strong enough to ensure that $\mathbb{N} - u$ contained any even numbers still to be acquired. Use augmentation with *no* concrete variables but still a coupling invariant of $u \in \textbf{finset}\,\mathbb{N}$ to show that *Acquire* can be transformed to

$$t, u: [u \in \textbf{finset}\,\mathbb{N} \,, \; t \notin u_0 \wedge u = u_0 \cup \{t\}] .$$

How does that help with Exercise 16.2?

Ex. 17.15 ♡   Show that in the *Tag* module of Figure 16.1, the body of *Return* can be replaced by **skip**. *Hint*: Remember that you cannot transform just part of a module. Use new variable v and coupling invariant $u \subseteq v \wedge v \in \textbf{finset}\,\mathbb{N}$ to transform all of it. The appearance of changing only *Return* is then gained by renaming v back to u.

Ex. 17.16   (See Exercise 17.15). Why is $v \in \textbf{finset}\,\mathbb{N}$ necessary in the coupling invariant?

Ex. 17.17   Show that $Tag \sqsubseteq Tag'$ (Figures 16.1 and 17.1).

Ex. 17.18 ♡   Explain the effect of a data refinement with *no* concrete or abstract variables, but still a coupling invariant. *Hint*: Recall Exercise 17.16.

Ex. 17.19   Why isn't false a good idea for a coupling invariant? *Hint*: See Exercise 16.1.

Ex. 17.20 ♡   The example of Section 17.7.2 on data-refining specifications concerned removing an element a from a set as. What does the concrete version (in terms of aq) do if a is *not* in aq? Is that reasonable?

Ex. 17.21   Use the functional abstraction laws to do the data refinement of Section 17.6 in reverse: that is, show that the module of Figure 17.2 is a refinement of that in Figure 17.4. Does that mean that the modules are equal? How does equality differ from refinement?
  Hint: Convert the assignments to specifications first.

Ex. 17.22 ♡   In the example of Section 17.7.2 the function fr is left in the code, but considerable trouble was taken to remove ↑, ↓ and +. Why is fr acceptable but the others not?

Ex. 17.23   Why is it acceptable to use linear search in the example of Section 17.7.2, instead of the more efficient binary search?

Ex. 17.24 ♡   Let the abstract type be (again) a set as : **set** A and take the concrete type to be a pair aq : $\mathbf{seq}_N A$; n : $\mathbb{N}$ with the functional abstraction being $as = \mathsf{set}(aq{\uparrow}n)$. (Thus the data-type invariant is true.) Calculate data refinements for the following:

  1. a: $[as \neq \{\}\,,\ a \in as]$;
  2. a, as: $[as \neq \{\}\,,\ a \notin as \wedge \{a\} \cup as = as_0]$;
  3. $as := as \cup \{a\}$; $\{\#as \leq N\}$.

Hint: For the third, consider rewriting it as a specification.

Ex. 17.25 ♡   Justify the last step of the derivation of Section 17.7.4. What might replace the '???' ?

Ex. 17.26 ♡   Use *expand frame* 8.3 to derive a law analogous to *data-refine specification* 17.15 in which the abstract variable does not appear in the frame. Do not assume that *post* contains no a_0.

Ex. 17.27 ♡   Suggest an example where the abstract command does not include a in the frame, but the concrete refinement of it does nevertheless. (See Exercise 17.26.)

Ex. 17.28 ♡   A more abstract database type than those we investigated in Section 15.3 would be $K \nrightarrow D$, a partial function from keys K to data D. Give a specification, at that level, of a lookup operation which can be data-refined to the specification you gave as your answer to Exercise 15.6. Write down the coupling invariant and work through the data refinement.

Ex. 17.29 ♡   Section 15.8.2 presented an iterative tree-summing program whose code contained a sequence of trees. How might that be implemented in a more conventional language that had only fixed-size arrays (for sequences) and records-plus-pointers for trees? Would one have to change the specification?

Ex. 17.30   Is it a refinement to strengthen or to weaken coercions? (Recall Exercise 1.13.)

Ex. 17.31   Prove this equality:

> *Law 17.18* <u>merge coercions</u>
>
> $$[post]\,[post'] \quad = \quad [post \wedge post']\,.$$

     □

Ex. 17.32   Show that *augment assignment* 17.8 indeed follows from *augment assignment* 17.7.

Ex. 17.33   Prove this law:

> *Law 17.19* <u>introduce assumption</u>
>
> $$[post] \quad \sqsubseteq \quad [post]\,\{post\}.$$

     □

Ex. 17.34   Prove this law:

> *Law 17.20* <u>remove coercion</u>
>
> $$\{pre\}\,[pre] \quad \sqsubseteq \quad \{pre\}.$$

     □

Ex. 17.35 ♡   Prove this refinement:

$$
\begin{aligned}
&x := 1 \\
\sqsubseteq\ &\textbf{if } true \rightarrow x := 1 \\
&\quad [\!] \quad true \rightarrow x := -1 \\
&\textbf{fi}; \\
&[x \geq 0]\,.
\end{aligned}
$$
      (i)

If coercions were code, how would (i) above be executed? *Hint:* Consider backtracking.

Chapter 18

Case study: Majority voting

Although our goal in program development is to reach code, there are reasons one might want to go further: to increase efficiency is one; and a second reason is to translate from one programming language into another. In this chapter, an example more extended than usual, we show two successive program developments, both successful. But the first, too inefficient (quadratic complexity), provides the motivation for extra trouble and ingenuity pursued in the second (linear complexity).

From the second attempt, however, we go much further; a series of carefully chosen transformations in the spirit of Chapter 17 leads on to a program of unexpected simplicity.

18.1   Refinement of code

One of our early examples of alternation was the following program fragment, illustrating both nondeterminism and nontermination:

> **if** $2 \mid x \rightarrow x := x \div 2$
> **‖** $3 \mid x \rightarrow x := x \div 3$
> **fi** .

In spite of its being code, we may nevertheless need to refine it further, given the demands of a particular programming language. As we saw in Exercise 4.5, one possibility is

> $\sqsubseteq$ "*alternation guards 4.3*"
> > **if** $2 \mid x$ $\rightarrow x := x \div 2$
> > **‖** $\neg(2 \mid x) \rightarrow x := x \div 3$
> > **fi**
> $=$ "transliteration into C"
> > `if (x%2 == 0) x=x/2; else x=x/3;`

184

Note that the above is a proper refinement: the final program does not equal the original. If $x = 6$, the original program sets it either to 2 or to 3; but the refined program sets it to 2. If $x = 7$, the original program can abort; the refined program must terminate, setting it to 2.

The final phase of this chapter will be concerned with replacing code by code, sometimes by simple refinement as above, sometimes by transformation (as within modules). To begin, however, we set out the problem and follow a straightforward and innocent approach to its development.

18.2 Winning an election

The *strict majority* of a bag of values is that value occurring with frequency strictly more than half the size of the bag. If the values represented votes, the strict majority value would identify the candidate, if any, that had an absolute majority.

Not every bag has a strict majority (just as not every election has an absolute winner). For example, the strict majority in $\llbracket A, B, A, C, A \rrbracket$ is A, but neither the empty bag nor $\llbracket A, B, B, A \rrbracket$ has a strict majority.

To be more specific, we define three predicates: first sm for *strict majority*; then em for *exists majority*; and finally cm for *conditional majority*. It will be convenient in the code to use a sequence rather than a bag, and so we suppose a sequence $as : \mathbf{seq}\ T$ and value $x : T$, defining

$$
\begin{aligned}
\mathsf{sm}\ x\ as &\ \widehat{=}\ \ as.x > \#as/2 \\
\mathsf{em}\ as &\ \widehat{=}\ \ (\exists\, x : T \cdot \mathsf{sm}\ x\ as) \\
\mathsf{cm}\ x\ as &\ \widehat{=}\ \ \mathsf{em}\ as \Rightarrow \mathsf{sm}\ x\ as\ .
\end{aligned}
$$

(Recall from p.81 that $as.x$ is the number of occurrences of x in as, whether as is a set or a bag.)

The task of our program will be to find a strict majority if there is one, terminating whether there is one or not. (Thus if as contains no strict majority, the program may set x at random, but still must terminate.) Here is our abstract program:

$$
\begin{aligned}
&\mathbf{var}\ as : \mathbf{seq}_N\ T;\ \ x :\ T\cdot \\
&x\text{:}\ [\mathsf{cm}\ x\ as]\ .
\end{aligned}
$$

18.3 A straightforward attempt yields quadratic code

18.3.1 A simple invariant

We begin with our usual strategy, to establish the postcondition over longer and longer prefixes:

$\lVert$ **var** $i : \mathbb{N}$·

$\quad i := 0;$
$\quad$ **do** $i \neq N \rightarrow$
$\qquad$ **if** $\neg$ em $as{\uparrow}i \rightarrow x := as[i]$
$\qquad$ $[\!]$ sm x $as{\uparrow}i \rightarrow$ **skip**
$\qquad$ **fi**;
$\qquad i := i + 1$
$\quad$ **od**
$]\!|$

Figure 18.1 Summary of first refinements

$\sqsubseteq$ "iterate up" **var** $i : \mathbb{N}$·
$\quad i := 0;$
$\quad$ **do** $i \neq N \rightarrow$
$\qquad x \colon [\mathsf{cm}\, x\ as{\uparrow}i\ ,\ \mathsf{cm}\, x\ as{\uparrow}(i+1)]$; $\qquad\qquad$ $\triangleleft$
$\qquad i := i + 1$
$\quad$ **od**
$\sqsubseteq$ **if** $\neg$ em $as{\uparrow}i \rightarrow x \colon [\neg\,\mathsf{em}\ as{\uparrow}i\ ,\ \mathsf{cm}\, x\ as{\uparrow}(i+1)]$ $\qquad$ (i)
$\quad [\!]$ sm x $as{\uparrow}i \rightarrow x \colon [\mathsf{sm}\, x\ as{\uparrow}i\ ,\ \mathsf{cm}\, x\ as{\uparrow}(i+1)]$ $\qquad$ (ii)
$\quad$ **fi** .

Note how the alternation exploits the disjunction inherent in cm x $as{\uparrow}i$.

Now if there is no majority in $as{\uparrow}i$, then the only possible majority in $as{\uparrow}(i+1)$ is $as[i]$ itself. Hence

(i) $\sqsubseteq$ $x := as[i]$.

On the other hand, if x is the majority in $as{\uparrow}i$, then either it is the majority in $as{\uparrow}(i+1)$ as well (if $as[i] = x$) or there is no majority in $as{\uparrow}(i+1)$ at all (if $as[i] \neq x$). Hence

(ii) $\sqsubseteq$ **skip** .

The program so far is collected in Figure 18.1. Only the guards are left to do.

18.3.2   State transformation of local blocks

In Chapter 17, we showed how to transform the state of modules. The same techniques apply to local blocks.

$$
\begin{aligned}
&\|[\ \ \textbf{var} \ i, c : \mathbb{N}; \\
&\quad \ \textbf{initially} \ c = as\uparrow i.x \cdot \\[4pt]
&\quad \ i, c := 0, 0; \\
&\quad \ \textbf{do} \ i \neq N \rightarrow \\
&\quad\quad\quad \textbf{if} \ c \leq i/2 \rightarrow x, c := as[i], (as\uparrow i).as[i] \quad\quad\quad\quad\quad (\text{iii})\\
&\quad\quad\quad [\!] \ \ c > i/2 \rightarrow \textbf{skip} \\
&\quad\quad\quad \textbf{fi}; \\
&\quad\quad\quad \textbf{if} \ as[i] = x \rightarrow i, c := i + 1, c + 1 \\
&\quad\quad\quad [\!] \ \ as[i] \neq x \rightarrow i := i + 1 \\
&\quad\quad\quad \textbf{fi} \\
&\quad \ \textbf{od} \\
&\,]|
\end{aligned}
$$

Figure 18.2 Introduction of count c

Recall Figures 16.2 and 16.3. A local block can be made into a module, then transformed, then made back into a local block again. An initialisation may suddenly appear in the transformed block, of course. To simplify that, we introduce this abbreviation:

Abbreviation 18.1 local block initialisation

$$
\begin{aligned}
&\quad \ \|[\ \textbf{var} \ l : T; \ \textbf{initially} \ inv \cdot prog \ ]| \\
&\widehat{=} \ \ \|[\ \textbf{var} \ l : T \cdot l: [inv] \, ; \ prog \ ]| \ .
\end{aligned}
$$

□

(Abbreviation 18.1 also simplifies the translation between modules and local blocks.)

All the transformation laws of Chapter 17 carry over to local blocks. In fact, even more is possible for local blocks: the coupling invariant can refer to global variables as well (compare p.164 'any formula over the *local and exported* variables of the module'). But we do not need that here.

Now we apply the above to Figure 18.1. We add a variable $c : \mathbb{N}$ which counts the occurrences of x in the prefix $as\uparrow i$ examined so far: the coupling invariant is $c = as\uparrow i.x$. That gives the program of Figure 18.2. Though we include the initialisation, Abbreviation 18.1 shows it to be unnecessary: it is subsumed by the command $i, c := 0, 0$.

The law *alternation guards* 4.3 has allowed the two guards to be simplified dramatically, to $c \leq i/2$ and $c > i/2$. (See Exercise 18.5.) That leaves only the refinement of (iii):

$$
\begin{aligned}
(\text{iii}) \ \sqsubseteq \ &x := as[i]; \\
&c := as\uparrow i.x
\end{aligned}
$$

◁

```
⊑ "invariant c = as↑j.x ∧ j ≤ i"; var j : ℕ•
  j, c := 0, 0;
  do j ≠ i →
       if x = as[j] → c, j := c + 1, j + 1
       ∥ x ≠ as[j] → j := j + 1
       fi
  od.
```

We have reached code. But its time complexity is quadratic: due to the iteration appearing as a the refinement of (iii), the entire prefix $as↑i$ is re-examined to compute c for the newly chosen x.

18.4   A second attempt is faster

18.4.1   How to do better

The troublesome (iii) occurs in a command guarded by $\neg\,\mathsf{em}\ as↑i$, which we did not exploit. Can that reduce the time complexity? A crucial property of sm is that for any sequences as, as' and value x,

$$\mathsf{sm}\ x\ (as + \!\!+ as') \quad \Rightarrow \quad \mathsf{sm}\ x\ as \lor \mathsf{sm}\ x\ as' \ . \tag{18.1}$$

If x is a majority in a concatenation, then it must be a majority in one part or the other. Hence if x is a majority in as overall (that is, if $\mathsf{sm}\ x\ as$), but $as↑i$ has no majority (and $\neg\,\mathsf{em}\ as↑i$), then x must be a majority in the remainder $as↓i$ (thus $\mathsf{sm}\ x\ as↓i$). Thus under the given conditions, we can forget the prefix altogether!

A convenient consequence of the above is given in this lemma:

Lemma 18.1 For sequences as, as',

$$\neg\,\mathsf{em}\ as \land \mathsf{cm}\ x\ as' \quad \Rightarrow \quad \mathsf{cm}\ x\ (as + \!\!+ as') \ .$$

Proof: Note that $\neg\,\mathsf{em}\ as \Rightarrow \neg\,\mathsf{sm}\ x\ as$. Now we consider the two cases in $\mathsf{cm}\ x\ as'$.

First, if $\neg\,\mathsf{em}\ as'$, then by Property (18.1) we have $\neg\,\mathsf{em}(as + \!\!+ as')$, hence it follows that $\mathsf{cm}\ x\ (as + \!\!+ as')$.

Second, if $\mathsf{sm}\ x\ as'$ then for all $y \neq x$ we have $\neg\,\mathsf{sm}\ y\ as'$. Again by Property (18.1), for all $y \neq x$ that gives $\neg\,\mathsf{sm}\ y\ (as + \!\!+ as')$, hence finally $\mathsf{cm}\ x\ (as + \!\!+ as')$.
□

Lemma 18.1 leads us to this new development:

```
  x: [cm x as]
  ⊑ "Lemma 18.1"; var j : ℕ•
     x, j: [¬ em as[0→j] ∧ cm x as[j→N] ]
```

```
|[ var i, j, c : ℕ•

    i, j, c := 0, 0, 0;
    do i ≠ N →
        if c ≤ (i − j)/2 → j, x, c := i, as[i], 0
        ▯ c > (i − j)/2 → skip
        fi;
        if as[i] = x → i, c := i + 1, c + 1
        ▯ as[i] ≠ x → i := i + 1
        fi
    od
]|
```

Figure 18.3 Second attempt: linear code

$$\sqsubseteq \begin{cases} I \ \hat{=} \ \neg\mathsf{em}\ as[0{\to}j] \wedge \mathsf{cm}\ x\ as[j{\to}i] \\ \mathbf{var}\ i : \mathbb{N}\bullet \end{cases}$$

$$x, j, i \colon [I \wedge i = N]$$

$\sqsubseteq$ "invariant $I \wedge j \le i \le N$"
```
    i, j := 0, 0;
    do i ≠ N →
        if ¬em as[0→j] ∧ ¬em as[j→i] →
            x, j: [¬em as[0→j] ∧ ¬em as[j→i] , I[i\i + 1]]      (iv)
        ▯ ¬em as[0→j] ∧ sm x as[j→i] →
            x, j: [¬em as[0→j] ∧ sm x as[j→i] , I[i\i + 1]]      (v)
        fi;
        i := i + 1
    od
```

(iv) $\sqsubseteq \ j, x := i, as[i]$

(v) $\sqsubseteq \ \mathbf{skip}$.

Again we introduce c, this time with the coupling invariant $c = as[j{\to}i].x$; the result is Figure 18.3. Note that again *alternation guards* 4.3 is used to simplify the guards. (See Exercise 18.5.) Now the code has linear time complexity; but — as we see below — it can be simplified dramatically.

```
|[  var i, j, c : N; d : Z.

    i, j, c, d := 0, 0, 0, 0;
    do i ≠ N →
        if d ≤ 0 → j, x, c, d := i, as[i], 0, 0
        [] d > 0 → skip
        fi;
        if as[i] = x → i, c, d := i + 1, c + 1, d + 1
        [] as[i] ≠ x → i, d := i + 1, d - 1
        fi
    od
]|
```

Figure 18.4 Add variable d

18.5   Transformation of code

18.5.1   Representing two variables by one

The guards in Figure 18.3 can be further simplified by a state transformation. We introduce a single variable $d : \mathbb{Z}$ using the coupling invariant $d = 2c - (i - j)$; then we remove c, j. First, the guards become $d \leq 0$ and $d > 0$, and the resulting program is Figure 18.4. (The superfluous initialisation is omitted.) Then, removing the auxiliary c, j gives Figure 18.5.

18.5.2   Laws of distribution

Inspection of Figure 18.5 reveals that the two alternations are not independent: the $d \leq 0$ branch of the first cannot be followed by the $as[i] \neq x$ branch of the second. With the following distribution law we can exploit that:

Law 18.2 left-distribution of composition over alternation

$$\mathbf{if} \ ([\!]\ i \cdot G_i \to branch_i) \ \mathbf{fi}; \ prog$$
$$= \mathbf{if} \ ([\!]\ i \cdot G_i \to branch_i; \ prog) \ \mathbf{fi} \ .$$

□

First, we distribute $i := i + 1$ out of the second alternation; then we distribute the second alternation into the first. The result is Figure 18.6.

In the first branch, we now have assignments before an alternation. We can use the following law to simplify that:

$\lVert$ **var** $i : \mathbb{N};\ d : \mathbb{Z}$.

$\quad i, d := 0, 0;$
$\quad$ **do** $i \neq N \rightarrow$
$\qquad$ **if** $d \leq 0 \rightarrow x, d := as[i], 0$
$\qquad [\!]\ \ d > 0 \rightarrow$ **skip**
$\qquad$ **fi**;
$\qquad$ **if** $as[i] = x \rightarrow i, d := i + 1, d + 1$
$\qquad [\!]\ \ as[i] \neq x \rightarrow i, d := i + 1, d - 1$
$\qquad$ **fi**
$\quad$ **od**
$]\!|$

Figure 18.5 Remove auxiliary c, j

$\vdots$

if $d \leq 0 \rightarrow$
$\quad x, d := as[i], 0;$
$\quad$ **if** $as[i] = x \rightarrow d := d + 1$
$\quad [\!]\ \ as[i] \neq x \rightarrow d := d - 1$
$\quad$ **fi**
$[\!]\ \ d > 0 \rightarrow$
$\quad$ **if** $as[i] = x \rightarrow d := d + 1$
$\quad [\!]\ \ as[i] \neq x \rightarrow d := d - 1$
$\quad$ **fi**
fi;
$i := i + 1$
$\vdots$

Figure 18.6 Merge alternations

Law 18.3 right-distribution of assignment over alternation

$\qquad x := E;\ \ \textbf{if}\ ([\!]\ i \cdot G_i \rightarrow branch_i)\ \textbf{fi}$
$= \textbf{if}\ ([\!]\ i \cdot G_i[x \backslash E] \rightarrow x := E;\ branch_i)\ \textbf{fi}$.

$\square$

The result is Figure 18.7.

$$\vdots$$

if $d \leq 0 \rightarrow$
    if true $\rightarrow x, d := as[i], 0;\ \ d := d + 1$
    $[\!]$ false $\rightarrow x, d := as[i], 0;\ \ d := d - 1$
    fi
$[\!]\ \ d > 0 \rightarrow$
    if $as[i] = x \rightarrow d := d + 1$
    $[\!]\ \ as[i] \neq x \rightarrow d := d - 1$
    fi
fi

$$\vdots$$

Figure 18.7 Distribute assignment over alternation

18.5.3   Laws of alternation

The true and false guards of Figure 18.7 are handled with these laws; the result is
Figure 18.8, in which we have merged the assignments as well.

Law 18.4 <u>remove false guard</u>

    if $([\!]\ i \cdot G_i \rightarrow branch_i)$
    $[\!]$ false $\rightarrow branch$
    fi
$=$ **if** $([\!]\ i \cdot G_i \rightarrow branch_i)$ **fi** .

□

Law 18.5 <u>remove alternation</u>

    if true $\rightarrow branch$ **fi** $=$ $branch$.

□

    Now we flatten the alternations with the following law. The result is Figure 18.9.

Law 18.6 <u>flatten nested alternations</u>

    if $([\!]\ i \cdot G_i \rightarrow$ **if** $([\!]\ j \cdot H_j \rightarrow branch_{ij})$ **fi**$)$ **fi**
$=$ **if** $([\!]\ i, j \cdot G_i \wedge H_j \rightarrow branch_{ij})$ **fi** .

□

$\vdots$

if $d \leq 0 \rightarrow x, d := as[i], 1$
$[\!]\ d > 0 \rightarrow$
    if $as[i] = x \rightarrow d := d + 1$
    $[\!]\ as[i] \neq x \rightarrow d := d - 1$
    fi
fi

$\vdots$

Figure 18.8 Simplify alternation

$\vdots$

if $d \leq 0 \rightarrow x, d := as[i], 1$
$[\!]\ d > 0 \wedge as[i] = x \rightarrow d := d + 1$
$[\!]\ d > 0 \wedge as[i] \neq x \rightarrow d := d - 1$
fi

$\vdots$

Figure 18.9 Flatten nested alternations

18.5.4 Introducing invariants

Inspection of Figure 18.9, recalling its surrounding text, suggests that $d \geq 0$ is invariant. It is true initially, and is maintained by every assignment in the program. That takes us to Figure 18.10. Note that the type of d is now $\mathbb{N}$.

$\vdots$

if $d = 0 \rightarrow x, d := as[i], 1$
$[\!]\ d \neq 0 \wedge as[i] = x \rightarrow d := d + 1$
$[\!]\ d \neq 0 \wedge as[i] \neq x \rightarrow d := d \ominus 1$
fi

$\vdots$

Figure 18.10 Introduce invariant $d \geq 0$

194 *Case study: Majority voting*

$$\vdots$$

if $d = 0 \rightarrow x, d := as[i], d+1$
⫿ $d \neq 0 \wedge as[i] = x \rightarrow x, d := as[i], d+1$
⫿ $d \neq 0 \wedge as[i] \neq x \rightarrow d := d \ominus 1$
fi

$$\vdots$$

Figure 18.11 Exploit guards

$$\vdots$$

if $d = 0 \vee as[i] = x \rightarrow x, d := as[i], d+1$
⫿ $d \neq 0 \wedge as[i] \neq x \rightarrow d := d \ominus 1$
fi

$$\vdots$$

Figure 18.12 Collapse branches

In fact, invariant introduction is a special case of the add variable transformation: we introduce *no* variables, but have a coupling invariant nevertheless. The law *augment assignment* 17.8 reduces to checking that assignments preserve the invariant (the list c is empty); the law *augment guard* 17.9 allows the invariant to simplify the guards.

If we exploit the guards, we can reach Figure 18.11, in which we have made two branches identical. The following law then takes Figure 18.11 to Figure 18.12:

Law 18.7 collapse identical branches

$\quad$ **if** ($⫿ i \cdot G_i \rightarrow branch_i$)
$\quad$ ⫿ $G \rightarrow branch$
$\quad$ ⫿ $G' \rightarrow branch$
$\quad$ **fi**
$=$ **if** ($⫿ i \cdot G_i \rightarrow branch_i$)
$\quad$ ⫿ $G \vee G' \rightarrow branch$
$\quad$ **fi** .

□

```
|[  var i, d : N·

    i, d := 0, 0;
    do i ≠ N →
        if  d = 0 ∨ as[i] = x
            then x, d := as[i], d + 1
            else d := d ⊖ 1
        fi;
        i := i + 1
    od
]|
```

Figure 18.13 Simplified code

18.6 Simplified code

With Figure 18.12 we reach the end of the development. The code is collected in
Figure 18.13, where we use the conventional **if** ··· **then** ··· **else** ··· **end**.

Curiously, we have iterative code but have 'lost' the invariant. Where has it
gone?

The last invariant quoted was on p.189:

$$j \leq i \leq N$$
$$\neg \text{em } as[0 \rightarrow j]$$
$$\text{cm } x \ as[j \rightarrow i] \ .$$

Introducing c adds a conjunct to that; introducing d adds another:

$$j \leq i \leq N$$
$$\neg \text{em } as[0 \rightarrow j]$$
$$\text{cm } x \ as[j \rightarrow i]$$
$$c = as[j \rightarrow i].x$$
$$d = 2c - (i - j) \ .$$

Removing c, j removes them from the invariant, leaving this:

$$\exists \, c, j : \mathbb{N} \cdot \begin{pmatrix} j \leq i \leq N \\ \neg \text{em } as[0 \rightarrow j] \\ \text{cm } x \ as[j \rightarrow i] \\ c = as[j \rightarrow i].x \\ d = 2c - (i - j) \end{pmatrix} . \tag{18.2}$$

Since an invariant is unaffected by refinements to the iteration *body*, formula (18.2)
is the invariant for the final program. (See Exercise 18.6.)

18.7   Exercises

Ex. 18.1 ♡   (From p.186) Prove that

$$\neg\, \mathsf{em}\ as{\uparrow}i \quad\Rightarrow\quad \mathsf{cm}\ as[i]\ as{\uparrow}(i+1)\ .$$

Ex. 18.2   (From p.186) Prove that

$$\mathsf{sm}\ x\ as{\uparrow}i \quad\Rightarrow\quad \mathsf{cm}\ x\ as{\uparrow}(i+1)\ .$$

Ex. 18.3   Why isn't **initially** false a good idea in a local block? *Hint*: Recall *local block initialisation* 18.1.

Ex. 18.4 ♡   (From p.187) Work through the details of showing that transformation is valid for local blocks. *Hint*: Introduce a module with a single parameterless procedure, called once.

Ex. 18.5 ♡   Check the claims made about simplifying guards (pp. 187 and 189).

Ex. 18.6   Show that the monstrous formula (18.2) entails

$$i \le N$$
$$as[0{\to}i].x \le (i+d)/2$$
$$\text{for all } y \ne x \quad as[0{\to}i].y \le (i-d)/2\ .$$

Using that as an invariant, develop the code of Figure 18.13 directly.

Ex. 18.7   Use *alternation guards* 4.3, *remove false guard* 18.4, and *remove alternation* 18.5 to prove this law:

> *Law 18.8* <u>select true guard</u>
>
>   **if** ($[\!]\ i \cdot G_i \to branch_i$)
> $[\!]$ true $\to branch$
>   **fi**
>
> $\sqsubseteq branch$.
>
>   □

Chapter 19

Origins and conclusions

The idea of our refinement calculus originated with Ralph Back [Bac80], and was reinvented by Joseph Morris [Mor87] and by me [Mor88d]. In each case the context was E.W. Dijkstra's *weakest precondition calculus* [Dij76]. Similar ideas were put forward by Dershowitz [Der83].

Much work has been done since the crucial first step of considering both specifications and code to be programs. The effect has been to simplify, and make more regular, much of the detail of constructing programs; and there are significant implications for the practice of software engineering generally.

For example, none of the programs developed in this book has comments in its code. Indeed, many of the developments never present the complete code at all; and the result would probably be unreadable if they did.

Proper commenting and laying out of code is important when there is no rigorous development history of the program: then, the code is all we have. If the source code of a compiled program were discarded after its development, then certainly commenting and layout of the machine code would be important.

Now we know, though, that code is not meant to be read: it is meant to be executed by computer. And we have rigorous development histories: they can be found, for example, in the case study chapters. In each of those there is a sequence of refinement steps, every one justified by a refinement law, whose validity is independent of the surrounding English text. The histories have the initial, abstract, program at their beginning, and the final executable code is easily (even mechanically) recoverable from them, at the end. They reveal the structure of the program as well: logically related sections of code are identified simply by finding a common ancestor. Furthermore, the development histories allow those programs to be modified safely.

Return for example to the square root case study of Chapter 7, whose code is collected in Figure 19.1. The comment suggests a possible modification: could we choose some other p? The development history, collected in Figure 19.2, gives the answer: the commented command in the code can be replaced by $p := r+1$ without

```
|[ var q : N·
   q, r := s + 1, 0;
   do r + 1 ≠ q →
      |[ var p : N·
         p := (q + r) ÷ 2;      (* Choose p between r and q. *)
         if s < p² → q := p
         [] s ≥ p² → r := p
         fi
      ]|
   od
]|
```

Figure 19.1 Square root code (Chapter 7)

---

affecting the program's correctness. The validity of the following refinement step is all that is needed, and the rest of the program can be completely ignored:

$$p: [r + 1 < q \ , \ r < p < q] \quad \sqsubseteq \quad p := r + 1 \ .$$

No comment could ever have that credibility.

There are still good reasons for collecting code. One is that certain optimisations are not possible until logically separate fragments are found to be executed close together. That is like a peephole optimiser's removing redundant loads to registers from compiler-generated machine code: the opportunity is noticed only when the machine code is assembled together. And those activities have more in common, for both are carried out without any knowledge of the program's purpose. It is genuine post-processing.

For us, the documentation is the English text accompanying the development history (including the quoted decorations on individual refinement steps). Because it plays no role in the correctness of the refinements, we are free to tailor it to specific needs. For teaching, it reveals the strategies used; for production programs, it might contain hints for later modification ('Binary chop').

What of testing and debugging? They are still necessary. Three larger case studies, in the remaining chapters, are presented after these conclusions because they are significantly harder than the case studies earlier. The code of the first was collected, transliterated by hand,[1] and then tested.

There was an error in the transliteration: a multiple assignment $x, y := E, F$ was translated in error to $x := E; \ y := F$ (the expression F contained x). However, such errors are easily detected, and even avoided, by incorporating the checks in an automated transliterator.

---

[1] The programming language was Modula-2.

$\textbf{var } r, s : \mathbb{N}\text{\small{•}}$

$r := \lfloor \sqrt{s} \rfloor$

$= \; r\text{:} \, [r^2 \leq s < (r+1)^2]$

$\sqsubseteq \; \textbf{var } q : \mathbb{N}\text{\small{•}}$

$\quad q, r\text{:} \, [r^2 \leq s < q^2 \wedge r + 1 = q]$

$\sqsubseteq \; I \; \hat{=} \; r^2 \leq s < q^2\text{\small{•}}$

$\quad q, r\text{:} \, [I \wedge r + 1 = q]$

$\sqsubseteq \; q, r\text{:} \, [I] \, ;$ $\hspace{6cm}$ (iii)

$\quad q, r\text{:} \, [I \, , \, I \wedge r + 1 = q]$ $\hspace{5cm}$ ◁

$\sqsubseteq \; \textbf{do } r + 1 \neq q \; \rightarrow$

$\qquad q, r\text{:} \, [r + 1 \neq q \, , \, I \, , \, q - r < q_0 - r_0]$ $\hspace{3cm}$ ◁

$\quad \textbf{od}$

$\sqsubseteq \; \textbf{var } p : \mathbb{N}\text{\small{•}}$

$\quad p\text{:} \, [r + 1 < q \, , \, r < p < q] \, ;$ $\hspace{4.5cm}$ (iv)

$\quad q, r\text{:} \, [r < p < q \, , \, I \, , \, q - r < q_0 - r_0]$ $\hspace{2.5cm}$ ◁

$\sqsubseteq \; \textbf{if } s < p^2 \rightarrow q\text{:} \, [s < p^2 \wedge p < q \, , \, I \, , \, q < q_0]$ $\hspace{1.5cm}$ (v)

$\quad \mathbin{[\!]} \; s \geq p^2 \rightarrow r\text{:} \, [s \geq p^2 \wedge r < p \, , \, I \, , \, r_0 < r]$ $\hspace{1.5cm}$ (vi)

$\quad \textbf{fi}$

(iii) $\sqsubseteq \; q, r := s + 1, 0$

(iv) $\sqsubseteq \; p := (q + r) \div 2$ $\quad$ 'Binary chop.'

(v) $\sqsubseteq \; q := p$

(vi) $\sqsubseteq \; r := p$.

Figure 19.2 Square root development history

A second error was due to a single mistake in the development, and that was found by checking the refinement steps in detail without reading the English text. Thus it is the *development* that is debugged: the thought of checking the code itself was shockingly unpleasant — and in any case it was not at all clear how it worked.

Those were the only errors, and 'it ran third time'. But the point had been made: mathematical rigour cannot eliminate mistakes entirely.

Nevertheless it does reduce their likelihood dramatically.

Chapter 20

Case study: A paragraph problem

20.1 Even paragraphs

This case study, the first of three major studies with which we conclude, is based on [Bir86]; like the two to follow, it is quite a lot more ambitious than our earlier examples.

The problem itself seems simple: it is just the laying out of words into lines and paragraphs. Compare the paragraphs of Figures 20.1 and 20.2. In *simple* paragraphs, like Figure 20.1, each line is filled as much as possible before moving on to the next. As a consequence, the minimum number of lines is used; but a long word arriving near the end of a line can cause a large gap there.

In *even* paragraphs, like Figure 20.2, such gaps are reduced: space is distributed over earlier lines in order to increase the length of a later line which would otherwise be very short. We will develop a program that produces even paragraphs.

To start, we forget the actual words and just consider their lengths. Let the sequence of word lengths to be laid out be ws, of type $\mathbf{seq}_N \, \mathbb{N}$. We have a maximum line width of M (characters), and we assume that all (word) lengths are non-zero and no more than M:

$$(\forall \, w : ws \cdot 0 < w \leq M) \ .$$

A *paragraph* of ws is a sequence of lines, and each line is a sequence of words. For paragraph $pss : \mathbf{seq} \, \mathbf{seq} \, \mathbb{N}$ (remember we are considering only lengths, not actual words), we have these conditions:

1. The paragraph pss contains exactly the lengths in ws, in their original order: $\mathsf{fl} \, pss = ws$. The function fl, *flatten*, is defined as follows:

    $$\mathsf{fl} \, pss \ \widehat{=} \ (+\!\!\!+ \, ls : pss) \ .$$

2. Each line of the paragraph contains at least one but no more than M characters: $(\forall \, ls : pss \cdot 0 < \sum ls \leq M)$. We abbreviate that $\mathsf{ok} \, pss$. The function $\sum$ is defined as follows:

```
⊣Compare the paragraphs of Figure 20.1 and      ⊢
⊣Figure 20.2. In simple paragraphs, like Figure⊢
⊣20.1, each line is filled as much as possible ⊢
⊣before moving on to the next. As a            ⊢
⊣consequence, the minimum number of lines is    ⊢
⊣used; but a long word arriving near the end of⊢
⊣a line can cause a large gap there.            ⊢
```

Figure 20.1 Simple paragraph

```
⊣Compare the paragraphs of Figure 20.1 and      ⊢
⊣Figure 20.2. In simple paragraphs, like        ⊢
⊣Figure 20.1, each line is filled as much as    ⊢
⊣possible before moving on to the next. As a    ⊢
⊣consequence, the minimum number of lines is    ⊢
⊣used; but a long word arriving near the end of⊢
⊣a line can cause a large gap there.            ⊢
```

Figure 20.2 Even paragraph

$$\sum ls \ \hat{=} \ (+w : ls) \ .$$

Suppose for example that $ws = \langle 2, 1, 1, 3 \rangle$, and $M = 3$. Here are three paragraphs of ws:

$$\langle \langle 2, 1 \rangle, \langle 1 \rangle, \langle 3 \rangle \rangle \quad \text{(simple)}$$
$$\langle \langle 2 \rangle, \langle 1, 1 \rangle, \langle 3 \rangle \rangle \quad \text{(even)}$$
$$\langle \langle 2 \rangle, \langle 1 \rangle, \langle 1 \rangle, \langle 3 \rangle \rangle \quad \text{(neither simple nor even)}.$$

Figures 20.1 and 20.2 are paragraphs of the same words. But Figure 20.2 minimises the waste of the paragraph, where the *waste* is the size of the largest gap left in any of its lines except the last:

$$\mathsf{wt} \, pss \ \hat{=} \ (\sqcup ls : \mathsf{fr} \, pss \cdot M - \sum ls) \ .$$

(Recall that fr takes the front of a sequence.) Now the *minimum waste* mw of a sequence of word lengths is the least waste found in any of its paragraphs:

$$\mathsf{mw} \, ws \ \hat{=} \ (\sqcup pss \mid \mathsf{fl} \, pss = ws \wedge \mathsf{ok} \, pss \cdot \mathsf{wt} \, pss) \ .$$

The paragraph of Figure 20.1 has waste 12; the waste of Figure 20.2 is only 7, which is minimal in that width for those words.

Our first step is to derive a program that calculates mw ws.

20.2　The minimum waste

Here is the abstract program that calculates the waste that an even paragraph would have.

> **var** $ws : \mathbf{seq}_N \, \mathbb{N};$
> $mw, M : \mathbb{N};$
>
> **and** $ws \neq \langle\rangle \wedge (\forall\, w : ws \cdot 0 < w \leq M) \cdot$
>
> $mw := \mathsf{mw}\, ws \; .$

The invariant expresses the conditions on ws and M: that ws is non-empty, no word length in ws is 0, and no word length in ws exceeds M.

Rather than consider larger and larger prefixes of ws, we consider suffixes. That is because the last line is treated specially: it does not contribute to the waste. So we introduce a sequence sf (*suffixes*) to contain the minimum wastes of all suffixes of ws; the needed value will be $sf[0]$ finally.

> $\sqsubseteq$ **var** $sf : \mathbf{seq}_N \, \mathbb{N} \cdot$
> $sf \colon [(\forall\, i \mid 0 \leq i < N \cdot sf[i] = \mathsf{mw}(ws{\downarrow}i))] \,;$　　　　◁
> $mw := sf[0] \; .$

The next few steps are the usual ones for developing a iteration. Note however that the initialisation is $j := N - 1$; that is because $\mathsf{mw}\,\langle\rangle$ is not defined.

> $\sqsubseteq\; I \;\hat{=}\; (\forall\, i \mid j \leq i < N \cdot sf[i] = \mathsf{mw}(ws{\downarrow}i)) \wedge j < N \cdot$
> $sf \colon [I[j\backslash 0]]$
> $\sqsubseteq$ **var** $j : \mathbb{N} \cdot$
> $j, sf[N-1] := N - 1, 0;$
> $j, sf \colon [j = N - 1 \,,\, I \,,\, j = 0]$　　　　◁
> $\sqsubseteq$ "iterate down"
> $\quad$ **do** $j \neq 0 \to$
> $\qquad j := j - 1;$
> $\qquad sf \colon [I[j\backslash j + 1] \,,\, I]$　　　　　　　　　(i)
> $\quad$ **od** .

Now we must change sf, but it is clear that we need change it only at index j. So we introduce a new variable x to be finally assigned to $sf[j]$. That allows the first command below to leave sf out of the frame.

> (i) $\sqsubseteq$ **var** $x : \mathbb{N} \cdot$
> $\quad x \colon [I[j\backslash j + 1] \,,\, x = \mathsf{mw}(ws{\downarrow}j)] \,;$　　　　　　(ii)
> $\quad sf[j] := x \; .$

To make progress now, we must look more closely at $\mathsf{mw}(ws{\downarrow}j)$. From the precondition we have $j + 1 < N$, and we proceed

$$\mathsf{mw}(ws{\downarrow}j)$$
$$= (\sqcap pss \mid \mathsf{fl}\, pss = ws{\downarrow}j \wedge \mathsf{ok}\, pss \cdot \mathsf{wt}\, pss)$$
$$= \text{``because } j < N, \text{ and so } ws{\downarrow}j \text{ cannot be empty''}$$
$$(\sqcap ls, pss' \mid \quad \mathsf{fl}(\langle ls \rangle \mathbin{+\!\!+} pss') = ws{\downarrow}j \wedge \mathsf{ok}(\langle ls \rangle \mathbin{+\!\!+} pss')$$
$$\cdot\ \mathsf{wt}(\langle ls \rangle \mathbin{+\!\!+} pss'))\ .$$

In the last step, we replaced the bound variable pss by a concatenation $\langle ls \rangle \mathbin{+\!\!+} pss'$, using as justification that pss was not empty. The step is valid because the non-empty lists pss and the pairs ls, pss' can be put into 1-to-1 correspondence.

To avoid proliferating names, we now rename pss' to pss again, and continue:

$$= (\sqcap ls, pss \mid \quad \mathsf{fl}(\langle ls \rangle \mathbin{+\!\!+} pss) = ws{\downarrow}j \wedge \mathsf{ok}(\langle ls \rangle \mathbin{+\!\!+} pss)$$
$$\cdot\ \mathsf{wt}(\langle ls \rangle \mathbin{+\!\!+} pss))$$
$$= \text{``by definition of fl and ok''}$$

$$(\sqcap ls, pss \mid \left\{ \begin{array}{l} ls \mathbin{+\!\!+} \mathsf{fl}\, pss = ws{\downarrow}j \\ \mathsf{ok}\, pss \\ 0 < \sum ls \le M \end{array} \right. \cdot\ \mathsf{wt}(\langle ls \rangle \mathbin{+\!\!+} pss))\ .$$

Now we replace ls by its length k. Again, there is a 1-to-1 correspondence, since for any k, there is only one ls of length k satisfying $ls \mathbin{+\!\!+} \mathsf{fl}\, pss = ws{\downarrow}j$. That gives

$$= \text{``replacing } ls \text{ by its length } k\text{''}$$

$$(\sqcap k, pss \mid \left\{ \begin{array}{l} 0 < k \le N - j \\ \mathsf{fl}\, pss = ws{\downarrow}(j + k) \\ \mathsf{ok}\, pss \\ \sum ws{\downarrow}j{\uparrow}k \le M \end{array} \right. \cdot\ \mathsf{wt}(\langle ws{\downarrow}j{\uparrow}k \rangle \mathbin{+\!\!+} pss))\ .$$

Now we will use the definition of wt, but it is defined only for non-empty sequences! That means the case $k = N - j$, which makes pss empty, must be handled carefully.

If $\sum ws{\downarrow}j \le M$, then k can take the value $N - j$ in the distributed minimum above: $\sum ws{\downarrow}j{\uparrow}k \le M$ will be true even when $k = N - j$. But then pss will be empty, and the waste $\mathsf{wt}(\langle ws{\downarrow}j{\uparrow}k \rangle \mathbin{+\!\!+} pss)$ will be 0. Since all wastes are at least 0, the whole expression simplifies to that value:

$$= \mathbf{Case}\ \sum ws{\downarrow}j \le M$$
$$0\ .$$

In the other case, we can of course exclude $k = N - j$ since it is dealt with in the first case. We have then, by definition of wt,

$$= \mathbf{Case}\ \sum ws{\downarrow}j > M$$

$$(\sqcap k, pss \mid \left\{ \begin{array}{l} 0 < k < N - j \\ \mathsf{fl}\, pss = ws{\downarrow}(j + k) \\ \mathsf{ok}\, pss \\ \sum ws{\downarrow}j{\uparrow}k \le M \end{array} \right. \cdot \left\{ \begin{array}{l} M - \sum ws{\downarrow}j{\uparrow}k \\ \sqcup\ \ \mathsf{wt}\, pss \end{array} \right.)$$

$=$ "nesting the minima"
$$(\sqcap k \mid 0 < k < N - j \wedge \sum ws{\downarrow}j{\uparrow}k \leq M \cdot$$
$$(\sqcap pss \mid \mathsf{fl}\,pss = ws{\downarrow}(j + k) \wedge \mathsf{ok}\,pss \cdot$$
$$(M - \sum ws{\downarrow}j{\uparrow}k) \sqcup \mathsf{wt}\,pss))$$

$=$ "distributing $\sqcup$ out of $\sqcap$"
$$\left(\sqcap k \mid 0 < k < N - j \wedge \sum ws{\downarrow}j{\uparrow}k \leq M \cdot \right.$$
$$M - \sum ws{\downarrow}j{\uparrow}k$$
$$\left. \sqcup \; (\sqcup pss \mid \mathsf{fl}\,pss = ws{\downarrow}(j + k) \wedge \mathsf{ok}\,pss \cdot \mathsf{wt}\,pss)\right)$$

$=$ "definition of mw"
$$(\sqcap k \mid 0 < k < N - j \wedge \sum ws{\downarrow}j{\uparrow}k \leq M \cdot$$
$$(M - \sum ws{\downarrow}j{\uparrow}k) \sqcup \mathsf{mw}\,ws{\downarrow}(j + k))$$

$=$ "replace k by $k - j$"
$$(\sqcap k \mid j < k < N \wedge \sum ws[j{\to}k] \leq M \cdot$$
$$(M - \sum ws[j{\to}k]) \sqcup \mathsf{mw}(ws{\downarrow}k)) \;.$$

With the above, we have defined $\mathsf{mw}(ws{\downarrow}j)$ in terms of the minimum waste $\mathsf{mw}(ws{\downarrow}k)$ of shorter suffixes; we can now return to the development of the program. Since the range condition $\sum ws[j{\to}k] \leq M$ is less likely to be true for greater values of k, we start k at $j + 1$ and increase it. In our invariant also will be the sum s of the segment $ws[j{\to}k]$ considered so far.

The case distinction will be made *after* we have calculated the minimum above, since then the sum $\sum ws{\downarrow}j$ will be available in s. So we continue

(ii) $\sqsubseteq$ **var** $n, s : \mathbb{N} \cdot$
$$x, n, s : [I[j{\backslash}j + 1]\,,\; x = \mathsf{mw}(ws{\downarrow}j)]$$
$$\sqsubseteq X \widehat{=} \left(\sqcap k \mid \left\{\begin{array}{l} j < k < n \\ \sum ws[j{\to}k] \leq M \end{array}\right. \cdot \left\{\begin{array}{l} M - \sum ws[j{\to}k] \\ \sqcup \;\; \mathsf{mw}(ws{\downarrow}k) \end{array}\right.\right)$$
$$J \widehat{=} I[j{\backslash}j + 1] \wedge x = X \wedge s = \sum ws[j{\to}n] \wedge j + 1 \leq n \leq N \cdot$$
$$n, s, x := j + 1, ws[j], M\,;$$
$$n, s, x : [J\,,\; J \wedge (n = N \vee s > M)]\,; \qquad\qquad\qquad \triangleleft$$
$$\textbf{if } s \leq M \to x := 0$$
$$[\!]\;\; s > M \to \textbf{skip}$$
$$\textbf{fi}$$
$\sqsubseteq$ "invariant J, variant $N - n$"
$$\textbf{do } n \neq N \wedge s \leq M \to$$
$$s, x : [n \neq N \wedge s \leq M \wedge J\,,\; J[n{\backslash}n + 1]]\,; \qquad\qquad \triangleleft$$
$$n := n + 1$$
$$\textbf{od}$$
$\sqsubseteq s, x := s + ws[n], x \sqcap ((M - s) \sqcup sf[n]) \;.$

That completes the development of this section. In the next section we finish the job, finding not only the minimum waste but a paragraph that produces it.

20.3   Producing the even paragraph

Let the predicate ep, *even paragraph*, be defined as follows:

$$\text{ep } ws \ pss \ \hat{=} \ ws = pss = \langle \rangle \vee \begin{cases} \text{fl } pss = ws \\ \text{ok } pss \\ \text{wt } pss = \text{mw } ws \ . \end{cases}$$

We then have an abstract program for producing a minimum-waste paragraph of a sequence of lengths ws:

> **var** $ws : \text{seq}_N \ \mathbb{N}$;
> $\quad M : \mathbb{N}$;
> $\quad pss : \text{seq seq } \mathbb{N}$;
>
> **and** $ws \neq \langle \rangle \wedge (\forall \, w : ws \cdot 0 < w \leq M) \cdot$
>
> pss: $[\text{ep } ws \ pss]$.

This time we consider prefixes of ws; the even paragraph will be produced as we go. The invariant is 'if pss were extended by an even paragraph qss of the remaining text $ws{\downarrow}i$, the result $pss \,+\!\!+\, qss$ would be an even paragraph of the whole text ws'. Here is the first step:

$$\sqsubseteq \begin{cases} \mathbf{var} \ i : \mathbb{N} \\ I \ \hat{=} \ \begin{cases} (\forall \, qss \cdot \text{ep}(ws{\downarrow}i) \ qss \Rightarrow \text{ep } ws \ (pss \,+\!\!+\, qss)) \\ i \leq N \end{cases} \end{cases} .$$

> $i, pss := 0, \langle \rangle$;
> i, pss: $[I \ , \ I \wedge i = N]$ ◁
> $\sqsubseteq$ "invariant I, variant $N - i$"
> **do** $i \neq N \rightarrow$
> $\quad\quad i, pss$: $[i \neq N \ , \ I \ , \ i_0 < i]$ ◁
> **od** .

Unusually, increasing i above will not necessarily just be a matter of adding 1: the next line of pss could be longer than that. Instead, we introduce a variable j to find the new value of i; the next line of pss is then $ws[i{\rightarrow}j]$.

> $\sqsubseteq$ **var** $j : \mathbb{N}\cdot$
> j: $[i \neq N \wedge I \ ,$
> $\quad \left(\forall \, qss \cdot \begin{cases} \text{ep}(ws{\downarrow}j) \ qss \\ \Rightarrow \text{ep } ws \ (pss \,+\!\!+\, \langle ws[i{\rightarrow}j]\rangle \,+\!\!+\, qss) \end{cases} \right) \quad \Big];$ (iii)
> $\quad\quad\quad\quad\quad i < j \leq N$
> $i, pss := j, pss \,+\!\!+\, \langle ws[i{\rightarrow}j]\rangle$.

(iii) $\sqsubseteq$ "Exercise 20.1"

$$j\colon \left[\, i < N \;,\; \left(\forall\, qss \cdot \left\{ \begin{array}{l} \mathsf{ep}(ws{\downarrow}j)\ qss \\ \Rightarrow\ \mathsf{ep}(ws{\downarrow}i)\ (\langle ws[i{\rightarrow}j]\rangle +\!\!+ qss) \\ i < j \le N \end{array} \right. \right) \right]\,.$$

The program above finds a *first* line in a paragraph of $ws{\downarrow}i$ (which the development has shown to be the *next* line in a paragraph of ws). If we know the minimum waste of $ws{\downarrow}i$, and all its suffixes, then that line is easily found: its sum is less than M, and we must have either $j = N$ or

$$\mathsf{mw}(ws{\downarrow}i) \ge (M - \sum ws[i{\rightarrow}j]) \sqcup \mathsf{mw}(ws{\downarrow}j)\,.$$

That leads to

$$\sqsubseteq E(j) \; \hat{=} \; (M - \sum ws[i{\rightarrow}j]) \sqcup \mathsf{mw}(ws{\downarrow}j)\cdot$$

$$j\colon \left[\, i < N \;,\; \begin{array}{c} i < j \le N \\ \sum ws[i{\rightarrow}j] \le M \\ j = N \vee \mathsf{mw}(ws{\downarrow}i) \ge E(j) \end{array} \right]\,.$$

There may be several choices for the next line — but if we take the shortest, we know its length can be no greater than M. Thus we strengthen the postcondition:

$$\sqsubseteq j\colon \left[\, i < N \;,\; \begin{array}{c} i < j \le N \\ (\forall\, k \cdot i < k < j \Rightarrow \mathsf{mw}(ws{\downarrow}i) < E(k)) \\ j = N \vee \mathsf{mw}(ws{\downarrow}i) \ge E(j) \end{array} \right]\,.$$

Introducing a variable s to hold the length of the developing line (used in $E(j)$), we continue

$$\sqsubseteq \left\{ \begin{array}{l} \mathbf{var}\ s : \mathbb{N} \\ J \; \hat{=} \; \left\{ \begin{array}{l} i < j \le N \\ (\forall\, k \cdot i < k < j \Rightarrow \mathsf{mw}(ws{\downarrow}i) < E(k)) \cdot \\ s = \sum ws[i{\rightarrow}j] \end{array} \right. \end{array} \right.$$

$$\quad j, s\colon [\, i < N \;,\; J \wedge (j = N \vee \mathsf{mw}(ws{\downarrow}i) \ge E(j))]$$
$$\sqsubseteq\ j, s := i + 1, ws[i];$$
$$\quad j, s\colon [\, J \;,\; J \wedge (j = N \vee \mathsf{mw}(ws{\downarrow}i) \ge E(j))] \qquad\qquad \triangleleft$$
$$\sqsubseteq\ \text{"invariant } J\text{, variant } N - j\text{"}$$
$$\quad \mathbf{do}\ j \ne N \wedge \mathsf{mw}(ws{\downarrow}i) < E(j) \rightarrow$$
$$\qquad j, s := j + 1, s + ws[j]$$
$$\mathbf{od}\,.$$

And that completes the development — nearly. We still have the expressions $\mathsf{mw}(ws{\downarrow}i)$ and $\mathsf{mw}(ws{\downarrow}j)$ (in $E(j)$) in the guard of the iteration. But the program of Section 20.2 establishes

$$(\forall\, i \mid 0 \leq i \leq N \cdot \mathsf{mw}(ws{\downarrow}i) = sf[i])\ ,$$

and so by sequentially composing the two programs we can replace the guard with

$$j \neq N \wedge sf[i] < (M - s) \sqcup sf[j]\ .$$

And that does complete the development.

20.4   Exercises

Ex. 20.1 ♡   Recall Specification (iii) (p.205). Its postcondition says

> If the paragraph so far *pss* is extended by the line $ws[i{\rightarrow}j]$, and then by any even paragraph *qss* of what remains $ws{\downarrow}j$, the result is an even paragraph of the entire input *ws*.

The postcondition of its following refinement says

> The line $ws[i{\rightarrow}j]$, if extended by an even paragraph *qss* of what remains, is an even paragraph of the remaining input $ws{\downarrow}i$.

Explain informally why the refinement is valid, then check it rigorously using *strengthen postcondition* and *weaken precondition*.

Ex. 20.2   Collect the code developed in this chapter. Determine its time complexity in terms of M and N. Is it linear? Quadratic? Worse?
   Hint: The sum s must increase on each inner iteration.

Ex. 20.3 ♡   Although there may be several even paragraphs of a single sequence of words, the code we developed is deterministic. Where, in the development, was the nondeterminism removed?

Ex. 20.4 ♡   Modify the code of Exercise 20.2 so that, using the module of Figure 20.3, it actually reads and writes words from input and output. Your final program should not contain any variables of type **seq seq** $\cdots$ (except *css* within the module *Words*).
   Hint: Don't forget to account for spaces between words.

```
module Words;
    var css : seq seq CHAR;

    procedure GetWord (result w : ℕ)  ≙
    |[  var cs : seq CHAR·
        if   eof → w := 0
        []  ¬eof →
                input cs;
                css := css ⧺ ⟨cs⟩;
                w := #cs
        fi
    ]|;

    procedure PutWord
    ≙ output hd css;
        css := tl css;

    procedure PutLine
    ≙ output nl
end
```

The character nl takes output to a new line.

Figure 20.3 Input/output module for words

Chapter 21

Case study: The largest rectangle under a histogram

The case study of this chapter is a notoriously tricky development, and the several approaches to it include using auxiliary sequences or intermediate tree structures. Here however we use proper (not tail-) recursion, for which simple variables suffice.[1]

The problem is to find the area of the largest rectangle under a given histogram, as illustrated in Figures 21.1 and 21.2. The straightforward complexity of the problem is given by the number of possible bases for the rectangle ($\approx N^2$) times the cost of examining each to determine its height ($\approx N$) — a cubic algorithm, in other words.

A divide-and-conquer approach, in which we split the problem into smaller pieces, will lead us first to $N \log N$ complexity. But, with some effort, we shall do even better than that.

21.1   Laying the groundwork

Assume we have a sequence of non-negative integers $hs : \mathbf{seq}_N \mathbb{N}$ that represents a *histogram*, as in Figure 21.1, under which we are to find the largest rectangular area, as in Figure 21.2. Since the base of a largest rectangle is sufficient to determine it completely (since it should be as high as the histogram will allow), we consider the problem to be the finding of that base, represented below as a pair of indices l and h denoting its start and end:

$$(\sqcup l, h : \mathbb{N} \mid l \leq h \leq N \cdot (h - l) \times \sqcap hs[l{\rightarrow}h]) \ .$$

In fact, we will need to be more general, looking for largest rectangular areas under subsegments $hs[i{\rightarrow}j]$ of the histogram; thus we define natural number $\mathsf{lr}(i, j)$ to be the largest rectangular area under the histogram $hs[i{\rightarrow}j]$ —

---

[1]Naturally the solutions are related, since each approach more or less encodes the structures found in the others.

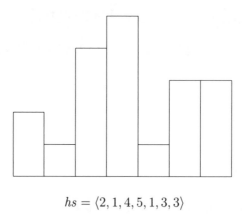

$$hs = \langle 2, 1, 4, 5, 1, 3, 3 \rangle$$

Figure 21.1 Example histogram

$$\mathsf{lr}(i,j) \;\mathrel{\hat{=}}\; (\sqcup l, h \mid i \leq l \leq h \leq j \cdot (h - l) \times \sqcap hs[l{\rightarrow}h])$$

— and with that specify our program

$$a := \mathsf{lr}(0, N) \;, \qquad\qquad\qquad\qquad\qquad\qquad (\mathrm{i})$$

in which the variable $a : \mathbb{N}$ will contain the result.

21.2   Divide and conquer

A divide-and-conquer approach to this problem suggests finding a division of hs into two pieces such that solutions to the pieces can be combined into a solution for the whole. In fact we shall be especially interested in splitting at minimum values of hs, because of the following property of lr:

> If $hs[min]$ is a minimum value in hs, then the largest area of a rectangle under hs is the maximum of
>
> 1. the largest under $hs[0{\rightarrow}min]$,
> 2. the largest under $hs[min + 1{\rightarrow}N]$ and
> 3. the area given by base N and height $hs[min]$.

Thus we need only find a minimum element $hs[min]$ of hs, and then solve recursively the subproblems $hs[0{\rightarrow}min]$ and $hs[min+1{\rightarrow}N]$ on either side. The property above then gives us the solution for the whole.

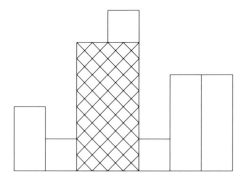

Rectangle under $\langle 2, 1, 4, 5, 1, 3, 3 \rangle$

Figure 21.2 Largest rectangle

A rough estimate for the average time required by the above approach, in terms of N the size of hs, gives the recurrence

$$\text{time}\, N \leq N + 2 \times \text{time}(N/2)\ ,$$

which leads to $\text{time}\, N \preceq N \log N$. (Think of the fact that the sequence can be halved approximately $\log N$ times, and the time taken altogether on each level is still proportional to the original N.)

With some iteration as well we can do even better than $N \log N$, however. We begin by seeking to maintain a 'running maximum' as longer and longer initial segments of hs are considered. Our first step is therefore the usual

$$\text{(i)} \quad \sqsubseteq \; \textbf{var}\ i : \mathbb{N}\text{\textbf{.}}$$

$$a, i := 0, 0;$$
$$\textbf{do}\ i \neq N \rightarrow$$
$$\qquad a, i \colon [i \neq N\ ,\ i \leq N \wedge a = \text{lr}(0, i)\ ,\ i_0 < i] \qquad\qquad \text{(ii)}$$
$$\textbf{od}\ .$$

But now we become more adventurous: bearing the property above in mind, we might be interested in increasing i in the iteration body by more than just 1. If $hs[i]$ becomes a minimum value for the longer segment — that is, if i is increased to some j perhaps greater than $i + 1$, and we have that $hs[i]$ is a minimum value of the segment $hs[0{\rightarrow}j]$ — then it is particularly easy to re-establish $a = \text{lr}(0, j)$, provided we can calculate $\text{lr}(i + 1, j)$ as required by Item 2 of the property. Thus we proceed

(ii) $\sqsubseteq$ **var** $b, j : \mathbb{N} \cdot$

$$\left[\begin{array}{c} b, j \\ \hline i < N \\ \hline i < j \leq N \\ hs[i] \leq hs[0 \rightarrow j] \\ b = \mathsf{lr}(i+1, j) \end{array}\right] ;$$

$a, i := a \sqcup b \sqcup j \times hs[i], j$.

We have of necessity adopted an alternative layout for specifications in which the components appear in the same order, but vertically instead of horizontally, and new line is interpreted as conjunction.[2]

The first command sets j as suggested, and the second re-establishes the invariant.

The conjunct $b = \mathsf{lr}(i+1, j)$ in the first command is where we foreshadow a recursion, since it is effectively solving our original problem but on a smaller segment. Given that $a = \mathsf{lr}(0, i)$ (which was Item 1), that $b = \mathsf{lr}(i+1, j)$ (given in Item 2) and the explicit calculation $j \times hs[i]$, it can be seen that the assignment command does re-establish the invariant $a = \mathsf{lr}(0, i)$ for the now-larger i.

But it is not as simple as that, unfortunately; we do have a problem. The first command above is infeasible, because its postcondition implies $hs[i] \leq hs[0 \rightarrow i]$, something which assignments only to b and j cannot affect.

21.3   Strengthening invariants to restore feasibility

The dead end is only apparent. If $hs[i] \leq hs[0 \rightarrow j]$ is in the postcondition, but cannot necessarily be established by changing only b and j, then the 'missing conjunct' $hs[i] \leq hs[0 \rightarrow i]$ must come from the precondition. How do we put it there? (*Strengthening* the precondition is not an example of refinement!)

A similar problem occurs in proofs by mathematical induction, when the proof that the inductive hypothesis holds at $i+1$, given its truth at i, does not go through. If the truth at i does imply truth at $i+1$, but the proof cannot be found, then either the approach is unnecessarily difficult or the mathematician insufficiently skilled. For us that would correspond to a *feasible* iteration body that we nevertheless could not see how to develop further. If on the other hand the truth at i does *not* imply truth at $i + 1$, then the inductive hypothesis may be too weak; strengthening it makes its assumption at i more powerful, but the obligation to re-prove it at $i + 1$ becomes accordingly more difficult. That corresponds to an iteration body that is *in*feasible: strengthening the invariant then strengthens the precondition (as we wanted, and makes development easier), but also strengthens the postcondition (making development more difficult).

In both cases, induction and iteration, the necessary strengthening is usually not

---

[2]That is rather like a Z *schema*, but with a frame.

apparent until the first attempt at proof or development has already failed; and thus excursions like the above in Section 21.2 are not fruitless. In our case we have discovered that we need the extra conjunct $hs[i] \leq hs[0{\to}i]$ in the precondition, and so we simply place it in the invariant and try again: our iteration body (ii) becomes (ii') below, and we resume from there, performing the same first steps as before:

$$\sqsubseteq \left[\begin{array}{c} \dfrac{a,\,i}{\begin{array}{c} i \neq N \\ \hline i \leq N \\ a = \mathsf{lr}(0,i) \\ hs[i] \leq hs[0{\to}i] \\ \hline i_0 < i \end{array}} \end{array}\right] \tag{ii'}$$

$$\sqsubseteq \mathbf{var}\ b,j : \mathbb{N}\cdot$$

$$\left[\begin{array}{c} \dfrac{b,\,j}{\begin{array}{c} i < N \\ a = \mathsf{lr}(0,i) \\ hs[i] \leq hs[0{\to}i] \\ \hline i < j \leq N \\ a = \mathsf{lr}(0,i) \\ hs[j] \leq hs[0{\to}j] \\ hs[i] \leq hs[0{\to}j] \\ b = \mathsf{lr}(i+1,j) \end{array}} \end{array}\right]\ ; \qquad\qquad \triangleleft$$

$$a,i := a \sqcup b \sqcup j \times hs[i],\, j$$

$$\sqsubseteq \left[\begin{array}{c} \dfrac{b,\,j}{\begin{array}{c} i < N \\ \hline i < j \leq N \\ hs[i] \leq hs[i+1{\to}j] \\ hs[j] \leq hs[i] \\ b = \mathsf{lr}(i+1,j) \end{array}} \end{array}\right]\ . \tag{iii}$$

The only non-immediate reasoning above relies on the implication

$$hs[i] \leq hs[0{\to}i] \wedge hs[i] \leq hs[i+1{\to}j] \wedge hs[j] \leq hs[i]$$
$$\Rightarrow\ hs[j] \leq hs[0{\to}j] \wedge hs[i] \leq hs[0{\to}j]\ .$$

Remember that $hs[j]$ lies just beyond the segment $hs[0{\to}j]$, and that the first conjunct $hs[i] \leq hs[0{\to}i]$ of the antecedent comes from the precondition.

The interesting thing about the last step is that a possible recursion has popped up: our original problem is an instance of (iii), provided we define 'formally' that $hs[-1]$ and $hs[N]$ are both -1 (any negative number would do). That is because setting i to -1 initially will force (iii) to establish $j = N$: the postcondition contains $hs[j] \leq hs[i]$, and we know that $hs[0{\to}N] \geq 0$, and j cannot be -1. (It must be strictly greater than i.) That is, the postcondition then implies

$$b = \mathsf{lr}(0,N)\ ,$$

making b the value we are looking for.

That is all the excuse we need for a recursive procedure.

21.4   Introducing recursion

Because our original problem has reappeared in (iii), we now aim explicitly for recursion by making it a procedure. With some foresight,[3] we provide three parameters:

$$\textbf{procedure } \mathit{Hist} \textbf{ (value } i : \mathbb{Z}; \textbf{ result } b, j : \mathbb{Z})$$
$$\mathrel{\widehat{=}} \text{(iii)} .$$

Since our problem is now more general than before, however, we will need a generalisation of the property we exploited earlier; it is

$$\begin{aligned}
\mathsf{lr}(l, h) &= 0, \text{ if } l = h; \text{ and} \\
\mathsf{lr}(l, h) &= \mathsf{lr}(l, i) \sqcup \mathsf{lr}(i + 1, h) \sqcup hs[i] \times (h - l) , \\
&\quad \text{provided } l \le i < h \wedge hs[i] \le hs[l \!\to\! h].
\end{aligned}$$

Our original version of this simply had $l = 0$ and $h = N$.

Carrying on, the variant is i, and it is already (in the precondition of (iii) above) strictly bounded above by N:

(iii) $\sqsubseteq$ **variant** I is i·

$$\left[\begin{array}{c} b, j \\ \hline i = I < N \\ \hline i < j \le N \\ hs[i] \le hs[i + 1 \!\to\! j] \\ hs[j] \le hs[i] \\ b = \mathsf{lr}(i + 1, j) . \end{array}\right]$$

And, forewarned by our having had to strengthen the invariant above, we choose here an invariant 'stronger than the obvious' in that it includes the conjunct $hs[j] \le hs[i + 1 \!\to\! j]$. The iteration will establish (the negation of its guard) that $hs[j] \le hs[i]$, giving

$\sqsubseteq$ "invariant is middle formula of iteration body"

---

[3]The prophesy is only apparent, since we would later discover in any case what the parameters should be.

$b, j := 0, i + 1;$
do $hs[j] > hs[i] \rightarrow$

$$\left[\begin{array}{c} b, j \\ \hline hs[j] > hs[i] \\ \hline I < j \leq N \\ hs[i] \leq hs[i + 1 \rightarrow j] \\ hs[j] \leq hs[i + 1 \rightarrow j] \\ b = \mathsf{lr}(i + 1, j) \\ \hline j_0 < j \end{array}\right] \qquad \triangleleft$$

od
$\sqsubseteq$ **var** $c, k : \mathbb{N}\cdot$

$$\left[\begin{array}{c} c, k \\ \hline I < j < N \\ \hline j < k \leq N \\ hs[j] \leq hs[j + 1 \rightarrow k] \\ hs[k] \leq hs[j] \\ c = \mathsf{lr}(j + 1, k) \end{array}\right] ; \qquad \triangleleft$$
$b, j := b \sqcup c \sqcup (k - i - 1) \times hs[j], k .$

It has to be admitted that the second step above conceals a certain amount of detailed working out of implications. But it was not altogether necessary to see beforehand that they *would* work out, since the first stage of our development had already suggested that we proceed that way, with the following assignment given just a transliteration of the one we met before.

One genuinely obscure step, however, is the apparent strengthening of the pre-condition, from $j \leq N$ to $j < N$. That is necessary to match the offered recursion, where $i < N$ occurs in the precondition; and it is justified by the fact that if $hs[j] > hs[i]$, then j cannot be N.

And that's it: we finish off with

$\sqsubseteq$ *Hist* $(j, c, k) .$

21.5 Wrapping up

We have now reached code, if by a slightly circuitous route. The first stage of the development produced an iteration body which generalised the original problem; with that encouragement, we were able to continue the development by introducing a recursion. Rather than calling the procedure within the iteration, however, we now exploit the generalisation by discarding the outer iteration, replacing the whole thing by a procedure call. In other words, we redo the first part of our development in a stroke:

$a := \mathsf{lr}(0, N)$

procedure *Hist* (**value** $i : \mathbb{Z}$; **result** $b, j : \mathbb{Z}$) $\triangleq$
$[\![$ **var** $c, k : \mathbb{N}\cdot$
$\quad b, j := 0, i + 1;$
$\quad$ **do** $hs[j] > hs[i] \rightarrow$
$\qquad$ *Hist* $(j, c, k);$
$\qquad b, j := b \sqcup c \sqcup (k - i - 1) \times hs[j], k$
$\quad$ **od**
$]\!]$

with 'main program' $[\![$ **var** $j : \mathbb{Z} \cdot Hist\ (-1, a, j)\ ]\!]$.

Figure 21.3 Collected code.

$$\sqsubseteq \begin{cases} \text{assume } hs[-1] = hs[N] = -1 \\ \textbf{var } j : \mathbb{N} \end{cases}.$$

$\boxed{\text{Specification (iii) above}}$
$\sqsubseteq Hist\ (-1, a, j)$.

The declaration of j is necessary only to supply the third parameter of the procedure call: the result returned there is not used.

That concludes the development, and the code is shown in Figure 21.3. Exercise 21.1 investigates whether all this effort has improved the execution time over the straightforward $N \log N$.

21.6   Exercises

Ex. 21.1 ♡   What is the running time of the algorithm, in terms of the size of hs? Count calls of *Hist*. *Hint*: What values of i are passed successively to *Hist* as the algorithm executes?

Ex. 21.2 ♡   Specify and develop a program that finds 'the largest true rectangle' in a two-dimensional array of Boolean values: the largest area of any rectangle, within the array, that contains only **true** values.

Ex. 21.3 ♡   Specify and develop a program that finds 'the largest true *square*' in a two-dimensional array of Boolean values: the largest area of any square, within the array, that contains only **true** values. *Hint*: There may be a much simpler approach than was required for the largest true rectangle. What is the essential property of a square that prevents that simpler approach working for rectangles as well?

Chapter 22

Case study: A mail system

This final case study contains little in the way of intricate algorithm development, and not a single iterative invariant: it is a case study in specification itself.

In our earlier examples we did not have to worry about the construction of the specification: it was given at the outset, usually of a program fragment or a single procedure. In this chapter however we concern ourselves with the specification of a whole 'system', which in our terms is a module encapsulating a state and all operations on it. The increased size and possible complexity means that we cannot take even our starting point for granted.

Electronic mail systems, our subject, have their main features in common but vary a lot in the detail. Thus our initial specification, in Figure 22.1, is more or less just the bare minimum that electronic mail could be said to comprise. But the immediately following two sections nevertheless discuss deficiencies apparent even at that level of abstraction, and propose design changes to avoid them.

Design changes are seldom without hazard, and several 'opportunities' arise on our way to Figure 22.10, the 'final' specification, for changes that if implemented would sooner or later prove disastrous. The dangers are revealed by exhaustive — and sometimes exhausting — application of the rigorous techniques now at our disposal: assumptions, coercions, refinement and above all data refinement.

The message of those sections is twofold: that even the apparently simple Figure 22.10 is too complex a specification to accept without some degree of rigorous analysis; and that one way of producing even a simple specification is to develop it in small steps from one that is simpler still.

The second part of the chapter makes the first few development steps, from Figure 22.10 towards a conventional implementation of electronic mail in terms of asynchronous delivery of message packets. The concurrency involved is limited, but still enough to capture the notion of system actions carried out 'in the background' without the participation of the users.

The result of the development, delivered in Figure 22.15, is laden with the details of headers, unique identifiers, packets and transmission delay — a very long way from the simple beginnings to which shortly we turn.

A warning is appropriate before we start: much of the low-level working is detailed enough to skip at first reading, and just the beginning and end of 'refinement chains' may be sufficient in many cases to maintain the continuity of the narrative.

22.1   A first specification

The system will provide just three procedures for passing messages:

- *Send*: A message and set of intended recipients are supplied; a 'unique' identifier is returned for that transmission. The identifier is used to refer to the message while it remains in the system.
- *Receive*: The set of identifiers is returned for mail that has been received by a given user, but not yet read.
- *Read*: The message text corresponding to a given identifier is presented to its recipient, and the message is removed from the system.

Generally the system works as follows. A user *me* sends a message *msg* to a group *tos* of other users using Procedure *Send*; its result parameter *id* provides a unique reference to that transmission, which could be used by the sender, for example, to enquire after the status of a message or even to cancel it. (See Exercises 22.1 and 22.2.)

Procedure *Receive* is called by potential recipients who wish to know whether mail has been sent to them. Its result is a set *ids* of transmission identifiers that refer to messages sent to them that they have not yet read.

Supplying an identifier to Procedure *Read* will return the message text associated with the identifier, and delete that message from the system.

Naturally the above brief description leaves a lot unsaid. Can a user send a message to himself? What happens for example if an invalid identifier is supplied to *Read*? Can a message be read by a user to whom it was *not* sent? Does the deleting of a message, once read in *Read*, remove copies of it sent to other recipients?

It is extremely unlikely that an informal specification like the one above, no matter how extensive, could ever answer all such questions. Even rigorous specifications, like the one we shall see shortly, are limited. But they do have a significant advantage: their terms of reference are unambiguous, and within their declared terms their answers are unambiguous[1] as well.

To construct an abstract module consistent with the informal description above — our version of 'rigorous specification' here — we begin by choosing types. Let users come from a type *Usr*, messages from *Msg* and identifiers from *Id*. The state of the system could then be given by the two variables

---

[1]We regard nondeterminism in a specification as an unambiguous indication of freedom in the design.

$$msgs : Id \nrightarrow Msg \quad \text{and} \quad sent : Usr \leftrightarrow Id \ ,$$

in which the partial function *msgs* associates message identifiers with the corresponding message text, and the relation *sent* records the (identifiers of) messages sent but not yet read. By making *sent* a proper relation we allow many users (many possible recipients) to be associated with a single identifier: that is how we shall deal with 'broadcasts', in which the same message is sent to many different users.

For the procedure *Send* we have the following parameters: which user is sending the message; the message itself; to which users it is being sent; and (as a result parameter) the identifier that subsequently can be used to refer to it. Here is the procedure heading:

> **procedure** *Send* (**value** *me* : *Usr*; *msg* : *Msg*; *tos* : **set** *Usr*;
> **result** *id* : *Id*) .

Within the procedure we first have a new identifier selected, which then will be associated both with the message and with the set of recipients. We use simply $i\colon [i \notin \mathsf{dom}\ msgs]$ for the selection, on the understanding that *Id* must be an infinite set so that the supply of unused identifiers can never 'run out'. That does raise several problems — but its simplicity is so appealing that we shall do it nevertheless.

The first problem is that the above specification is infeasible: if executed in a state in which $\mathsf{dom}\ msgs = Id$ (meaning 'all identifiers in use'), its postcondition is false. Informally we note however that if *Id* is infinite the module can never reach such a state (provided *msgs* is initially empty); more rigorously, we could argue as in Exercise 17.14, showing that $\mathsf{dom}\ msgs \in \mathbf{finset}\ Id$ is invariant for the module, and by data refinement therefore being able to introduce $\mathsf{dom}\ msgs \subset Id$ into the precondition.

The second problem, however, is that we cannot after all provide an infinite type *Id*: the identifiers may have to be recovered.[2] But we will see much about that later, and so for now leave things as they are.

Once the identifier is selected it is a straightforward matter to construct the necessary links to the recipients and the message text, and the body of the procedure is as a whole

> $id\colon [id \notin \mathsf{dom}\ msgs]$;
> $msgs[id] := msg$;
> $sent := sent \cup (tos \times \{id\})$.

Note that the assignment $msgs[id] := msg$ is just an abbreviation for the lengthier $msg := msg[id := msg]$, and in particular that *id* need not be in the domain of

---

[2] It is not altogether certain that they must, since for example using 64-bit unique identifiers would be sufficient to support a traffic of one message per millisecond for more than 500 million years. But other resource implications may make recovery of identifiers appropriate nevertheless.

msgs for that to be meaningful. (See Exercise 9.14; in fact the previous command ensures that *id* is *not* in the domain of *msgs*.)

Note also that in this simple system we are not bothering to record the sender of the message.

For the procedure *Receive* we need only return for user *me* the set of identifiers of messages waiting in *sent* to be read, and for that we use $ids := sent[me]$. (Ignoring for now the warning in Section 9.6.2, that unlikely-looking application $sent[me]$ of a relation to an element we take as an abbreviation for $\{i : Id \mid (me, i) \in sent\}$.)

Finally, procedure *Read* must retrieve a message, given its identifier, and here we deal with some of the questions raised earlier. Suppose user *me* supplies identifier *id* legitimately — that is, that (me, id) is an element of *sent*, meaning that *me* is one of its intended recipients: then the message to be returned is found in *msgs*, and $msg := msgs[id]$ will retrieve it. But if the identifier *id* is not legitimate for *me*, what then? Making 'legitimacy' a precondition of the procedure (we need only include the assumption $\{(me, id) \in sent\}$ as its first command) would relieve the implementor of the obligation to deal with such matters: the procedure would simply abort if the request were not legitimate.

A more forgiving design would insist on termination in any case (not aborting, therefore); but it would allow any message whatsoever to be returned for illegitimate requests. That ranges from the helpful 'Identifier does not refer to a message that has been received.' through the cryptic '`MSGERR BAD ID`', finally to the mischievous option of returning likely-looking but wholly invented messages that were never sent. (That last could be useful if one user is suspected of trying to read messages intended for others.) Thus we use the specification

$$msg: [(me, id) \in sent \Rightarrow msg = msgs[id]] \ ,$$

leaving as the last detail the removal of the message from the system. The command $sent := sent - \{(me, id)\}$ does that, with the set subtraction as usual having no effect on *sent* if the pair $\{(me, id)\}$ is not there.

Straightforward initialisation to 'the system is empty' gives us finally the module of Figure 22.1.

22.2   Reuse of identifiers

We considered briefly above the possible implementation problems caused by our use of $id: [id \notin \mathsf{dom}\ msgs]$ in *Send*: that an unending supply of identifiers is required. Looking at *Read* in Figure 22.1, however, we can see that once a message has been read by all of its intended recipients, the antecedent $(me, id) \in sent \Rightarrow \cdots$ of the first command will never again be true, and so subsequent calls for the same identifier need not refer to *msgs* — the message texts can simply be invented. Thus, provided that at the end of *Read* we have $id \notin \mathsf{ran}\ sent$ (because the last (me, id) pair has just been removed), we can remove (id, msg) from *msgs*. That is

module *MailSys*
    var *msgs* : *Id* $\nrightarrow$ *Msg*;
        sent : *Usr* $\leftrightarrow$ *Id*·

    procedure *Send* (**value** *me* : *Usr*; *msg* : *Msg*; *tos* : **set** *Usr*;
                       result *id* : *Id*)
  $\hat{=}$ *id*: $[id \notin \mathsf{dom}\ msgs]$;
    msgs[*id*] := *msg*;
    sent := *sent* $\cup$ (*tos* $\times$ {*id*});

    procedure *Receive* (**value** *me* : *Usr*; **result** *ids* : **set** *Id*)
  $\hat{=}$ *ids* := *sent*[*me*];

    procedure *Read* (**value** *me* : *Usr*; *id* : *Id*; **result** *msg* : *Msg*)
  $\hat{=}$ *msg*: $[(me, id) \in sent \Rightarrow msg = msgs[id]]$;
    sent := *sent* $-$ {(*me*, *id*)};

    initially *msgs* = *sent* = {}
end

Figure 22.1 Initial specification of mail system

---

    procedure *Read* (**value** *me* : *Usr*; *id* : *Id*; **result** *msg* : *Msg*)
  $\hat{=}$ *msg*: $[(me, id) \in sent \Rightarrow msg = msgs[id]]$;
    sent := *sent* $-$ {(*me*, *id*)};
    msgs := ($\mathsf{ran}\ sent$) $\lhd$ *msgs* $\lhd$

Figure 22.2 Attempted recovery of *Id*'s

---

done with the $\lhd$-marked command in the revised *Read* shown in Figure 22.2, which removes all such pairs at once.

But on what basis have we been saying 'should' and 'can'? Are we changing the specification, or are we merely refining the original module of Figure 22.1? How do we find out?

The effect of the change is to make the state component *msgs* a smaller function than before, taking care however never to delete identifiers still in ran *sent*. We are therefore led to consider a data refinement in which the abstract variable is *msgs*, the concrete is *msgs'*, say, and the coupling invariant is

$$msgs' = (\text{ran } sent) \lhd msgs . \tag{22.1}$$

(In all of the data refinements of this chapter we shall use 'primed' names for concrete variables; when the result of the data refinement is presented (and thus the abstract variables are gone), we simply remove the primes. That will help prevent a proliferation of names.)

We begin our data refinement with the last command of *Read*:

$$sent := sent - \{(me, id)\}$$

becomes "*augment assignment 17.8*"

$$\{msgs' = (\text{ran } sent) \lhd msgs\};$$
$$sent, msgs' := sent - \{(me, id)\}, ?;$$
$$[msgs' = (\text{ran } sent) \lhd msgs]$$

$\sqsubseteq$ "see below"

$$\{msgs' = (\text{ran } sent) \lhd msgs\};$$
$$sent := sent - \{(me, id)\};$$
$$[(\text{ran } sent) \lhd msgs' = (\text{ran } sent) \lhd msgs] ;$$
$$msgs' := (\text{ran } sent) \lhd msgs'$$

$\sqsubseteq$ "see below"

$$\{msgs' = (\text{ran } sent) \lhd msgs\};$$
$$\left[\begin{array}{l} (\text{ran}(sent - \{(me, id)\})) \lhd msgs' \\ = \;\; (\text{ran}(sent - \{(me, id)\})) \lhd msgs \end{array} \right];$$
$$sent := sent - \{(me, id)\};$$
$$msgs' := (\text{ran } sent) \lhd msgs'$$

$\sqsubseteq$ "*remove coercion 17.20 mainly*"

$$sent := sent - \{(me, id)\};$$
$$msgs' := (\text{ran } sent) \lhd msgs' .$$

Thus $msgs' := (\text{ran } sent) \lhd msgs'$ has appeared, as desired.

The comments 'see below' refer to the first of the following two laws, used for moving coercions 'forward' through a program:

Law 22.1 <u>advance coercion</u>

$$w := E \; [post] \quad = \quad [post[w \backslash E]] \;\; w := E .$$

$\square$

Law 22.2 <u>advance assumption</u>

$$w := E \; \{pre\} \quad = \quad \{pre[w \backslash E]\} \;\; w := E .$$

$\square$

Law 22.1 is often used to move a coercion forward through a program until it is 'cancelled' by an earlier, and weaker, assumption (as in *remove coercion 17.20*, given that it is a refinement to weaken an assumption).

For the rest of the module, things are straightforward until finally we reach the first command of *Send*. There, we have

$id\colon [id \notin \mathsf{dom}\ msgs]$

$becomes$ "*augment specification* 17.6"

$$\left[\begin{array}{c} id, msgs' \\ \hline msgs' = (\mathsf{ran}\ sent) \lhd msgs \\ \hline msgs' = (\mathsf{ran}\ sent) \lhd msgs \\ id \notin \mathsf{dom}\ msgs \end{array}\right]$$

$=$ "$msgs,\ sent$ not in frame, thus $msgs'$ cannot change"

$id\colon [msgs' = (\mathsf{ran}\ sent) \lhd msgs\ ,\ id \notin \mathsf{dom}\ msgs]$

$becomes$ "*diminish specification* 17.12"

$$\left[\begin{array}{c} id \\ \hline (\exists\ msgs \cdot msgs' = (\mathsf{ran}\ sent) \lhd msgs) \\ \hline (\forall\ msgs_0 \cdot msgs' = (\mathsf{ran}\ sent) \lhd msgs_0 \Rightarrow id \notin \mathsf{dom}\ msgs_0) \end{array}\right]$$

$=$ "simplify precondition"

$$\left[\begin{array}{c} id \\ \hline \mathsf{dom}\ msgs' \subseteq \mathsf{ran}\ sent \\ \hline (\forall\ msgs_0 \cdot msgs' = (\mathsf{ran}\ sent) \lhd msgs_0 \Rightarrow id \notin \mathsf{dom}\ msgs_0) \end{array}\right]$$

$=$ "simplify postcondition"[3]

$id\colon [\mathsf{dom}\ msgs' \subseteq \mathsf{ran}\ sent\ ,\ id \in \mathsf{ran}\ sent - \mathsf{dom}\ msgs']$.

We have been reasoning with equality rather than refinement $\sqsubseteq$, because we want to be sure of finding a concrete command if there is one. (Using $\sqsubseteq$ we might accidentally introduce infeasible behaviour and thus miss a data refinement that would actually have been acceptable.)

In the last step, refinement $\sqsubseteq$ is not difficult to show. (The antecedent gives $\mathsf{dom}\ msgs' = \mathsf{ran}\ sent \cap \mathsf{dom}\ msgs_0$, and thus that $\mathsf{ran}\ sent - \mathsf{dom}\ msgs'$ and $\mathsf{dom}\ msgs_0$ are disjoint.) But for the equality we need also the reverse refinement $\sqsupseteq$; for that we choose an arbitrary $m\colon Msg$ and define $large \mathrel{\widehat{=}} Id \times \{m\}$, whose domain is all of Id. Taking $msgs_0$ to be $msgs' \cup (\mathsf{ran}\ sent) \lhd large$ satisfies the antecedent, and the consequent is then equivalent to $id \in \mathsf{ran}\ sent - \mathsf{dom}\ msgs'$.

But alas it has all in any case been for nothing, since our conclusion is *not* feasible: the precondition allows $\mathsf{dom}\ msgs' = \mathsf{ran}\ sent$, making the postcondition false. Not having shown refinement with this particular coupling invariant does not of course mean that no other would work; but it does encourage us to look more closely at whether we *are* after all performing refinement.

In fact we are not proposing a refinement: the concrete module can return the same id from *Send* on separate occasions, which is something the abstract module cannot do. But does it really matter? See Figure 22.3 (and Exercise 22.3).

---

[3]Some of these comments conceal quite a lot of non-trivial predicate calculation, in this case discussed below. Similarly, 'routine' steps in engineering design sometimes generate quite tough integrals to be calculated. But the *principles* remain simple.

Persistent problems with electronic funds transfer led to chaos recently in the financial markets. The cause was traced to code in which the ordinary electronic mail system had been used to generate the unique identifiers needed for funds transfers.

Noticing that the specification of the mail system guarenteed never to repeat an identifier, a programmer had obtained them as needed by broadcasting null messages to no-one. (Such 'empty broadcasts' were, not surprisingly, particularly efficient and generated no network traffic.)

The mail system originally was implemented with such a large set of possible identifiers it was thought they would never run out. Use grew so rapidly, however, that recently the system was upgraded to recover old identifiers — yet it was not verified that the new system was a refinement of the original, and in fact it was not. Had the absence of refinement been noticed, the well-established principles of the Institute of Systems and Software Engineering would then have required a routine check to be made for dependencies on the original behaviour.

The institutions affected are suing for damages; meanwhile the financial community waits anxiously for other effects to come to light.

Figure 22.3

22.3   A second specification: reuse

We are forced to admit that reusing identifiers requires a *change* in the specification that is *not* a refinement of it. Having to accept therefore that we are still in the 'design stage', we consider a simpler change with the same effect: we leave *Read* in its original state, changing *Send* instead so that 'new' identifiers are chosen in fact simply outside the range of *sent* (since it is precisely the identifiers in *sent* that refer to messages not yet read by all recipients). The result is shown in Figure

module *MailSys*
    var *msgs* : *Id* ↦ *Msg*;
       sent : *Usr* ↔ *Id*·

    procedure *Send* (**value** *me* : *Usr*; *msg* : *Msg*; *tos* : **set** *Usr*;
                     result *id* : *Id*)
   ≙ *id*: [*id* ∉ ran *sent*] ;   ◁
     msgs[*id*] : = *msg*;
     sent : = *sent* ∪ (*tos* × {*id*});

    procedure *Receive* (**value** *me* : *Usr*; **result** *ids* : **set** *Id*)
   ≙ *ids* : = *sent*[*me*];

    procedure *Read* (**value** *me* : *Usr*; *id* : *Id*; **result** *msg* : *Msg*)
   ≙ *msg*: [(*me*, *id*) ∈ *sent* ⇒ *msg* = *msgs*[*id*]] ;
     sent : = *sent* − {(*me*, *id*)};

    initially *msgs* = *sent* = {}
end

Figure 22.4 Reuse of identifiers

22.4, with the altered command marked.

A slightly unhelpful aspect of this new specification, and of the earlier attempt, now comes to light: it is that the reuse of identifiers is enabled by *Read* as soon as (*me*, *id*) is removed from *sent*. In an eventual implementation that would probably require communication, in some form, from the receiver back to the sender. Our first specification did not require that, since the generation of identifiers was managed locally in *Send*, an essentially self-contained activity.

A second unrealistic aspect of this specification is that messages arrive instantly at the destination: a *Receive* no matter how quickly after a *Send* will return the identifier of the newly sent message, and this too is unlikely to be implementable in practice.

Thus we are led to consider a third version of our specification.

22.4   A third specification: delay

In order to allow delay between sending a message and receiving it, one might think of altering *Receive* as shown in Figure 22.5: only some, not necessarily all, of

procedure *Receive* (**value** *me* : *Usr*; **result** *ids* : **set** *Id*)
   $\widehat{=}$ *ids*: [*ids* $\subseteq$ *sent*[*me*]]   ◁

Figure 22.5 Attempt at specifying delayed receipt

the identifiers of sent messages are returned by *Receive*. The rest are 'in transit'.

But if the subset returned is chosen afresh on each occasion, then messages could be received only later to be 'unreceived' again. In order to specify that once a message is received it stays received, we must introduce an extra variable *recd* that records which messages have been received already. That would be necessary in any case to make *Read* sensitive to whether a message has been received or not.

Thus while *Send* will use *sent* as before, in *Read* we find the new variable *recd* instead. The transfer of messages between *sent* and *recd* occurs in *Receive*, as shown in Figure 22.6. Note that in *Read* both *sent* and *recd* must have (*me*, *id*) removed: if left in *recd* the message could be read again; if removed from *recd* but left in *sent* it could be received again; and if left in both its identifier would never be recovered.

The effect of the marked command in *Receive* is to allow *recd* to increase arbitrarily up to and including *sent*. (That includes not increasing at all.) As written, however, the command is infeasible: one cannot achieve $recd_0 \subseteq recd \subseteq sent$ while changing only *recd*, unless $recd \subseteq sent$ already. Fortunately $recd \subseteq sent$ is an invariant of the module: as before, a data refinement could introduce it explicitly, allowing the command to be replaced by

   recd: [*recd* $\subseteq$ *sent* , $recd_0 \subseteq recd \subseteq sent$] .

In the interests of brevity, however, we leave it as it is.

We will not attempt to show that Figure 22.6 refines our earlier Figure 22.4: indeed it cannot, because with our new module the program fragment

   Send (*me*, *msg*, {*you*}, *id*); *Receive* (*you*, *ids*)

can terminate with *id* $\notin$ *ids* (because *id* is still in transit), and in our earlier module that is not possible. Nevertheless we should investigate carefully what we have done: is delay the *only* change we have made?

For our investigation, we go back and alter (but do not necessarily *refine*) our 'prompt' module of Figure 22.4 to express our minimum expectations of introducing delay. First, we must accept that *Receive* will not return *all* identifiers of messages sent, and so we use in this 'mock-up' the alternative procedure in Figure 22.5. Second, we split *Read* into two procedures: one for reading received messages, and the other for reading (or attempting to read) not-yet-received ones. The former should behave as *Read* does in Figure 22.4; the latter should return a randomly chosen message, but change nothing else. The result is shown in Figure 22.7.

module *MailSys*
  var *msgs* : *Id* $\nrightarrow$ *Msg*;
    sent, *recd* : *Usr* $\leftrightarrow$ *Id*·

  procedure *Send* (**value** *me* : *Usr*; *msg* : *Msg*; *tos* : **set** *Usr*;
                result *id* : *Id*)
  $\hat{=}$ *id*: [*id* $\notin$ ran *sent*];
    msgs[*id*] := *msg*;
    sent := *sent* $\cup$ (*tos* $\times$ {*id*});

  procedure *Receive* (**value** *me* : *Usr*; **result** *ids* : **set** *Id*)
  $\hat{=}$ *recd*: [*recd*$_0$ $\subseteq$ *recd* $\subseteq$ *sent*]; $\lhd$
    ids := *recd*[*me*];

  procedure *Read* (**value** *me* : *Usr*; *id* : *Id*; **result** *msg* : *Msg*)
  $\hat{=}$ *msg*: [(*me*, *id*) $\in$ *recd* $\Rightarrow$ *msg* = *msgs*[*id*]];
    sent, *recd* := *sent* $-$ {(*me*, *id*)}, *recd* $-$ {(*me*, *id*)};

  initially *msgs* = *sent* = *recd* = {}
end

Figure 22.6 Delayed receipt of messages

We should be quite clear about the role of Figure 22.7: it is not a refinement of Figure 22.4 (a customer having specified a prompt mail system will not accept an implementation containing delay); nor is it even a satisfactory specification of a system with delay (it is too weak). It is only the most we can say about delay while retaining the state of Figure 22.4.

Because we constructed our system with delay (Figure 22.6) essentially by guess-work, we are now double-checking against Figure 22.7 to see whether it has those 'reasonable' properties *at least*.

To compare Figure 22.6 with Figure 22.7, we must make the same distinction in Figure 22.6 between reading received messages and attempting to read not-yet-received ones. We can do that with a pair of coercions.

Recall that a coercion [*post*] behaves like **skip** if *post* holds, and like **magic** otherwise: if *post* does not hold then [*post*] is essentially 'unexecutable'. We make our procedures *ReadReceived* and *ReadNotReceived* from Figure 22.6 by exploiting that unexecutability. The body of *ReadReceived* will be as for *Read* but with an initial coercion expressing 'the message has been received':

module *MailSys*
  var *msgs* : $Id \nrightarrow Msg$;
    sent : $Usr \leftrightarrow Id$·

  procedure *Send* (**value** *me* : *Usr*; *msg* : *Msg*; *tos* : **set** *Usr*;
                 result *id* : *Id*)
  $\triangleq$ *id*: $[id \notin \mathsf{ran}\, sent]$;
    $msgs[id] := msg$;
    $sent := sent \cup (tos \times \{id\})$;

  procedure *Receive* (**value** *me* : *Usr*; **result** *ids* : **set** *Id*)
  $\triangleq$ *ids*: $[ids \subseteq sent[me]]$;

  procedure *ReadReceived* (**value** *me* : *Usr*; *id* : *Id*;
                         result *msg* : *Msg*)
  $\triangleq$ *msg*: $[(me, id) \in sent \Rightarrow msg = msgs[id]]$;
    $sent := sent - \{(me, id)\}$;

  procedure *ReadNotReceived* (**value** *me* : *Usr*; *id* : *Id*;
                            result *msg* : *Msg*)
  $\triangleq$ **choose** *msg*;

  initially $msgs = sent = \{\}$
end

Figure 22.7 Delay 'mock-up' — compare Figure 22.4

$[(me, id) \in recd]$;
msg: $[(me, id) \in recd \Rightarrow msg = msgs[id]]$;
$sent, recd := sent - \{(me, id)\}, recd - \{(me, id)\}$.

Naturally, we can use the coercion to simplify the rest of the procedure; we continue from immediately above:

$=$ "*introduce assumption 17.19*"
  $[(me, id) \in recd]$;
  $\{(me, id) \in recd\}$;
  msg: $[(me, id) \in recd \Rightarrow msg = msgs[id]]$;
  $sent, recd := sent - \{(me, id)\}, recd - \{(me, id)\}$
$=$ "*absorb assumption 1.8*"

$$[(me, id) \in recd] \, ;$$
$$msg \colon [(me, id) \in recd \,, \; (me, id) \in recd \Rightarrow msg = msgs[id]] \, ;$$
$$sent, recd := sent - \{(me, id)\}, recd - \{(me, id)\}$$
$$= \text{``Note this is equality''}^4$$
$$[(me, id) \in recd] \, ;$$
$$msg := msgs[id];$$
$$sent, recd := sent - \{(me, id)\}, recd - \{(me, id)\} \, .$$

If disinclined to work through the above, one could simply note that the coercion $(me, id) \in recd$ simplifies the following postcondition to $msg = msgs[id]$.

The body of *ReadNotReceived* will have the opposite coercion added, and we are able to simplify it as follows: the coercion can by *introduce assumption* 17.19 spawn an assumption which can then be distributed throughout the procedure body, exploiting the fact that almost all commands there change none of its variables. We have

$$[(me, id) \notin recd] \, ;$$
$$msg \colon [(me, id) \in recd \Rightarrow msg = msgs[id]] \, ;$$
$$sent, recd := sent - \{(me, id)\}, recd - \{(me, id)\}$$
$$= [(me, id) \notin recd] \, ;$$
$$\{(me, id) \notin recd\};$$
$$msg \colon [(me, id) \in recd \Rightarrow msg = msgs[id]] \, ;$$
$$\{(me, id) \notin recd\};$$
$$sent, recd := sent - \{(me, id)\}, recd - \{(me, id)\}$$
$$= \text{``}\begin{cases} remove\ assumption\ 1.10 \\ absorb\ assumption\ 1.8 \\ leading\ assignment\ 8.5 \end{cases}\text{''}$$
$$[(me, id) \notin recd] \, ;$$
$$msg \colon [(me, id) \notin recd \,, \; (me, id) \in recd \Rightarrow msg = msgs[id]] \, ;$$
$$sent := sent - \{(me, id)\};$$
$$recd \colon [(me, id) \notin recd \,, \; recd = recd_0 - \{(me, id)\}]$$
$$\sqsubseteq [(me, id) \notin recd] \, ;$$
$$msg \colon [\mathsf{true}] \, ;$$
$$sent := sent - \{(me, id)\};$$
$$\mathbf{skip}$$
$$\sqsubseteq [(me, id) \notin recd] \, ;$$
$$\mathbf{choose}\ msg;$$
$$sent := sent - \{(me, id)\} \, .$$

The result of all of these changes is shown in Figure 22.8, and we now — finally — investigate whether Figure 22.7 is refined by Figure 22.8. We choose as coupling invariant $recd \subseteq sent$, with $recd$ being our concrete variable; we have no abstract variable.

---

[4]For simple refinement, rather than equality, the precondition would not have been necessary.

module *MailSys*
  var *msgs* : $Id \nrightarrow Msg$;
      sent, recd : $Usr \leftrightarrow Id$·

  procedure *Send* (**value** *me* : *Usr*; *msg* : *Msg*; *tos* : **set** *Usr*;
                  result *id* : *Id*)
  $\hat{=}$ *id*: $[id \notin$ ran *sent*] ;
      msgs[*id*] := *msg*;
      sent := *sent* $\cup$ (*tos* $\times$ {*id*});

  procedure *Receive* (**value** *me* : *Usr*; **result** *ids* : **set** *Id*)
  $\hat{=}$ *recd*: $[recd_0 \subseteq recd \subseteq sent]$;
      ids := *recd*[*me*];

  procedure *ReadReceived* (**value** *me* : *Usr*; *id* : *Id*;
                          result *msg* : *Msg*)
  $\hat{=}$ $[(me, id) \in recd]$;
      msg := *msgs*[*id*];
      sent, recd := *sent* $-$ {(*me, id*)}, *recd* $-$ {(*me, id*)};

  procedure *ReadNotReceived* (**value** *me* : *Usr*; *id* : *Id*;
                            result *msg* : *Msg*)
  $\hat{=}$ $[(me, id) \notin recd]$;
      choose *msg*;
      sent := *sent* $-$ {(*me, id*)};

  initially *msgs* = *sent* = *recd* = {}
end

Figure 22.8 Delayed receipt of messages, with 'split' *Read*

Procedure *Send* we can look at informally: imagine that abstract and concrete states are coupled as above, and that we execute the abstract *Send* on the abstract state and the concrete *Send* on the concrete state. Of the variables appearing in the coupling invariant, only *sent* is modified, having *tos* $\times$ {*id*} added to it in both cases. As *sent* is therefore not made smaller (actually it is made strictly bigger, but that follows from earlier statements and we do not need it), the coupling invariant is maintained. We need also check that if the concrete *Send* can abort then so can the abstract (but neither can), and that all concrete results (*id* in this case) are possible also for the abstract: they are, as the choice of *id* depends only on *sent*, unaffected by the data refinement.

For procedure *Receive* we reason

$$ids: [ids \subseteq sent[me]]$$

becomes

$$ids, recd: [recd \subseteq sent \ , \ recd \subseteq sent \wedge ids \subseteq sent[me]]$$

$\sqsubseteq$ *"following assignment 3.5"*

$$recd: [recd \subseteq sent \ , \ recd \subseteq sent \wedge recd[me] \subseteq sent[me]] \ ;$$ ◁
$$ids := recd[me]$$

$\sqsubseteq$ $recd: [recd_0 \subseteq recd \subseteq sent]$.

Procedure *ReadReceived* has two commands; for the first we proceed

$$msg: [(me, id) \in sent \Rightarrow msg = msgs[id]]$$

becomes

$$\left[\begin{array}{c} \underline{msg, recd} \\ \underline{recd \subseteq sent} \\ \underline{recd \subseteq sent} \\ (me, id) \in sent \Rightarrow msg = msgs[id] \end{array} \right]$$

$\sqsubseteq$ *"assignment 5.2"*

$$msg := msgs[id]$$

$\sqsubseteq$ *"introduce coercion 17.3"*

$$[(me, id) \in recd] \ ;$$
$$msg := msgs[id] \ ,$$

and for the second command we have

$$sent := sent - \{(me, id)\}$$

becomes *"augment assignment 17.7"*

$$\{recd \subseteq sent\};$$
$$sent, recd := sent - \{(me, id)\}, ?;$$
$$[recd \subseteq sent]$$

$\sqsubseteq$ *"advance coercion 22.1"*

$$\{recd \subseteq sent\};$$
$$[recd - \{(me, id)\} \subseteq sent - \{(me, id)\}] \ ;$$
$$sent, recd := sent - \{(me, id)\}, recd - \{(me, id)\}$$

$\sqsubseteq$ $\left"\begin{cases} \text{weaken assumption} \\ remove\ coercion\ 17.20 \quad\quad " \\ remove\ assumption\ 1.10 \end{cases}\right.$

$$sent, recd := sent - \{(me, id)\}, recd - \{(me, id)\} \ .$$

Finally we deal with *ReadNotReceived*:

choose *msg*

becomes

$$\{recd \subseteq sent\};$$
$$msg, recd := ?, ?;$$
$$[recd \subseteq sent] \ .$$

And here we have a problem. Our target code, in *ReadNotReceived* of Figure 22.8, appears to alter *sent*; the above code does not. Doing our best to aim for the code we want, we introduce the beginnings of our assignment to *sent* and continue:

$= $ "sent: $[sent = sent_0] = $ **skip**"

$$\{recd \subseteq sent\};$$
$$msg, recd := ?, ?;$$
$$sent: [sent = sent_0] \ ;$$
$$[recd \subseteq sent]$$
$= $ "following assignment 3.5"
$$\{recd \subseteq sent\};$$
$$msg, recd := ?, ?;$$
$$[sent - \{(me, id)\} = sent] \ ;$$
$$sent := sent - \{(me, id)\};$$
$$[recd \subseteq sent]$$
$= $ "advance coercion 22.1"
$$\{recd \subseteq sent\};$$
$$[(me, id) \notin sent] \ ;$$
$$msg, recd := ?, ?;$$
$$[recd \subseteq sent - \{(me, id)\}] \ ;$$
$$sent := sent - \{(me, id)\}$$
$\sqsubseteq$ "because $recd := ? \sqsubseteq$ **skip**"
$$\{recd \subseteq sent\};$$
$$[(me, id) \notin sent] \ ;$$
$$[recd \subseteq sent - \{(me, id)\}] \ ;$$
choose *msg*;
$$sent := sent - \{(me, id)\}$$
$\sqsubseteq [(me, id) \notin sent] \ ;$
choose *msg*;
$$sent := sent - \{(me, id)\} \ .$$

The last step of removing the assertion loses us no generality, since *recd* no longer appears in the following code. The earlier refinement of $recd := ?$ to **skip** was forced by the fact that *recd* is unchanged by the code of Figure 22.8.

The coercion $[(me, id) \notin sent]$, however, is not the one we want. It is too strong, and we can do nothing about it: stronger coercions cannot be refined into weaker ones. Thus our actual behaviour differs from our desired behaviour precisely when those two coercions differ: when $(me, id) \notin recd$ (from Figure 22.8) but $(me, id) \in sent$ (negating the above).

The appellants withdrew today in the *CMSK* (Common Mail-System Kernel) case, after it was shown that the specification of the system indeed allowed accidental deletion of messages before they had been read. Unexplained message loss had been widely reported and documented in the user community, and in a joint action by users of *CMSK* it was claimed that since the specification guaranteed no loss, the manufacturer was liable for damages.

In a rare move in such cases, the manufacturer showed that its own specification did after all allow such undesirable behaviour, in particular when message identifiers were used for reading before they had been registered as received: a randomly chosen message was in that case returned to the user, and the legitimate message was deleted from the system.

Users generally are now looking more closely at the published specification of *CMSK*, the future of which has been thrown into in doubt.

Figure 22.9

Thus we have not been able to show that Figure 22.8 refines 22.7, and must conclude therefore that our introduction of delay, in Figure 22.6, may have brought with it some unexpected consequences. Does that matter? Consider Figure 22.9 (and Exercise 22.4).

Now it is clear that the problem was essentially a coding trick that came back to haunt us: in the original specification of *Read* we allowed the command

$$sent := sent - \{(me, id)\}$$

to be executed even when (me, id) is not an element of *sent*. Later that became, without our noticing it, "executing $sent := sent - \{(me, id)\}$ even when (me, id) is not an element of *recd*" — altogether different, quite dangerous, and hard to detect without some kind of formal analysis.

We remedy matters by using more straightforward coding in *Read*, as shown in Figure 22.10. If we now performed the above analysis, the concrete procedure

module *MailSys*
  var *msgs* : *Id* $\nrightarrow$ *Msg*;
    sent, *recd* : *Usr* $\leftrightarrow$ *Id*·

  procedure *Send* (**value** *me* : *Usr*; *msg* : *Msg*; *tos* : **set** *Usr*;
                 result *id* : *Id*)
  $\widehat{=}$ *id*: [*id* $\notin$ ran *sent*] ;
    msgs[*id*] := *msg*;
    sent := *sent* $\cup$ (*tos* $\times$ {*id*});

  procedure *Receive* (**value** *me* : *Usr*; **result** *ids* : **set** *Id*)
  $\widehat{=}$ *recd*: [*recd*$_0$ $\subseteq$ *recd* $\subseteq$ *sent*] ;
    ids := *recd*[*me*];

  procedure *Read* (**value** *me* : *Usr*; *id* : *Id*; **result** *msg* : *Msg*)
  $\widehat{=}$ **if** (*me*, *id*) $\in$ *recd* $\rightarrow$
      msg := *msgs*[*id*];
      sent, *recd* := *sent* − {(*me*, *id*)}, *recd* − {(*me*, *id*)}
    [] (*me*, *id*) $\notin$ *recd* $\rightarrow$ **choose** *msg*
    fi;

  initially *msgs* = *sent* = *recd* = {}
end

Figure 22.10 The 'final' specification

ReadNotReceived would simply be

  [(*me*, *id*) $\notin$ *recd*] ;
  choose *msg* ,

which we could reach without difficulty by direct refinement from Figure 22.7.

22.5 A first development: asynchronous delivery

With Figure 22.10 we have — finally — a specification that describes a reasonably realistic system in which messages may take some time to be delivered. We take it as our 'final' specification. (Why the quotes? Very few specifications are never changed, final or not.)

Our first move towards implementation will be concerned with the 'delay' built in to Procedure *Receive* of Figure 22.10. That describes the user's-eye view of it,

procedure *Deliver* $\;\hat{=}\;$ *recd*: $[recd_0 \subseteq recd \subseteq sent]$

procedure *Receive* (**value** *me* : *Usr*; **result** *ids* : **set** *Id*)
$\hat{=}$ *ids* := *recd*[*me*]

Figure 22.11 Asynchronous delivery, modifying Figure 22.10

but of course the delay does not necessarily happen in *Receive* itself; that is only where it is noticed.

Through the implementor's eyes instead, we would see messages moving towards their destination even while no user-accessible procedures are called. The subset relation in *recd* $\subseteq$ *sent* merely reflects the effect of calling *Receive* before they have arrived.

Our first development step is to introduce asynchronous message delivery, 'in the background'. Not having refinement rules for concurrency, however, we proceed informally: the actual delivery *recd*: $[recd_0 \subseteq recd \subseteq sent]$ is relocated from Procedure *Receive* into a new procedure *Deliver* which, it is understood, is called 'by the operating system' to move messages about. (Calls of *Deliver* are not even seen by the users.) The result is shown in Figure 22.11; note that *Deliver* needs no parameters.

With such a modest excursion into concurrency as this new module represents, we need only require that in an actual implementation there never be destructive interference between apparently concurrent calls on the procedures: a simple way of doing that is to introduce mutual exclusion so that at any time at most one procedure is active within it. In fact we would need to do that in any case — even without asynchronous delivery — if we were to share the mail system module between concurrently executing users.

Although we admit we are not strictly speaking implementing a refinement, we still should strive for as much confidence as possible in justifying the new behaviour, having learned our lessons in the scenarios of Figures 22.3 and 22.9 above. The key change, the new procedure, is not visible to users at all; it is called, 'in between' users' access to the module, by the operating system. Can we isolate that change, bringing the rest within the reach of our rigorous techniques?

If we were to add an 'asynchronous' procedure *Deliver* to our specification, Figure 22.10, we would only have to make its body **skip** to be sure that the change would not affect the users' perception of the module's behaviour. (We would have to ignore however the possibility that *Deliver* could be called 'so often' that users' access to *MailSys* is forever delayed, just as we have already ignored such starvation of one user by another.) Thus to justify the step we have just taken, we go back and add

procedure *Deliver* $\hat{=}$ **skip**

to Figure 22.10, and attempt to show that Figure 22.11 is a refinement of that. To find a coupling invariant, imagine executions of the abstract and concrete *Deliver* together: we can see that even if *recd* and *recd'* were equal beforehand, afterwards the concrete *recd'* could have grown. Thus we choose *recd* as abstract variable, introduce concrete variable *recd'*, and couple the two with

$$recd \subseteq recd' \subseteq sent \ .$$

We look at the procedures in turn, taking a slightly informal view where matters seem clear enough.

As earlier, we can look at *Send* informally: since *sent* is only increased, the coupling invariant cannot be broken. For *Deliver* we must introduce a statement allowing *recd'* to grow, and we reason as follows:

skip
becomes "augment specification 17.6"
$$recd' : [recd \subseteq recd' \subseteq sent \ , \ recd \subseteq recd' \subseteq sent]$$
$$\sqsubseteq \ recd' : [recd'_0 \subseteq recd' \subseteq sent] \ .$$

In *Receive* we must on the other hand *remove* the statement affecting *recd*. We have first

$$recd : [recd_0 \subseteq recd \subseteq sent]$$
becomes "augment specification 17.6"

$$\left[\begin{array}{c} recd, recd' \\ \hline \frac{recd \subseteq recd' \subseteq sent}{recd \subseteq recd' \subseteq sent} \\ recd_0 \subseteq recd \subseteq sent \end{array} \right]$$

$\sqsubseteq$ **skip** .

Note that it is in that last step that we need $recd' \subseteq sent$ in the coupling invariant.

The second command is $ids := recd[me]$ and here, apparently, we have a problem. Naturally, we want for its concrete equivalent $ids := recd'[me]$, but with our coupling invariant $recd \subseteq recd' \subseteq sent$ we cannot show that the *ids* returned by the concrete *Receive* could have been returned also by the abstract. If *recd* and *recd'* differ initially — and they may — then the concrete and abstract *ids* will differ also.

On the other hand, we see that if the coupling invariant holds at the beginning of the whole procedure, then any concrete choice of *ids* can be mimicked by the abstract: the first abstract command could after all establish that $recd = recd'$. Thus we can sidestep this difficulty by going back and data-refining the two commands together, as follows:

$$recd : [recd_0 \subseteq recd \subseteq sent] \ ;$$
$$ids := recd[me]$$

$$= recd, ids: [recd_0 \subseteq recd \subseteq sent \land ids = recd[me]]$$

becomes "augment specification 17.6"

$$\left[\begin{array}{c} recd, ids, recd' \\ \hline \begin{array}{c} recd \subseteq recd' \subseteq sent \\ \hline recd \subseteq recd' \subseteq sent \\ recd_0 \subseteq recd \subseteq sent \\ ids = recd[me] \end{array} \end{array} \right]$$

$\sqsubseteq$ "again using $recd' \subseteq sent$"

$$recd, ids := recd', recd'[me]$$

becomes "diminish assignment 17.13"

$$ids := recd'[me] .$$

In *Read*, however, we have a problem we cannot sidestep. The guards of the alternation make essential use of *recd*: we cannot replace them by guards involving *recd'* only, as *recd'* is essentially an arbitrary superset of *recd*. We are stuck.

The difference between that and our earlier problem, with *Receive*, is that the abstract *Receive* allowed a nondeterministic alteration of *recd*: deliveries could occur there. But deliveries cannot occur in our abstract *Read*. Does it really matter? See Figure 22.12 (and Exercise 22.5).

Thus our Figure 22.11 is not a refinement of Figure 22.10 with its extra

procedure *Deliver* $\hat{=}$ **skip** .

We are forced instead to add a third variable *deld* for 'delivered', independent of *sent* and *recd*. Our proposed concrete module is shown in Figure 22.13.

To show refinement between the extended Figure 22.10 and Figure 22.13, our coupling invariant is $read \subseteq deld' \subseteq sent$; there are no abstract variables. Arguing informally, we can see that *Send* is successfully data-refined, since *sent* is only increased. Similarly in *Read*, variables *sent*, *deld'* and *recd* are decreased 'in step'. For Procedure *Deliver* we have

skip

becomes "augment specification 17.6"

$$deld': [recd \subseteq deld' \subseteq sent , recd \subseteq deld' \subseteq sent]$$
$$\sqsubseteq deld': [deld'_0 \subseteq deld' \subseteq sent] .$$

Note that even though the last command appears miraculous, we can as in Section 22.4 introduce a module invariant, in this case $deld' \subseteq sent$ (direct from the coupling invariant in fact), that would allow us to write

$$deld': [deld' \subseteq sent , deld'_0 \subseteq deld' \subseteq sent]$$

if we wished to.

Finally, for *Receive* we have

$$recd: [recd_0 \subseteq recd \subseteq sent]$$

A large-scale computer fraud was discovered today, involving an accounting loophole in the national electronic mail system.

It had been noticed that messages could be read before their delivery was reported. Believing their own specification, however, the mail authority had installed accounting software only at the actual point of reporting delivery. Thus 'unreported' messages could be read free of charge.

The loophole was exploited by a company that offered greatly reduced rates on bulk electronic mail. Its customers' messages would be collected and sent all at once as a single very long message. The identifier returned would then be sent as the body of an immediately following very short message. Since the mail system tended to allow short messages to overtake long ones, the second message was often delivered before the first: the identifier it contained would then be used to read the first, by-passing report of delivery — and bypassing charging as well. The occasional failure of the second message to overtake the first was easily covered by the enormous profit made overall.

Figure 22.12

becomes *"augment specification 17.6"*

$$\left[\frac{recd, deld'}{\begin{array}{c} recd \subseteq deld' \subseteq sent \\ \hline recd \subseteq deld' \subseteq sent \\ recd_0 \subseteq recd \subseteq sent \end{array}} \right]$$

$\sqsubseteq \; recd := deld' \; .$

and our data-refinement is proved. We therefore accept Figure 22.13 as our first development step, introducing asynchronous delivery of messages.

module *MailSys*
   var *msgs* : $Id \nrightarrow Msg$;
      sent, deld, recd : $Usr \leftrightarrow Id\cdot$

   procedure *Send* (**value** *me* : *Usr*; *msg* : *Msg*; *tos* : **set** *Usr*;
                      result *id* : *Id*)
  $\hat{=}$ *id*: $[id \notin \mathsf{ran}\, sent]$;
     $msgs[id] := msg$;
     $sent := sent \cup (tos \times \{id\})$;

   procedure *Deliver*
  $\hat{=}$ *deld*: $[deld_0 \subseteq deld \subseteq sent]$

   procedure *Receive* (**value** *me* : *Usr*; **result** *ids* : **set** *Id*)
  $\hat{=}$ $recd := deld$;
     $ids := recd[me]$;

   procedure *Read* (**value** *me* : *Usr*; *id* : *Id*; **result** *msg* : *Msg*)
  $\hat{=}$ **if** $(me, id) \in recd \rightarrow$
        $msg := msgs[id]$;
        $sent, deld, recd := sent - \{(me, id)\},$
                          $deld - \{(me, id)\},$
                          $recd - \{(me, id)\}$
    $\llbracket$ $(me, id) \notin recd \rightarrow$ **choose** *msg*
    fi;

   initially $msgs = sent = deld = recd = \{\}$
end

Figure 22.13 Asynchronous delivery — corrected

22.6   A second development: acknowledgements

In spite of our having introduced asynchronous delivery, the system is still centralised: variables *sent*, *deld* and *recd* each represent information that in a running system would probably be physically distributed. In particular, the execution of $sent := sent - \{(me, id)\}$ in *Read* can make an identifier available 'instantaneously' for reallocation by id: $[id \notin \mathsf{ran}\, sent]$ in *Send*.

We remedy those implementation problems as follows. A new variable *used* will be introduced to record which identifiers may not yet be (re-)allocated. That frees *sent* to represent, not *all* of the $Usr \times Id$ pairs in use, but now only those that have been sent but not yet delivered. Similarly *deld* will now represent those delivered but not yet read. Finally, a new variable *ackd* will contain pairs that have been read but are not yet available for reuse. (In effect they are acknowledgements 'on the way back'.) That last breaks the 'instantaneous' link referred to above.

The abstract variables are *sent* and *deld* (leaving *recd* as it is); the concrete are *used'*, *sent'*, *deld'* and *ackd'*; and the coupling invariant is

$$sent = sent' \cup deld' \cup recd$$
$$deld = deld' \cup recd$$
$$used' = sent \cup ackd'$$

disjoint $sent'\ deld'\ recd\ ackd'$.

We have thus a functional coupling invariant, with a data-type invariant showing that the four sets listed are disjoint. The third conjunct can be seen as part of the data-type invariant by taking the first conjunct into account. (Replace *sent* in the third conjunct by $sent' \cup deld' \cup recd$.)

We begin the data refinement with *Send* (of Figure 22.13). In its first command we can replace *sent* by *used'*, since the coupling invariant gives us that $sent \subseteq used'$. The second command is unaffected. For the third we recall in an assumption that $id \notin \text{ran } sent$ was established by the first, and then we reason

$$\{id \notin \text{ran } sent\};$$
$$sent := sent \cup (tos \times \{id\})$$

becomes "$\left\{ \begin{array}{l} \text{simple specification 8.1} \\ \text{data-refine specification 17.15} \end{array} \right.$ "

$$\left[\begin{array}{c} \underline{\qquad used',\, sent',\, deld',\, ackd' \qquad} \\ id \notin \text{ran}(sent' \cup deld' \cup recd) \\ used' = sent' \cup deld' \cup recd \cup ackd' \\ \text{disjoint } sent'\ deld'\ recd\ ackd' \\ \hline used' = sent' \cup deld' \cup recd \cup ackd' \\ \text{disjoint } sent'\ deld'\ recd\ ackd' \\ sent' \cup deld' \cup recd = sent'_0 \cup deld'_0 \cup recd \cup (tos \times \{id\}) \\ deld' \cup recd = deld'_0 \cup recd \end{array} \right]$$

$\sqsubseteq$

$$\left[\begin{array}{c} \underline{\qquad used',\, sent' \qquad} \\ id \notin \text{ran}(sent' \cup deld' \cup recd) \\ \text{disjoint } sent'\ deld'\ recd\ ackd' \\ \hline used' = used'_0 \cup (tos \times \{id\}) \\ \text{disjoint } sent'\ deld'\ recd\ ackd' \\ sent' = sent'_0 \cup (tos \times \{id\}) \end{array} \right]$$

$\sqsubseteq sent',\, used' := sent \cup (tos \times \{id\}),\, used' \cup (tos \times \{id\})$.

In *Deliver* we have

$$deld : [deld_0 \subseteq deld \subseteq sent]$$

becomes "*data-refine specification* 17.15"

$$
\left[
\begin{array}{c}
used', deld', sent', ackd' \\
\hline
used' = sent' \cup deld' \cup recd \cup ackd' \\
\text{disjoint } sent'\ deld'\ recd\ ackd' \\
\hline
used' = sent' \cup deld' \cup recd \cup ackd' \\
\text{disjoint } sent'\ deld'\ recd\ ackd' \\
sent' \cup deld' = sent'_0 \cup deld'_0 \\
deld'_0 \subseteq deld'
\end{array}
\right]
$$

$\sqsubseteq$ **var** $muis, auis : Usr \leftrightarrow Id\cdot$

$muis, auis : [muis \subseteq sent' \wedge auis \subseteq ackd']$;
$sent', ackd' := sent' - muis, ackd' - auis;$
$deld', used' := deld' \cup muis, used' - auis$

The local variables *muis* and *auis* represent the arrival of new messages and acknowledgements respectively; the former are added to *deld'*, and the latter deleted from *used'*.

In *Receive* we have

$recd := deld$

becomes

$$
\left[
\begin{array}{c}
recd, deld' \\
\hline
\text{disjoint } deld'\ recd \\
\hline
deld'_0 \cup recd_0 = deld' \cup recd \\
\text{disjoint } deld'\ recd \\
recd = deld'_0 \cup recd_0
\end{array}
\right]
$$

$\sqsubseteq deld', recd := \{\}, recd \cup deld'$,

and the second command is unchanged.

Finally, in *Read* we need be concerned only with the assignments to the three sets, and we will need that $(me, id) \in recd$ (which we have from the guard); thus we proceed

$\{(me, id) \in recd\};$
$sent, deld, recd := sent - \{(me, id)\},$
$\qquad\qquad\qquad deld - \{(me, id)\},$
$\qquad\qquad\qquad recd - \{(me, id)\}$

becomes

$$
\left[
\begin{array}{c}
recd, ackd' \\
\hline
(me, id) \in recd \\
\text{disjoint } recd\ ackd' \\
\hline
recd_0 \cup ackd'_0 = recd \cup ackd' \\
\text{disjoint } recd\ ackd' \\
recd = recd_0 - \{(me, id)\}
\end{array}
\right]
$$

$\sqsubseteq recd, ackd' := recd - \{(me, id)\}, ackd' \cup \{(me, id)\}$.

The result is Figure 22.14.

module *MailSys*
    var *msgs* : *Id* $\nrightarrow$ *Msg*;
        used, sent, deld, recd, ackd : *Usr* $\leftrightarrow$ *Id*·

    procedure *Send* (**value** *me* : *Usr*; *msg* : *Msg*; *tos* : **set** *Usr*;
                    result *id* : *Id*)
    $\triangleq$ *id*: [*id* $\notin$ ran *used*] ;
        msgs[*id*] := *msg*;
        sent, used := *sent* $\cup$ (*tos* $\times$ {*id*}), *used* $\cup$ (*tos* $\times$ {*id*});

    procedure *Deliver*
    $\triangleq$ |[**var** *muis, auis* : *Usr* $\leftrightarrow$ *Id*·
            muis, auis: [*muis* $\subseteq$ *sent* $\wedge$ *auis* $\subseteq$ *ackd*] ;
            sent, ackd := *sent* $-$ *muis, ackd* $-$ *auis*;
            deld, used := *deld* $\cup$ *muis, used* $-$ *auis*
        ]|;

    procedure *Receive* (**value** *me* : *Usr*; **result** *ids* : **set** *Id*)
    $\triangleq$ *deld, recd* :={}, *recd* $\cup$ *deld*;
        ids := *recd*[*me*];

    procedure *Read* (**value** *me* : *Usr*; *id* : *Id*; **result** *msg* : *Msg*)
    $\triangleq$ **if** (*me, id*) $\in$ *recd* $\rightarrow$
            msg := *msgs*[*id*];
            recd, ackd := *recd* $-$ {(*me, id*)}, *ackd* $\cup$ {(*me, id*)}
        [] (*me, id*) $\notin$ *recd* $\rightarrow$ **choose** *msg*
        fi;

    initially *msgs* = *used* = *sent* = *deld* = *recd* = *ackd* = {}
end

Figure 22.14 Acknowledgements and distribution

22.7   The final development: packets

In a real mail system it would be the messages themselves that moved from place to place, not just their identifiers, and it finally is time to develop our specification in that direction. We introduce a type *Pkt* to represent both messages and acknowledgements; the new concrete variables will be *sets* of those and the procedures will, after data refinement, move packets between them:

type *From* $\hat{=}$ *Usr*;
To $\hat{=}$ *Usr*;
Pkt $\hat{=}$ msg *Id From To Msg* | ack *Id From To* .

The type synonyms *From* and *To* are introduced to make the use of the two *Usr* fields clear.

To express our coupling invariant — to recover the abstract variables from the new concrete sets — we must define several projection functions that extract sets of *Usr* $\times$ *Id* pairs from sets of packets:

mui, aui, ui : set *Pkt* $\rightarrow$ (*Usr* $\leftrightarrow$ *Id*)

mui *pp* $\hat{=}$ $\{i : Id; f : From; t : To; m : Msg \mid$ msg $i\ f\ t\ m \in pp \cdot (t, i)\}$
aui *pp* $\hat{=}$ $\{i : Id; f : From; t : To \mid$ ack $i\ f\ t \in pp \cdot (t, i)\}$
ui *pp* $\hat{=}$ mui *pp* $\cup$ aui *pp* .

We will need to express also that any given *Usr* $\times$ *Id* pair is represented uniquely in a set of packets — that is, that there are never two distinct packets with the same pair:

ui1 *pp* $\hat{=}$ $(\forall\, p, p' : pp \cdot$ ui$\{p\} =$ ui$\{p'\} \Rightarrow p = p')$.

And finally, we need a projection function to extract the message texts from our packets:

im : set *Pkt* $\rightarrow$ (*Id* $\leftrightarrow$ *Msg*)

im *pp* $\hat{=}$ $\{i : Id; f : From; t : To; m : Msg \mid$ msg $i\ f\ t\ m \in pp \cdot (i, m)\}$.

Our abstract *sent* and *ackd* will be represented by the single concrete *sent'*, representing the packets of either kind in transit, with the tags msg and ack available to separate them; the coupling invariant is straightforward, if a bit lengthy:

sent = mui *sent'*
deld = mui *deld'*
recd = mui *recd'*
ackd = aui *sent'*

ui1(*sent'* $\cup$ *deld'* $\cup$ *recd'*)

msgs $\supseteq$ im(*sent'* $\cup$ *deld'* $\cup$ *recd'*) .

The last conjunct states that our sets of packets do contain message bodies consistent with *msgs* — and our aim is to remove *msgs*.

Data refinement of *Send*, *Receive* and *Read* is straightforward; and since the coupling invariant allows *msgs*[*id*] in *Read* to be recovered from *recd*, we find that *msgs* has become auxiliary and that we can remove it. It can be removed from *Send* in any case.

For *Deliver* we first rewrite our abstract program slightly, anticipating that *sent* and *ackd* will be collected together:

$$
\begin{aligned}
&\mathsf{|[}\ \ \mathbf{var}\ muis, auis : Usr \leftrightarrow Id\cdot \\
&\qquad muis, auis\colon [muis \subseteq sent' \land auis \subseteq ackd]\,; \\
&\qquad sent, ackd := sent - muis, ackd - auis; \\
&\qquad deld, used := deld \cup muis, used - auis \\
&\mathsf{]|} \\
= &\mathsf{|[}\ \ \mathbf{var}\ uis, muis, auis : Usr \leftrightarrow Id\cdot \\
&\qquad uis\colon [uis \subseteq sent]\,; \\
&\qquad muis, auis := uis \cap sent, uis \cap ackd; \\
&\qquad sent, ackd := sent - uis, ackd - auis; \\
&\qquad deld, used := deld \cup muis, used - auis\ . \\
&\mathsf{]|}
\end{aligned}
$$

For the data refinement we introduce concrete local variables pp, mpp and app to replace the abstract local variables uis, $muis$ and $auis$, with coupling invariant

$$ \mathsf{ui}\ pp = uis \land \mathsf{mui}\ mpp = muis \land \mathsf{aui}\ app = auis\ . $$

The assignment $sent, ackd := \cdots$ will be data-refined to a single assignment to $sent'$, because it effectively represents the union of $sent$ and $ackd$.

The result — our final module — is in Figure 22.15.

22.8   Exercises

Ex. 22.1 ♡   Modify the original specification of Figure 22.1 to include a procedure *Cancel* that can be used to remove all unreceived copies of a message from the system. Does the specification contain enough detail to prevent 'unauthorised' removal?

Ex. 22.2   Modify the original specification of Figure 22.1 to include a procedure *Unread* that can be used to determine which users have not yet read a given message.

Ex. 22.3 ♡   Explain precisely how the specification of Figure 22.1, as amended in Figure 22.2, could have led to the scenario described in Figure 22.3.

Ex. 22.4   Explain precisely how the module of Figure 22.6 could have behaved as suggested in the scenario described in Figure 22.9.

Ex. 22.5   Explain precisely how the module of Figure 22.10, as amended in Figure 22.11, could have behaved as suggested in the scenario described in Figure 22.12.

Ex. 22.6   Imagine a building with one lift serving several floors. Outside the lift door, on each floor, is a panel of buttons and lights with one button/light pair for each floor. Inside the lift are no buttons or lights at all.

module *MailSys*
   type *From* $\triangleq$ *Usr*;
        To $\triangleq$ *Usr*;
        Pkt $\triangleq$ msg *Id From To Msg* | ack *From To Id*;

   var *used* : *Usr* $\leftrightarrow$ *Id*;
      sent, deld, recd : **set** *Pkt·*

   procedure *Send* (**value** *me* : *Usr*; *msg* : *Msg*; *tos* : **set** *Usr*;
                 result *id* : *Id*)
 $\triangleq$ *id*: $[id \notin$ ran *used*] ;
   used := *used* $\cup$ (*tos* $\times$ $\{id\}$);
   sent := *sent* $\cup$ $\{t : tos \mid$ msg *id me t msg*$\}$;

   procedure *Deliver*
 $\triangleq$ |[**var** *pp, mpp, app* : **set** *Pkt·*
     pp: $[pp \subseteq sent]$;
     sent := *sent* $-$ *pp*;
     mpp, app := *pp* $\cap$ ran msg, *pp* $\cap$ ran ack;
     deld, used := *deld* $\cup$ *mpp*, *used* $-$ ui *app*
   ]|;

   procedure *Receive* (**value** *me* : *Usr*; **result** *ids* : **set** *Id*)
 $\triangleq$ *deld, recd* := $\{\}$, *recd* $\cup$ *deld*;
   ids := (ui *recd*)[*me*];

   procedure *Read* (**value** *me* : *Usr*; *id* : *Id*; **result** *msg* : *Msg*)
 $\triangleq$ |[**var** *p* : *Pkt*; *u* : *Usr*; ·
     if $(me, id) \in$ ui *recd* $\rightarrow$
        p, f, msg: [*p* = msg *id f me msg* $\wedge$ *p* $\in$ *recd*] ;
        recd, sent := *recd* $- \{p\}$, *sent* $\cup$ $\{$ack *id f me*$\}$
     $[\!]$ $(me, id) \notin$ ui *recd* $\rightarrow$ **choose** *msg*
     fi
   ]|;

   initially *used* = *sent* = *deld* = *recd* = $\{\}$
end

Figure 22.15 A refinement of Figure 22.10

To use the lift one presses the button, next to the doors, for the desired destination; the corresponding light should light if it is not lit already. When the doors open, one enters the lift in the hope that it will eventually visit that destination (whose light should be lit).

Design a module based on the type

$$Floor \ \hat{=} \ 0 {\rightarrow} F$$

that contains these procedures with the meanings informally indicated:

- *Press* (**value** $f, b : Floor$) — Press button b outside the lift doors on floor f. (Called by lift user.)
- *Check* (**value** $f, l : Floor$; **result** $b : Boolean$) — Check whether the light l on floor f is lit. (Called by lift user.)
- *Visit* (**result** $f : Floor$) — Close the doors, select a floor f 'randomly' which it would be useful to visit, go there, and open the doors. (Called by lift operator.)

Hint: There are probably unanswered questions about the informal specification above; answer them yourself. Consider using set-valued variables inside the module.

Ex. 22.7   Let T be a set of *telephones* connected to an exchange that supports conference calls, so that collections of (people using) telephones can hold group conversations.

Declare a variable *xns* of appropriate type that could represent the set of conversations in progress at any moment; write then, in English *and* in mathematics, an invariant that ensures there is no telephone in more than one conversation.

Now suppose *rqs* is to represent the set of conversations requested but not in progress (thus 'pending'). Specify and justify an operation (with the default pre-condition, true)

$$xns, rqs: [???]$$

that connects as many new conversations as is possible without disturbing existing conversations. Note that the invariant over *xns* must be respected. *Hint*: The set *xns* should be made locally maximal in some sense.

Then use the structures above to supply (abstract) program text for the informally described module in Figure 22.16. (You need not fill in *Connect*, already specified in the text above.)

Finally, give a sensible definition of a new procedure *Chat* (**value** $t : T$) that causes t immediately to join a single 'chat line', able then to converse with all others that have not executed *HangUp* since they last executed *Chat*. Modify your other definitions if necessary (but the less, the better).

Ex. 22.8 ♡   Show that Figure 22.10, the 'final' specification, is refined by Figure 22.17. Is that a problem?

---

module *TelephoneExchange*
   var *xns* : ???
      rqs : ???.

   procedure *Request* (**value** *tt* : ???)
   $\hat{=}$ "Request a conversation *tt*";

   procedure *Connect* $\hat{=}$ "described in the text";

   procedure *Converse* (**value** *t* : *T*;
                     result *tt* : ???)
   $\hat{=}$ "Identify *all* participants in any conversation involving *t*";

   procedure *HangUp* (**value** *t* : *T*)
   $\hat{=}$ "Withdraw *t* from any conversation in which it is involved";

   initially "no conversations"
end

Note that

- A single telephone may be part of many requests (but of at most one conversation).
- *Connect* may be thought of as being executed at suitable moments by the exchange itself.
- *HangUp* should allow other participants in a conversation to continue.

Figure 22.16 Telephone module

---

module *MailSys*
    var *used* : **set** *Id*;

    procedure *Send* (**value** *me* : *Usr*; *msg* : *Msg*; *tos* : **set** *Usr*;
                            result *id* : *Id*)
    $\hat{=}$ *id*: $\notin$ *used*;
       used : $=$ *used* $\cup$ {*id*};

    procedure *Receive* (**value** *me* : *Usr*; **result** *ids* : **set** *Id*)
    $\hat{=}$ *ids* : ={};

    procedure *Read* (**value** *me* : *Usr*; *id* : *Id*; **result** *msg* : *Msg*)
    $\hat{=}$ **choose** *msg*
end

Figure 22.17 An unexpected implementation

Chapter 23

Semantics

23.1 Introduction

'Semantics' means meaning. In this final chapter we look back and examine the mathematical meaning of our program development method.

There are several reasons for taking an interest in foundations. The first, for the new reader in this subject, is to provide references to the research from which this style of program development has arisen.

The second reason is to address the nervous reader: Why are these dozens of laws necessarily consistent? Where have they come from? Why do they, or indeed does refinement itself, have any connection with real programming?

Questions like those should not be asked during program development, for there it is already too late; those who only *apply* the method need not read this chapter. But those who *select* a program development method regard such questions as crucial: they have to be sure that it works.

The answers are usually given by deciding first of all on a reasonable way of viewing programs — in fact, a mathematical model for them. That model should correspond closely with the way that computers operate, so that there is no doubt about its appropriateness. (Otherwise the questions will only have been moved, not answered.) Then the laws are checked, one by one, against the model. If the check is passed, and one has accepted the model, then by that very fact one has accepted the law also. As an example, we check *assignment* 5.2 in Section 23.3.3 below.

Our mathematical model is the predicate transformer, popularised by E.W. Dijkstra [Dij76]. The treatment of it below is brief, even condensed; for the novice, pursuit of the introductory references is probably essential. Any of [Dij76, Gri81, Heh84, Bac86, DF88] is a good starting point.

23.2   Predicate transformers

In Section 1.4.3 the operation of a specification was described as follows:

> *If* the initial state satisfies the precondition *then* change only the variables listed in the frame so that the resulting final state satisfies the postcondition.

In fact, that description could apply to the behaviour of any command: if for *any* postcondition we know which preconditions will guarantee termination in a final state satisfying the postcondition, then we say that we know the meaning of the command.

For command *prog* and postcondition $\mathcal{A}$, let

$$wp(prog, \mathcal{A})$$

be the *weakest* precondition sufficient to ensure termination in a state described by $\mathcal{A}$. In that way we can see *prog* as a predicate transformer, because it transforms the postcondition $\mathcal{A}$ into the weakest precondition $wp(prog, \mathcal{A})$. And with it we know the meaning of *prog*: a precondition $\mathcal{B}$ will guarantee that *prog* terminates in a state described by $\mathcal{A}$ precisely when

$$\mathcal{B} \quad \Rightarrow \quad wp(prog, \mathcal{A}) \ .$$

For example, the meaning of $x := x + 1$ is a predicate transformer that takes the postcondition $x > 0$ to the precondition $x \geq 0$, because that precondition is the weakest one whose truth initially guarantees termination of $x := x + 1$ and truth of $x > 0$ finally. Thus $x \geq 0$ is the weakest precondition of $x := x + 1$ with respect to $x > 0$, and we write

$$wp(x := x + 1, x > 0) \quad \equiv \quad x \geq 0 \ . \tag{23.1}$$

The next section gives the meaning of our program development method in terms of predicate transformers.

23.3   Semantic definitions

23.3.1   Guarded commands

Semantics for the ordinary guarded commands are introduced in [Dij76] and repeated in [Heh84, Gri81]. In [Bac86], similar definitions are given for Pascal. Here for example we give the semantics of assignment:

Definition 23.1 <u>assignment</u> For any postcondition $\mathcal{A}$,

$$wp(w := E, \mathcal{A}) \ \widehat{=} \ \mathcal{A}[w\backslash E] \ .$$

□

$$wp(\textbf{skip}, \mathcal{A}) \quad \hat{=} \quad \mathcal{A}$$
$$wp(\textbf{abort}, \mathcal{A}) \quad \hat{=} \quad \textsf{false}$$
$$wp(x := E, \mathcal{A}) \quad \hat{=} \quad \mathcal{A}[x \backslash E]$$
$$wp(P; Q, \mathcal{A}) \quad \hat{=} \quad wp(P, wp(Q, \mathcal{A}))$$

$$wp(\textbf{if } ([\!]i \cdot G_i \rightarrow P_i) \textbf{ fi}, \mathcal{A})$$
$$\hat{=} \qquad (\vee i \cdot G_i)$$
$$\wedge \quad (\wedge i \cdot G_i \Rightarrow wp(P_i, \mathcal{A}))$$

Iteration **do** $\cdots$ **od** is a special case of recursion, dealt with in Section 23.3.9.

Figure 23.1 Predicate transformers for guarded commands

With Definition 23.1 we verify the claim (23.1) above:

$$wp(x := x + 1, x > 0)$$
$$\equiv \quad \text{``assignment 23.1''}$$
$$(x > 0)[x \backslash x + 1]$$
$$\equiv \quad x + 1 > 0$$
$$\equiv \quad x \geq 0 \ .$$

Figure 23.1 gives predicate transformers for all the basic guarded commands except iteration.

23.3.2   Specifications

Our most significant extension to the ordinary guarded commands is the specification, and this is its meaning:

Definition 23.2 <u>specification</u>

$$wp(w: [pre \ , \ post], \mathcal{A}) \quad \hat{=} \quad pre \wedge (\forall w \cdot post \Rightarrow \mathcal{A}) [v_0 \backslash v] \ ,$$

where the substitution $[v_0 \backslash v]$ replaces *all* initial variables by corresponding final variables.
□

Note that initial variables v_0 never occur in postconditions $\mathcal{A}$.

As an example of the above, suppose we use $x := x \pm 1$ to abbreviate

$$x: [x = x_0 + 1 \vee x = x_0 - 1] \ .$$

Then we have

$$
\begin{aligned}
& wp(x := x \pm 1, \mathcal{A}) \\
\equiv\ & wp(x\colon [x = x_0 + 1 \lor x = x_0 - 1], \mathcal{A}) \\
\equiv\ & \textsf{true} \land (\forall\, x \cdot (x = x_0 + 1 \lor x = x_0 - 1) \Rightarrow \mathcal{A})\, [x_0 \backslash x] \\
\equiv\ & \text{``Predicate laws A.34, A.65''} \\
& (\forall\, x \cdot x = x_0 + 1 \Rightarrow \mathcal{A})\, [x_0 \backslash x] \land (\forall\, x \cdot x = x_0 - 1 \Rightarrow \mathcal{A})\, [x_0 \backslash x] \\
\equiv\ & \text{``Predicate law A.56''} \\
& \mathcal{A}[x \backslash x_0 + 1][x_0 \backslash x] \land \mathcal{A}[x \backslash x_0 - 1][x_0 \backslash x] \\
\equiv\ & \text{``}\mathcal{A}\text{ contains no } x_0\text{''} \\
& \mathcal{A}[x \backslash x + 1] \land \mathcal{A}[x \backslash x - 1] \ .
\end{aligned}
$$

'Specifications' were first added to the guarded command language in [Bac78, Bac80], though not in our form; in particular, miracles were not allowed (see Section 23.3.6 below). Later they appeared in [Mee79]; most recently they appear in [Mor87, MR87, Mor88d, Bac88]. References [MR87, Mor88d] are closest to this book.

23.3.3   Refinement

Refinement $\sqsubseteq$ is a relation between commands (just as $\le$ is a relation between numbers): for any commands *prog1* and *prog2*, either *prog1* $\sqsubseteq$ *prog2* holds or it does not. This is the definition:

Definition 23.3 <u>refinement</u> For any commands *prog1* and *prog2*, we say that *prog1* is refined by *prog2*, writing *prog1* $\sqsubseteq$ *prog2*, exactly when for all postconditions $\mathcal{A}$ we have

$$
wp(prog1, \mathcal{A}) \quad \Rightarrow \quad wp(prog2, \mathcal{A}) \ .
$$

□

Definition 23.3 is used in all approaches to the refinement calculus (for example [Bac80, MR87, Mor87, Mor88d]), and in other places as well [Heh84, Abr87]. It seems to be the only reasonable definition for sequential program development based on weakest preconditions.

With our definitions so far, we can see refinement in action. For example, it is easy to verify both of these:

$$
\begin{aligned}
x := x \pm 1 \ &\sqsubseteq\ x := x + 1 \\
x := x \pm 1 \ &\sqsubseteq\ x := x - 1 \ .
\end{aligned}
$$

More interesting, however, is showing the proof of one of our laws. Suppose we have $w = w_0 \land pre \Rightarrow post[w \backslash E]$, the proviso of *assignment* 5.2; then we reason

$$wp(w\colon [pre\ ,\ post]\,,\mathcal{A})$$

$\equiv$ "specification 23.2"
$$pre \wedge (\forall\, w \cdot post \Rightarrow \mathcal{A})\,[v_0 \backslash v]$$

$\equiv$ "Predicate law A.56; *pre* contains no v_0"
$$(\forall\, v_0 \cdot v_0 = v \Rightarrow pre \wedge (\forall\, w \cdot post \Rightarrow \mathcal{A}))$$

$\Rightarrow$ "assumed proviso; v_0 includes w_0"
$$(\forall\, v_0 \cdot v_0 = v \Rightarrow post[w \backslash E] \wedge (\forall\, w \cdot post \Rightarrow \mathcal{A}))$$

$\Rightarrow$ "Predicate law A.86"
$$(\forall\, v_0 \cdot v = v_0 \Rightarrow post[w \backslash E] \wedge (post[w \backslash E] \Rightarrow \mathcal{A}[w \backslash E]))$$

$\Rightarrow$ $(\forall\, v_0 \cdot v = v_0 \Rightarrow \mathcal{A}[w \backslash E])$

$\equiv$ "$\mathcal{A}$, E contain no v_0"
$$\mathcal{A}[w \backslash E]$$

$\equiv$ "assignment 23.1"
$$wp(w := E, \mathcal{A})\ .$$

With that, and *refinement* 23.3, we have proved *assignment* 5.2.

But we have done more: we have shown how to prove a law which formerly we had to take on faith. Such proofs have been used to establish the consistency of all the laws in this book, ensuring that no contradictions can occur. And new laws can be added, supported by similar proofs.

23.3.4 Local variables

Local variable declarations are code, and their meaning is this:

Definition 23.4 <u>local variable</u>

$$wp(|[\ \textbf{var}\ x \cdot prog\ ]|, \mathcal{A})\ \widehat{=}\ (\forall\, x \cdot wp(prog, \mathcal{A}))\,,$$

provided $\mathcal{A}$ contains no free x.
□

Definition 23.4 is well known but not often quoted. The proviso, similar to others below, is easily circumvented by renaming x in *prog* to some other fresh variable.

Typed local variables are discussed in Section 23.3.11.

23.3.5 Logical constants

Logical constant declarations are *not* code, but they have meaning nevertheless:

Definition 23.5 <u>logical constant</u>

$$wp(|[\ \textbf{con}\ x \cdot prog\ ]|, \mathcal{A})\ \widehat{=}\ (\exists\, x \cdot wp(prog, \mathcal{A}))\,,$$

provided $\mathcal{A}$ contains no free x.
□

Definition 23.5 is not so well known; it appears in [MG90]. In [Mor] it is introduced specifically for procedures. Our use of it is independent of procedures: we make precise the long-established use of logical constants for referring in the postcondition to initial values. Other uses have been discovered, in data refinement [MG90] for example.

As noted in [MG90], logical constants do not satisfy E.W. Dijkstra's Property 3 [Dij76, p.18]: that is, they do not distribute conjunction.

23.3.6 Feasibility

A command is feasible if it obeys the *Law of the Excluded Miracle* [Dij76, p.18]. That gives the following definition:

Definition 23.6 <u>feasibility</u> Command *prog* is *feasible* exactly when

$$wp(prog, \mathsf{false}) \quad \equiv \quad \mathsf{false} \ .$$

Otherwise it is *infeasible*.
□

Infeasible commands, because they break the law, are called *miracles*. They were introduced in [Mor87, Mor88d], and in [Nel89] (but not for refinement). Miracles are used also in [Abr87], and in [Mor88b] for data refinement.

It is easy to show that miracles refine only to miracles (just apply the definitions above), and hence never to code: E.W. Dijkstra's law paraphrased reads 'all code is feasible'.

23.3.7 Annotations

These definitions follow from the above, given *assumption* 1.6 and *coercion* 17.1. Assumptions are defined independently in [Mor87, Bac88, MV89]; coercions are defined in [MV89].

Definition 23.7 <u>assumption</u>

$$wp(\{pre\}, \mathcal{A}) \ \ \widehat{=} \ \ pre \wedge \mathcal{A} \ .$$

□

Definition 23.8 <u>coercion</u> Provided *post* contains no initial variables,

$$wp([post], \mathcal{A}) \ \ \widehat{=} \ \ post \Rightarrow \mathcal{A} \ .$$

□

All assertions are feasible; no coercion is feasible except [true].

23.3.8   Substitutions

The following definitions come from [Mor88c]:

Definition 23.9 <u>substitution by value</u>

$$wp(prog[\textbf{value } f\backslash E], \mathcal{A}) \;\; \widehat{=} \;\; wp(prog, \mathcal{A})[f\backslash E] \;,$$

provided f does not occur free in $\mathcal{A}$.
□

Definition 23.10 <u>substitution by result</u>

$$wp(prog[\textbf{result } f\backslash a], \mathcal{A}) \;\; \widehat{=} \;\; (\forall f \cdot wp(prog, \mathcal{A}[a\backslash f])) \;,$$

provided f does not occur free in $\mathcal{A}$.
□

Definition 23.11 <u>substitution by value-result</u>

$$wp(prog[\textbf{value result } f\backslash a], \mathcal{A}) \;\; \widehat{=} \;\; wp(prog, \mathcal{A}[a\backslash f])[f\backslash a],$$

provided f does not occur free in $\mathcal{A}$.
□

Those three definitions account for all the simple substitution laws of Chapter 11. Procedures and parameters are treated in [Bac87, Mor] also.

23.3.9   Recursion

This is the standard definition:

Definition 23.12 <u>recursion</u>   Let $\mathcal{C}(p)$ be a program fragment in which the name p appears. Then

$$\textbf{re } p \cdot \mathcal{C}(p) \textbf{ er}$$

is the *least-refined* program *fix* such that $\mathcal{C}(\textit{fix}) = \textit{fix}$.
□

Take **re** $p \cdot p$ **er**, for example. Since $prog = prog$ holds for all programs $prog$, the *fix* in Definition 23.12 is in this case the least-refined of all programs: it is **abort**.

Definition 23.12 gives indirectly the meaning of iteration, since iteration can be viewed as a certain kind of recursion:

$$\textbf{do } G \to prog \textbf{ od} \;\;\; = \;\;\; \textbf{re } P\cdot$$
$$\textbf{if } G \textbf{ then } prog; \; P \textbf{ fi}$$
$$\textbf{er} \;.$$

The meaning above generalises the standard meaning of iteration [Dij76, Gri81] in a way first explored in [Boo82]. Recursion is treated in [Nel89], and recursive procedures in [Bac87, Mor]. Recursion is much used in [Heh84].

23.3.10   Data refinement

Data refinement is abundantly defined; our definition appears in [GM91, Mor88a, Mor89, MG90, CU89]:

Definition 23.13 <u>data refinement</u>   Let a be a list of variables called *abstract*, let c be a list of variables called *concrete*, and let I be a formula called the *coupling invariant*. Then command $progA$ is data-refined to $progC$ by a, c, I exactly when for all postconditions $\mathcal{A}$ not containing c we have

$$(\exists\, a \cdot I \wedge wp(progA, \mathcal{A})) \quad \Rightarrow \quad wp(progC, (\exists\, a \cdot I \wedge \mathcal{A})) \,.$$

□

The approach of Chapter 17 is based mainly on [Mor88a, MG90].

23.3.11   Types

A precise treatment of types, and invariants, appears in [MV89], where the semantic function wp is extended to take them into account. The effect is roughly as follows.

Typed local variable and logical constant declarations are a combination of an untyped declaration and the imposition of a local invariant in which the type information appears. For example, the typed declaration $n : \mathbb{N}$ appears as $n \in \mathbb{N}$ in the local invariant. At any point in a program, the surrounding local invariants are conjoined and called the *context*, and the semantic function wp takes that context as an extra argument.

In a context C, commands behave as if C were assumed initially (aborting otherwise), and they are guaranteed to establish C if they terminate. For specifications, that effect is gained by imagining the context conjoined to both pre- and postcondition. Thus in the context $x \geq 0$ we have

$$
\begin{aligned}
&\quad x := x \pm 1 \\
&= \ x\colon [x = x_0 + 1 \vee x = x_0 - 1] \\
&= \ \text{``impose invariant in pre- and postcondition''} \\
&\quad\quad x\colon [x \geq 0 \ , \ x \geq 0 \wedge (x = x_0 + 1 \vee x = x_0 - 1)] \\
&= \ \textbf{if } x > 0 \rightarrow x := x - 1 \\
&\quad \ [\!]\ \ x \geq 0 \rightarrow x := x + 1 \\
&\quad \textbf{fi} \ .
\end{aligned}
$$

(The last equality can be shown using weakest preconditions directly; our laws would show only refinement.)

Note that the alternation above can abort when $x < 0$ initially, and when $x = 0$ initially the possibility $x := x - 1$ is automatically avoided.

Commands that cannot avoid breaking the invariant go ahead and break it, but establish it too: thus they are miracles. For example, in the same context we have

$$x := -1$$
$$= x \colon [x = -1]$$
$$= \text{``impose invariant in pre- and postcondition''}$$
$$x \colon [x \geq 0 \,,\; x \geq 0 \wedge x = -1]$$
$$= x \colon [x \geq 0 \,,\; \mathsf{false}] \;.$$

Thus $x := -1$, normally called ill-typed, is just a miracle when the declaration $x : \mathbb{N}$ is in effect: type checking is just feasibility checking.

Local invariants resulting from type declarations are called *implicit*; those introduced by **and** are called *explicit*. Explicit local invariants are not code; they are removed by laws that distribute them through compound programs towards atomic components. Removing a local invariant immediately surrounding, say, an assignment amounts only to checking that the assignment preserves it.

Appendix A

Some laws for predicate calculation

This collection of laws is drawn from [MS89].

A.1 Some propositional laws

Throughout this section $\mathcal{A}$, $\mathcal{B}$ are $\mathcal{C}$ denote formulae of predicate calculus. The laws are *propositional* because they do not deal with the quantification or substitution of variables.

A.1.1 Conjunction and disjunction

The propositional connectives for conjunction, $\wedge$, and disjunction, $\vee$, are idempotent, commutative, associative and absorptive, and they distribute through each other.

Idempotence of $\wedge$ and $\vee$
Conjunction and disjunction are *idempotent* connectives:
$$\mathcal{A} \wedge \mathcal{A} \quad \equiv \quad \mathcal{A} \quad \equiv \quad \mathcal{A} \vee \mathcal{A} . \tag{A.1}$$

Commutativity of $\wedge$ and $\vee$
Conjunction and disjunction are *commutative* connectives:
$$\mathcal{A} \wedge \mathcal{B} \quad \equiv \quad \mathcal{B} \wedge \mathcal{A} \tag{A.2}$$
$$\mathcal{A} \vee \mathcal{B} \quad \equiv \quad \mathcal{B} \vee \mathcal{A} . \tag{A.3}$$

Associativity of $\wedge$ and $\vee$
Conjunction and disjunction are *associative* connectives:
$$\mathcal{A} \wedge (\mathcal{B} \wedge \mathcal{C}) \quad \equiv \quad (\mathcal{A} \wedge \mathcal{B}) \wedge \mathcal{C} \tag{A.4}$$

$$\mathcal{A} \vee (\mathcal{B} \vee \mathcal{C}) \;\equiv\; (\mathcal{A} \vee \mathcal{B}) \vee \mathcal{C} \;. \tag{A.5}$$

Laws A.1 to A.5 mean that we can ignore duplication, order and bracketing in conjunctions $\mathcal{A} \wedge \mathcal{B} \wedge \cdots \wedge \mathcal{C}$ and disjunctions $\mathcal{A} \vee \mathcal{B} \vee \cdots \vee \mathcal{C}$.

Absorption laws
Sometimes terms can be removed immediately from expressions involving both conjunctions and disjunctions. This is *absorption*:

$$\mathcal{A} \wedge (\mathcal{A} \vee \mathcal{B}) \;\equiv\; \mathcal{A} \;\equiv\; \mathcal{A} \vee (\mathcal{A} \wedge \mathcal{B}) \;. \tag{A.6}$$

Distributive laws
The *distribution* of $\wedge$ through $\vee$ is similar to the distribution of multiplication over addition in arithmetic. But in logic distribution goes both ways, so that $\vee$ also distributes through $\wedge$:

$$\mathcal{A} \wedge (\mathcal{B} \vee \mathcal{C}) \;\equiv\; (\mathcal{A} \wedge \mathcal{B}) \vee (\mathcal{A} \wedge \mathcal{C}) \tag{A.7}$$
$$\mathcal{A} \vee (\mathcal{B} \wedge \mathcal{C}) \;\equiv\; (\mathcal{A} \vee \mathcal{B}) \wedge (\mathcal{A} \vee \mathcal{C}) \;. \tag{A.8}$$

A.1.2 Constants and negation

Units and zeroes
In ordinary multiplication, $a \times 1 = a$ and $a \times 0 = 0$. We say therefore that 1 is a *unit* and 0 a *zero* of multiplication. Similarly, the predicate constant true is the unit of $\wedge$ and the zero of $\vee$:

$$\mathcal{A} \wedge \mathsf{true} \;\equiv\; \mathcal{A} \tag{A.9}$$
$$\mathcal{A} \vee \mathsf{true} \;\equiv\; \mathsf{true} \;. \tag{A.10}$$

The constant false is the unit of $\vee$ and the zero of $\wedge$:

$$\mathcal{A} \wedge \mathsf{false} \;\equiv\; \mathsf{false} \tag{A.11}$$
$$\mathcal{A} \vee \mathsf{false} \;\equiv\; \mathcal{A} \;. \tag{A.12}$$

Negation as complement
Negation $\neg$ acts as a *complement*:

$$\neg\mathsf{true} \;\equiv\; \mathsf{false} \tag{A.13}$$
$$\neg\mathsf{false} \;\equiv\; \mathsf{true} \tag{A.14}$$
$$\mathcal{A} \wedge \neg\mathcal{A} \;\equiv\; \mathsf{false} \tag{A.15}$$
$$\mathcal{A} \vee \neg\mathcal{A} \;\equiv\; \mathsf{true} \;. \tag{A.16}$$

Furthermore it is an *involution*:

$$\neg\neg\mathcal{A} \;\equiv\; \mathcal{A} \;. \tag{A.17}$$

And it satisfies de Morgan's laws:

$$\neg(\mathcal{A} \wedge \mathcal{B}) \;\equiv\; \neg\mathcal{A} \vee \neg\mathcal{B} \tag{A.18}$$

$$\neg(\mathcal{A} \vee \mathcal{B}) \;\equiv\; \neg\mathcal{A} \wedge \neg\mathcal{B} \;. \tag{A.19}$$

Further absorptive laws

With negation, we have two more absorptive laws:

$$\mathcal{A} \vee (\neg\mathcal{A} \wedge \mathcal{B}) \;\equiv\; \mathcal{A} \vee \mathcal{B} \tag{A.20}$$

$$\mathcal{A} \wedge (\neg\mathcal{A} \vee \mathcal{B}) \;\equiv\; \mathcal{A} \wedge \mathcal{B} \;. \tag{A.21}$$

A.1.3   Normal forms

A formula is in *disjunctive normal form* if it is a finite disjunction of other formulae each of which is, in turn, a *conjunction* of simple formulae. *Conjunctive normal form* is defined complementarily.

Laws A.7, A.8, A.18 and A.19 allow us to convert any proposition to either disjunctive or conjunctive normal form, as we choose, and laws A.15 and A.16 serve to remove adjacent complementary formulae. For example,

$$\mathcal{A} \wedge \neg(\mathcal{B} \wedge \mathcal{C} \wedge \mathcal{A})$$

$\equiv$ "Predicate law A.18"

$$\mathcal{A} \wedge (\neg\mathcal{B} \vee \neg\mathcal{C} \vee \neg\mathcal{A})$$

$\equiv$ "Predicate law A.7"

$$(\mathcal{A} \wedge \neg\mathcal{B}) \vee (\mathcal{A} \wedge \neg\mathcal{C}) \vee (\mathcal{A} \wedge \neg\mathcal{A})$$

$\equiv$ "Predicate law A.15"

$$(\mathcal{A} \wedge \neg\mathcal{B}) \vee (\mathcal{A} \wedge \neg\mathcal{C}) \vee \mathsf{false}$$

$\equiv$ "Predicate law A.12"

$$(\mathcal{A} \wedge \neg\mathcal{B}) \vee (\mathcal{A} \wedge \neg\mathcal{C}) \;.$$

The second formula above is in conjunctive normal form and the third, fourth, and fifth are in disjunctive normal form.

A.1.4   Implication

Implication $\Rightarrow$ satisfies the law

$$\mathcal{A} \Rightarrow \mathcal{B} \;\equiv\; \neg\mathcal{A} \vee \mathcal{B} \;, \tag{A.22}$$

and that leads on to these laws:

$$\mathcal{A} \Rightarrow \mathcal{A} \;\equiv\; \mathsf{true} \tag{A.23}$$

$$\mathcal{A} \Rightarrow \mathcal{B} \;\equiv\; \neg(\mathcal{A} \wedge \neg\mathcal{B}) \tag{A.24}$$

$$\neg(\mathcal{A} \Rightarrow \mathcal{B}) \;\equiv\; \mathcal{A} \wedge \neg\mathcal{B} \tag{A.25}$$

$$\mathcal{A} \Rightarrow \mathcal{B} \;\equiv\; \neg\mathcal{B} \Rightarrow \neg\mathcal{A} \;. \tag{A.26}$$

The last above is called the *contrapositive law*. Useful special cases of those are

$$\mathcal{A} \Rightarrow \text{true} \;\equiv\; \text{true} \tag{A.27}$$

$$\text{true} \Rightarrow \mathcal{A} \;\equiv\; \mathcal{A} \tag{A.28}$$

$$\mathcal{A} \Rightarrow \text{false} \;\equiv\; \neg\mathcal{A} \tag{A.29}$$

$$\text{false} \Rightarrow \mathcal{A} \;\equiv\; \text{true} \tag{A.30}$$

$$\mathcal{A} \Rightarrow \neg\mathcal{A} \;\equiv\; \neg\mathcal{A} \tag{A.31}$$

$$\neg\mathcal{A} \Rightarrow \mathcal{A} \;\equiv\; \mathcal{A} \;. \tag{A.32}$$

These next two laws distribute implication $\Rightarrow$ through conjunction and disjunction:

$$\mathcal{C} \Rightarrow (\mathcal{A} \wedge \mathcal{B}) \;\equiv\; (\mathcal{C} \Rightarrow \mathcal{A}) \wedge (\mathcal{C} \Rightarrow \mathcal{B}) \tag{A.33}$$

$$(\mathcal{A} \vee \mathcal{B}) \Rightarrow \mathcal{C} \;\equiv\; (\mathcal{A} \Rightarrow \mathcal{C}) \wedge (\mathcal{B} \Rightarrow \mathcal{C}) \tag{A.34}$$

$$\mathcal{C} \Rightarrow (\mathcal{A} \vee \mathcal{B}) \;\equiv\; (\mathcal{C} \Rightarrow \mathcal{A}) \vee (\mathcal{C} \Rightarrow \mathcal{B}) \tag{A.35}$$

$$(\mathcal{A} \wedge \mathcal{B}) \Rightarrow \mathcal{C} \;\equiv\; (\mathcal{A} \Rightarrow \mathcal{C}) \vee (\mathcal{B} \Rightarrow \mathcal{C}) \;. \tag{A.36}$$

Extra laws of implication
The following laws are useful in showing that successive hypotheses may be conjoined or even reversed:

$$\mathcal{A} \Rightarrow (\mathcal{B} \Rightarrow \mathcal{C}) \;\equiv\; (\mathcal{A} \wedge \mathcal{B}) \Rightarrow \mathcal{C} \;\equiv\; \mathcal{B} \Rightarrow (\mathcal{A} \Rightarrow \mathcal{C}) \;. \tag{A.37}$$

And the next law is the basis of definition by cases:

$$(\mathcal{A} \Rightarrow \mathcal{B}) \wedge (\neg\mathcal{A} \Rightarrow \mathcal{C}) \;\equiv\; (\mathcal{A} \wedge \mathcal{B}) \vee (\neg\mathcal{A} \wedge \mathcal{C}) \;. \tag{A.38}$$

A.1.5 Equivalence

Equivalence satisfies this law:

$$\mathcal{A} \Leftrightarrow \mathcal{B} \;\equiv\; (\mathcal{A} \Rightarrow \mathcal{B}) \wedge (\mathcal{B} \Rightarrow \mathcal{A}) \tag{A.39}$$

$$\equiv\; (\mathcal{A} \wedge \mathcal{B}) \vee \neg(\mathcal{A} \vee \mathcal{B}) \tag{A.40}$$

$$\equiv\; \neg\mathcal{A} \Leftrightarrow \neg\mathcal{B} \;. \tag{A.41}$$

Also we have these:

$$\mathcal{A} \Leftrightarrow \mathcal{A} \;\equiv\; \text{true} \tag{A.42}$$

$$\mathcal{A} \Leftrightarrow \neg\mathcal{A} \;\equiv\; \text{false} \tag{A.43}$$

$$\mathcal{A} \Leftrightarrow \text{true} \;\equiv\; \mathcal{A} \tag{A.44}$$

$$\mathcal{A} \Leftrightarrow \text{false} \;\equiv\; \neg\mathcal{A} \tag{A.45}$$

$$\mathcal{A} \Rightarrow \mathcal{B} \;\equiv\; \mathcal{A} \Leftrightarrow (\mathcal{A} \wedge \mathcal{B}) \tag{A.46}$$

$$\mathcal{B} \Rightarrow \mathcal{A} \;\equiv\; \mathcal{A} \Leftrightarrow (\mathcal{A} \vee \mathcal{B}) \tag{A.47}$$

$$\mathcal{A} \vee (\mathcal{B} \Leftrightarrow \mathcal{C}) \;\equiv\; (\mathcal{A} \vee \mathcal{B}) \Leftrightarrow (\mathcal{A} \vee \mathcal{C}) \;. \tag{A.48}$$

Equivalence is commutative and associative

$$\mathcal{A} \Leftrightarrow \mathcal{B} \;\equiv\; \mathcal{B} \Leftrightarrow \mathcal{A} \tag{A.49}$$
$$\mathcal{A} \Leftrightarrow (\mathcal{B} \Leftrightarrow \mathcal{C}) \;\equiv\; (\mathcal{A} \Leftrightarrow \mathcal{B}) \Leftrightarrow \mathcal{C}\,, \tag{A.50}$$

and, from Laws A.46 and A.47, it satisfies E.W. Dijkstra's *Golden Rule*:

$$\Rightarrow \mathcal{A} \wedge \mathcal{B} \Leftrightarrow \mathcal{A} \Leftrightarrow \mathcal{B} \Leftrightarrow \mathcal{A} \vee \mathcal{B}\,. \tag{A.51}$$

A.2   Some predicate laws

In this section we consider laws concerning the universal and existential quantifiers, $\forall$ and $\exists$. Although for most practical purposes we wish the quantification to be *typed*

$$(\forall\, x : T \cdot \mathcal{A})$$
$$(\exists\, x : T \cdot \mathcal{A})\,,$$

where T denotes a type and $\mathcal{A}$ is a formula, for simplicity we state our laws using untyped quantifications:

$$(\forall\, x \cdot \mathcal{A})$$
$$(\exists\, x \cdot \mathcal{A})\,.$$

Each can be converted to a law for typed quantification by uniform addition of type information, *provided the type is non-empty*. These laws enable us to convert between the two styles:

$$(\forall x : T \cdot \mathcal{A}) \;\equiv\; (\forall x \cdot x \in T \Rightarrow \mathcal{A}) \tag{A.52}$$
$$(\exists x : T \cdot \mathcal{A}) \;\equiv\; (\exists x \cdot x \in T \wedge \mathcal{A})\,, \tag{A.53}$$

where the simple formula $x \in T$ means 'x is in the set T'.

For more general constraints than typing, we have these abbreviations as well, which include a range formula $\mathcal{R}$:

$$(\forall x : T \mid \mathcal{R} \cdot \mathcal{A}) \;\equiv\; (\forall x \cdot x \in T \wedge \mathcal{R} \Rightarrow \mathcal{A}) \tag{A.54}$$
$$(\exists x : T \mid \mathcal{R} \cdot \mathcal{A}) \;\equiv\; (\exists x \cdot x \in T \wedge \mathcal{R} \wedge \mathcal{A})\,, \tag{A.55}$$

Note that A.52 and A.54 introduce implication, but A.53 and A.55 introduce conjunction.

A.2.1   Substitution

Recall (p.8) that we write substitution of a term E for a variable x in a formula $\mathcal{A}$ as

$\mathcal{A}[x\backslash E]$,

and we write the multiple substitution of terms E and F for variables x and y respectively as

$\mathcal{A}[x, y\backslash E, F]$.

In simple cases, such substitutions just replace the variable by the term. In more complex cases, however, we must take account of whether variables are free or bound. Suppose, for example, that $\mathcal{A}$ is the formula $(\exists\, x \cdot x \neq y) \wedge x = y$; then

$$\mathcal{A}[x\backslash y] \quad \text{is} \quad (\exists\, x \cdot x \neq y) \wedge y = y \ ,$$
$$\text{but} \quad \mathcal{A}[y\backslash x] \quad \text{is} \quad (\exists\, z \cdot z \neq x) \wedge x = x \ .$$

The variable z is *fresh*, not appearing in $\mathcal{A}$. In the first case, $x \neq y$ is unaffected because *that* occurrence of x is bound by $\exists\, x$. Indeed, since we could have used any other letter (except y) without affecting the meaning of the formula — and it would not have been replaced in that case — we do not replace it in this case either. The occurrence of x in $x = y$ is free, however, and the substitution occurs.

In the second case, since both occurrences of y are free, both are replaced by x. But on the left we must not 'accidentally' quantify over the newly introduced x — $(\exists\, x \cdot x \neq x)$ would be wrong — so we change (before the substitution) the bound x to a fresh variable z.

Finally, note that multiple substitution can differ from successive substitution:

$$\mathcal{A}[y\backslash x][x\backslash y] \quad \text{is} \quad (\exists\, z \cdot z \neq y) \wedge y = y$$
$$\text{but} \quad \mathcal{A}[y, x\backslash x, y] \quad \text{is} \quad (\exists\, z \cdot z \neq x) \wedge y = x \ .$$

A.2.2 The one-point laws

These laws allow quantifiers to be eliminated in many cases. They are called 'one-point' because the bound variable is constrained to take one value exactly. If x does not occur (free) in the term E, then

$$(\forall\, x \cdot x = E \Rightarrow \mathcal{A}) \ \equiv \mathcal{A}[x\backslash E] \equiv \ (\exists\, x \cdot x = E \wedge \mathcal{A}) \ . \tag{A.56}$$

If the type T in Laws A.52 and A.53 is finite, say $\{a, b\}$, we have the similar

$$(\forall\, x : \{a, b\} \cdot \mathcal{A}) \ \equiv \ \mathcal{A}[x\backslash a] \wedge \mathcal{A}[x\backslash b] \tag{A.57}$$
$$(\exists\, x : \{a, b\} \cdot \mathcal{A}) \ \equiv \ \mathcal{A}[x\backslash a] \vee \mathcal{A}[x\backslash b] \ . \tag{A.58}$$

Those can be extended to larger (but still finite) types $\{a, b, \cdots, z\}$. We are led to think, informally, of universal and existential quantification as infinite conjunction and disjunction respectively over all the constants of our logic:

$$(\forall\, x : \mathbb{N} \cdot \mathcal{A}) \quad \text{represents} \quad \mathcal{A}(0) \wedge \mathcal{A}(1) \cdots$$
$$(\exists\, x : \mathbb{N} \cdot \mathcal{A}) \quad \text{represents} \quad \mathcal{A}(0) \vee \mathcal{A}(1) \cdots$$

A.2.3 Quantifiers alone

Quantification is idempotent:

$$(\forall\, x \cdot (\forall\, x \cdot \mathcal{A})) \;\equiv\; (\forall\, x \cdot \mathcal{A}) \tag{A.59}$$
$$(\exists\, x \cdot (\exists\, x \cdot \mathcal{A})) \;\equiv\; (\exists\, x \cdot \mathcal{A}) \;. \tag{A.60}$$

Extending de Morgan's laws A.18 and A.19, we have

$$\neg\,(\forall\, x \cdot \mathcal{A}) \;\equiv\; (\exists\, x \cdot \neg\mathcal{A}) \tag{A.61}$$
$$\neg\,(\exists\, x \cdot \mathcal{A}) \;\equiv\; (\forall\, x \cdot \neg\mathcal{A}) \;. \tag{A.62}$$

A.2.4 Extending the commutative laws

These laws extend the commutativity of $\wedge$ and $\vee$:

$$(\forall\, x \cdot (\forall\, y \cdot \mathcal{A})) \;\equiv\; (\forall\, x, y \cdot \mathcal{A}) \equiv\; (\forall\, y \cdot (\forall\, x \cdot \mathcal{A})) \tag{A.63}$$
$$(\exists\, x \cdot (\exists\, y \cdot \mathcal{A})) \;\equiv\; (\exists\, x, y \cdot \mathcal{A}) \equiv\; (\exists\, y \cdot (\exists\, x \cdot \mathcal{A})) \;. \tag{A.64}$$

A.2.5 Quantifiers accompanied

Extending the associative and previous laws,

$$(\forall\, x \cdot \mathcal{A} \wedge \mathcal{B}) \;\equiv\; (\forall\, x \cdot \mathcal{A}) \wedge (\forall\, x \cdot \mathcal{B}) \tag{A.65}$$
$$(\exists\, x \cdot \mathcal{A} \vee \mathcal{B}) \;\equiv\; (\exists\, x \cdot \mathcal{A}) \vee (\exists\, x \cdot \mathcal{B}) \tag{A.66}$$
$$(\exists\, x \cdot \mathcal{A} \Rightarrow \mathcal{B}) \;\equiv\; (\forall\, x \cdot \mathcal{A}) \Rightarrow (\exists\, x \cdot \mathcal{B}) \;. \tag{A.67}$$

Here are weaker laws (using $\Rightarrow$ rather than $\equiv$) which are nonetheless useful:

$$(\forall\, x \cdot \mathcal{A}) \;\Rightarrow\; (\exists\, x \cdot \mathcal{A}) \tag{A.68}$$
$$(\forall\, x \cdot \mathcal{A}) \vee (\forall\, x \cdot \mathcal{B}) \;\Rightarrow\; (\forall\, x \cdot \mathcal{A} \vee \mathcal{B}) \tag{A.69}$$
$$(\forall\, x \cdot \mathcal{A} \Rightarrow \mathcal{B}) \;\Rightarrow\; (\forall\, x \cdot \mathcal{A}) \Rightarrow (\forall\, x \cdot \mathcal{B}) \tag{A.70}$$
$$(\exists\, x \cdot \mathcal{A} \wedge \mathcal{B}) \;\Rightarrow\; (\exists\, x \cdot \mathcal{A}) \wedge (\exists\, x \cdot \mathcal{B}) \tag{A.71}$$
$$(\exists\, x \cdot \mathcal{A}) \Rightarrow (\exists\, x \cdot \mathcal{B}) \;\Rightarrow\; (\exists\, x \cdot \mathcal{A} \Rightarrow \mathcal{B}) \tag{A.72}$$
$$(\exists\, y \cdot (\forall\, x \cdot \mathcal{A})) \;\Rightarrow\; (\forall\, x \cdot (\exists\, y \cdot \mathcal{A})) \;. \tag{A.73}$$

A.2.6 Manipulation of quantifiers

If a variable has no free occurrences, its quantification is superfluous:

$$(\forall\, x \cdot \mathcal{A}) \;\equiv \mathcal{A} \quad \text{if } x \text{ is not free in } \mathcal{A} \tag{A.74}$$
$$(\exists\, x \cdot \mathcal{A}) \;\equiv \mathcal{A} \quad \text{if } x \text{ is not free in } \mathcal{A} \;. \tag{A.75}$$

Other useful laws of this kind are the following, many of which are specialisations of laws A.65 to A.67. In each case, x must not be free in the formula $\mathcal{N}$:

$$(\forall\, x \cdot \mathcal{N} \wedge \mathcal{B}) \quad\equiv\quad \mathcal{N} \wedge (\forall\, x \cdot \mathcal{B}) \tag{A.76}$$

$$(\forall\, x \cdot \mathcal{N} \vee \mathcal{B}) \quad\equiv\quad \mathcal{N} \vee (\forall\, x \cdot \mathcal{B}) \tag{A.77}$$

$$(\forall\, x \cdot \mathcal{N} \Rightarrow \mathcal{B}) \quad\equiv\quad \mathcal{N} \Rightarrow (\forall\, x \cdot \mathcal{B}) \tag{A.78}$$

$$(\forall\, x \cdot \mathcal{A} \Rightarrow \mathcal{N}) \quad\equiv\quad (\exists\, x \cdot \mathcal{A}) \Rightarrow \mathcal{N} \tag{A.79}$$

$$(\exists\, x \cdot \mathcal{N} \wedge \mathcal{B}) \quad\equiv\quad \mathcal{N} \wedge (\exists\, x \cdot \mathcal{B}) \tag{A.80}$$

$$(\exists\, x \cdot \mathcal{N} \vee \mathcal{B}) \quad\equiv\quad \mathcal{N} \vee (\exists\, x \cdot \mathcal{B}) \tag{A.81}$$

$$(\exists\, x \cdot \mathcal{N} \Rightarrow \mathcal{B}) \quad\equiv\quad \mathcal{N} \Rightarrow (\exists\, x \cdot \mathcal{B}) \tag{A.82}$$

$$(\exists\, x \cdot \mathcal{A} \Rightarrow \mathcal{N}) \quad\equiv\quad (\forall\, x \cdot \mathcal{A}) \Rightarrow \mathcal{N} \;. \tag{A.83}$$

Bound variables can be renamed, as long as the new name does not conflict with existing names:

$$(\forall\, x \cdot \mathcal{A}) \equiv (\forall\, y \cdot \mathcal{A}[x\backslash y]) \quad \text{if } y \text{ is not free in } \mathcal{A} \tag{A.84}$$

$$(\exists\, x \cdot \mathcal{A}) \equiv (\exists\, y \cdot \mathcal{A}[x\backslash y]) \quad \text{if } y \text{ is not free in } \mathcal{A} \;. \tag{A.85}$$

Finally, we have for any term E,

$$(\forall\, x \cdot \mathcal{A}) \quad\Rightarrow\quad \mathcal{A}[x\backslash E] \tag{A.86}$$

$$\mathcal{A}[x\backslash E] \quad\Rightarrow\quad (\exists\, x \cdot \mathcal{A}) \;. \tag{A.87}$$

If A is true for all x, then it is true for E in particular; and if A is true for E, then certainly it is true for some x.

Appendix B

Answers to some exercises

Those adopting the book for teaching may obtain a complete set of answers from the publisher.

Chapter 1

Answer 1.1 (p.13) The number of refinement steps has nothing to do with closeness to code. *Refinement* is a relation between the meanings of programs; *code* is a description of the way in which programs can be written. Here is a refinement '*from* code':

$$\mathbf{abort} \quad \sqsubseteq \quad y\colon \left[0 \le x \le 9 \ , \ y^2 = x\right].$$

Answer 1.2 (p.13) The new specification is the following:

$$y\colon \left[x \le 9 \ , \ (x < 0 \Rightarrow y = 0) \land (x \ge 0 \Rightarrow y^2 = x)\right].$$

Note that the original could abort if $x < 0$ initially.

Answer 1.4 (p.13) The valid ones are 1, 4, 5 and 7. (But you need *strengthen postcondition* 5.1 to show number 7.)

Answer 1.7 (p.14) On the left, the client cannot assume that x will not change; on the right, he can. But what is wrong with the following counter argument?

> On the right, the client cannot assume that x will change; on the left, he can.

Answer 1.8 (p.14)

$$x \leq 9 \Rightarrow (\exists\, y : \mathbb{R} \cdot (x < 0 \Rightarrow y = 0) \wedge (x \geq 0 \Rightarrow y^2 = x))$$
$\Leftarrow$ "Exercise 2.9"
$$(\exists\, y : \mathbb{R} \cdot (x < 0 \Rightarrow y = 0) \wedge (x \geq 0 \Rightarrow y^2 = x))$$
$\Leftarrow$ "Exercise 2.11"
$$(x < 0 \Rightarrow (\exists\, y : \mathbb{R} \cdot y = 0)) \wedge (x \geq 0 \Rightarrow (\exists\, y : \mathbb{R} \cdot y^2 = x))$$
$\equiv$ $\mathsf{true} \wedge (x \geq 0 \Rightarrow (\exists\, y : \mathbb{R} \cdot y^2 = x))$
$\equiv$ "property of $\mathbb{R}$"
true .

Answer 1.10 (p.14) From *feasibility* 1.4, we must prove that

$$x \geq 0 \quad \Rightarrow \quad \left(\exists\, y : \mathbb{R} \cdot y^2 = x \wedge y > 0\right).$$

But that is not true, since the right-hand side is equivalent to $x > 0$.

Informally, the program, when $x = 0$, must establish $y = 0$ (because $0^2 = 0$) and $y > 0$ (in the postcondition) simultaneously.

Answer 1.11 (p.14) It is feasible (false implies anything); it is never guaranteed to terminate. Hence it is **abort**. That it can change w is suggested by the remark on p.12 concerning the behaviour of **abort**. See also Exercise 8.8.

Answer 1.12 (p.14) Executing a false assumption causes the program to abort, and that does change the program (unless it would have aborted anyway). But a false assumption can be placed at a point which is never executed; there, it has no effect (and little value).

Answer 1.13 (p.14) Assumptions may be weakened; the program is refined because it assumes less.

Answer 1.14 (p.14)

$\{pre'\}\ \{pre\}$
$=$ "*assumption* 1.6"
$\{pre'\};\ : [pre\ ,\ \mathsf{true}]$
$=$ "*absorb assumption* 1.8"
$: [pre' \wedge pre\ ,\ \mathsf{true}]$
$=$ "*assumption* 1.6"
$\{pre' \wedge pre\}$.

Answer 1.17 (p.15) Remember that anything is refined (trivially) by itself.

Answer 1.18 (p.15) The law *strengthen postcondition* 1.1 requires $post \Rightarrow \mathsf{true}$; the law *weaken precondition* 1.2 requires $\mathsf{false} \Rightarrow pre$. Both hold.

Chapter 2

Answer 2.3 (p.25)   The propositional formulae are 1 and 7.   Number 2 is a variable; number 3 is an English word. Number 6 is a statement about two simple formulae.

Answer 2.5 (p.26)

1. $(\forall\, i : \mathbb{Z} \cdot \text{even } i \vee \text{odd } i)$
2. $(\forall\, m : \mathbb{N} \cdot \text{odd } m \Rightarrow (\exists\, n : \mathbb{N} \cdot \text{even } n \wedge m = n + 1))$
3. $(\exists\, i : \mathbb{Z} \cdot \text{even } i \wedge \neg (\exists\, n : \mathbb{N} \cdot \text{odd } n \wedge i = n + 1))$
4. $(\forall\, n : \mathbb{N} \cdot 0 \leq n)$
5. $\neg (\exists\, i : \mathbb{Z} \cdot (\forall\, j : \mathbb{Z} \cdot i \leq j))$
6. $(\forall\, r : \mathbb{R} \cdot r > 0 \Rightarrow (\exists\, s : \mathbb{R} \cdot 0 < s < r))$

Answer 2.6 (p.26) $(\exists\, y \cdot (\forall\, x \cdot \mathcal{A} \Rightarrow x = y))$.

Answer 2.8 (p.26)   We have for the first formula

$\mathcal{A}$	$\mathcal{B}$	$\mathcal{A}$	$\Rightarrow$	$(\mathcal{B}$	$\Rightarrow$	$\mathcal{A})$
true	true	true	true	true	true	true
true	false	true	true	false	true	true
false	true	false	true	true	false	false
false	false	false	true	false	true	false
			↑			

The indicated column is all true.
   The other formulae are done similarly.

Answer 2.9 (p.26)   Exercise 2.8 showed that $\mathcal{A} \Rightarrow (\mathcal{B} \Rightarrow \mathcal{A})$ is true in all states; that's what $\mathcal{A} \Rightarrow \mathcal{B} \Rightarrow \mathcal{A}$ means.

Answer 2.10 (p.26)

$(\exists\, x \cdot (\mathcal{A} \Rightarrow \mathcal{B}) \wedge (\neg \mathcal{A} \Rightarrow \mathcal{C}))$
$\equiv$ "Predicate law A.38"
$(\exists\, x \cdot \mathcal{A} \wedge \mathcal{B} \vee \neg \mathcal{A} \wedge \mathcal{C})$
$\equiv$ "Predicate law A.66"
$(\exists\, x \cdot \mathcal{A} \wedge \mathcal{B}) \vee (\exists\, x \cdot \neg \mathcal{A} \wedge \mathcal{C})$.

Answer 2.12 (p.26)

$(\exists\, a \cdot (\forall\, b \cdot \mathcal{A}))$
$\equiv$ "Predicate law A.74"
$(\forall\, b \cdot (\exists\, a \cdot (\forall\, b \cdot \mathcal{A})))$

⇒   "Predicate law A.86"
  $(\forall\, b \cdot (\exists\, a \cdot \mathcal{A}))$.

The converse is not true. (Try it.)

Chapter 3

Answer 3.3 (p.34)

$\quad x\colon [x = X \ , \ x = X^4]$
$\sqsubseteq$ "*sequential composition 3.3*"
$\quad x\colon [x = X \ , \ x = X^2]\,;$ $\qquad\qquad\qquad\qquad$ (i)
$\quad x\colon [x = X^2 \ , \ x = X^4]$ $\qquad\qquad\qquad\qquad$ (ii)
(i) $\sqsubseteq\ x := x^2$
(ii) $\sqsubseteq\ x := x^2$.

Answer 3.6 (p.34)

$\quad x,y,t\colon [x = X \wedge y = Y \ , \ x = Y \wedge y = X]$
$\sqsubseteq$ "*sequential composition 3.3*"
$\quad x,y,t\colon [x = X \wedge y = Y \ , \ t = Y \wedge y = X]\,;$
$\quad x,y,t\colon [t = Y \wedge y = X \ , \ x = Y \wedge y = X]$
$\sqsubseteq$ "*assignment 1.3*"
$\quad x,y,t\colon [x = X \wedge y = Y \ , \ t = Y \wedge y = X]\,;$ $\qquad\qquad\qquad$ ◁
$\quad x := t$
$\sqsubseteq$ "*sequential composition 3.3*"
$\quad x,y,t\colon [x = X \wedge y = Y \ , \ x = X \wedge t = Y]\,;$
$\quad x,y,t\colon [x = X \wedge t = Y \ , \ t = Y \wedge y = X]$
$\sqsubseteq$ "*assignment 1.3*"
$\quad t := y\,;$
$\quad y := x$.

Answer 3.7 (p.35)

$\quad x,y,t := y,x,?$
$\sqsubseteq$ "*open assignment 3.1*"
$\quad x,y,t := y,x,y$
$=$ "aim for leading $t := y$"
$\quad x,y,t := t[t \backslash y], x, y$
$=$ "*leading assignment 3.6*"
$\quad t := y\,;$
$\quad x,y := t,x$

$\quad$ = "special case of Law 3.6; t contains no y"
$\qquad t := y;$
$\qquad y := x;$
$\qquad x := t \,.$

Answer 3.8 (p.35)

$\qquad w, x\colon [pre \;,\; post]$
$\quad \sqsubseteq$ *"sequential composition 3.3"*
$\qquad w, x\colon [pre \;,\; post[x \backslash E]]\,;$
$\qquad w, x\colon [post[x \backslash E] \;,\; post]$ $\qquad\qquad\qquad\qquad$ ◁
$\quad \sqsubseteq\; x := E \,.$

Chapter 4

Answer 4.1 (p.39)

$\qquad x := \mathsf{abs}\, y$
$\quad \sqsubseteq$ **if** $y \geq 0 \to x\colon [y \geq 0 \;,\; x = \mathsf{abs}\, y]$ $\qquad\qquad$ (i)
$\qquad \llbracket\ y \leq 0 \to x\colon [y \leq 0 \;,\; x = \mathsf{abs}\, y]$ $\qquad\qquad$ (ii)
$\qquad$ **fi**
(i) $\sqsubseteq\; x := y$
(ii) $\sqsubseteq\; x := -y \,.$

Answer 4.4 (p.39) Write *prog* as $w\colon [pre \;,\; post]$, and use *absorb assumption* 1.8 everywhere. Then use *weaken precondition* 1.2 and the fact that $\mathcal{A} \Rrightarrow \mathcal{B}$ implies $\mathcal{A} \Rrightarrow \mathcal{A} \land \mathcal{B}$.

Chapter 5

Answer 5.2 (p.47) Let I abbreviate the invariant $n \neq 0 \land (\mathsf{pt}\, N \Leftrightarrow \mathsf{pt}\, n)$. The development then continues

$\quad \sqsubseteq\; n\colon [I \;,\; I \land \neg(2 \mid n)]$
$\quad \sqsubseteq$ "invariant I, variant n"
$\qquad$ **do** $2 \mid n \to$
$\qquad\qquad n\colon [2 \mid n \;,\; n \neq 0 \land (\mathsf{pt}\, N \Leftrightarrow \mathsf{pt}\, n) \;,\; 0 \leq n < n_0]$ $\qquad$ ◁
$\qquad$ **od**

$\sqsubseteq \ n := n \div 2 \ .$

It is the same code as before.

Answer 5.3 (p.47) The laws used are *sequential composition* 3.3 and *strengthen postcondition* 1.1. Continuing,

(i) $\sqsubseteq$ *"assignment 1.3"*

$\quad f := 1$

(ii) $\sqsubseteq$ *"invariant $f \times n! = F$, variant n"*

$\quad$ **do** $n \neq 0 \rightarrow$

$\qquad n, f \colon [n \neq 0 \ , \ f \times n! = F \ , \ 0 \leq n < n_0]$ ◁

$\quad$ **od**

$\sqsubseteq$ *"following assignment 3.5"*

$\quad n, f \colon [n \neq 0 \wedge f \times n! = F \ ,$
$\qquad f \times (n-1)! = F \wedge 0 \leq n-1 < n_0] \ ;$ ◁
$\quad n := n - 1$

$\sqsubseteq$ *"contract frame 5.4"*

$\quad f \colon [n \neq 0 \wedge f \times n! = F \ , \ f \times (n-1)! = F]$

$\sqsubseteq$ *"weaken precondition 1.2"*

$\quad f \colon [f \times n \times (n-1)! = F \ , \ f \times (n-1)! = F]$

$\sqsubseteq$ *"assignment 1.3"*

$\quad f := f \times n \ .$

Answer 5.4 (p.47) First we strengthen the postcondition, then we weaken the precondition. The conditions of *strengthen postcondition* 5.1 require

$(0 \leq x \leq 9)[y \backslash y_0] \wedge (0 \leq x \Rightarrow y^2 = x)$
$\Rightarrow \ y^2 = x \ .$

The law *weaken precondition* 1.2 requires the trivial $0 \leq x \leq 9 \Rightarrow$ true. Together they give the derivation

$\quad y \colon [0 \leq x \leq 9 \ , \ y^2 = x]$
$\sqsubseteq$ *"strengthen postcondition 5.1"*
$\quad y \colon [0 \leq x \leq 9 \ , \ 0 \leq x \Rightarrow y^2 = x]$
$\sqsubseteq$ *"weaken precondition 1.2"*
$\quad y \colon [y^2 = x] \ .$

Why is the order of the laws (5.1 before 1.2) important?

Answer 5.5 (p.48)

1. Use *assignment* 5.2: the condition is $y > x_0 \Rightarrow y > x_0$.
2. Use *assignment* 5.2: the condition is $x_0 < 0 \Rightarrow -x_0 > x_0$.

3. Use *assignment* 5.2: the condition is $\mathsf{true} \Rightarrow y_0 = y_0 \wedge x_0 = x_0$.

4. Use *assignment* 5.2: the condition is $x_0 = X + 1 \Rightarrow x_0 + 1 = X + 2$.

5. $\qquad x\colon [x = X + 1 \,,\, x = X + 2]$

$\qquad\qquad \sqsubseteq$ *"strengthen postcondition 5.1"*, $x_0 = X + 1 \wedge x = x_0 + 1 \Rightarrow x = X + 2$

$\qquad\quad x\colon [x = X + 1 \,,\, x = x_0 + 1]$

$\qquad\qquad \sqsubseteq$ *"weaken precondition 1.2"*

$\qquad\quad x\colon [x = x_0 + 1]$.

6. $\qquad x\colon [x = x_0 + 2]$

$\qquad\qquad \sqsubseteq \mathbf{con}\ X \cdot$

$\qquad\quad x\colon [x = x_0 + 1] \,;$

$\qquad\quad x\colon [x = X + 1 \,,\, x = X + 2]$ $\qquad\qquad\qquad\qquad\qquad \triangleleft$

$\qquad\qquad \sqsubseteq$ *"as in 5 above"*

$\qquad\quad x\colon [x = x_0 + 1]$.

This required the more advanced *sequential composition* 8.4. What did you use?

Answer 5.6 (p.48) The law would be as follows:

Law B.1 <u>initialised iteration</u> Provided *inv* contains no initial variables,

$$w\colon [pre \,,\, inv \wedge \neg G]$$

$\sqsubseteq w\colon [pre \,,\, inv] \,;$

$\qquad \mathbf{do}\ G \rightarrow w\colon [G \wedge inv \,,\, inv \wedge (0 \leq V < V_0)]\ \mathbf{od}$.

$\square$

The expression V is the variant.

Answer 5.8 (p.48) Conjuncts (5.8) and (5.9) of the invariant are sufficient to ensure requirement (5.7) of a fair handing-out, taking into account that the iteration body is executed exactly C times.

For requirement (5.6) it would be enough to know that $s = 0$ on termination, since conjunct (5.10) of the invariant then suffices. Unfortunately, the negated guard gives us $c = 0$, not $s = 0$.

We choose a slightly different invariant therefore, to get around that problem. Since by the quoted properties of $\lfloor\ \rfloor$ we have

$$\lfloor S/C \rfloor \leq \lfloor s/c \rfloor \equiv \lfloor S/C \rfloor \leq s/c \,,$$

and similarly for (5.9), we replace (5.8) and (5.9) by the single

$$c \times \lfloor S/C \rfloor \leq s \leq c \times \lceil S/C \rceil \,. \tag{B.1}$$

Then $c = 0$ (from termination of the iteration) together with (B.1), gives us $s = 0$, which is what we needed.

Now we must consider maintenance of the invariant. Conjunct (5.10) is maintained by the combination of 'hand out t' and $s := s - t$ in the body. For (B.1) we must show that the iteration body refines

$$c, s, t: [(B.1) , (B.1)] . \tag{i}$$

Following assignment gives us

$$\text{(i)} \sqsubseteq t: [(B.1) , (c - 1) \times \lfloor S/C \rfloor \le s - t \le (c - 1) \times \lceil S/C \rceil] \tag{ii}$$
$$c, s := c - 1, s - t$$

and, leaving aside the 'hand out', we could strengthen the postcondition to reach

$$\text{(ii)} \sqsubseteq t: [\lfloor s/c \rfloor \le t \le \lceil s/c \rceil]$$

provided

$$
\begin{aligned}
& \lfloor s/c \rfloor \le t \le \lceil s/c \rceil \\
\wedge \quad & c \times \lfloor S/C \rfloor \le s \le c \times \lceil S/C \rceil \\
\Rightarrow \quad & (c - 1) \times \lfloor S/C \rfloor \le s - t \le (c - 1) \times \lceil S/C \rceil .
\end{aligned}
\tag{B.2}
$$

Claim (B.2) is really the core of the problem; it is the key mathematical fact, finally extracted from the details of programming. To finish off, consider the following:

$$
\begin{aligned}
& (c - 1) \times \lfloor S/C \rfloor \le s - t \\
\Leftarrow \quad & \text{``} t \le \lceil s/c \rceil \text{ in antecedent''} \\
& (c - 1) \times \lfloor S/C \rfloor \le s - \lceil s/c \rceil \\
\equiv \quad & \lceil s/c \rceil \le s - (c - 1) \times \lfloor S/C \rfloor \\
\equiv \quad & \text{``property of } \lceil \ \rceil \text{''} \\
& s/c \le s - (c - 1) \times \lfloor S/C \rfloor \\
\equiv \quad & \text{``iteration guard ensures } c \ne 0 \text{''} \\
& (c - 1) \times \lfloor S/C \rfloor \le (c - 1) \times s/c \\
\Leftarrow \quad & \text{``even when } c = 1!\text{''} \\
& \lfloor S/C \rfloor \le s/c \\
\equiv \quad & \text{``} c \ne 0 \text{ again''} \\
& c \times \lfloor S/C \rfloor \le s ,
\end{aligned}
$$

which is given to us in the antecedent of Claim (B.2): it is part of the invariant. The other inequality is handled similarly.

This has been a simple problem, but not an easy one; and that is often the case. Finding an invariant, and then discovering an inexorable proof that it is the *correct* invariant, can take a very long time. In spite of that, one should aim to make the resulting reasoning so clear and polished that its *checking* is very short. Then — and only then — is the correctness of the program finally 'obvious'.

Chapter 6

Answer 6.3 (p.61) It follows from $n \in \mathbb{N} \wedge z = n \Rightarrow z \geq 0$.

Answer 6.5 (p.61) We would use **var** $c : \mathbb{N}$; **and** $c = 3$. The remaining difference is that we can assign to such constants, and that is feasible as long as the value assigned is the value it already has. That cannot be checked automatically by a compiler, so conventional languages allow **const** declarations in code only by prohibiting assignments to them altogether.

Answer 6.6 (p.61) Yes. Use of the law *assignment* 1.3 requires true $\wedge n \in \mathbb{N} \Rightarrow (-1)^2 = 1$. The assignment is infeasible, however, and in Section 6.6 that was called ill-typed.

Answer 6.7 (p.61)

1. Infeasible: z might be negative.
2. Feasible: $\mathbb{N} \subseteq \mathbb{Z}$.
3. Feasible.
4. Infeasible: even if positive, an integer need not have an integral square root.
5. Feasible: If c is a complex root of unity, then c and $1/c$ are conjugates.

Answer 6.10 (p.62) Unfold the iteration *twice*, as shown on p.42. The first execution of the body establishes $E < e$; the second requires $E = e$, and so can abort (which it shouldn't).

Chapter 7

Answer 7.2 (p.66) See Figure 19.1.

Answer 7.4 (p.66) The formula $p < q$ is implied by the previous precondition. The 'increasing variant' was originally $(q - r) < (q_0 - r_0)$; contracting the frame gave $(q - r) < (q - r_0)$; then strengthening the postcondition gave $r_0 < r$.

Chapter 8

Answer 8.2 (p.72) It is unnecessary because if x is not in the frame, its initial and final values are equal. Here is the proof of equality:

$$w: [pre , post]$$
$$= \text{``expand frame 8.3''}$$
$$w, x: [pre , post \wedge x = x_0]$$
$$= w, x: [pre , post[x_0 \backslash x] \wedge x = x_0]$$
$$= \text{``expand frame 8.3''}$$
$$w: [pre , post[x_0 \backslash x]] .$$

Answer 8.4 (p.73) Note first that $pre[w \backslash w_0] \Rightarrow (\exists w \cdot pre)$, from Predicate law A.87. Then we have

$$w: [pre , post]$$
$$\sqsubseteq \text{``strengthen postcondition 5.1''}$$
$$w: [pre , (\exists w \cdot pre) \Rightarrow post]$$
$$\sqsubseteq \text{``strengthen postcondition 1.1''}$$
$$w: [pre , (\exists w \cdot pre) \wedge post]$$
$$\sqsubseteq \text{``strengthen postcondition 5.1''}$$
$$w: [pre , post] .$$

Answer 8.5 (p.73) The result is this law:

Law B.2 <u>sequential composition</u>

$$w, x: [pre , post]$$
$$\sqsubseteq x: [pre , mid];$$
$$w, x: [mid , post].$$

The formula *mid* must not contain initial variables; and *post* must not contain x_0.

□

Law B.2 allows initial variables w_0 in post, since the first command $x: [pre , mid]$ in the composition does not change them. In contrast, *sequential composition* 3.3 allows no initial variables at all.

Answer 8.7 (p.73)

$$w: [\mathsf{true} , \mathsf{false}]$$
$$\sqsubseteq \text{``contract frame 5.4''}$$
$$: [\mathsf{true} , \mathsf{false}] \qquad = \mathbf{magic}$$
$$\sqsubseteq \text{``expand frame 8.3''}$$
$$w: [\mathsf{true} , \mathsf{false} \wedge w = w_0]$$
$$\sqsubseteq w: [\mathsf{true} , \mathsf{false}].$$

Chapter 9

Answer 9.2 (p.91)

1. $\{n : \mathbb{N} \cdot n^2\}$
2. $\left\{i, j, k : \mathbb{N} \cdot 2^i 3^j 4^k\right\}$
3. $\mathbb{N}^{++} - \{i, j : \mathbb{N}^{++} \cdot i \times j\}$, where $\mathbb{N}^{++} \;\hat{=}\; \{k : \mathbb{N} \mid k \geq 2\}$
4. $\{c : \mathbb{C} \mid c^n = 1\}$

Answer 9.3 (p.91)   Using the alternative definition, the promoted relation is transitive if the original relation is. But this law, for example, no longer holds:

$$s1 \odot s2 \wedge s1' \subseteq s1 \wedge s2' \subseteq s2 \quad \Rightarrow \quad s1' \odot s2' \ .$$

We retain the original definition, therefore.

Answer 9.6 (p.91)

$$\begin{aligned}
\{\mid \mathsf{true} \cdot x\} &= \{x\} \\
\{\mid \mathsf{false} \cdot x\} &= \{\} \\
\langle i : 0 {\to} n \cdot x \rangle &= \underbrace{\langle x, x, \cdots, x \rangle}_{n \text{ times}} .
\end{aligned}$$

Answer 9.7 (p.91)   The definition is $\prod q \;\hat{=}\; (\times x : q)$. The empty product $\prod \langle \rangle$ is 1, because 1 is the identity of multiplication.

Answer 9.10 (p.91)   It gives the size of the set. The same applies to bags and sequences.

Answer 9.16 (p.92)   The placement of the well-definedness assumption allows abortion explicitly in any case in which $as[i]$ is 'undefined', and there are two cases: when the iteration is encountered for the first time; and when the guard is re-evaluated after an execution of the iteration body.

For the refinement, we have

$$\begin{aligned}
&i{:}\,[a \in as \ , \ a = as[i]] \\
&\sqsubseteq \text{``}I \;\hat{=}\; a \in as{\downarrow}i\text{''} \\
&\quad i{:}\,[a \in as \ , \ I]; && \text{(i)} \\
&\quad i{:}\,[I \ , \ I \wedge a = as[i]] && \text{(ii)} \\
&\text{(i)} \sqsubseteq \text{``}w{:}\,[pre \ , \ post] \sqsubseteq w{:}\,[pre \ , \ post]; \{post\}\text{''} \\
&\quad i := 0; \\
&\quad \{I\} && \triangleleft \\
&\sqsubseteq \text{``}weaken\ precondition\ 1.2\text{''} \\
&\quad \{i < N\}
\end{aligned}$$

(ii) $\sqsubseteq$ **do** $a \neq as[i] \rightarrow$
$\qquad i: [a \neq as[i] , I , i_0 < i \leq N]$ $\qquad\qquad\qquad\qquad\qquad$ ◁
$\qquad$ **od**
$\quad \sqsubseteq$ "as above"
$\qquad i: [a \neq as[i] , I , i_0 < i \leq N]$ $\qquad\qquad\qquad\qquad$ (iii)
$\qquad \{I\}$ $\qquad\qquad\qquad\qquad\qquad\qquad\qquad\qquad\qquad$ ◁
$\quad \sqsubseteq \{i < N\}$
(iii) $\sqsubseteq i := i + 1$.

Although some of the above manipulations of assumptions do not follow easily from the laws we have so far, they should be intuitively plausible: since $w: [pre , post]$ establishes *post*, one can sequentially compose on the right with $\{post\}$, which behaves like **skip** in those circumstances. A 'nice' formal derivation of that step would be

$\qquad i: [a \in as , a \in as{\downarrow}i]$
$\quad \sqsubseteq \{a \in as{\downarrow}0\} \; i := 0$
$\quad \sqsubseteq$ "*advance assumption* 22.2 backwards"
$\qquad i := 0;$
$\qquad \{a \in as{\downarrow}i\} ,$

using a law postponed until Chapter 22 (though not a very complicated one).

Evaluation of $as[i]$ when $i = N$ is 'now' acceptable because the assumptions $\{i < N\}$ abort in that case anyway, and so it matters not at all what the implementation might do with $as[N]$.

The general rule connecting invariants and possibly 'undefined' iteration guards is that the invariant should imply the well-definedness condition of the guard. Requiring those conditions explicitly as assumptions in the code has the effect of forcing the developer to use just such an invariant.

Answer 9.17 (p.93) The specification terminates unconditionally, but the program aborts at the first assumption when (for example) $N = 0$. The refinement by that fact alone is invalid. (Look for *simple* counter examples.)

Operationally, the code of Exercise 9.15 under the conditions of Exercise 9.16 is inappropriate because evaluation of the iteration guard could fail (and cause abortion) when $i = N$. See Exercise 13.3 for one of the well-known ways around that problem.

Chapter 10

Answer 10.1 (p.100) The main step is *leading assignment* 8.5, after writing true as $(k = 0)[k \backslash 0]$. But the refinement is operationally obvious anyway: after assigning 0 to k, the precondition $k = 0$ may be assumed.

Answer 10.2 (p.100)

1. If $P{\uparrow}l \not\leq P[l]$, then $P{\uparrow}l$ cannot be empty; hence l cannot be 0. Thus the greatest element $P[l \ominus 1]$ of $P{\uparrow}l$ (which is sorted) must exceed $P[l]$. The converse is immediate.

2. For any sequence q such that up q, we have $x \leq q$ iff $x \leq q[0]$. Apply that to $P{\downarrow}l$, noting that up $P \backslash \{l \ominus 1\}$ implies up $P{\downarrow}l$.

3. From the other conjuncts, we have $P[l] < P[l \ominus 1] \leq P{\downarrow}(l+1)$.

Answer 10.4 (p.100) The guard $\neg J$ is $P{\uparrow}l \not\leq P[l]$, and that was simplified in Answer 10.2 to $l \neq 0 \wedge P[l \ominus 1] > P[l]$. We can perform that simplification here as well, because the invariant was in the precondition at the point the iteration was developed.

Answer 10.5 (p.100) It is $L[as \backslash as[l := t]]$; that is, it is as before if we imagine as with its lth element replaced by t.

Since the changed program does not maintain the local invariant, it must be removed first.

Answer 10.6 (p.101) If the sequence contains repeated elements initially, no amount of sorting is going to make them go away: a strictly ascending sequence cannot result, no matter what code we use.

The step in error is the refinement of (iv) to a swap. Conjuncts J and K will have been modified to be strict —

$$
\begin{aligned}
J &\mathrel{\hat{=}} P{\uparrow}l < P[l] \\
K &\mathrel{\hat{=}} P[l] < P{\uparrow}(l+1)
\end{aligned}
$$

— and the K part of the invariant is not maintained by the swap. (Check it!)

Answer 10.10 (p.101) There's no good reason why not. But one should avoid the impression that a strategy must be officially a 'law' in order to be valid, or useful.

Answer 10.11 (p.101) The meaning of the program is unaffected by the difference between $k-1$ and $k \ominus 1$, since the assignment is executed only when $k > 0$, and there the two alternatives are equal. The only disadvantage in using $k-1$ is that *if* variable k is typed as a natural number (instead of, say, as an integer), *and* automatic type checking is performed (the kind that can't 'notice' that $k > 0$ in the iteration body), *then* the statement will be rejected as ill-typed: a conservative, but at least a safe, judgement.

The disadvantage of using $k \ominus 1$ is that it would have distracted attention from the main issue, down iteration itself.

Chapter 11

Answer 11.1 (p.115)

1.
$$(a := f + 1)[\textbf{value } f \backslash a]$$

$$= \ |[\quad \textbf{var } l \cdot$$
$$l := a;$$
$$a := l + 1$$
$$]|$$

$$= \ a := a + 1 \ .$$

2.
$$(f := a + 1)[\textbf{result } f \backslash a]$$

$$= \ |[\quad \textbf{var } l \cdot$$
$$l := a + 1;$$
$$a := l$$
$$]|$$

$$= \ a := a + 1 \ .$$

3.
$$(f := a + 1)[\textbf{value result } f \backslash a]$$

$$= \ |[\quad \textbf{var } l \cdot$$
$$l := a;$$
$$l := a + 1;$$
$$a := l$$
$$]|$$

$$= \ a := a + 1 \ .$$

4.
$$(f := f + 1)[\textbf{value result } f \backslash a]$$

$$= \ |[\quad \textbf{var } l \cdot$$
$$l := a;$$
$$l := l + 1;$$
$$a := l$$
$$]|$$

$$= \ a := a + 1 \ .$$

Answer 11.2 (p.115)

1.
$$n := (n + 1)!$$

$$= \ |[\quad \textbf{var } a, f \cdot$$
$$a := f;$$
$$f := a!;$$
$$n := f$$
$$]|$$

$$\sqsubseteq \ (f := a!)[\textbf{value } a; \textbf{result } f \backslash n + 1, n] \ .$$

2.
$$a:> a$$
$$= \ [\![\ \textbf{var } l\cdot$$
$$l:= a;$$
$$a:> l$$
$$]\!]$$
$$\sqsubseteq \ a: [a > b] \, [\textbf{value } b\backslash a] \ .$$

3.
$$x: [x \neq 0 \ , \ x = 1/x_0]$$
$$\sqsubseteq \ x: [(p \neq 0)[p\backslash x] \ , \ (x = 1/p_0)[p_0\backslash x_0]]$$
$$\sqsubseteq \ [\![\ \textbf{var } p, q\cdot$$
$$p:= x;$$
$$q: [p \neq 0 \ , \ q \times p = 1];$$
$$x:= q$$
$$]\!]$$
$$\sqsubseteq \ q: [p \neq 0 \ , \ q \times p = 1] \, [\textbf{value } p; \, \textbf{result } q\backslash x, x] \ .$$

Answer 11.3 (p.115)

$$x: [0 \leq x \ , \ x^2 = x_0]$$
$$\sqsubseteq \ [\![\ \textbf{var } a, b : \mathbb{R}\cdot$$
$$a, b, x: [0 \leq x \ , \ x^2 = x_0]$$
$$]\!]$$
$$\sqsubseteq \ \textit{``following assignment 3.5''}$$
$$[\![\ \textbf{var } a, b : \mathbb{R}\cdot$$
$$a, b, x: [0 \leq x \ , \ b^2 = x_0];$$
$$x:= b$$
$$]\!]$$
$$\sqsubseteq \ \textit{``leading assignment 8.5; contract frame 5.4''}$$
$$[\![\ \textbf{var } a, b : \mathbb{R}\cdot$$
$$a:= x;$$
$$b: [0 \leq a \ , \ b^2 = a_0];$$
$$x:= b$$
$$]\!]$$
$$\sqsubseteq \ \textit{Sqrts } (x, x) \ .$$

Answer 11.4 (p.115) Variable a has been captured. Here is the correct use of the Copy Rule:

$$[\![\ \textbf{procedure } \textit{One} \ \hat{=} \ a:= 1 \cdot [\![\ \textbf{var } a \cdot \textit{One} \ ]\!] \ ]\!]$$
$$\sqsubseteq \ [\![\ \textbf{procedure } \textit{One} \ \hat{=} \ a:= 1 \cdot [\![\ \textbf{var } b \cdot \textit{One} \ ]\!] \ ]\!]$$
$$\sqsubseteq \ [\![\ \textbf{var } b \cdot a:= 1 \ ]\!]$$
$$\sqsubseteq \ a:= 1 \ .$$

Answer 11.6 (p.116) Using a local invariant makes this easier; otherwise, just carry the bag-condition through. We have

$$p, q, r: \left[\begin{array}{c} p \leq q \leq r \\ \llbracket p, q, r \rrbracket = \llbracket p_0, q_0, r_0 \rrbracket \end{array} \right]$$
$\sqsubseteq$ **con** B; **and** $B = \llbracket p, q, r \rrbracket$.

$p, q, r: [p \leq q \leq r]$
$\sqsubseteq$ *"sequential composition 3.3"*

$$\begin{array}{ll} p, q, r: [p \leq q] ; & \text{(i)} \\ p, q, r: [p \leq q \ , \ p \leq r \wedge q \leq r] ; & \text{(ii)} \\ p, q, r: [p \leq r \wedge q \leq r \ , \ p \leq q \leq r] & \text{(iii)} \end{array}$$

(i) $\sqsubseteq p, q := p \sqcap q, p \sqcup q$
(ii) $\sqsubseteq q, r := q \sqcap r, q \sqcup r$
(iii) $\sqsubseteq p, q := p \sqcap q, p \sqcup q$.

The three commands are just an unfolded insertion sort; the invariant is maintained trivially.

Answer 11.7 (p.116) It is given in Section 6.2.3.

Chapter 12

Answer 12.2 (p.122)

$$\neg \, \mathsf{hi} \, k$$
$$\equiv \quad (\exists j : l {\rightarrow} k \cdot k \rightsquigarrow j \wedge as[k] > as[j]) \ .$$

From J, however, we have $\mathsf{ph}(l{\rightarrow}h - \{k\})$, so the j whose existence is asserted above must be either $2k+1$ or $2k+2$. Thus we continue

$$\equiv \quad \left\{ \begin{array}{l} 2k+1 < h \wedge as[k] > as[2k+1] \\ \vee \quad 2k+2 < h \wedge as[k] > as[2k+2] \ . \end{array} \right.$$

Answer 12.4 (p.122) We assume that all variables range over strictly positive values. From the definition of $\lim_{N\to\infty}$, we have

$$(\forall \, c \cdot (\exists \, M \cdot (\forall \, N \cdot N \geq M \Rightarrow \mathsf{f} \, N / \mathsf{g} \, N \leq c))) \, .$$

By Predicate law A.68 we conclude that

$$(\exists \, c, M \cdot (\forall \, N \cdot N \geq M \Rightarrow \mathsf{f} \, N \leq c \times \mathsf{g} \, N)) \, ,$$

which is just $\mathsf{f} \preceq \mathsf{g}$. It remains to show that $\mathsf{f} \not\succeq \mathsf{g}$, and we proceed

$$\neg\,(\exists\, c, M \cdot (\forall\, N \cdot N \geq M \Rightarrow \mathsf{g}\, N \leq c \times \mathsf{f}\, N))$$

$\equiv$ "Predicate laws A.61, A.62"
$$(\forall\, c, M \cdot (\exists\, N \cdot N \geq M \wedge \mathsf{f}\, N < 1/c \times \mathsf{g}\, N))$$

$\Leftarrow$ "take $d = 1/2c$"
$$(\forall\, d, M \cdot (\exists\, N \cdot N \geq M \wedge \mathsf{f}\, N \leq d \times \mathsf{g}\, N))$$

$\Leftarrow$ "Lemma B.1 below"
$$(\forall\, d \cdot (\exists\, M \cdot (\forall\, N \cdot N \geq M \Rightarrow \mathsf{f}\, N \leq d \times \mathsf{g}\, N)))$$

$\equiv$ the formula above.

In fact, Lemma B.1 is the interesting part of this exercise:

Lemma B.1 If $\mathcal{A}$ does not contain free M, then

$$(\exists\, M \cdot (\forall\, N \cdot N \geq M \Rightarrow \mathcal{A})) \Rightarrow (\forall\, M \cdot (\exists\, N \cdot N \geq M \wedge \mathcal{A})).$$

Proof:

$$(\exists\, M \cdot (\forall\, N \cdot N \geq M \Rightarrow \mathcal{A}))$$

$\equiv$ "L fresh; Predicate law A.74"
$$(\forall\, L \cdot (\exists\, M \cdot (\forall\, N \cdot N \geq M \Rightarrow \mathcal{A})))$$

$\Rightarrow$ "Predicate law A.86"
$$(\forall\, L \cdot (\exists\, M \cdot L \sqcup M \geq M \Rightarrow \mathcal{A}[N \backslash L \sqcup M]))$$

$\equiv$ "$L \sqcup M \geq M$ is identically true"
$$(\forall\, L \cdot (\exists\, M \cdot \mathcal{A}[N \backslash L \sqcup M]))$$

$\equiv$ "$L \sqcup M \geq L$ is identically true"
$$(\forall\, L \cdot (\exists\, M \cdot L \sqcup M \geq L \wedge \mathcal{A}[N \backslash L \sqcup M]))$$

$\Rightarrow$ "Predicate law A.87"
$$(\forall\, L \cdot (\exists\, M, N \cdot N \geq L \wedge \mathcal{A}))$$

$\equiv$ "Predicate laws A.75, A.84; L, M not free in $\mathcal{A}$"
$$(\forall\, M \cdot (\exists\, N \cdot N \geq M \wedge \mathcal{A})).$$

$\square$

Answer 12.8 (p.123) They do not obey the usual rules for equality: we can have $\mathsf{f} = O(\mathsf{h})$ and $\mathsf{g} = O(\mathsf{h})$, but $\mathsf{f} = \mathsf{g}$ does not follow. The intended meaning is $\mathsf{f} \in O(\mathsf{h})$, where $O(\mathsf{h}) \triangleq \{\mathsf{f} \mid \mathsf{f} \preceq \mathsf{h}\}$.

Answer 12.10 (p.123) Time complexity N is 'faster than' $2N$, though both are linear. Similarly, Quick Sort is faster than Heap Sort by some constant factor, on average. Incidentally, Quick Sort has worst-case complexity N^2, but in the worst case Heap Sort is still $N \log N$.

Chapter 13

Answer 13.1 (p.130) No. That *es* is finite is used when defining the variant to be #*es*, since that must be an integer.

(For those with some knowledge of set theory: The variant can be any ordinal-valued function, even infinite. But in developing iteration or recursion we depend on a strict decrease of the variant:

$$\#(es - \{e\}) < \#es.$$

That is not true when #*es* is infinite; instead, the two expressions are equal.)

Answer 13.2 (p.130)

> **procedure** *Fact'*(**value** $m, k : \mathbb{N}$) $\;\widehat{=}\; f := m! \times k$
> $\sqsubseteq$ **variant** M **is** $m \cdot$
>   **if** $m = 0 \rightarrow f := k$
> $[\!]\;\; m > 0 \rightarrow \{0 < m = M\}\, f := m! \times k$ ◁
>   **fi**
> $\sqsubseteq$ $f\colon [0 \le m \ominus 1 < M \;,\; f = (m \ominus 1)! \times m \times k]$
> $\sqsubseteq$ *Fact'* $(m \ominus 1, m \times k)$.

Chapter 14

Answer 14.1 (p.135) See Figure B.1.

Answer 14.2 (p.135) The defining properties of the Gray code treat cases $n = 0$, $n = 1$, and $n \ge 2$; the code should do the same.

Answer 14.6 (p.135)

> $\alpha, \omega\colon [\omega = \mathsf{rv}\,\alpha_0]$
> $\sqsubseteq$ **rewrite**;
> $\alpha, \omega\colon [\omega = \omega_0 \,+\!\!\!+\, \mathsf{rv}\,\alpha_0]$ ◁
> $\sqsubseteq$ **re** R **variant** N **is** $\#\alpha \cdot$
> $\alpha, \omega\colon [\#\alpha = N \;,\; \omega = \omega_0 \,+\!\!\!+\, \mathsf{rv}\,\alpha_0]$
> $\sqsubseteq$ **if**   eof $\rightarrow$ **skip**
> $[\!]\;\; \neg$eof $\rightarrow$
> $\alpha, \omega\colon [\alpha \neq \langle\rangle \wedge \#\alpha = N \;,\; \omega = \omega_0 \,+\!\!\!+\, \mathsf{rv}\,\alpha_0]$ ◁
>   **fi**
> $\sqsubseteq$ **var** $e : E \cdot$
> $\alpha, \omega, e\colon [\#\,\mathsf{tl}\,\alpha < N \;,\; \omega = \omega_0 \,+\!\!\!+\, \mathsf{rv}\,\mathsf{tl}\,\alpha_0 \,+\!\!\!+\, \langle\mathsf{hd}\,\alpha_0\rangle]$

n	$\mathbf{gc}\, n$	binary
0	0	0
1	1	1
2	1 1	1 0
3	1 0	1 1
4	1 1 0	1 0 0
5	1 1 1	1 0 1
6	1 0 1	1 1 0
7	1 0 0	1 1 1
8	1 1 0 0	1 0 0 0
9	1 1 0 1	1 0 0 1
10	1 1 1 1	1 0 1 0
11	1 1 1 0	1 0 1 1
12	1 0 1 0	1 1 0 0
13	1 0 1 1	1 1 0 1
14	1 0 0 1	1 1 1 0
15	1 0 0 0	1 1 1 1

Figure B.1 Gray codes

$\sqsubseteq$ **input** e;
$\quad \alpha, \omega: [\#\alpha < N \ , \ \omega = \omega_0 \mathbin{+\mkern-8mu+} \mathsf{rv}\, \alpha_0 \mathbin{+\mkern-8mu+} \langle e \rangle]$ ◁
$\sqsubseteq \alpha, \omega: [\#\alpha < N \ , \ \omega \mathbin{+\mkern-8mu+} \langle e \rangle = \omega_0 \mathbin{+\mkern-8mu+} \mathsf{rv}\, \alpha_0 \mathbin{+\mkern-8mu+} \langle e \rangle]$;   ◁
$\quad$ **output** e
$\sqsubseteq R$.

Chapter 15

Answer 15.2 (p.150)

1. $Buf \ \hat{=}\ \mathsf{empty} \mid \mathsf{full}\, \mathbb{N}$
2. $Tree \ \hat{=}\ \mathsf{tip}\, \mathbb{R} \mid \mathsf{node}\ Tree\ Tree$
3. violet | indigo | blue | green | yellow | orange | red

Answer 15.3 (p.150)

$\quad$ **if** nn **is** $\mathsf{ok}\, n \rightarrow nn := \mathsf{ok}(n+1)$ **fi** 'increments' n is if is not undefined, and aborts otherwise.

Answer 15.4 (p.150) The specification is $d: [k \text{ in } db \Rightarrow \text{full } k \; d \in db]$.

Answer 15.6 (p.150) The specification is

> **if** $\neg(k \text{ in } db) \rightarrow d := \text{undefined}$
> $[\![\ \ k \text{ in } db \quad \rightarrow d: [\text{full } k \; d \in db]$
> **fi**

Why is the overall specification feasible even though the body of the second branch, on its own, is not?

Answer 15.9 (p.150) The reasoning would continue

$\equiv$ "Predicate law A.56"
   $paradox \in \text{set } TooBig \wedge \text{several } paradox \notin paradox$,

establishing a contradiction, since the first conjunct follows from the definition of *paradox*. Our only remaining assumption is that the definition of *TooBig* was meaningful, which we must now abandon.

Answer 15.14 (p.152) It is a strict partial order, and $\subseteq$ is a non-strict partial order. Whether it is well founded depends on the set over which it is defined: over **set** $\mathbb{N}$ it is not well founded; but over **finset** $\mathbb{N}$ it is.

Answer 15.16 (p.152)

> $\quad r, s := \text{rv } s, ?$
> $\sqsubseteq \textbf{con } R\cdot$
> $\quad r, s: [R = \text{rv } s , \; r = R]$
> $\sqsubseteq r := \langle\rangle;$
> $\quad r, s: [R = \text{rv } s +\!\!+ r , \; R = \text{rv } s +\!\!+ r \wedge s = \langle\rangle]$ $\qquad\qquad\qquad$ ◁
> $\sqsubseteq \textbf{do } s \text{ is } h{:}t \rightarrow r, s := h{:}r, t \textbf{ od }$.

Answer 15.18 (p.152) This development requires two stacks of trees, say $ntl1$ and $ntl2$, with invariant 'the frontiers are equal so far':

$$\left(\exists F : \textbf{seq } X \cdot \begin{array}{l} F1 = F +\!\!+ (+\!\!+nt : ntl1 \cdot \text{frontier } nt) \\ F2 = F +\!\!+ (+\!\!+nt : ntl2 \cdot \text{frontier } nt) \end{array}\right) ,$$

where $F1$ and $F2$ are logical constants equal to the frontiers of $nt1$ and $nt2$ respectively.

The iteration has four alternatives, corresponding to the four possibilities for the tops of the two stacks when considered together; it should terminate when either or both of the stacks is empty.

This algorithm is a good example of one in which for space efficiency (two) explicit stacks are needed, rather than recursion. (Other options are coroutines, or a lazy functional language.)

Answer 15.19 (p.153) We give an argument for each of the two cases. First we have

$\quad$ sizelt ntl

$=\quad$ "alternation guard"
$\quad$ sizelt(empty:ntl'

$=\quad$ "definition sizelt"
$\quad$ sizet empty $+$ sizelt ntl'

$=\quad$ "definition sizet"
$\quad$ $1 +$ sizelt ntl'

$>\quad$ sizelt ntl' .

For the second we have

$\quad$ sizelt ntl

$=\quad$ "alternation guard"
$\quad$ sizelt(node n' $nt1$ $nt2$:ntl'

$=\quad$ "definition sizelt"
$\quad$ sizet(node n' $nt1$ $nt2$) $+$ sizelt ntl'

$=\quad$ "definition sizet"
$\quad$ $1 +$ sizet $nt1 +$ sizet $nt2 +$ sizelt ntl'

$=\quad$ "definition sizet"
$\quad$ $1 +$ sizelt($nt1$:$nt2$:ntl')

$>\quad$ sizelt($nt1$:$nt2$:ntl') .

Chapter 16

Answer 16.2 (p.161) Change *Acquire* to read

$$t, u: [u \neq \mathbb{N} , \; t \notin u_0 \wedge 2 \mid t \wedge u = u_0 \cup \{t\}] \;.$$

That refines the original specification, hence the new procedure refines the old, hence the new module refines the old.

But it is not feasible, because it is forced to return an even number even when u might contain only odd numbers. See Chapter 17 for a way to get around that — surely, beginning with an infinite supply of integers both even and odd, one should never run out!

module *Random*;
    var $n : \mathbb{N}$;

    procedure *Acquire* (**result** $t : \mathbb{N}$)
    $\mathrel{\widehat{=}} n := (A \times n) \bmod B$;
        $t := n$;

    procedure *Return* (**value** $t : \mathbb{N}$)
    $\mathrel{\widehat{=}}$ **skip**;

    initially $n = S$
end

The constants $A, B, S : \mathbb{N}$ determine the precise values returned.

Figure B.2 Random number module

Answer 16.4 (p.162) See Figure B.2; it does not refine *Tag*, because pseudo-random sequences eventually repeat.

Answer 16.5 (p.162) In Figure 16.7, yes: Part 3 of *refine module* 16.2 allows it. But in Figure 16.8, that change would affect the exported procedure $P1$ in a way not allowed by *refine module* 16.2. Hence in Figure 16.8, no.

Answer 16.6 (p.162) Originally *Out* assigned 0 to n, given the specific actual procedure *In* supplied; after the change, it assigned 1 to n instead. The new module *does* refine the old module, but the new behaviour does not refine the old behaviour.

    The explanation is that the $n := 0$ behaviour, though guaranteed given the actual procedure *In*, represented a resolution of nondeterminism in the implementation which cannot be depended on by clients. Indeed the behaviour could be changed at any time by a junior programmer who knows no more than to link imported procedures to actual procedures that refine them, and that he need not ask permission to do so.

Chapter 17

Answer 17.4 (p.179) For the first, we have by *diminish specification* 17.11,

$$x: [(\forall a_0 \cdot (\exists a \cdot x = a_0))]$$
$$\sqsubseteq x: [(\forall a_0 \cdot x = a_0)] \ . \tag{i}$$

For the second, we have

$$x: [(\forall\, a_0 \cdot (\exists\, a \cdot x = a))]$$
$$\sqsubseteq\ x: [\text{true}]$$
$$\sqsubseteq\ \textbf{choose}\ x\ .$$

The first results in the infeasible (i): we cannot have x equal to *all* values of a_0! But a is not auxiliary in the given specification anyway, since the final value of x depends on the initial value of a. So we should expect infeasibility.

The second refines to code.

Answer 17.5 (p.179) The invariant is $N = l + m \times n$.

The augmented program is

$$l, m, n, l', m' := 0, 1, N, 0, M;$$
$$\textbf{do}\ n \neq 0 \rightarrow$$
$$\quad \textbf{if even}\ n\ \rightarrow m, n, m' := 2 \times m, n \div 2, 2 \times m'$$
$$\quad [\!]\ \ \textbf{odd}\ n\ \ \rightarrow l, n, l' := l + m, n - 1, l' + m'$$
$$\quad \textbf{fi}$$
$$\textbf{od}\ .$$

Since the original program established $l = N$, the augmented program will establish $l' = M \times N$ (as well).

To determine which variables are *auxiliary*, as far as the calculation of l' is concerned, we do the opposite: collect the essential variables. Variable n is essential, because it occurs in guards, and it is given that l' is essential. From the assignment $l' := l' + m'$ we find that we need m' as well, but the process stops there: thus l and m are auxiliary. After removing them, then renaming (of l' to l and m' to m), we get

$$n, l, m := N, 0, M;$$
$$\textbf{do}\ n \neq 0 \rightarrow$$
$$\quad \textbf{if even}\ n\ \rightarrow n, m := n \div 2, 2 \times m$$
$$\quad [\!]\ \ \textbf{odd}\ n\ \ \rightarrow n, l := n - 1, l + m$$
$$\quad \textbf{fi}$$
$$\textbf{od}\ .$$

Answer 17.8 (p.180) If the constant A were a matrix, division by $A - 1$ would no longer be a simple matter.

Answer 17.9 (p.180) We have by *diminish specification* 17.12

$$x: [(\exists\, a \cdot pre)\ ,\ (\forall\, a \cdot pre_0 \Rightarrow post)]$$
$$\sqsubseteq\ \text{``Predicate laws A.74, A.75''}$$
$$x: [pre\ ,\ pre_0 \Rightarrow post]$$

$\sqsubseteq$ *"strengthen postcondition 5.1"*

w: $[pre\ ,\ post]$.

Thus such specifications are unaffected.

Answer 17.10 (p.181) Here are the two laws:

Law B.3 <u>augment assumption</u> The assumption $\{pre\}$ becomes $\{pre \wedge CI\}$.

Proof:

$\qquad \{pre\}$

$= : [pre\ ,\ \text{true}]$.

Then by *augment specification* 17.6 that *becomes*

$\qquad c: [pre \wedge CI\ ,\ CI]$

$\sqsubseteq : [pre \wedge CI\ ,\ CI]$.

$\sqsubseteq$ *"strengthen postcondition 5.1"*

$\qquad : [pre \wedge CI\ ,\ \text{true}]$

$= \{pre \wedge CI\}$.

$\square$

Law B.4 <u>diminish assumption</u> The assumption $\{pre\}$ is diminished to $\{(\exists\, a : A \cdot pre)\}$.

Proof:

$\qquad = : [pre\ ,\ \text{true}]$

Then by *diminish specification* 17.12 that becomes

$\qquad c: [(\exists\, a : A \cdot pre)\ ,\ (\forall\, a \cdot pre_0 \Rightarrow \text{true})]$

$\sqsubseteq : [(\exists\, a : A \cdot pre)\ ,\ \text{true}]$

$= \{(\exists\, a : A \cdot pre)\}$.

$\square$

Answer 17.11 (p.181) Here are the two laws:

Law B.5 <u>augment coercion</u> The coercion $[post]$ becomes $[CI \Rightarrow post]$.

Proof:

$\qquad [post]$

$= : [post]$

becomes *"augment specification 17.6"*

$\qquad : [CI\ ,\ CI \wedge post]$

$$\sqsubseteq : [CI \Rightarrow post]$$
$$= [CI \Rightarrow post] .$$

$\square$

Law B.6 <u>diminish coercion</u> The coercion $[post]$ *becomes* $[(\forall a : A \cdot post)]$.
Proof:

$\sqsubseteq [post]$

$= : [post]$

becomes "*diminish specification* 17.12"

$\qquad c\colon [(\exists\, a : A \cdot \mathbf{true})\ ,\ (\forall\, a \cdot \mathbf{true} \Rightarrow post)]$

$\sqsubseteq\ c\colon [(\forall\, a : A \cdot post)]$

$= [(\forall\, a : A \cdot post)] .$

$\square$

Answer 17.13 (p.181) The law *augment guard* 17.9 gives the new guards $n \neq 0$ and $n = 0$ directly; the law *alternation guards* 4.3 is then unnecessary! The other data refinements are as before.

Answer 17.14 (p.181) The effect of the augmentation is to add $u \in \mathbf{finset}\,\mathbb{N}$ as an invariant of every command: in particular,

$$t, u\colon [u \neq \mathbb{N}\ ,\ t \notin u_0 \wedge u = u_0 \cup \{t\}]$$
becomes $t, u\colon [u \neq \mathbb{N}\ ,\ u \in \mathbf{finset}\,\mathbb{N}\ ,\ t \notin u_0 \wedge u = u_0 \cup \{t\}] .$
$\qquad \sqsubseteq$ "$u \cup \{t\}$ is finite if u is"
$$t, u\colon [u \in \mathbf{finset}\,\mathbb{N}\ ,\ t \notin u_0 \wedge u = u_0 \cup \{t\}] .$$

The effect on Exercise 16.2 is to allow us to include $u \in \mathbf{finset}\,\mathbb{N}$ in the precondition before we strengthen the postcondition with $2 \mid t$. Feasibility is maintained.

Answer 17.15 (p.181) After adding v we have Figure B.3; removing u gives Figure B.4. See also Exercise 17.16.

Answer 17.18 (p.181) The data-type invariant (such as imposed by **and**) of the module is strengthened; the augmentation laws simply ensure that it is maintained.

Answer 17.20 (p.182) The concrete iteration **do** $aq[n] \neq a \rightarrow n := n + 1$ **od** would fail to terminate if a were not in aq. It *is* reasonable, since the abstract command could abort in that case.

Answer 17.22 (p.182) There is no hard-and-fast answer to questions like that: it depends on what your 'compiler' (or reader) will accept. In this case, one might

module *Tag*
   var u, v : **set** $\mathbb{N}$;

   procedure *Acquire* (**result** t : $\mathbb{N}$)
   $\hat{=}\ u, t, v\colon [u \neq \mathbb{N}\ ,\ u \subseteq v \wedge v \in \textbf{finset}\,\mathbb{N}\ ,\ t \notin u_0 \wedge u = u_0 \cup \{t\}]$;

   procedure *Return* (**value** t : $\mathbb{N}$)
   $\hat{=}\ u, v := u - \{t\}, v$;

   initially $u = \{\} \wedge u \subseteq v \wedge v \in \textbf{finset}\,\mathbb{N}$
end

Figure B.3 Augmented module (Exercise 17.15)

---

module *Tag*
   var v : **set** $\mathbb{N}$;

   procedure *Acquire* (**result** t : $\mathbb{N}$)
   $\hat{=}\ t, v\colon [v \neq \mathbb{N}\ ,\ t \notin v_0 \wedge v = v_0 \cup \{t\}]$;

   procedure *Return* (**value** t : $\mathbb{N}$)
   $\hat{=}\ v := v$;

   initially $v = \{\}$
end

Figure B.4 Diminished module (Exercise 17.15)

---

be thinking of a further data refinement to a fixed-length sequence and an integer 'end-of-sequence' pointer. The data refinement of fr then is trivial.

Answer 17.24 (p.182) The refinements are

1. $a := aq[a]$;
2. $a, n := as[n-1], n-1$; and
3. $\{n < N\}\ aq[n], n := a, n+1$.

Answer 17.25 (p.182) Binary search is a suitable finishing off of the derivation. (See Exercise 10.7).

Answer 17.26 (p.182)

$$w\colon [pre\ ,\ post]$$
$$\sqsubseteq\ \text{``expand frame 8.3''}$$
$$w, a\colon [pre\ ,\ post \wedge a = a_0]$$
$$becomes\ \text{``data-refine specification 17.15''}$$
$$w, c\colon [pre[a \backslash \mathsf{af}\ c]\ ,\ \mathsf{dti}\ c\ ,\ post[a_0, a \backslash \mathsf{af}\ c_0, \mathsf{af}\ c] \wedge \mathsf{af}\ c = \mathsf{af}\ c_0]$$
$$\sqsubseteq\ \text{``contract frame 5.4''}$$
$$w\colon [pre[a \backslash \mathsf{af}\ c]\ ,\ \mathsf{dti}\ c\ ,\ post[a_0, a \backslash \mathsf{af}\ c_0, \mathsf{af}\ c]]\ .$$

The effect is exactly as before, so that *data-refine specification* 17.15 can be used even when a does not occur in the abstract frame. Note however that the c_0 in the postcondition can be replaced by c, since c is not in the concrete frame.

Of more interest however is the use of *contract frame* 5.4, where a proper refinement occurs. The conjunct $\mathsf{af}\ c = \mathsf{af}\ c_0$, effectively strengthened to $c = c_0$ by *contract frame* 5.4, allows considerable freedom in adjusting the concrete representation. (See Exercise 17.27).

Answer 17.27 (p.182) Implementing $a \in as$, where the concrete representation is an *unordered* sequence aq, might result in bringing a to the front of the sequence aq so that it would be found more quickly on a subsequent search.

Answer 17.28 (p.182) Assuming a declaration $adb : K \nrightarrow D$, the specification would be

```
if k ∉ dom adb → d := undefined
 ▯ k ∈ dom adb → d := ok adb k
fi .
```

The coupling invariant is $adb = \{k : K; d : d \mid \mathsf{full}\ k\ d \in db\}$. Note that it is functional.

Answer 17.29 (p.183) If the array were fixed-size, then there would be an upper limit on the number of trees it could contain; with the given algorithm the size needed would depend on the depth of the original tree. Thus the specification would indeed need modification, including a precondition limiting the depth of the tree nt.

That taken care of, the data-refinement is simple. The abstract variable is ntl, and the concrete say would be $nta : \mathbf{seq}_N\ Tree;\ h : \mathbb{N}$ with coupling invariant $ntl = nta{\uparrow}h \wedge h \leq N$. The resulting code is shown in Figure B.5.

That leaves the records and pointers. Since the original tree nt is not modified, one could represent it and its subtrees by pointers to their root nodes: the array nta would then become a fixed-length sequence of pointers to records.

```
|[ var nta : seq_N Tree; h : N·
   nta[0], h := ⟨nt⟩, 1;
   do h ≠ 0 →
      if nta[h − 1] is
         empty → h := h − 1
      [] (node n′ nt1 nt2) →
            n, nta[h − 1], nta[h], h := n + n′, nt1, nt2, h + 1
      fi

   od
]|
```

Figure B.5 Iterative tree-summing with fixed-size array

Answer 17.35 (p.183) These are the refinement steps:

$$x := 1$$
⊑ *"simple specification 8.1"*
$$x: [x = 1]$$
⊑ $x: [(x = 1 \lor x = -1) \land x \geq 0]$
⊑ *"absorb coercion 17.2 (backwards)"*
$$x: [x = 1 \lor x = -1];$$ ◁
$$[x \geq 0]$$ (i)
⊑ *"alternation 4.1, assignment 1.3"*
    if true → $x := 1$
    [] true → $x := -1$
    fi .

The coercion (i) would test for $x \geq 0$, and force *backtracking* to the earlier non-deterministic choice if the test failed. 'Eventually' the correct branch $x := 1$ would be taken, and the coercion would then behave like **skip**.

Chapter 18

Answer 18.1 (p.196) If ¬ em $as{\uparrow}i$, then for all x we have

$$(as{\uparrow}i).x \leq i/2 .$$

Hence for all x not equal to $as[i]$, we have

$$(as{\uparrow}(i + 1)).x \leq (i + 1)/2 .$$

Thus the only possible majority in $as{\uparrow}(i+1)$ is $as[i]$ itself.

Answer 18.4 (p.196) We have these equalities:

$$\begin{aligned}
&\quad \| [\ \mathbf{var}\ x \cdot prog\ ]\| \\
&= \| [\ \mathbf{var}\ x;\ \mathbf{procedure}\ P \mathrel{\hat{=}} prog\cdot \\
&\qquad\quad P \\
&\quad]\| \\
&= \| [\ \ \mathbf{module}\ M \\
&\qquad\qquad \mathbf{var}\ x; \\
&\qquad\qquad \mathbf{procedure}\ P \mathrel{\hat{=}} prog \\
&\qquad\quad \mathbf{end}\cdot \\
\\
&\qquad\quad P \\
&\quad]\|\ .
\end{aligned}$$

The transformation is carried out on the interior of module M, and the above process reversed.

Answer 18.5 (p.196) For p.187, we need two steps. First, the invariant $c = as{\uparrow}i.x$ is conjoined to the guards. Then we must show that

$$\begin{array}{lll}
1. & & (\neg\,\mathsf{em}\ as{\uparrow}i \wedge c = as{\uparrow}i.x) \\
& \vee & (\mathsf{sm}\ x\ as{\uparrow}i \wedge c = as{\uparrow}i.x) \\
\\
& \Rrightarrow & \mathsf{true} \\
2. & & ((\neg\,\mathsf{em}\ as{\uparrow}i \wedge c = as{\uparrow}i.x) \\
& \vee & (\mathsf{sm}\ x\ as{\uparrow}i \wedge c = as{\uparrow}i.x)) \\
& \wedge & c \le i/2 \\
\\
& \Rrightarrow & \neg\,\mathsf{em}\ as{\uparrow}i \wedge c = as{\uparrow}i.x \\
3. & & ((\neg\,\mathsf{em}\ as{\uparrow}i \wedge c = as{\uparrow}i.x) \\
& \vee & (\mathsf{sm}\ x\ as{\uparrow}i \wedge c = as{\uparrow}i.x)) \\
& \wedge & c > i/2 \\
\\
& \Rrightarrow & \mathsf{sm}\ x\ as{\uparrow}i \wedge c = as{\uparrow}i.x\ .
\end{array}$$

For p.189, the procedure is similar.

Chapter 20

Answer 20.1 (p.207) The refinement is valid because, in seeking to minimise overall waste **wt**, we cannot do better than to minimise **wt** for what remains.

That is not a property of all waste functions, but it is of wt. Is it a property of this one?

$$\text{wt1 } pss \ \hat{=} \ (+ls : \text{fr } pss \cdot M - \sum ls)$$

What kind of paragraph results from minimising wt1?

The refinement of (ii) is proved by *strengthen postcondition*, then (trivially) *weaken precondition*. What we must show is of the form

$$(\forall \, qss \cdot \mathcal{A} \Rightarrow \mathcal{B}) \quad \Rightarrow \quad (\forall \, qss \cdot \mathcal{A} \Rightarrow \mathcal{C}),$$

and that follows from just $\mathcal{B} \Rightarrow \mathcal{C}$ by propositional reasoning and distribution of $\Rightarrow$ through $\forall \, qss$. The precondition of (ii) contains I, which by instantiating qss to $\langle ws[i{\rightarrow}j]\rangle \mathbin{+\!\!+} qss$ (Predicate law A.86) gives

$$\begin{aligned}
&\text{ep}(ws{\downarrow}i) \, (\langle ws[i{\rightarrow}j]\rangle \mathbin{+\!\!+} qss) \\
\Rightarrow \ &\text{ep } ws \ (pss \mathbin{+\!\!+} \langle ws[i{\rightarrow}j]\rangle \mathbin{+\!\!+} qss) \ .
\end{aligned}$$

That is exactly what is required.

Answer 20.3 (p.207) It is removed when the *shortest* next line is taken.

Answer 20.4 (p.207) Procedure *GetWord* is used to fill the sequence ws, in each case assigning $w+1$ to account for a following blank. The line width M is increased by 1 to allow for the blank following the last word on a line.

In the code of the second half, pss is removed. The command $j, s := j+1, s+ws[j]$ is followed by *PutWord* and $pss := pss \mathbin{+\!\!+} \langle ws[i{\rightarrow}j]\rangle$ is replaced by *PutLine*.

Chapter 21

Answer 21.1 (p.216) The time is linear in the size of hs.

For a given call of *Hist*, let I be the value it receives through its formal parameter i, and let J be the value it returns through its formal parameter J. Note first that $I < J$: the procedure is guaranteed to return J greater than the I it received.

Then consider the number of further calls made by *Hist* (to itself): it is no more than $J - I - 1$ (arguing recursively), and so any call to *Hist* accounts for at most $J - I$ calls in all (including the initial one).

Since for the initial call we have $I = -1$, and the J returned cannot exceed N, we have limited the total number of calls to $N + 1$.

Answer 21.2 (p.216) Consider successively longer 'row prefixes' of the rectangle, maintaining the invariant that the largest true rectangle of the prefix is known. Re-establishing the invariant for one further row is done by finding the largest rectangle under the histogram formed by 'true columns' above the new row.

The heights of columns in the histogram above successive rows can form part of the invariant also, leading to overall time complexity linear in the area of the array.

Answer 21.3 (p.216)   This problem is much easier than Exercise 21.2, though the complexity is still linear in the area of the array. One considers 'lower-right corners' of possible squares element-by-element along rows. Knowing the height of a 'true column' above the current element, the length of the 'true suffix' of the part of the current row ending in that element, and finally the size of the largest true square for the element immediately left and above it, is sufficient to re-establish the invariant that the largest true square is known for all elements considered so far.

The difference between squares and rectangles is that if one square has less area than another, then it can be nested within the other. The same is not true of rectangles.

Chapter 22

Answer 22.1 (p.244)   Following the convention that all procedures have the identity of their user as the first parameter, the definition would be

$$\textbf{procedure } Delete \ (\textbf{value } me : Usr; \ id : Id)$$
$$\mathrel{\hat{=}} sent := sent \vartriangleright \{id\} \ .$$

'Unauthorised' deletion is possible by any user knowing the *id* of the message, and in practice that would be someone who has already received it. (The sender knows the *id*, but is 'authorised'.)

Including *me* always as a first parameter allows subsequent design changes without altering the interface — in this case, we might change the specification to record messages' senders, and alter *Cancel* to take that into account. Would it be a refinement?

Answer 22.3 (p.244)   The unfortunate programmer saw in the specification of *Send* that the new identifier was first chosen outside the set dom *msgs*, and then immediately added to it by $msgs[id] := msg$. Noticing that *msgs* was not assigned to elsewhere in the module, he reasoned correctly that Procedure *Send* never returned the same *id* twice. Rather than write a generator of unique identifiers himself, therefore, he simply used the one he had found.

The change represented by Figure 22.2 invalidated his second observation, for *msgs* is assigned to by the replacement *Read*, and in fact made smaller.

Answer 22.8 (p.246)   Remove *msgs*, *sent* and *recd* as abstract variables, and introduce the concrete variable *used*; the coupling invariant is ran *sent* $\subseteq$ *used'* .

Yes, it is a problem. If we do not address *time* explicitly, then we do not have the vocabulary with which to express 'prompt' delivery. And one extreme of not being prompt is not to deliver at all.

Beyond *any* mathematical specification are 'extra-mathematical' requirements that must be specified some other way. If informal requirements are not good enough in any particular case, then more sophisticated mathematical techniques must be used; where the mathematics stops, and informality begins, is a matter for taste and good judgement.

Appendix C

Summary of laws

The laws, definitions, and abbreviations appear below in alphabetical order. This appendix may be copied and distributed freely for educational use.

Law 1.8 *absorb assumption*   *p.12*
An assumption before a specification can be absorbed directly into its precondition.

$$\{pre'\}\ w\colon [pre\ ,\ post] \quad = \quad w\colon [pre' \wedge pre\ ,\ post]\ .$$

□

Law 17.2 *absorb coercion*   *p.165*
A coercion following a specification can be absorbed into its postcondition.

$$w\colon [pre\ ,\ post]\,;\ [post'] \quad = \quad w\colon [pre\ ,\ post \wedge post']\ .$$

□

Law 22.2 *advance assumption*   *p.222*

$$w := E\ \{pre\} \quad = \quad \{pre[w\backslash E]\}\ w := E\ .$$

□

Law 22.1 *advance coercion*   *p.222*

$$w := E\ [post] \quad = \quad [post[w\backslash E]]\ w := E\ .$$

□

Law 4.1 *alternation* p.37
If $pre \Rrightarrow GG$, then

$$w\colon [pre \ , \ post]$$
$$\sqsubseteq \mathbf{if} \ ([\!] \ i \cdot G_i \to w\colon [G_i \wedge pre \ , \ post]) \ \mathbf{fi} \ .$$

$\square$

Law 4.2 *alternation* p.39

$$\{(\vee \, i \cdot G_i)\} \ prog$$
$$= \ \mathbf{if} \ ([\!] \ i \cdot G_i \to \{G_i\} \ prog) \ \mathbf{fi} \ .$$

$\square$

Law 4.3 *alternation guards* p.40
Let GG mean $G_0 \vee \cdots \vee G_n$, and HH similarly. Then provided

1. $GG \Rrightarrow HH$, and
2. $GG \Rrightarrow (H_i \Rightarrow G_i)$ for each i separately,

this refinement is valid:

$$\mathbf{if} \ ([\!] \ i \cdot G_i \to prog_i) \ \mathbf{fi} \quad \sqsubseteq \quad \mathbf{if} \ ([\!] \ i \cdot H_i \to prog_i) \ \mathbf{fi} \ .$$

$\square$

Law 1.3 *assignment* p.8
If $pre \Rrightarrow post[w \backslash E]$, then

$$w, x\colon [pre \ , \ post] \quad \sqsubseteq \quad w := E \ .$$

$\square$

Law 5.2 *assignment* p.44
If $(w = w_0) \wedge pre \Rrightarrow post[w \backslash E]$, then

$$w, x\colon [pre \ , \ post] \quad \sqsubseteq \quad w := E \ .$$

$\square$

Definition 23.1 *assignment* p.250
For any postcondition $\mathcal{A}$,

$$wp(w := E, \mathcal{A}) \ \mathrel{\widehat{=}} \ \mathcal{A}[w \backslash E] \ .$$

$\square$

Abbreviation 1.6 *assumption* p.11

$$\{pre\} \ \mathrel{\widehat{=}} \ \colon [pre \ , \ \mathsf{true}] \ .$$

$\square$

Definition 23.7 *assumption*   *p.254*

$$wp(\{pre\}, \mathcal{A}) \;\hat{=}\; pre \wedge \mathcal{A} \;.$$

□

Law 17.7 *augment assignment*   *p.167*
The assignment $w := E$ can be replaced by the fragment

$$\{CI\} \; w, c := E, ? \; [CI] \;.$$

□

Law 17.8 *augment assignment*   *p.167*
The assignment $w := E$ can be replaced by the assignment $w, c := E, F$ provided
that

$$CI \;\;\Rightarrow\;\; CI[w, c \backslash E, F] \;.$$

□

Law B.3 *augment assumption*   *p.289*
The assumption $\{pre\}$ *becomes* $\{pre \wedge CI\}$.
□

Law B.5 *augment coercion*   *p.289*
The coercion $[post]$ *becomes* $[CI \Rightarrow post]$.
□

Law 17.9 *augment guard*   *p.168*
The guard G may be replaced by G' provided that

$$CI \;\;\Rightarrow\;\; (G \Leftrightarrow G') \;.$$

□

Law 17.5 *augment initialisation*   *p.166*
The initialisation I *becomes* $I \wedge CI$.
□

Law 17.6 *augment specification*   *p.167*
The specification $w: [pre\ ,\ post]$ *becomes*

$$w, c: [pre\ ,\ CI\ ,\ post] \;.$$

□

Abbreviation 17.1 *coercion*   *p.165*
no initial variables,

$$[post] \;\hat{=}\; : [\mathsf{true}\ ,\ post] \;.$$

□

Definition 23.8 *coercion*   *p.254*

no initial variables,

$$wp([post], \mathcal{A}) \;\; \widehat{=} \;\; post \Rightarrow \mathcal{A} \; .$$

□

Law 18.7 *collapse identical branches*   *p.194*

$$\begin{aligned}
&\textbf{if } (\llbracket \; i \cdot G_i \to branch_i) \\
&\quad \llbracket \;\; G \to branch \\
&\quad \llbracket \;\; G' \to branch \\
&\textbf{fi} \\
= \;&\textbf{if } (\llbracket \; i \cdot G_i \to branch_i) \\
&\quad \llbracket \;\; G \vee G' \to branch \\
&\textbf{fi} \; .
\end{aligned}$$

□

Law 5.4 *contract frame*   *p.45*

$$w, x \colon [pre \;,\; post] \;\;\; \sqsubseteq \;\;\; w \colon [pre \;,\; post[x_0 \backslash x]] \; .$$

□

Definition 23.13 *data refinement*   *p.256*

Let a be a list of variables called *abstract*, let c be a list of variables called *concrete*, and let I be a formula called the *coupling invariant*. Then command *progA* is data-refined to *progC* by a, c, I exactly when for all postconditions $\mathcal{A}$ not containing c we have

$$(\exists \, a \cdot I \wedge wp(progA, \mathcal{A})) \;\;\; \Rrightarrow \;\;\; wp(progC, (\exists \, a \cdot I \wedge \mathcal{A})) \; .$$

□

Law 17.16 *data-refine assignment*   *p.177*

Under abstraction function af and data-type invariant dti, the assignment command $w, a \colon\!= E, F$ can be replaced by the assignment $w, c \colon\!= E, G$ provided that E and G contain no a, and that

$$\begin{aligned}
&\quad\quad \mathsf{dti}\, c \Rightarrow F[a \backslash \mathsf{af}\, c] = \mathsf{af}\, G \\
&\text{and} \quad \mathsf{dti}\, c \Rightarrow \mathsf{dti}\, G \; .
\end{aligned}$$

□

Law 17.17 *data-refine guard*   *p.178*

Under abstraction function af and data-type invariant dti, the guard G may be replaced by $G[a \backslash \mathsf{af}\, c] \wedge \mathsf{dti}\, c$, or if desired simply by $G[a \backslash \mathsf{af}\, c]$ on its own.

□

Law 17.14 *data-refine initialisation*   *p.175*

Under abstraction function af and data-type invariant dti, the initialisation I becomes

$$I[a \backslash \textsf{af } c] \wedge \textsf{dti } c \ .$$

$\square$

Law 17.15 *data-refine specification*   *p.176*

Under abstraction function af and data-type invariant dti, the specification $w, a\colon [pre \ , \ post]$ *becomes*

$$w, c\colon [pre[a \backslash \textsf{af } c] \ , \ \textsf{dti } c \ , \ post[a_0, a \backslash \textsf{af } c_0, \textsf{af } c]] \ .$$

$\square$

Abbreviation 1.5 *default precondition*   *p.11*

$$w\colon [post] \ \mathrel{\widehat{=}} \ w\colon [\textsf{true} \ , \ post] \ .$$

$\square$

Law 17.13 *diminish assignment*   *p.170*

If E contains no variables a, then the assignment $w, a := E, F$ can be replaced by the assignment $w := E$.

$\square$

Law B.4 *diminish assumption*   *p.289*

The assumption $\{pre\}$ is diminished to $\{(\exists\, a : A \cdot pre)\}$.

$\square$

Law B.6 *diminish coercion*   *p.290*

The coercion $[post]$ *becomes* $[(\forall\, a : A \cdot post)]$.

$\square$

Law 17.10 *diminish initialisation*   *p.168*

The initialisation I *becomes*

$$(\exists\, a : A \cdot I) \ .$$

$\square$

Law 17.11 *diminish specification*   *p.169*

The specification $w, a\colon [pre \ , \ post]$ *becomes*

$$w\colon [(\exists\, a : A \cdot pre) \ , \ (\forall\, a_0 : A \cdot pre_0 \Rightarrow (\exists\, a : A \cdot post))] \ ,$$

where pre_0 is $pre[w, a \backslash w_0, a_0]$. The frame beforehand *must* include a.

$\square$

Law 17.12 *diminish specification*   *p.169*
The specification $w\colon [pre\ ,\ post]$ *becomes*

$$w\colon [(\exists\, a : A \cdot pre)\ ,\ (\forall\, a : A \cdot pre_0 \Rightarrow post)]\ ,$$

where pre_0 is $pre[w\backslash w_0]$. The frame beforehand must not include a, and *post* must
not contain a_0.
□

Law 17.4 *establish assumption*   *p.166*
An assumption after a specification can be removed after suitable strengthening of
the precondition.

$$
\begin{aligned}
&w\colon [pre\ ,\ post];\ \{pre'\}\\
={}&w\colon [pre \wedge (\forall\, w \cdot post \Rightarrow pre')\,[w_0\backslash w]\ ,\ post]\ .
\end{aligned}
$$

□

Law 8.3 *expand frame*   *p.69*

$$w\colon [pre\ ,\ post]\quad=\quad w, x\colon [pre\ ,\ post \wedge x = x_0]\ .$$

□

Law 8.6 *expand frame*   *p.72*
For fresh constant X,

$$
\begin{aligned}
&w\colon [pre\ ,\ post]\\
\sqsubseteq{}&\mathbf{con}\ X\cdot\\
&w, x\colon [pre \wedge x = X\ ,\ post \wedge x = X]\,.
\end{aligned}
$$

□

Definition 1.4 *feasibility*   *p.10*
The specification $w\colon [pre\ ,\ post]$ is *feasible* iff

$$pre\quad\Rightarrow\quad (\exists\, w : T \cdot post)\ ,$$

where T is the type[1] of the variables w.
□

Definition 6.5 *feasibility*   *p.58*
The specification $w\colon [pre\ ,\ post]$ is *feasible* in context *inv* iff

$$(w = w_0) \wedge pre \wedge inv\quad\Rightarrow\quad (\exists\, w : T \cdot inv \wedge post),$$

where T is the type of w.
□

---

[1]In Chapter 6 the notion of type was generalised to include so-called 'local invariants', for
which a more comprehensive definition (6.5) of feasibility is appropriate.

Definition 23.6 *feasibility*   *p.254*
Command *prog* is *feasible* exactly when

$$wp(prog, \mathsf{false}) \quad \equiv \quad \mathsf{false} \ .$$

Otherwise it is *infeasible*.
□

Law 6.3 *fix initial value*   *p.56*
For any term E such that $pre \Rightarrow E \in T$, and fresh name c,

$$w\colon [pre \ , \ post]$$
$$\sqsubseteq \ \mathbf{con} \ c : T\boldsymbol{\cdot}$$
$$\quad w\colon [pre \wedge c = E \ , \ post] \ .$$

□

Law 18.6 *flatten nested alternations*   *p.192*

$$\mathbf{if} \ (\llbracket \ i \boldsymbol{\cdot} G_i \to \mathbf{if} \ (\llbracket \ j \boldsymbol{\cdot} H_j \to branch_{ij}) \ \mathbf{fi}) \ \mathbf{fi}$$
$$= \mathbf{if} \ (\llbracket \ i,j \boldsymbol{\cdot} G_i \wedge H_j \to branch_{ij}) \ \mathbf{fi} \ .$$

□

Law 3.5 *following assignment*   *p.32*
For any term E,

$$w, x\colon [pre \ , \ post]$$
$$\sqsubseteq \ w, x\colon [pre \ , \ post[x \backslash E]] \ ;$$
$$\quad x := E \ .$$

□

Abbreviation 8.2 *initial variable*   *p.69*
Occurrences of 0-subscripted variables in the postcondition of a specification refer to values held by those variables in the *initial* state. Let x be any variable, probably occurring in the frame w. If X is a fresh name, and T is the type of x, then

$$w\colon [pre \ , \ post]$$
$$\mathrel{\hat{=}} \ |[\ \mathbf{con} \ X : T \boldsymbol{\cdot} w\colon [pre \wedge x = X \ , \ post[x_0 \backslash X]] \ ]| \ .$$

□

Law B.1 *initialised iteration*   *p.272*
Provided *inv* contains no initial variables,

$$w\colon [pre \ , \ inv \wedge \neg G]$$
$$\sqsubseteq \ w\colon [pre \ , \ inv] \ ;$$
$$\quad \mathbf{do} \ G \to w\colon [G \wedge inv \ , \ inv \wedge (0 \le V < V_0)] \ \mathbf{od} \ .$$

□

Law 17.19 *introduce assumption* *p.183*

$$[post] \quad \sqsubseteq \quad [post] \, \{post\}.$$

□

Law 17.3 *introduce coercion* *p.165*
skip is refined by any coercion.

$$\textbf{skip} \quad \sqsubseteq \quad [post] \, .$$

□

Law 6.1 *introduce local variable* *p.55*
If x does not occur in w, *pre* or *post* then

$$w: [pre \, , \, post] \quad \sqsubseteq \quad |[\, \textbf{var} \, x : T; \textbf{and} \, inv \cdot w, x: [pre \, , \, post] \,]| \, .$$

□

Law 6.2 *introduce logical constant* *p.56*
If $pre \Rightarrow (\exists \, c : T \cdot pre')$, and c does not occur in w, *pre* or *post*, then

$$w: [pre \, , \, post]$$
$$\sqsubseteq \, \textbf{con} \, c : T \cdot$$
$$w: [pre' \, , \, post] \, .$$

If the optional type T is omitted, then the quantification in the proviso should be
untyped.
□

Law 5.5 *iteration* *p.45*
Let *inv*, the *invariant*, be any formula; let V, the *variant*, be any integer-valued
expression. Then if GG is the disjunction of the guards,

$$w: [inv \, , \, inv \wedge \neg GG]$$
$$\sqsubseteq \, \textbf{do} \, ([\!] \, i \cdot G_i \rightarrow w: [inv \wedge G_i \, , \, inv \wedge (0 \leq V < V_0)]) \, \textbf{od} \, .$$

Neither *inv* nor G_i may contain initial variables. The expression V_0 is $V[w \backslash w_0]$.
□

Law 3.6 *leading assignment* *p.35*
For disjoint w and x,

$$w, x := E, F[w \backslash E] \quad = \quad w := E; \; x := F \, .$$

□

Law 8.5 *leading assignment*   *p. 71*
For any expression E,

$$w, x: [pre[x \backslash E] \ , \ post[x_0 \backslash E_0]]$$
$$\sqsubseteq \ x := E;$$
$$w, x: [pre \ , \ post] \ .$$

The expression E_0 abbreviates $E[w, x \backslash w_0, x_0]$.
□

Law 18.2 *left-distribution of composition over alternation*   *p. 190*

$$\textbf{if} \ (\[\] \ i \cdot G_i \rightarrow branch_i) \ \textbf{fi}; \ prog$$
$$= \textbf{if} \ (\[\] \ i \cdot G_i \rightarrow branch_i; \ prog) \ \textbf{fi} \ .$$

□

Abbreviation 18.1 *local block initialisation*   *p. 187*

$$\|[\ \textbf{var} \ l : T; \ \textbf{initially} \ inv \cdot prog \ ]\|$$
$$\widehat{=} \ \|[\ \textbf{var} \ l : T \cdot l: [inv] ; \ prog \ ]\| \ .$$

□

Definition 23.4 *local variable*   *p. 253*

$$wp(\|[\ \textbf{var} \ x \cdot prog \ ]\|, \mathcal{A}) \ \widehat{=} \ (\forall \, x \cdot wp(prog, \mathcal{A})) \, ,$$

provided $\mathcal{A}$ contains no free x.
□

Definition 23.5 *logical constant*   *p. 253*

$$wp(\|[\ \textbf{con} \ x \cdot prog \ ]\|, \mathcal{A}) \ \widehat{=} \ (\exists \, x \cdot wp(prog, \mathcal{A})) \, ,$$

provided $\mathcal{A}$ contains no free x.
□

Law 1.9 *merge assumptions*   *p. 14*

$$\{pre'\} \ \{pre\} \ \ = \ \ \{pre' \wedge pre\} \ .$$

□

Law 17.18 *merge coercions*   *p. 183*

$$[post] \ [post'] \ \ = \ \ [post \wedge post'] \ .$$

□

Law 3.1 *open assignment* *p.29*
For any expression F,

$$w, x := E, ? \quad \sqsubseteq \quad w, x := E, F \ .$$

□

Definition 23.12 *recursion* *p.255*
Let $\mathcal{C}(p)$ be a program fragment in which the name p appears. Then

re $p \cdot \mathcal{C}(p)$ **er**

is the *least-refined* program *fix* such that $\mathcal{C}(fix) = fix$.
□

Law 16.1 *refine initialisation* *p.157*
If $init' \Rightarrow init$, then

initially $init \quad \sqsubseteq \quad$ **initially** $init'$.

□

Law 16.2 *refine module* *p.158*
Let E be the list of exported procedures from module M, I its imported procedures, and $init$ its initialisation. A module M' refines M if the following three conditions are satisfied:

1. Its exported variables are unchanged.
2. Its exported procedures E' refine E.
3. Its initialisation $init'$ refines $init$.

In addition, the following changes may be made provided the three conditions above are not invalidated as a result:

1. Its imported variables' declarations are weakened.
2. Its imported procedures I' are refined by I.
3. An imported procedure I is replaced by a *local* (neither imported nor exported) procedure I' that refines I.

□

Definition 23.3 *refinement* *p.252*
For any commands *prog1* and *prog2*, we say that *prog1* is refined by *prog2*, writing *prog1* $\sqsubseteq$ *prog2*, exactly when for all postconditions $\mathcal{A}$ we have

$$wp(prog1, \mathcal{A}) \quad \Rightarrow \quad wp(prog2, \mathcal{A}) \ .$$

□

Law 18.5 *remove alternation*   *p.192*

    if true → *branch* **fi**   =   *branch* .

□

Law 1.10 *remove assumption*   *p.15*
Any assumption is refined by **skip**.

    $\{pre\}$ ⊑   **skip** .

□

Law 17.20 *remove coercion*   *p.183*

    $\{pre\}\,[pre]$ ⊑ $\{pre\}$.

□

Law 18.4 *remove false guard*   *p.192*

    if ($[\!] \; i \cdot G_i \to branch_i$)
    $[\!]$ false → *branch*
    fi
  = **if** ($[\!] \; i \cdot G_i \to branch_i$) **fi** .

□

Law 7.1 *remove invariant*   *p.66*
Provided w does not occur in *inv*,

    $w\colon [pre\ ,\ inv\ ,\ post]$ ⊑ $w\colon [pre\ ,\ post]$.

□

Law 6.4 *remove logical constant*   *p.57*
If c occurs nowhere in program *prog*, then

    $|[\ $**con** $c : T \cdot prog\ ]|$ ⊑   *prog* .

□

Law 11.3 *result assignment*   *p.110*
Given a procedure declaration that refines

    procedure *Proc* (**result** $f : T$) $\hat{=}$ $w, f := E, F$,

with f not occurring in E or in F, we have the following refinement:

    $w, a := E, F$ ⊑   *Proc* (a) .

Variables a and f need not be different from each other, but w must be disjoint from both.

□

Law 11.4 *result specification* *p.111*

Given a procedure declaration that refines

$$\textbf{procedure } Proc \textbf{ (result } f : T) \ \hat{=} \ w, f \colon [pre \ , \ post[a \backslash f]] \ ,$$

with f not occurring in pre, and neither f nor f_0 occurring in $post$, we have the following refinement:

$$w, a \colon [pre \ , \ post] \quad \sqsubseteq \quad Proc \ (a) \ .$$

Again, variables a and f need not be different from each other, but w must be disjoint from both.

□

Law 18.3 *right-distribution of assignment over alternation* *p.191*

$$\begin{aligned} &x := E; \ \textbf{if } (\![\ i \cdot G_i \rightarrow branch_i) \ \textbf{fi} \\ = \ &\textbf{if } (\![\ i \cdot G_i[x \backslash E] \rightarrow x := E; \ branch_i) \ \textbf{fi} \ . \end{aligned}$$

□

Law 18.8 *select true guard* *p.196*

$$\begin{aligned} &\textbf{if } (\![\ i \cdot G_i \rightarrow branch_i) \\ &[\! \ \textbf{true} \rightarrow branch \\ &\textbf{fi} \\ &\sqsubseteq \ branch \ . \end{aligned}$$

□

Abbreviation 10.1 *sequence assignment* *p.99*

For any sequence as, if $0 \leq i, j \leq \# as$ then

$$as[i := E][j] \ \hat{=} \ \begin{array}{ll} E & \text{when} \ \ i = j \\ as[j] & \text{when} \ \ i \neq j \ . \end{array}$$

□

Law 3.3 *sequential composition* *p.31*

For any[2] formula mid,

$$w \colon [pre \ , \ post] \quad \sqsubseteq \quad w \colon [pre \ , \ mid] ; \ w \colon [mid \ , \ post] \ .$$

□

---

[2]Neither mid nor $post$, however, may contain 'initial variables', the subject of Chapter 8. Law B.2 replaces this law for the general case.

Law 8.4 *sequential composition*   *p.70*
For fresh constants X,

$$w, x\colon [pre \ , \ post]$$
$$\sqsubseteq \ \mathbf{con} \ X \cdot$$
$$x\colon [pre \ , \ mid] \, ;$$
$$w, x\colon [mid[x_0\backslash X] \ , \ post[x_0\backslash X]] \, .$$

The formula *mid* must not contain initial variables other than x_0.
□

Law B.2 *sequential composition*   *p.275*

$$w, x\colon [pre \ , \ post]$$
$$\sqsubseteq \ x\colon [pre \ , \ mid] \, ;$$
$$w, x\colon [mid \ , \ post] \, .$$

The formula *mid* must not contain initial variables; and *post* must not contain x_0.
□

Abbreviation 8.1 *simple specification*   *p.68*
For any relation $\odot$,

$$w\colon\odot E \quad = \quad w\colon [w \odot E_0] \, ,$$

where E_0 is $E[w\backslash w_0]$.
□

Law 1.7 *simple specification*   *p.11*
Provided E contains no w,

$$w := E \quad = \quad w\colon [w = E] \ .$$

If w and E are lists, then the formula $w = E$ means the equating of corresponding elements of the lists.
□

Law 3.2 *skip command*   *p.30*
If $pre \Rightarrow post$, then

$$w\colon [pre \ , \ post] \quad \sqsubseteq \quad \mathbf{skip}.$$

□

Law 5.3 *skip command*   *p.44*
If $(w = w_0) \wedge pre \Rightarrow post$, then

$$w\colon [pre \ , \ post] \quad \sqsubseteq \quad \mathbf{skip} \ .$$

□

Law 3.4 *skip composition*   *p.31*

For any program *prog*,

$$prog; \ \mathbf{skip} \quad = \quad \mathbf{skip}; \ prog \quad = \quad prog \ .$$

□

Definition 23.2 *specification*   *p.251*

$$wp(w\colon [pre \ , \ post], \mathcal{A}) \ \mathrel{\hat{=}} \ pre \wedge (\forall \, w \cdot post \Rightarrow \mathcal{A}) \, [v_0 \backslash v] \ ,$$

where the substitution $[v_0 \backslash v]$ replaces *all* initial variables by corresponding final variables.

□

Abbreviation 5.6 *specification invariant*   *p.46*

Provided *inv* contains no initial variables,

$$w\colon [pre \ , \ inv \ , \ post] \ \mathrel{\hat{=}} \ w\colon [pre \wedge inv \ , \ inv \wedge post] \ .$$

□

Law 1.1 *strengthen postcondition*   *p.7*

If $post' \Rightarrow post$, then

$$w\colon [pre \ , \ post] \quad \sqsubseteq \quad w\colon [pre \ , \ post'] \, .$$

□

Law 5.1 *strengthen postcondition*   *p.44*

If $pre[w \backslash w_0] \wedge post' \Rightarrow post$, then

$$w\colon [pre \ , \ post] \quad \sqsubseteq \quad w\colon [pre \ , \ post'] \ .$$

□

Definition 23.10 *substitution by result*   *p.255*

$$wp(prog[\mathbf{result} \ f \backslash a], \mathcal{A}) \ \mathrel{\hat{=}} \ (\forall \, f \cdot wp(prog, \mathcal{A}[a \backslash f])) \, ,$$

provided f does not occur free in $\mathcal{A}$.

□

Definition 23.9 *substitution by value*   *p.255*

$$wp(prog[\mathbf{value} \ f \backslash E], \mathcal{A}) \ \mathrel{\hat{=}} \ wp(prog, \mathcal{A})[f \backslash E] \ ,$$

provided f does not occur free in $\mathcal{A}$.

□

Definition 23.11 *substitution by value-result* $\qquad$ *p.255*

$$wp(prog[\textbf{value result } f\backslash a], \mathcal{A}) \;\hat{=}\; wp(prog, \mathcal{A}[a\backslash f])[f\backslash a],$$

provided f does not occur free in $\mathcal{A}$.

□

Law 15.1 *tagged alternation* $\qquad$ *p.139*

Let first, middle and last be tags from a typical type declaration

$\qquad$ first $A \cdots H \mid$ middle $I \cdots P \mid$ last $Q \cdots Z$.

Provided none of $a \cdots h, q \cdots z$ appear free in E or *prog*, this refinement is valid:

$\qquad \{E \text{ is first} \lor E \text{ is last}\}\ prog$
$\quad \sqsubseteq\ \textbf{if } E \textbf{ is}$
$\qquad\quad \text{first } a \cdots h \rightarrow \{E = \text{first } a \cdots h\}\ prog$
$\qquad\quad [\!]\ \text{last } q \cdots z\ \rightarrow \{E = \text{last } q \cdots z\}\ prog$
$\qquad \textbf{fi} .$

□

Law 15.2 *tagged iteration* $\qquad$ *p.145*

Let first, middle and last be tags from a type declaration

$\qquad Type \;\hat{=}\; \text{first } A \cdots H \mid \text{middle } I \cdots P \mid \text{last } Q \cdots Y$.

Provided none of $a \cdots h, q \cdots y$ appears free in z, *inv*, E, or V, this refinement is valid:

$\qquad z\colon [inv\ ,\ inv \land \neg(E \text{ is first} \lor E \text{ is last})]$
$\quad \sqsubseteq\ \textbf{do } E \textbf{ is}$
$\qquad\quad \text{first } a \cdots h \rightarrow z\colon [E = \text{first } a \cdots h\ ,\ inv\ ,\ V \oslash V_0]$
$\qquad\quad [\!]\ \text{last } q \cdots y \rightarrow z\colon [E = \text{last } q \cdots y\ ,\ inv\ ,\ V \oslash V_0]$
$\qquad \textbf{od} .$

The formula *inv* is the invariant, the expression V is the variant, and the relation $\oslash$ must be well-founded.

□

Law 11.1 *value assignment*   *p.108*
Given a procedure declaration that refines

$$\textbf{procedure } Proc \textbf{ (value } f : T) \;\;\hat{=}\;\; w, f := E, ? \; ,$$

we have the following refinement:

$$w := E[f\backslash A] \quad\sqsubseteq\quad Proc\;(A) \;.$$

The actual parameter A may be an expression, and it should have type T. (If it does not, the refinement remains valid but subsequent type checking will fail.) As usual, variables w and f must be disjoint.
□

Law 11.2 *value specification*   *p.109*
Given a procedure declaration that refines

$$\textbf{procedure } Proc \textbf{ (value } f : T) \;\;\hat{=}\;\; w, f \colon [pre \; , \; post] \; ,$$

with *post* containing no f (but possibly f_0), the following refinement is valid:

$$w \colon [pre[f\backslash A] \; , \; post[f_0\backslash A_0]] \quad\sqsubseteq\quad Proc\;(A) \; ,$$

where A_0 is $A[w\backslash w_0]$.
□

Law 11.5 *value-result assignment*   *p.113*
Given a procedure declaration that refines

$$\textbf{procedure } Proc \textbf{ (value result } f : T) \;\;\hat{=}\;\; w, f := E, F \; ,$$

we have the following refinement:

$$w, a := E[f\backslash a], F[f\backslash a] \quad\sqsubseteq\quad Proc\;(a) \;.$$

□

Law 11.6 *value-result specification*   *p.113*
Given a procedure declaration that refines

$$\textbf{procedure } Proc \textbf{ (value result } f : T) \;\;\hat{=}\;\; w, f \colon [pre \; , \; post[a\backslash f]] \; ,$$

with *post* not containing f, we have the following refinement:

$$w, a \colon [pre[f\backslash a] \; , \; post[f_0\backslash a_0]] \quad\sqsubseteq\quad Proc\;(a) \;.$$

□

Law 1.2 *weaken precondition*   p. 7
If $pre \Rightarrow pre'$, then

$$w: [pre \ , \ post] \quad \sqsubseteq \quad w: [pre' \ , \ post] \, .$$

□

References

[Abr87] J.-R. Abrial. Generalised substitutions. 26 Rue des Plantes, Paris 75014, France, 1987.

[Bac78] R.-J.R. Back. On the correctness of refinement steps in program development. Report A-1978-4, Department of Computer Science, University of Helsinki, 1978.

[Bac80] R.-J.R. Back. Correctness preserving program refinements: Proof theory and applications. Tract 131, Mathematisch Centrum, Amsterdam, 1980.

[Bac86] R. Backhouse. *Program Construction and Verification*. Prentice-Hall, 1986.

[Bac87] R.-J.R. Back. Procedural abstraction in the refinement calculus. Report Ser.A 55, Departments of Information Processing and Mathematics, Swedish University of Åbo, Åbo, Finland, 1987.

[Bac88] R.-J.R. Back. A calculus of refinements for program derivations. *Acta Informatica*, 25:593–624, 1988.

[Bir86] R.S. Bird. Transformational programming and the paragraph problem. *Science of Computer Programming*, 6:159–189, 1986.

[Boo82] H. Boom. A weaker precondition for loops. *ACM Transactions on Programming Languages and Systems*, 4:668–677, 1982.

[CU89] Wei Chen and J.T. Udding. Towards a calculus of data refinement. In J.L.A. van de Snepsheut, editor, *Lecture Notes in Computer Science 375: Mathematics of Program Construction*. Springer, June 1989.

[Der83] N. Dershowitz. *The Evolution of Programs*. Birkhäuser, 1983.

[DF88] E.W. Dijkstra and W.H.J. Feijen. *A Method of Programming*. Addison-Wesley, 1988.

[Dij76] E.W. Dijkstra. *A Discipline of Programming*. Prentice-Hall, Englewood Cliffs, 1976.

[Flo67]   R.W. Floyd. Assigning meanings to programs. In J.T. Schwartz, editor, *Mathematical Aspects of Computer Science*. American Mathematical Society, 1967.

[GM91]   P.H.B. Gardiner and C.C. Morgan. Data refinement of predicate transformers. *Theoretical Computer Science*, 87:143–162, 1991. Reprinted in [MV94].

[Gri81]   D. Gries. *The Science of Programming*. Springer, 1981.

[Hay93]   I.J. Hayes, editor. *Specification Case Studies*. Prentice-Hall, London, second edition, 1993.

[Heh84]   E.C.R. Hehner. *The Logic of Programming*. Prentice-Hall, London, 1984.

[Hoa69]   C.A.R. Hoare. An axiomatic basis for computer programming. *Communications of the ACM*, 12(10):576–580, 583, October 1969.

[Jon86]   C.B. Jones. *Systematic Software Development using VDM*. Prentice-Hall, 1986.

[Kin90]   S. King. *Z* and the refinement calculus. In *Proceedings of the 3rd VDM-Europe Symposium*, Kiel, 1990. Springer. Lecture Notes in Computer Science 428.

[Mee79]   L. Meertens. Abstracto 84: The next generation. In *Annual Conference*. ACM, 1979.

[MG90]   C.C. Morgan and P.H.B. Gardiner. Data refinement by calculation. *Acta Informatica*, 27:481–503, 1990. Reprinted in [MV94].

[Mor]   J.M. Morris. Invariance theorems for recursive procedures. Department of Computer Science, University of Glasgow.

[Mor87]   J.M. Morris. A theoretical basis for stepwise refinement and the programming calculus. *Science of Computer Programming*, 9(3):287–306, December 1987.

[Mor88a]   C.C. Morgan. Auxiliary variables in data refinement. *Information Processing Letters*, 29(6):293–296, December 1988. Reprinted in [MV94].

[Mor88b]   C.C. Morgan. Data refinement using miracles. *Information Processing Letters*, 26(5):243–246, January 1988. Reprinted in [MV94].

[Mor88c]   C.C. Morgan. Procedures, parameters, and abstraction: Separate concerns. *Science of Computer Programming*, 11(1):17–28, 1988. Reprinted in [MV94].

[Mor88d]   C.C. Morgan. The specification statement. *ACM Transactions on Programming Languages and Systems*, 10(3), July 1988. Reprinted in [MV94].

[Mor89]   J.M. Morris. Laws of data refinement. *Acta Informatica*, 26:287–308, 1989.

[MR87]   C.C. Morgan and K.A. Robinson. Specification statements and refinement. *IBM Journal of Research and Development*, 31(5), September 1987. Reprinted in [MV94].

[MS89]   C.C. Morgan and J.W. Sanders. Laws of the logical calculi. Technical Report PRG–78, Programming Research Group, 1989.

[MV89]   C.C. Morgan and T.N. Vickers. Types and invariants in the refinement calculus. *Science of Computer Programming*, 1989. A shorter version appears in LNCS 375, van de Snepsheut, J.L.A. (ed).

[MV94]   C.C. Morgan and T.N. Vickers, editors. *On the Refinement Calculus*. FACIT Series in Computer Science. Springer, 1994.

[Nel89]   G. Nelson. A generalization of Dijkstra's calculus. *ACM Transactions on Programming Languages and Systems*, 11(4):517–561, October 1989.

Index

Mathematical symbols and phrases occur first, in order of their appearance in the text; the remainder of the index is alphabetical. Bold page numbers are defining occurrences of the entry.

Abbreviations, definitions, and laws may be found either by number or alphabetically: laws for example appear by number under the heading 'Law', and they appear alphabetically as separate entries indicated by underlining.

REYNOLDS, J.C., *The Craft of Programming*
ROSCOE, A.W. (ed.), *A Classical Mind: Essays in honour of C.A.R. Hoare*
RYDEHEARD, D.E. and BURSTALL, R.M., *Computational Category Theory*
SLOMAN, M. and KRAMER, J., *Distributed Systems and Computer Networks*
SPIVEY, J.M., *The Z. Notation: A reference manual (2nd edn)*
TENNENT, R.D., *Principles of Programming Languages*
TENNENT, R.D., *Semantics of Programming Languages*
WATT, D.A., *Programming Language Concepts and Paradigms*
WATT, D.A., *Programming Language Processors*
WATT, D.A., WICHMANN, B.A. and FINDLAY, W., *ADA: Language and methodology*
WELSH, J. and ELDER, J., *Introduction to Modula 2*
WELSH, J. and ELDER, J., *Introduction to Pascal (3rd edn)*
WELSH, J., ELDER, J. and BUSTARD, D., *Sequential Program Structures*
WELSH, J. and HAY, A., *A Model Implementation of Standard Pascal*
WELSH, J. and McKEAG, M., *Structured System Programming*
WIKSTRÖM, Å., *Functional Programming Using Standard ML*